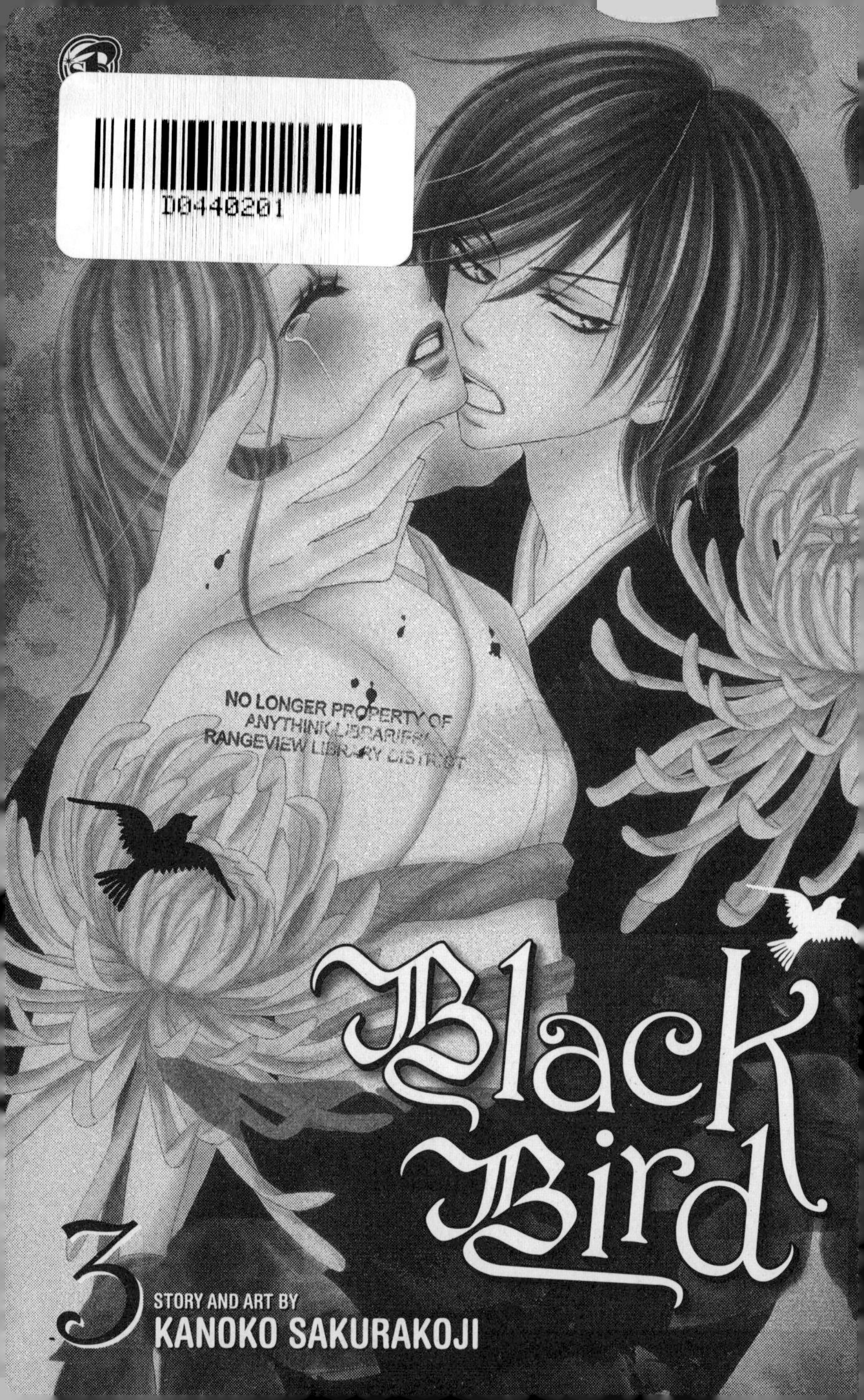
Black Bird
3
STORY AND ART BY
KANOKO SAKURAKOJI

Black Bird

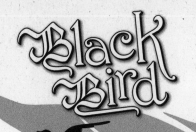

CONTENTS

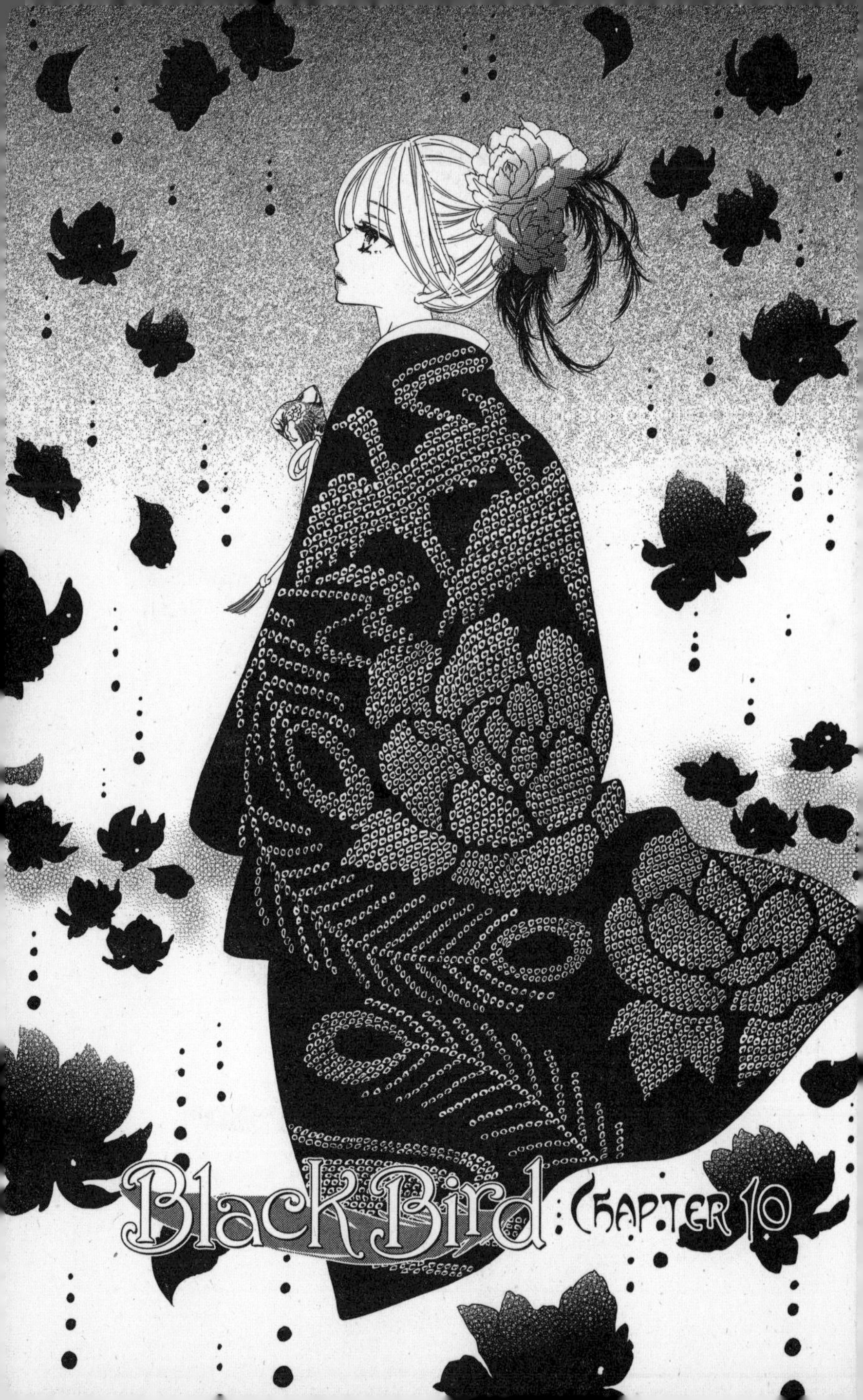
Black Bird
Chapter 10

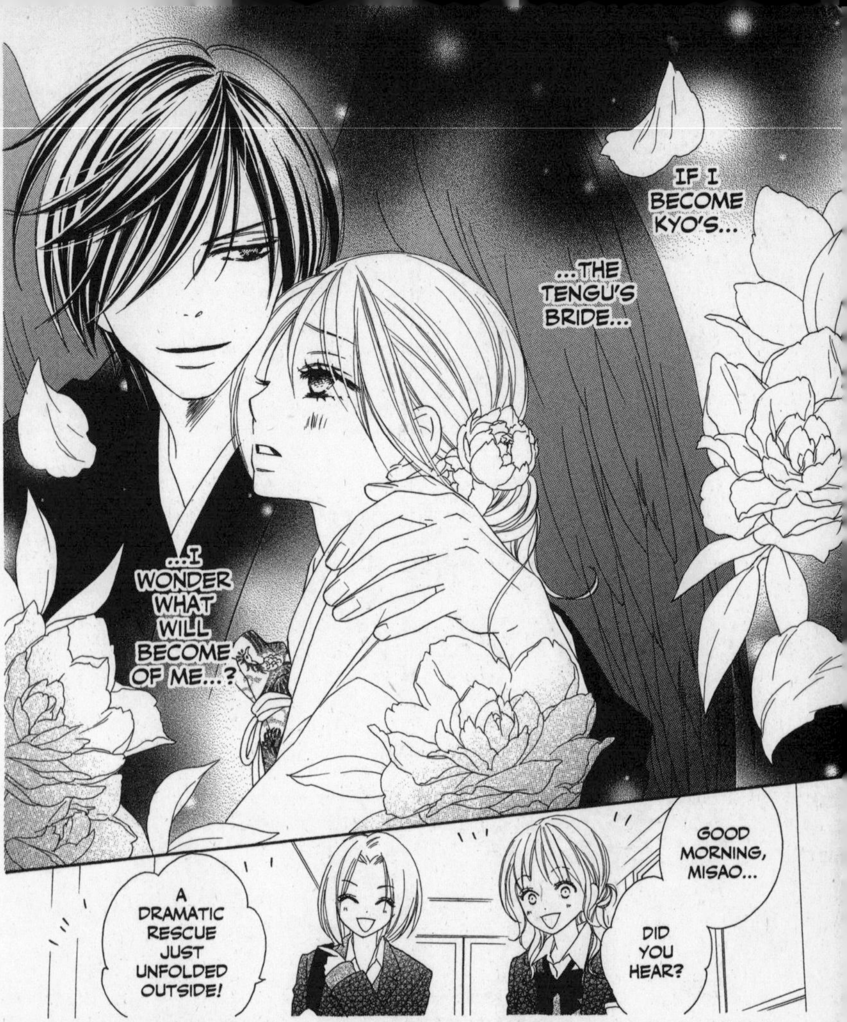
IF I BECOME KYO'S...
...THE TENGU'S BRIDE...
...I WONDER WHAT WILL BECOME OF ME...?
GOOD MORNING, MISAO...
DID YOU HEAR?
A DRAMATIC RESCUE JUST UNFOLDED OUTSIDE!

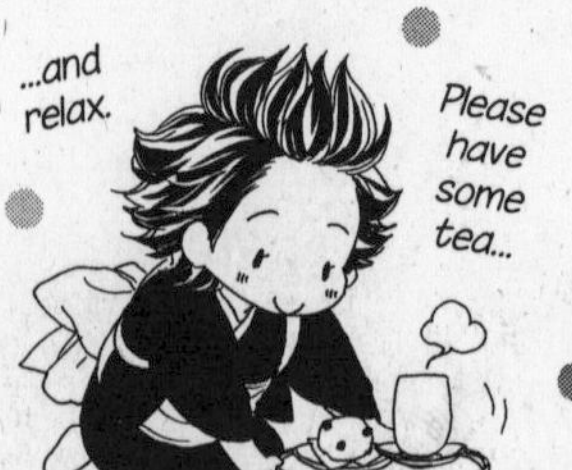
Please have some tea...
...and relax.

Hello, this is Sakurakoji. Thank you very much for picking up volume 3 of *Black Bird.* ♥

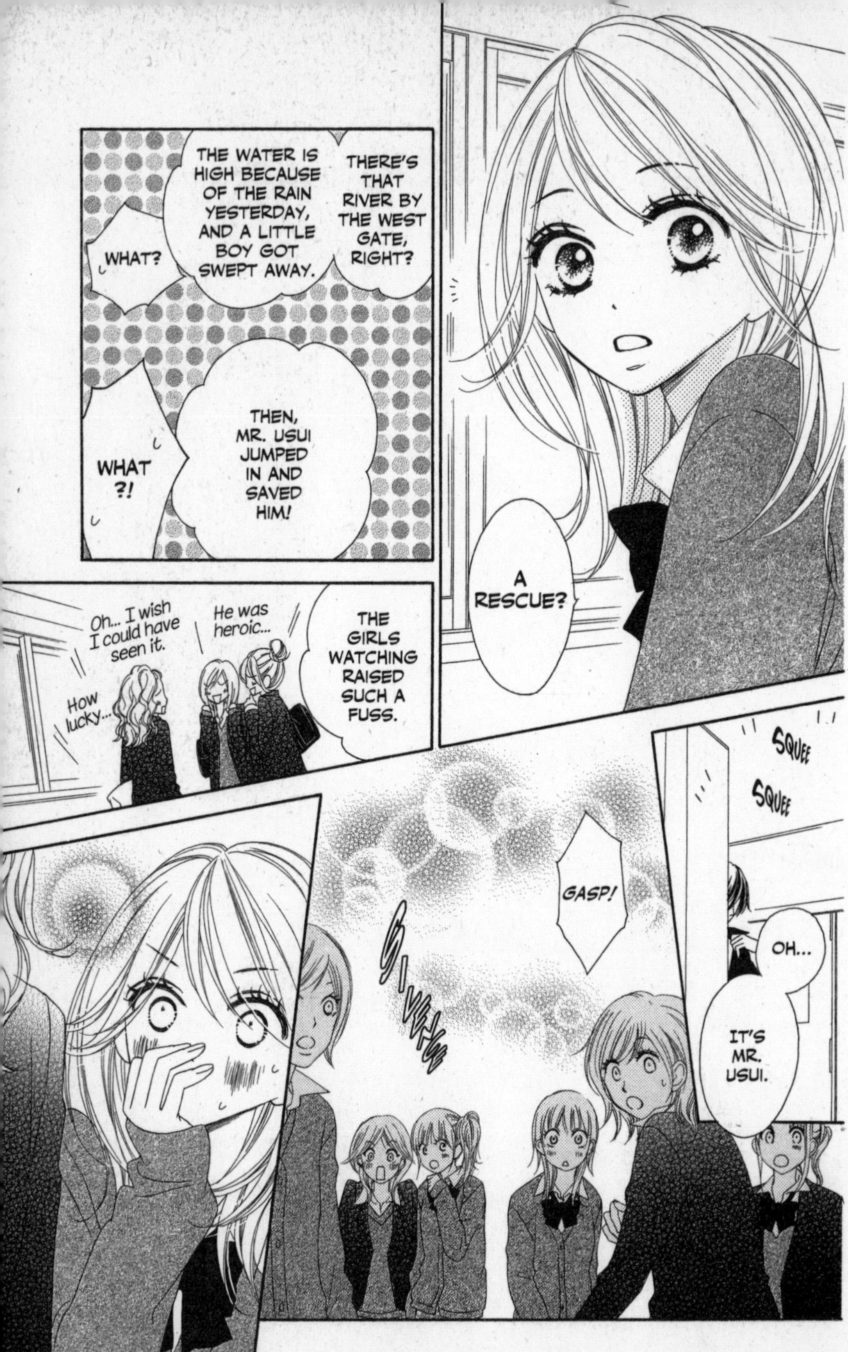
A RESCUE?
THERE'S THAT RIVER BY THE WEST GATE, RIGHT?
THE WATER IS HIGH BECAUSE OF THE RAIN YESTERDAY, AND A LITTLE BOY GOT SWEPT AWAY.
WHAT?
THEN, MR. USUI JUMPED IN AND SAVED HIM!
WHAT ?!
THE GIRLS WATCHING RAISED SUCH A FUSS.
He was heroic...
Oh... I wish I could have seen it.
How lucky...
SQUEE
SQUEE
OH...
IT'S MR. USUI.
GASP!

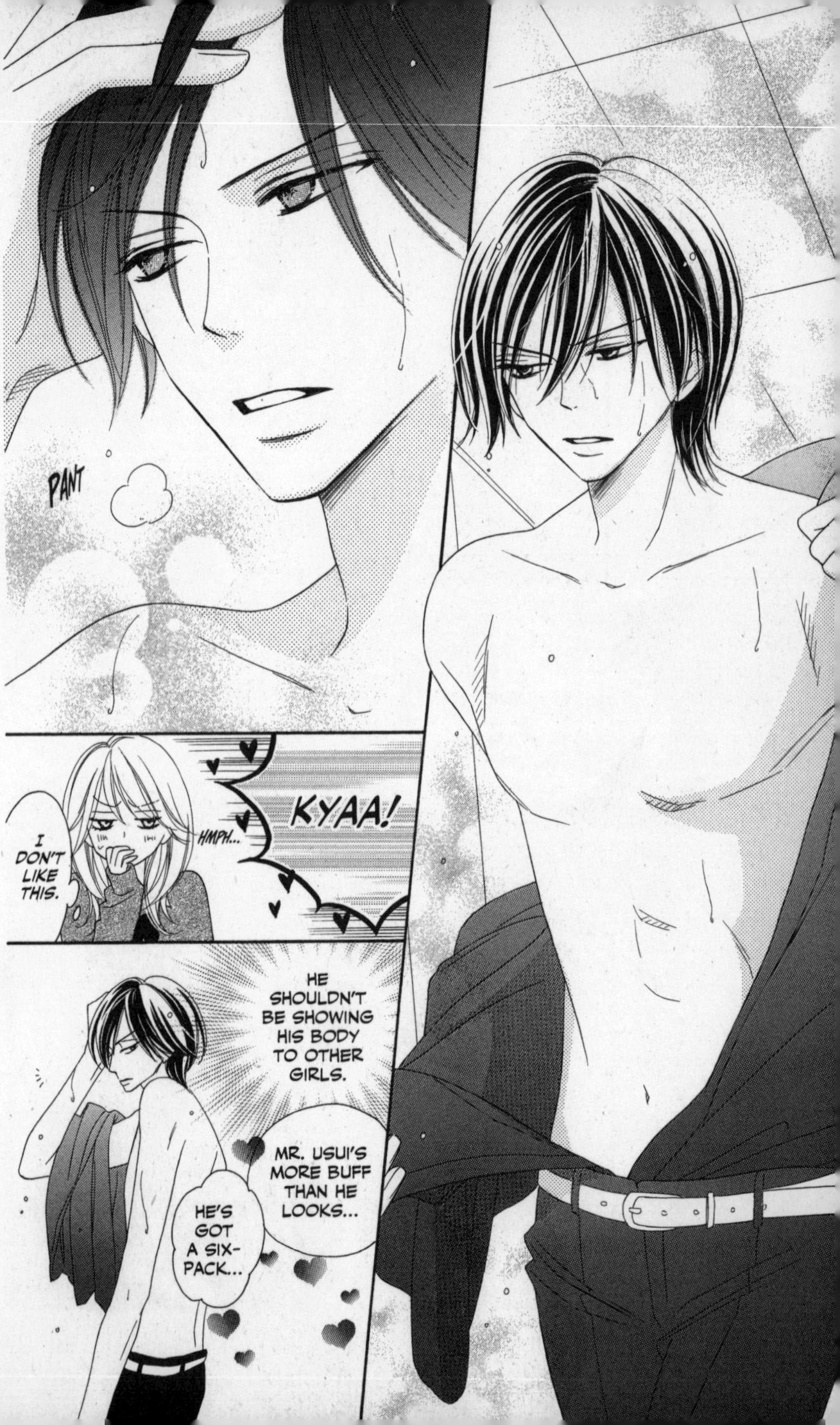
PANT
KYAA!
HMPH...
I DON'T LIKE THIS.
HE SHOULDN'T BE SHOWING HIS BODY TO OTHER GIRLS.
MR. USUI'S MORE BUFF THAN HE LOOKS...
HE'S GOT A SIX-PACK...

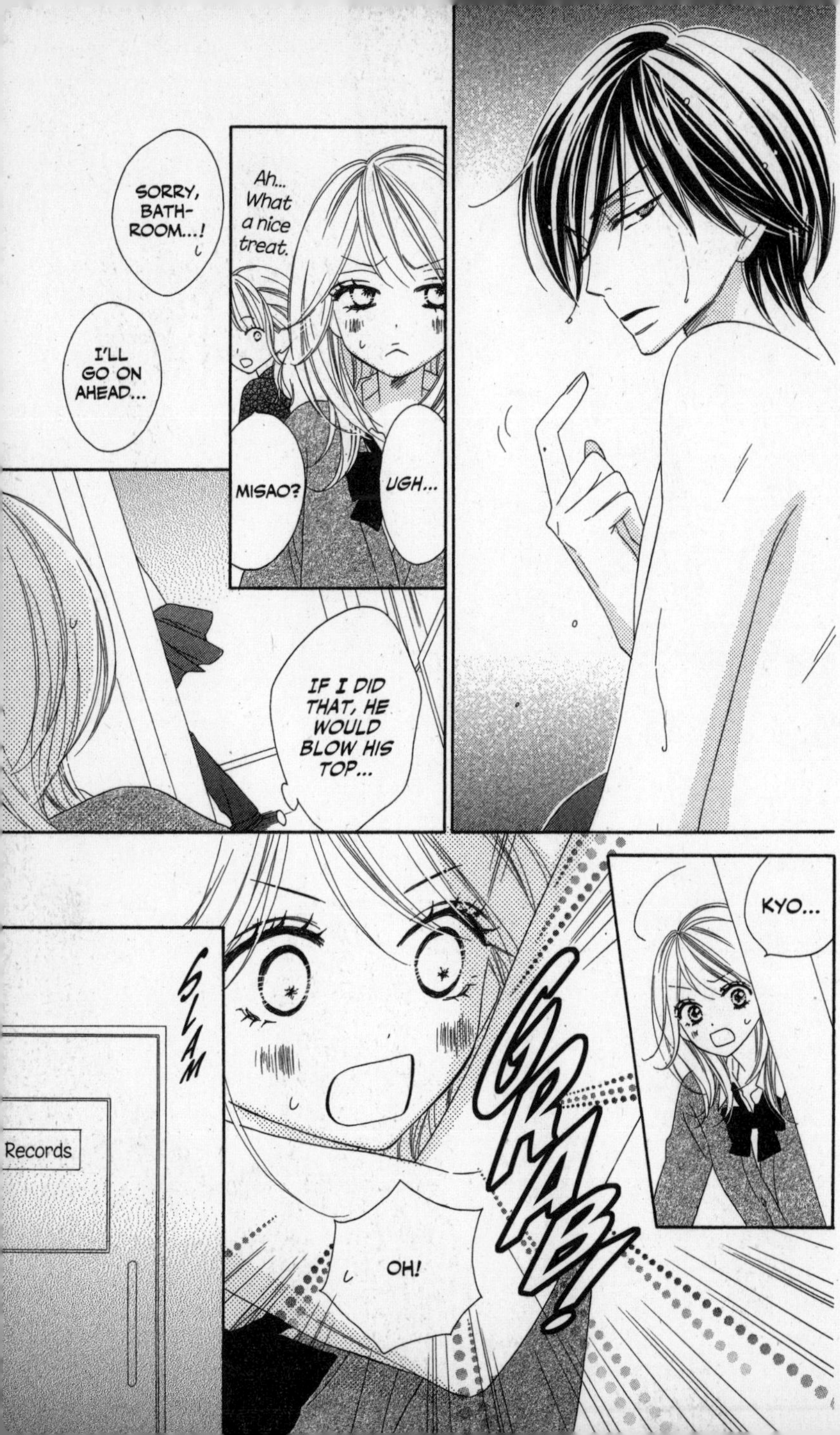

Ah... What a nice treat.
UGH...
MISAO?
SORRY, BATH-ROOM...!
I'LL GO ON AHEAD...
IF I DID THAT, HE WOULD BLOW HIS TOP...
KYO...
OH!
SLAM
Records

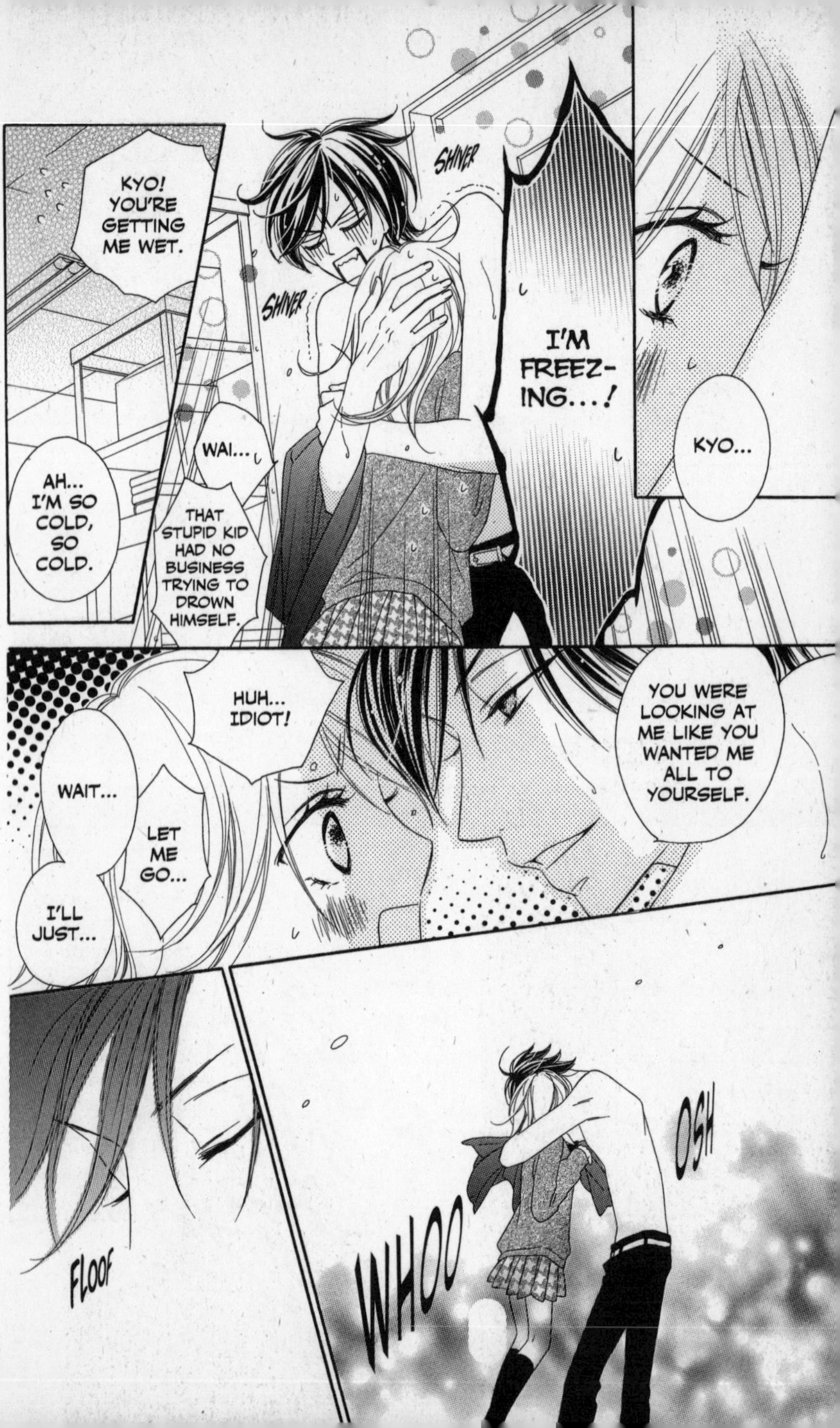
KYO...
I'M FREEZ-ING...!
SHIVER
SHIVER
WAI...
THAT STUPID KID HAD NO BUSINESS TRYING TO DROWN HIMSELF.
KYO! YOU'RE GETTING ME WET.
AH... I'M SO COLD, SO COLD.
YOU WERE LOOKING AT ME LIKE YOU WANTED ME ALL TO YOURSELF.
HUH... IDIOT!
WAIT...
LET ME GO...
I'LL JUST...
WHOOOSH
FLOOF

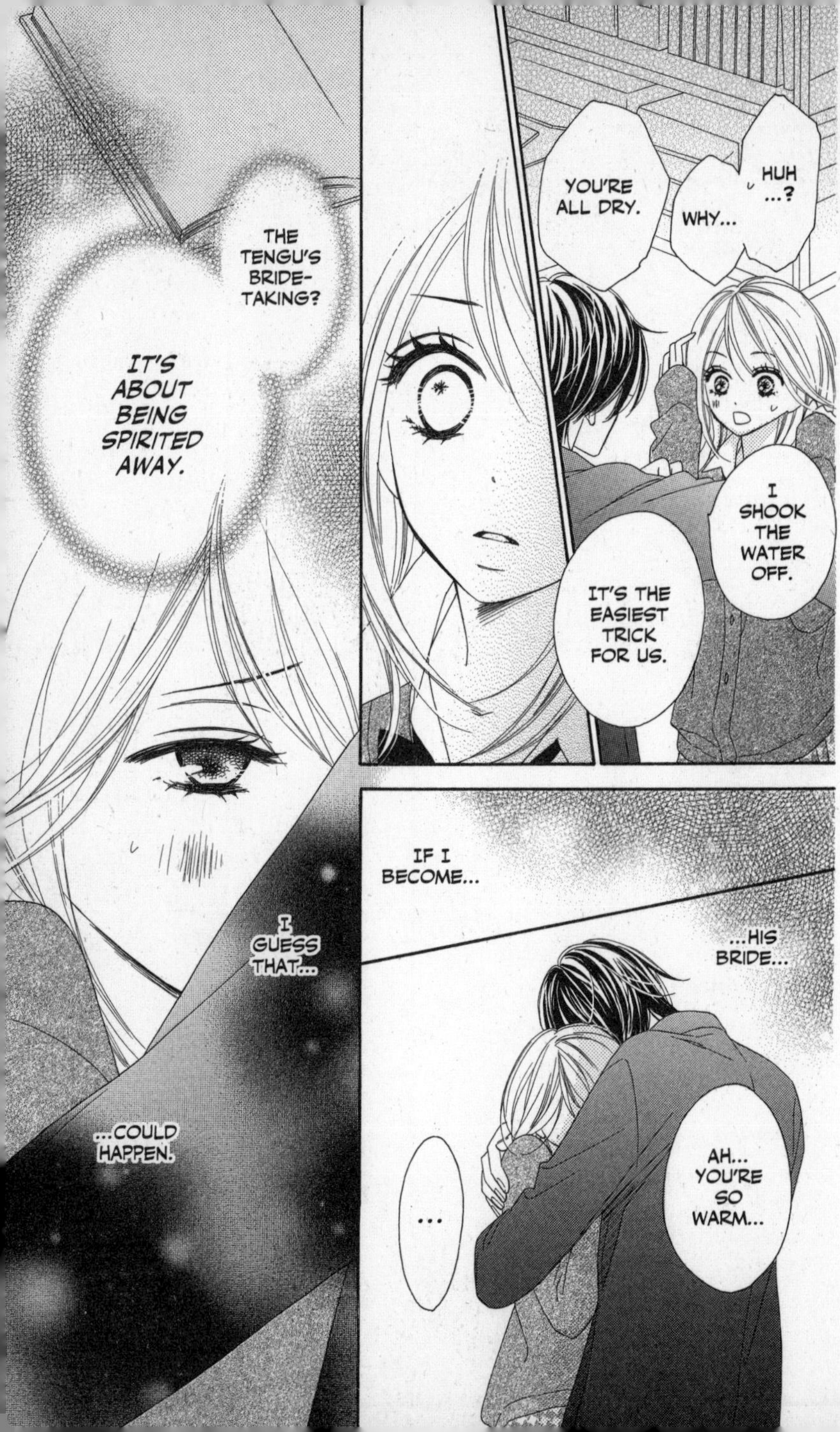
HUH ...?
WHY...
YOU'RE ALL DRY.
I SHOOK THE WATER OFF.
IT'S THE EASIEST TRICK FOR US.
IF I BECOME...
...HIS BRIDE...
AH... YOU'RE SO WARM...
...
THE TENGU'S BRIDE-TAKING?
IT'S ABOUT BEING SPIRITED AWAY.
I GUESS THAT...
...COULD HAPPEN.

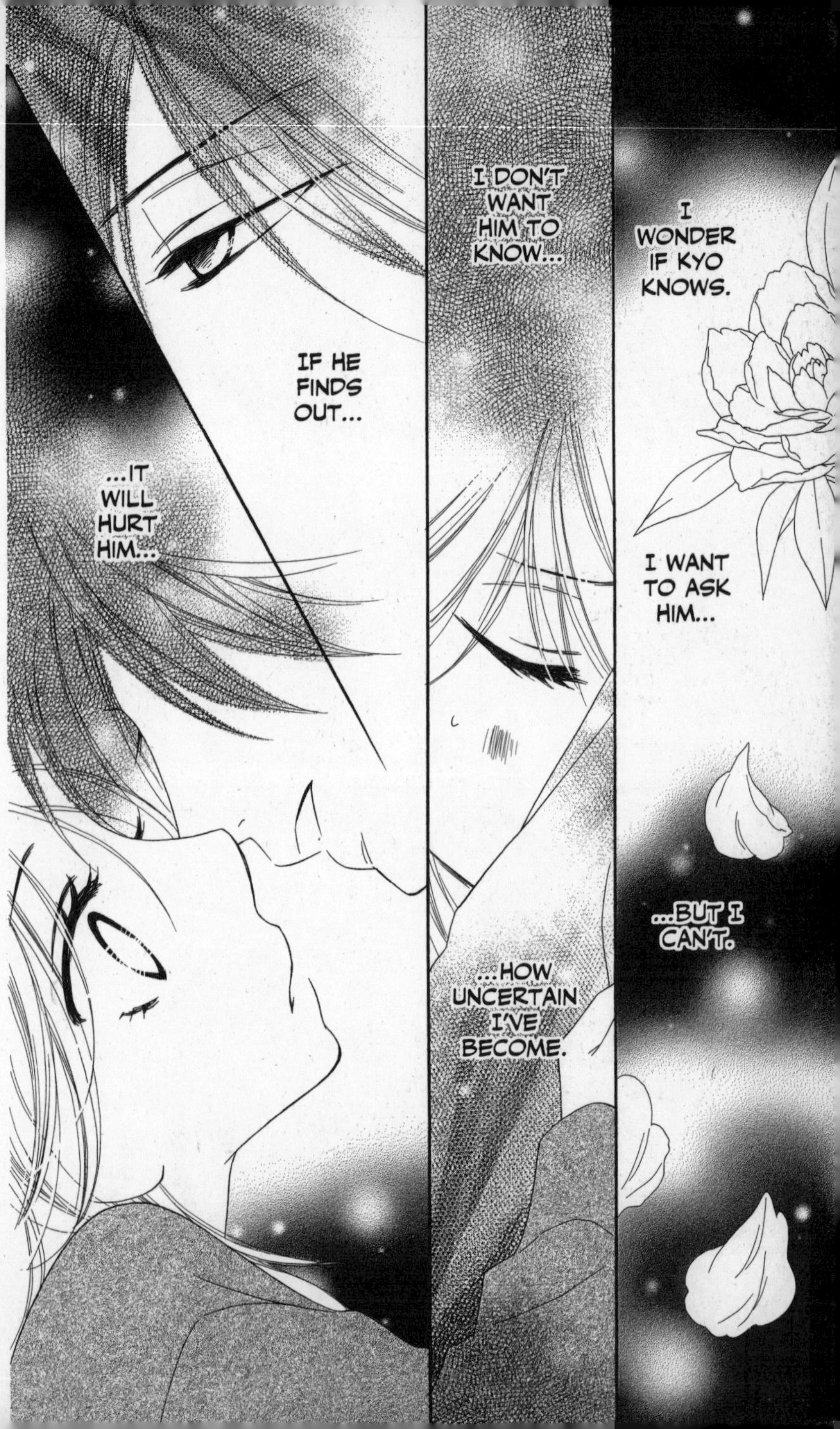
I WONDER IF KYO KNOWS.
I WANT TO ASK HIM...
...BUT I CAN'T.
I DON'T WANT HIM TO KNOW...
...HOW UNCERTAIN I'VE BECOME.
IF HE FINDS OUT...
...IT WILL HURT HIM...

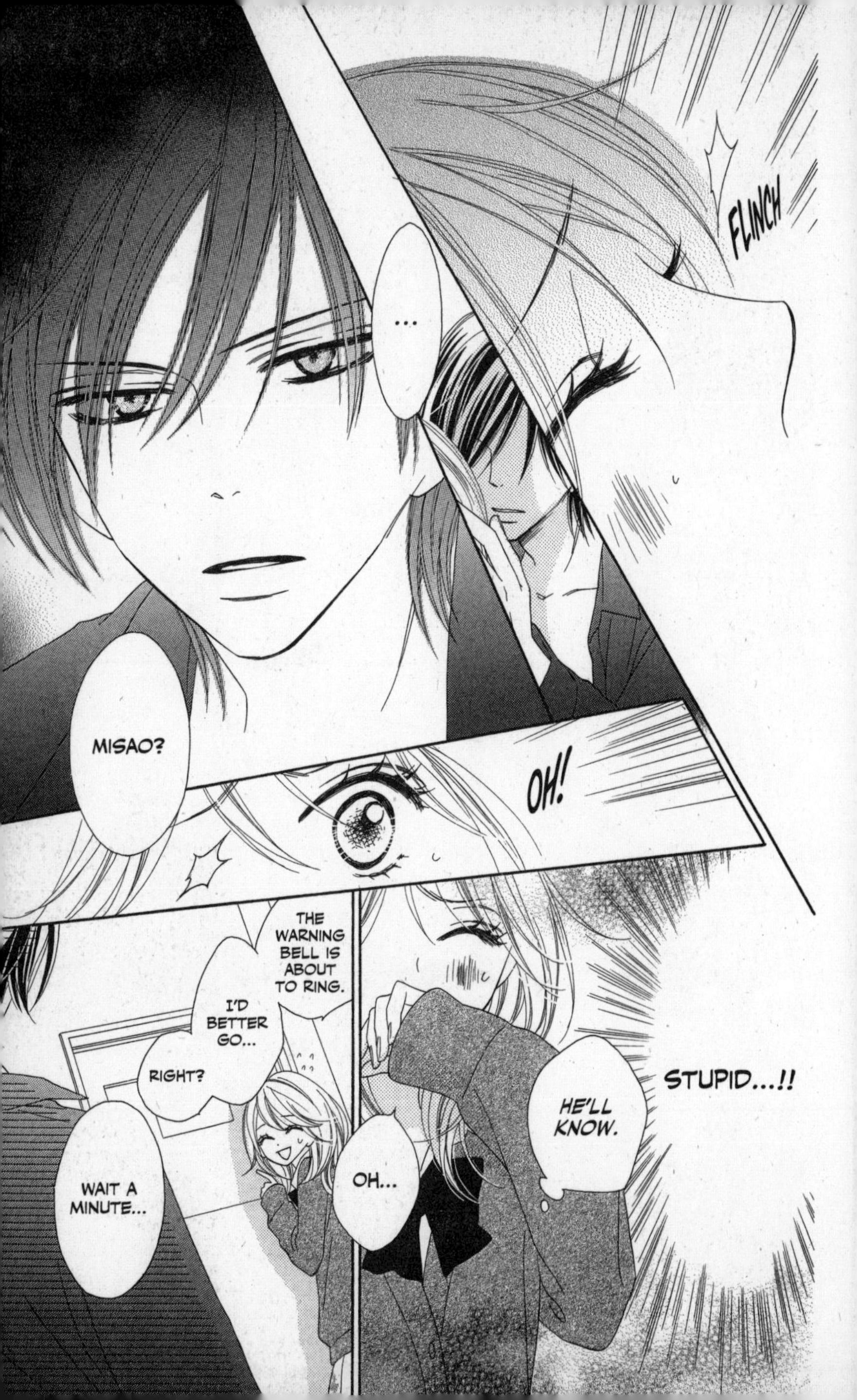
FLINCH
...
MISAO?
OH!
STUPID...!!
HE'LL KNOW.
OH...
THE WARNING BELL IS ABOUT TO RING.
I'D BETTER GO...
RIGHT?
WAIT A MINUTE...

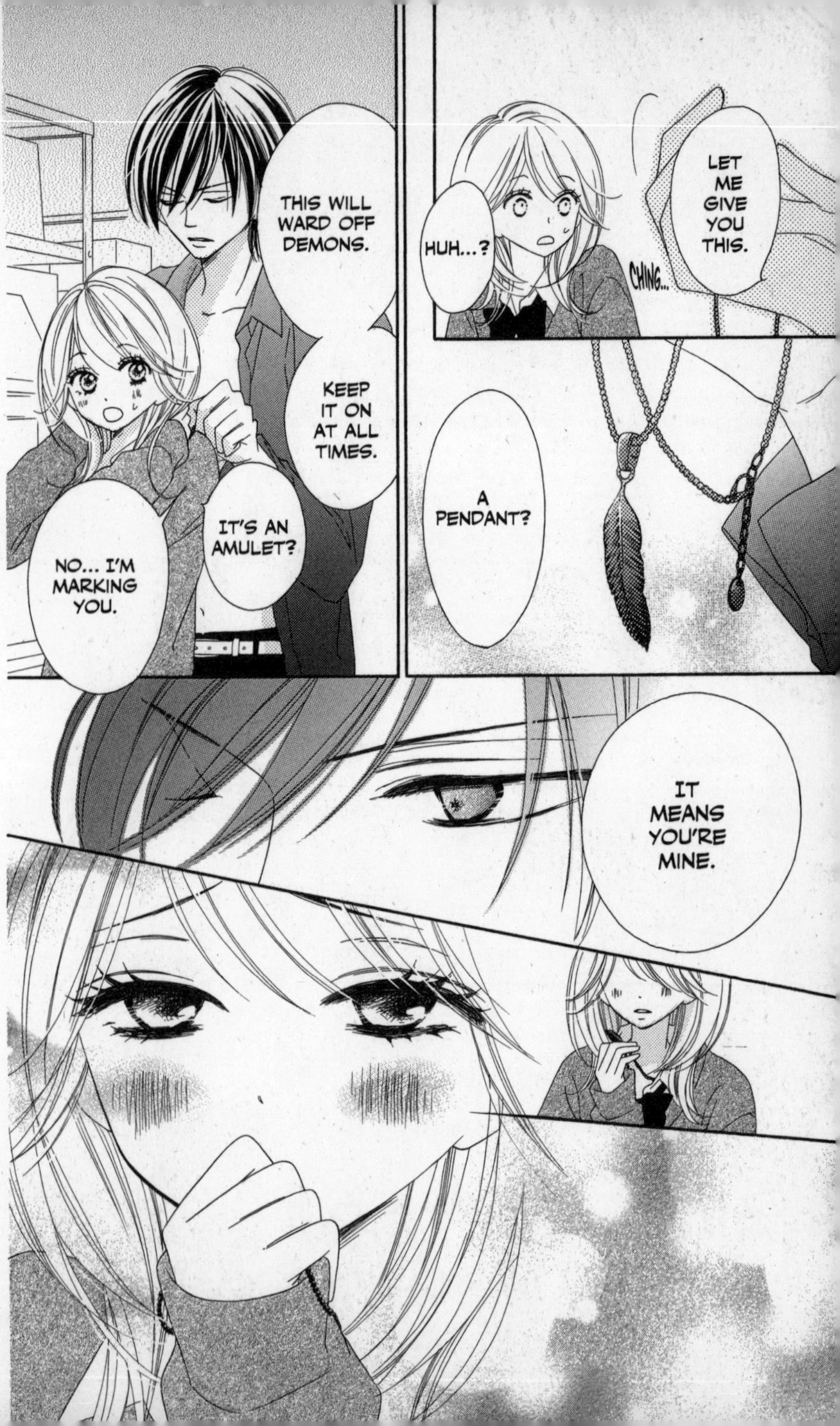
LET ME GIVE YOU THIS.
CHING...
HUH...?
A PENDANT?
THIS WILL WARD OFF DEMONS.
KEEP IT ON AT ALL TIMES.
IT'S AN AMULET?
NO... I'M MARKING YOU.
IT MEANS YOU'RE MINE.

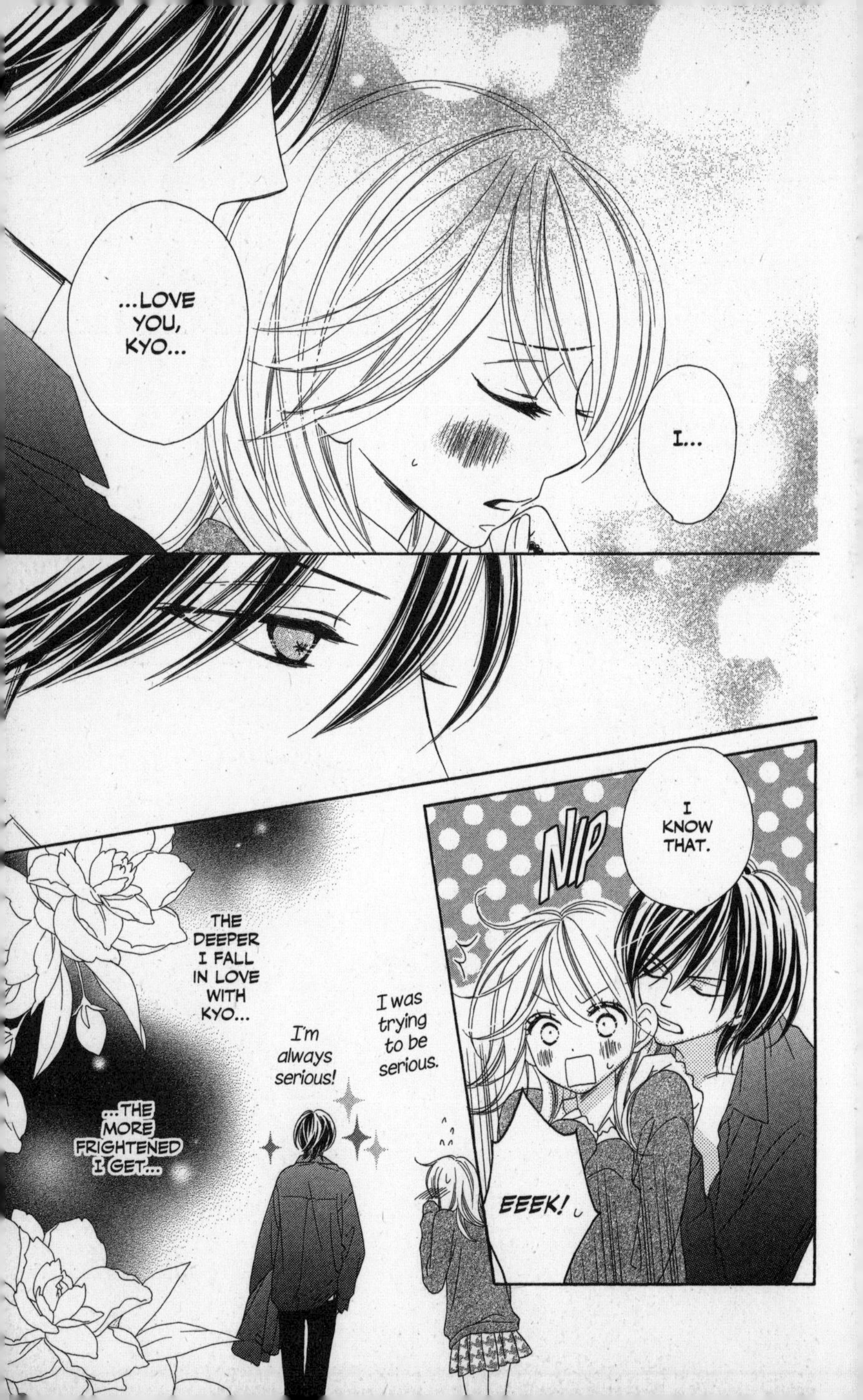

I...
...LOVE YOU, KYO...
I KNOW THAT.
NIP
EEEK!
I was trying to be serious.
I'm always serious!
THE DEEPER I FALL IN LOVE WITH KYO...
...THE MORE FRIGHTENED I GET...

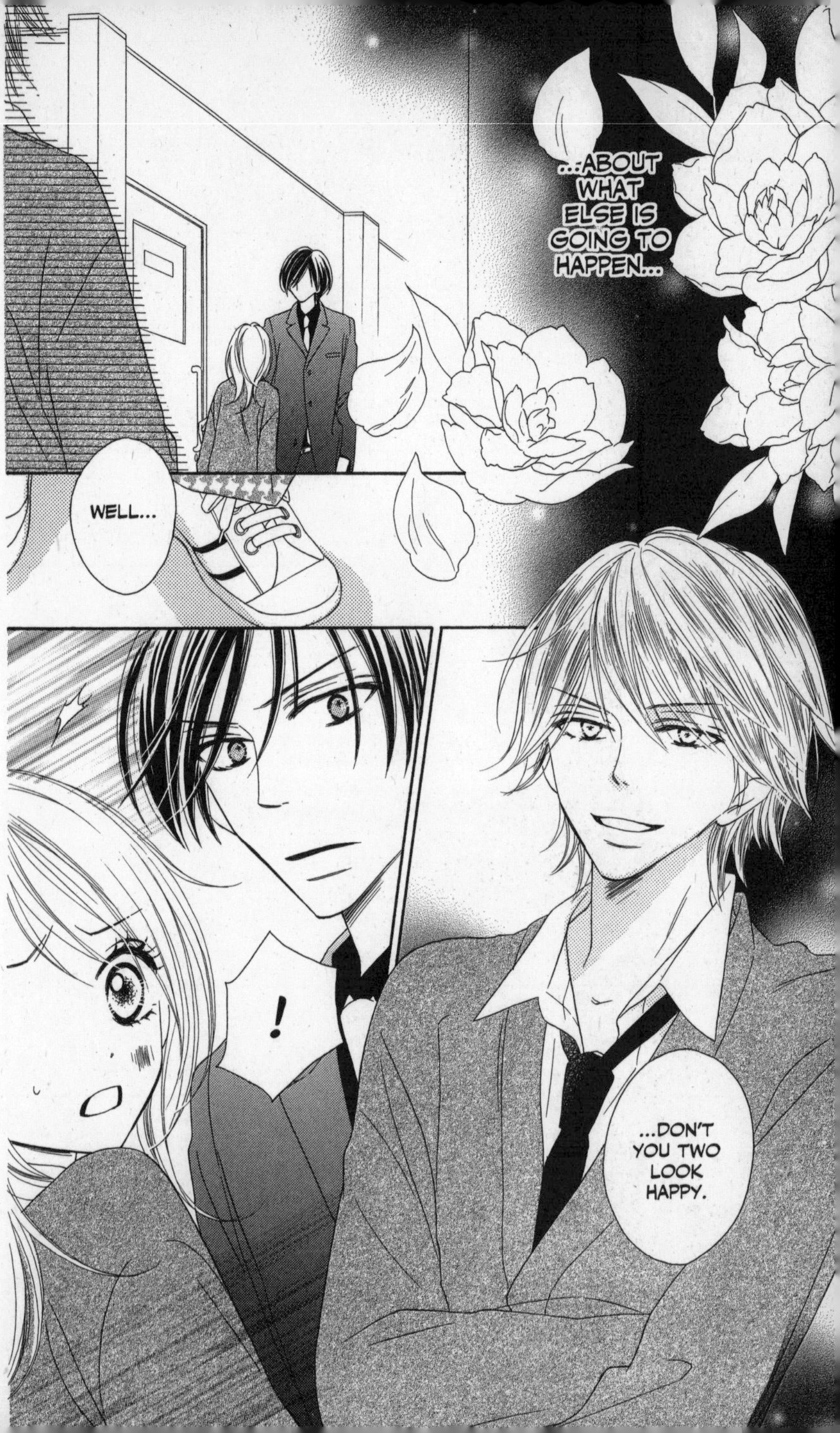
...ABOUT WHAT ELSE IS GOING TO HAPPEN...
WELL...
...DON'T YOU TWO LOOK HAPPY.
!

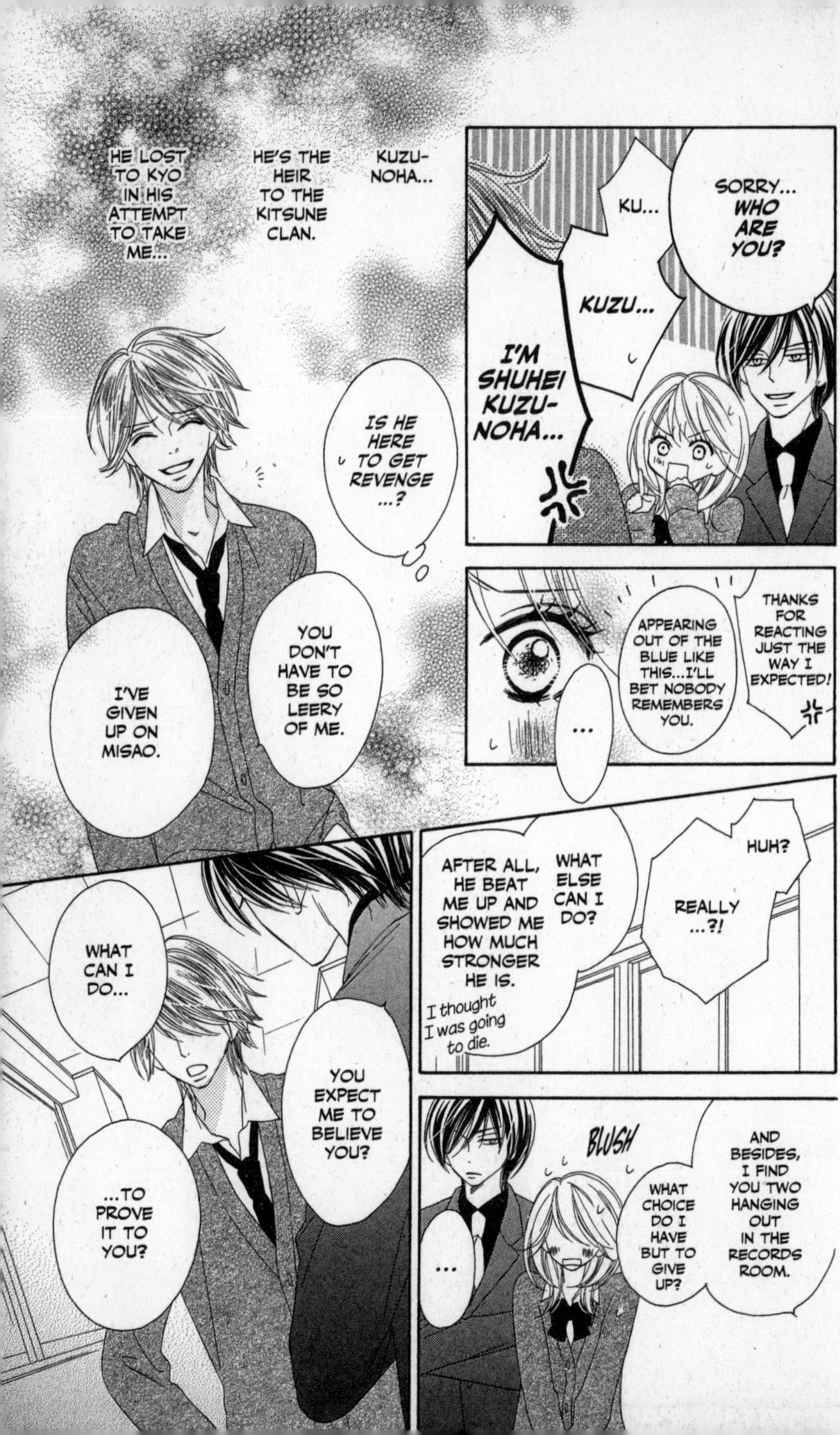
SORRY... WHO ARE YOU?
KU...
KUZU...
I'M SHUHEI KUZUNOHA...
THANKS FOR REACTING JUST THE WAY I EXPECTED!
APPEARING OUT OF THE BLUE LIKE THIS...I'LL BET NOBODY REMEMBERS YOU.
...
KUZUNOHA...
HE'S THE HEIR TO THE KITSUNE CLAN.
HE LOST TO KYO IN HIS ATTEMPT TO TAKE ME...
IS HE HERE TO GET REVENGE ...?
YOU DON'T HAVE TO BE SO LEERY OF ME.
I'VE GIVEN UP ON MISAO.
HUH?
REALLY ...?!
WHAT ELSE CAN I DO?
AFTER ALL, HE BEAT ME UP AND SHOWED ME HOW MUCH STRONGER HE IS.
I thought I was going to die.
AND BESIDES, I FIND YOU TWO HANGING OUT IN THE RECORDS ROOM.
BLUSH
WHAT CHOICE DO I HAVE BUT TO GIVE UP?
...
YOU EXPECT ME TO BELIEVE YOU?
WHAT CAN I DO...
...TO PROVE IT TO YOU?

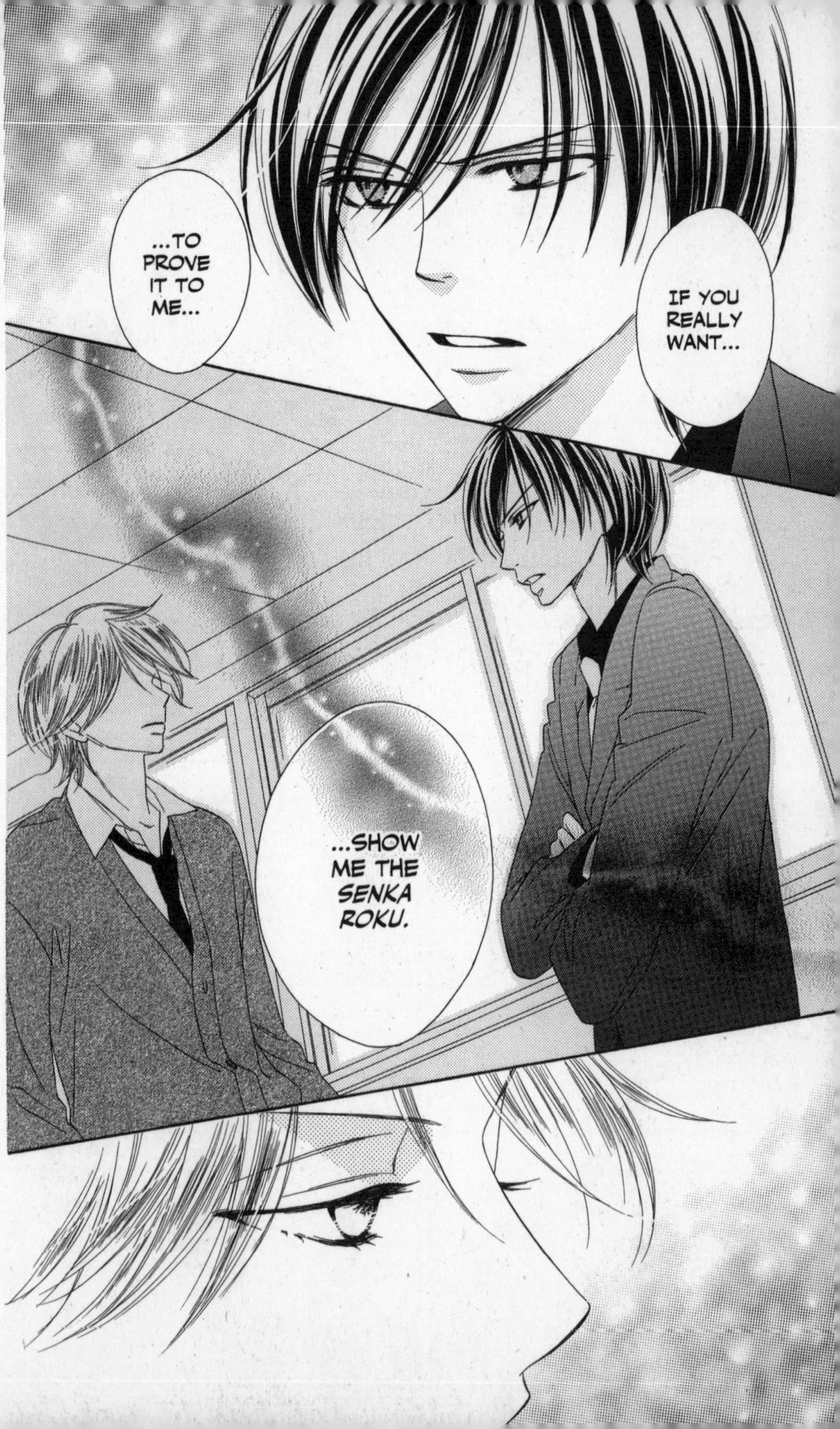
IF YOU REALLY WANT...
...TO PROVE IT TO ME...
...SHOW ME THE SENKA ROKU.

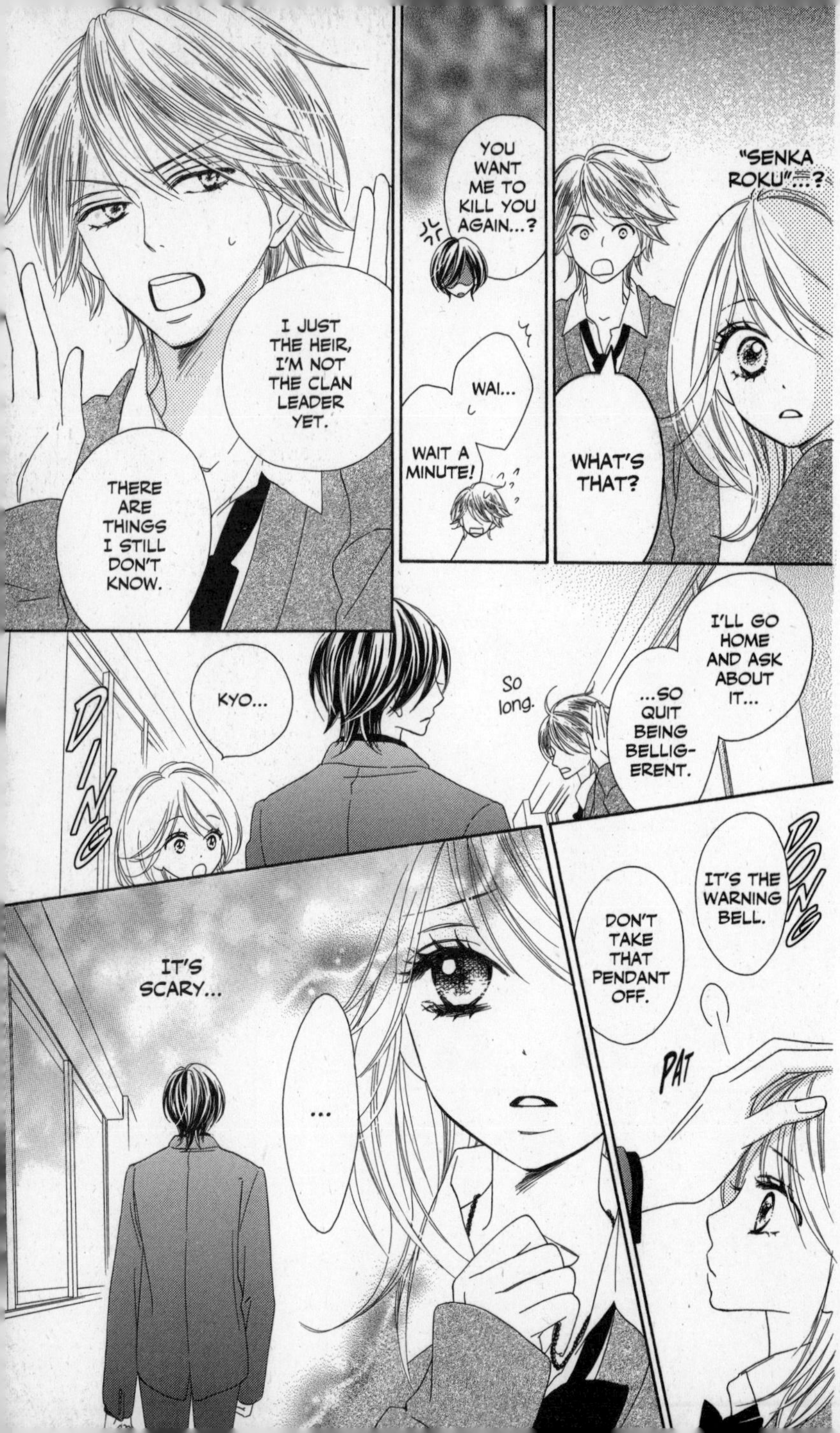
"SENKA ROKU"...?
WHAT'S THAT?
YOU WANT ME TO KILL YOU AGAIN...?
WAI...
WAIT A MINUTE!
I JUST THE HEIR, I'M NOT THE CLAN LEADER YET.
THERE ARE THINGS I STILL DON'T KNOW.
I'LL GO HOME AND ASK ABOUT IT...
...SO QUIT BEING BELLIG-ERENT.
So long.
DING
KYO...
DONG
IT'S THE WARNING BELL.
DON'T TAKE THAT PENDANT OFF.
PAT
IT'S SCARY...
...

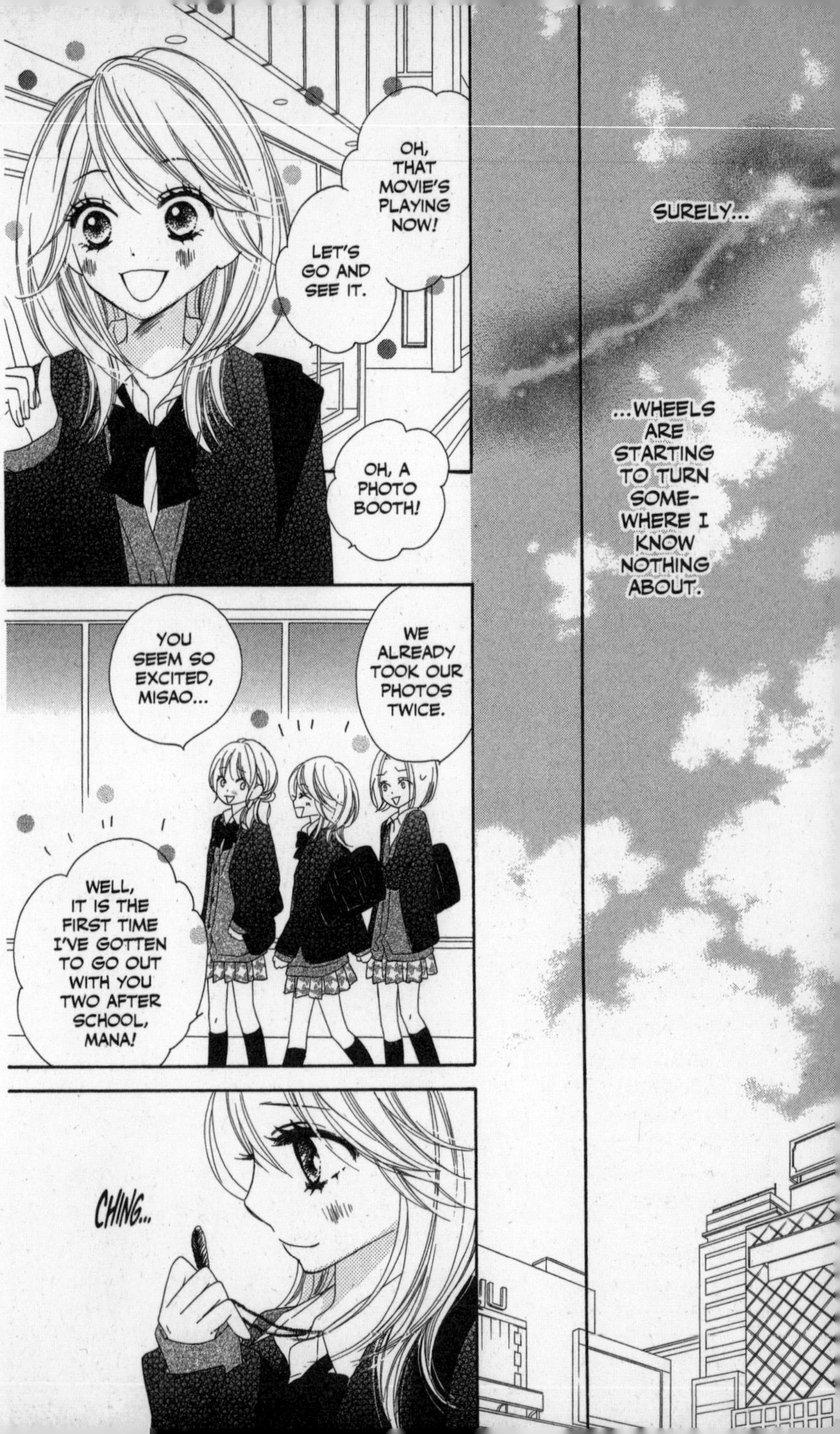
SURELY...
...WHEELS ARE STARTING TO TURN SOME-WHERE I KNOW NOTHING ABOUT.
OH, THAT MOVIE'S PLAYING NOW!
LET'S GO AND SEE IT.
OH, A PHOTO BOOTH!
WE ALREADY TOOK OUR PHOTOS TWICE.
YOU SEEM SO EXCITED, MISAO...
WELL, IT IS THE FIRST TIME I'VE GOTTEN TO GO OUT WITH YOU TWO AFTER SCHOOL, MANA!
CHING...

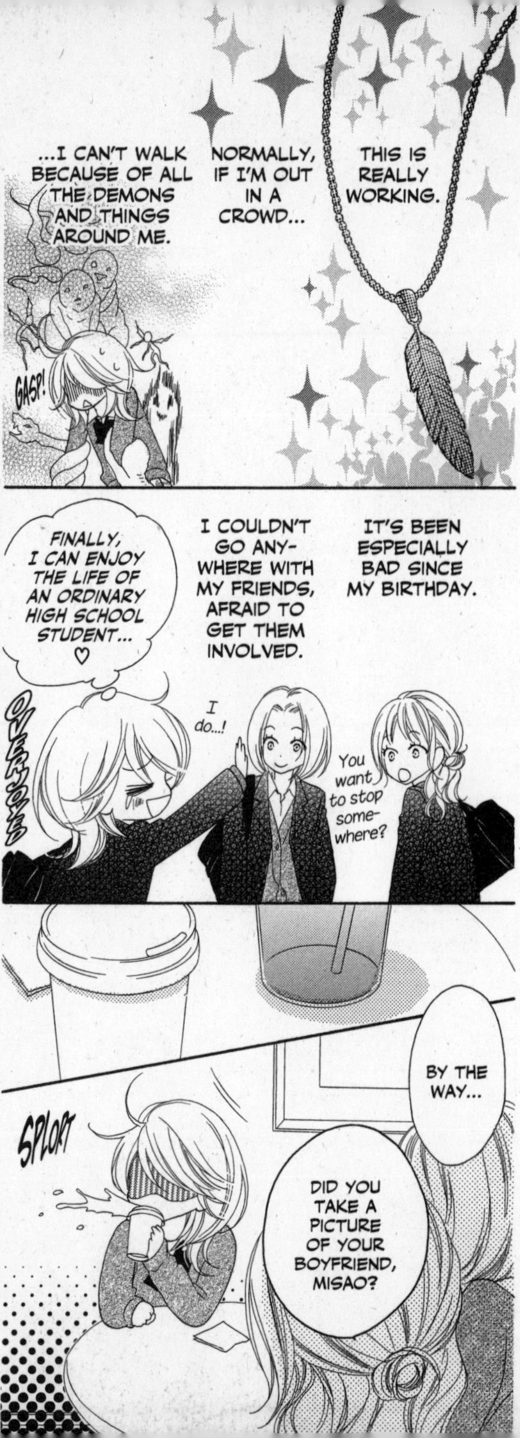
THIS IS REALLY WORKING.
NORMALLY, IF I'M OUT IN A CROWD...
...I CAN'T WALK BECAUSE OF ALL THE DEMONS AND THINGS AROUND ME.
GASP!
IT'S BEEN ESPECIALLY BAD SINCE MY BIRTHDAY.
I COULDN'T GO ANY-WHERE WITH MY FRIENDS, AFRAID TO GET THEM INVOLVED.
FINALLY, I CAN ENJOY THE LIFE OF AN ORDINARY HIGH SCHOOL STUDENT... ♡
OVERJOYED
You want to stop some-where?
I do...!
BY THE WAY...
DID YOU TAKE A PICTURE OF YOUR BOYFRIEND, MISAO?
SPLORT

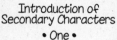

Introduction of Secondary Characters

• One •

Misao's Friends Mana (left) and Kana

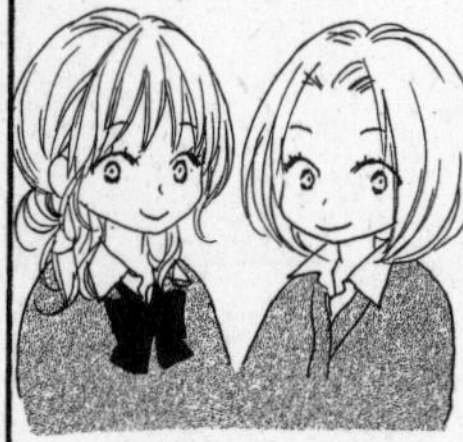

I had no intention of even mentioning their names in the story, so I wonder why I decided Mana's boyfriend was a college student, and Kana's boyfriend was a former middle-school classmate.

Incidentally, they are not twins.

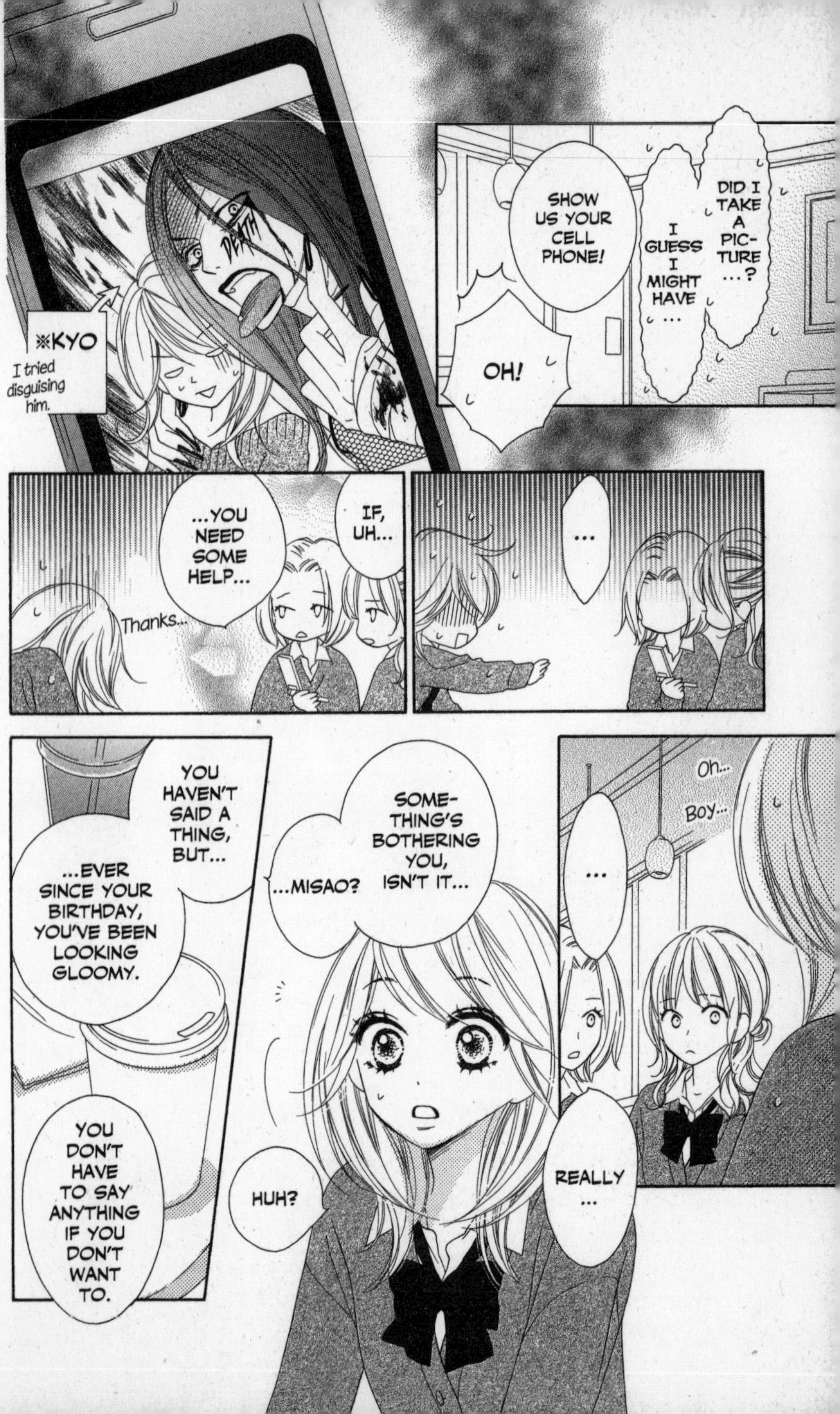
DID I TAKE A PIC-TURE...?
I GUESS I MIGHT HAVE...
SHOW US YOUR CELL PHONE!
OH!
DEATH
※KYO
I tried disguising him.
...
IF, UH...
...YOU NEED SOME HELP...
Thanks...
Oh... Boy...
...
REALLY...
SOME-THING'S BOTHERING YOU, ISN'T IT...
...MISAO?
YOU HAVEN'T SAID A THING, BUT...
...EVER SINCE YOUR BIRTHDAY, YOU'VE BEEN LOOKING GLOOMY.
HUH?
YOU DON'T HAVE TO SAY ANYTHING IF YOU DON'T WANT TO.

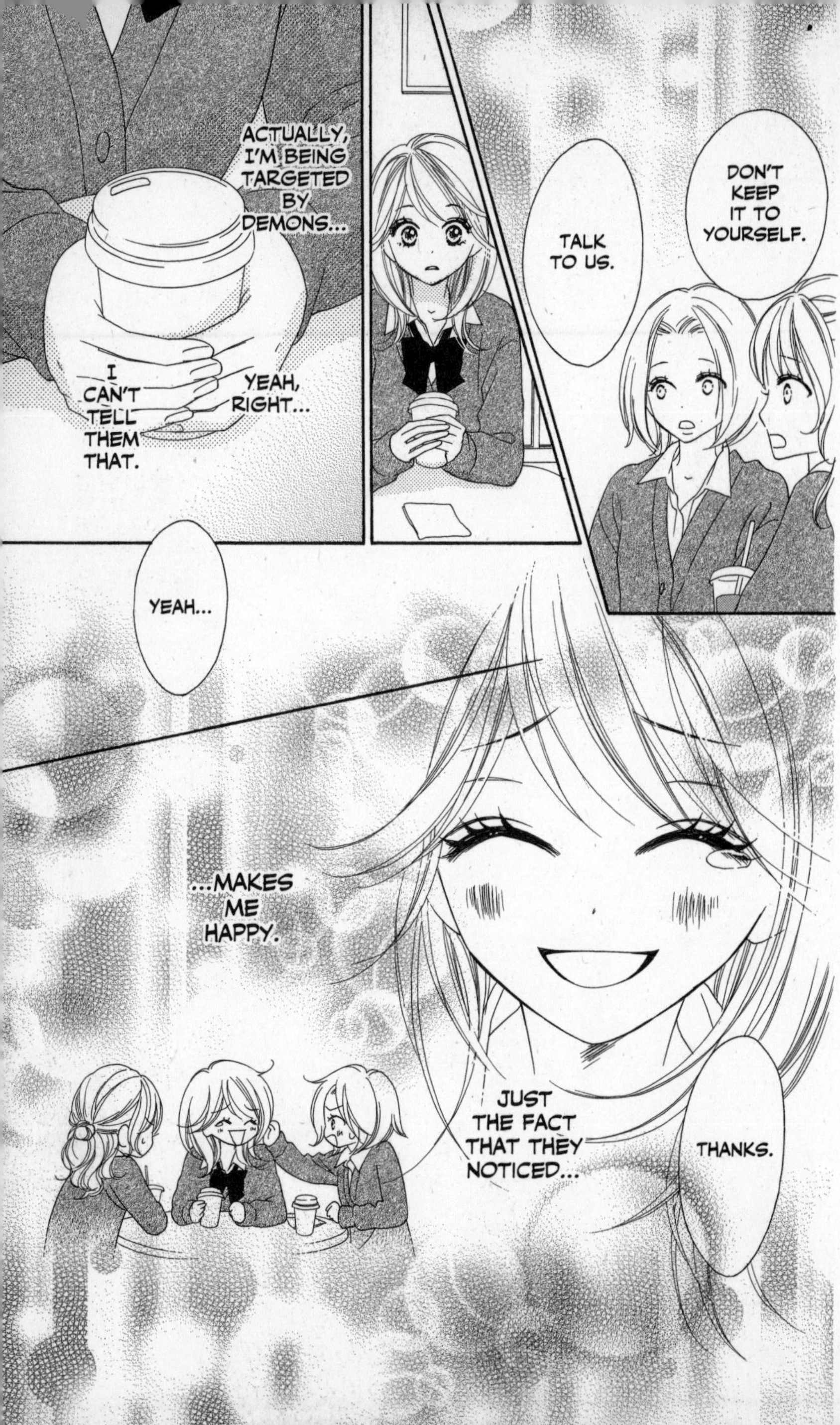

DON'T KEEP IT TO YOURSELF.
TALK TO US.
ACTUALLY, I'M BEING TARGETED BY DEMONS...
YEAH, RIGHT...
I CAN'T TELL THEM THAT.
YEAH...
THANKS.
JUST THE FACT THAT THEY NOTICED...
...MAKES ME HAPPY.

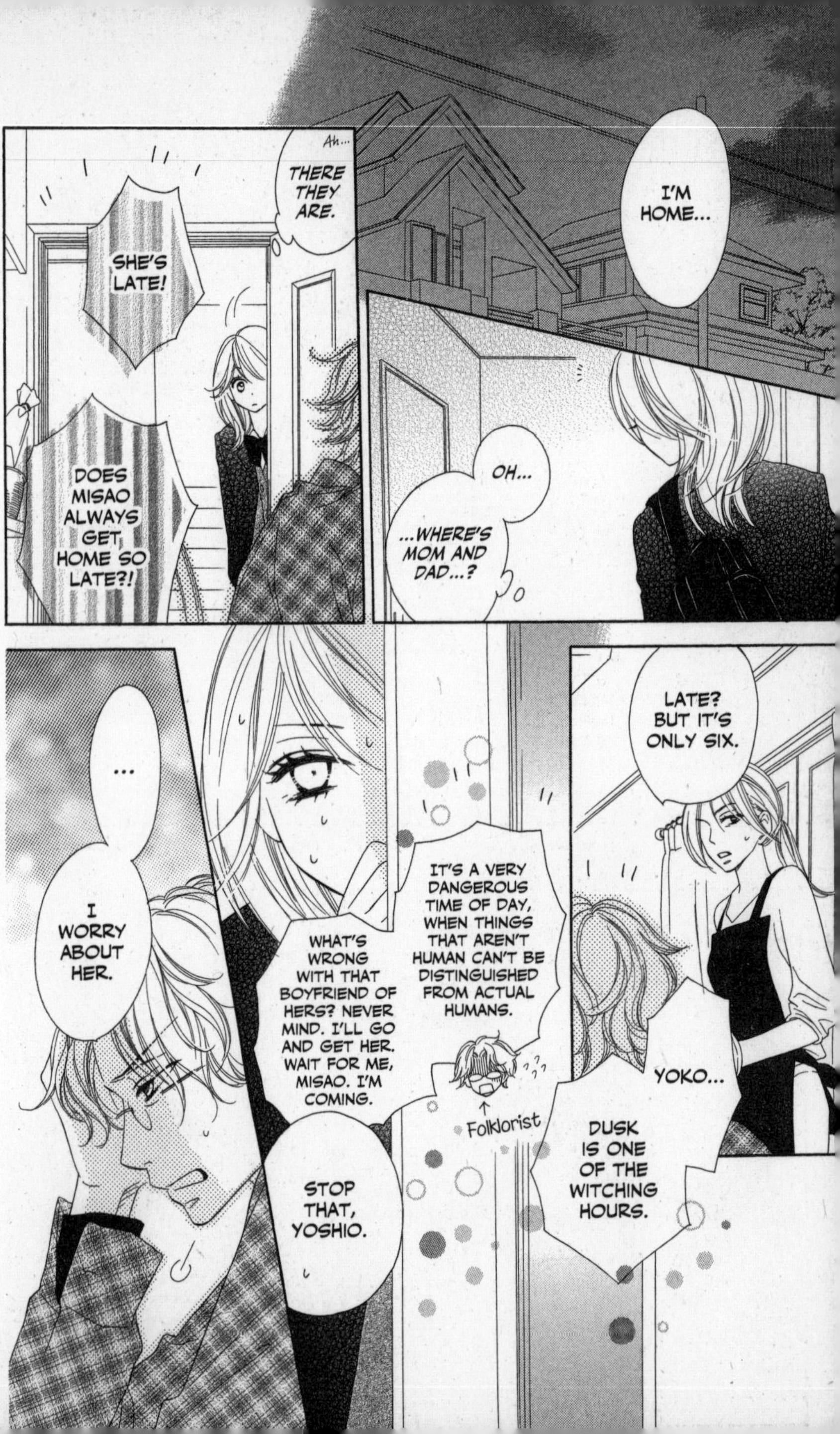
I'M HOME...
OH...
...WHERE'S MOM AND DAD...?
Ah...
THERE THEY ARE.
SHE'S LATE!
DOES MISAO ALWAYS GET HOME SO LATE?!
LATE? BUT IT'S ONLY SIX.
YOKO...
DUSK IS ONE OF THE WITCHING HOURS.
IT'S A VERY DANGEROUS TIME OF DAY, WHEN THINGS THAT AREN'T HUMAN CAN'T BE DISTINGUISHED FROM ACTUAL HUMANS.
Folklorist
WHAT'S WRONG WITH THAT BOYFRIEND OF HERS? NEVER MIND. I'LL GO AND GET HER. WAIT FOR ME, MISAO. I'M COMING.
STOP THAT, YOSHIO.
...
I WORRY ABOUT HER.

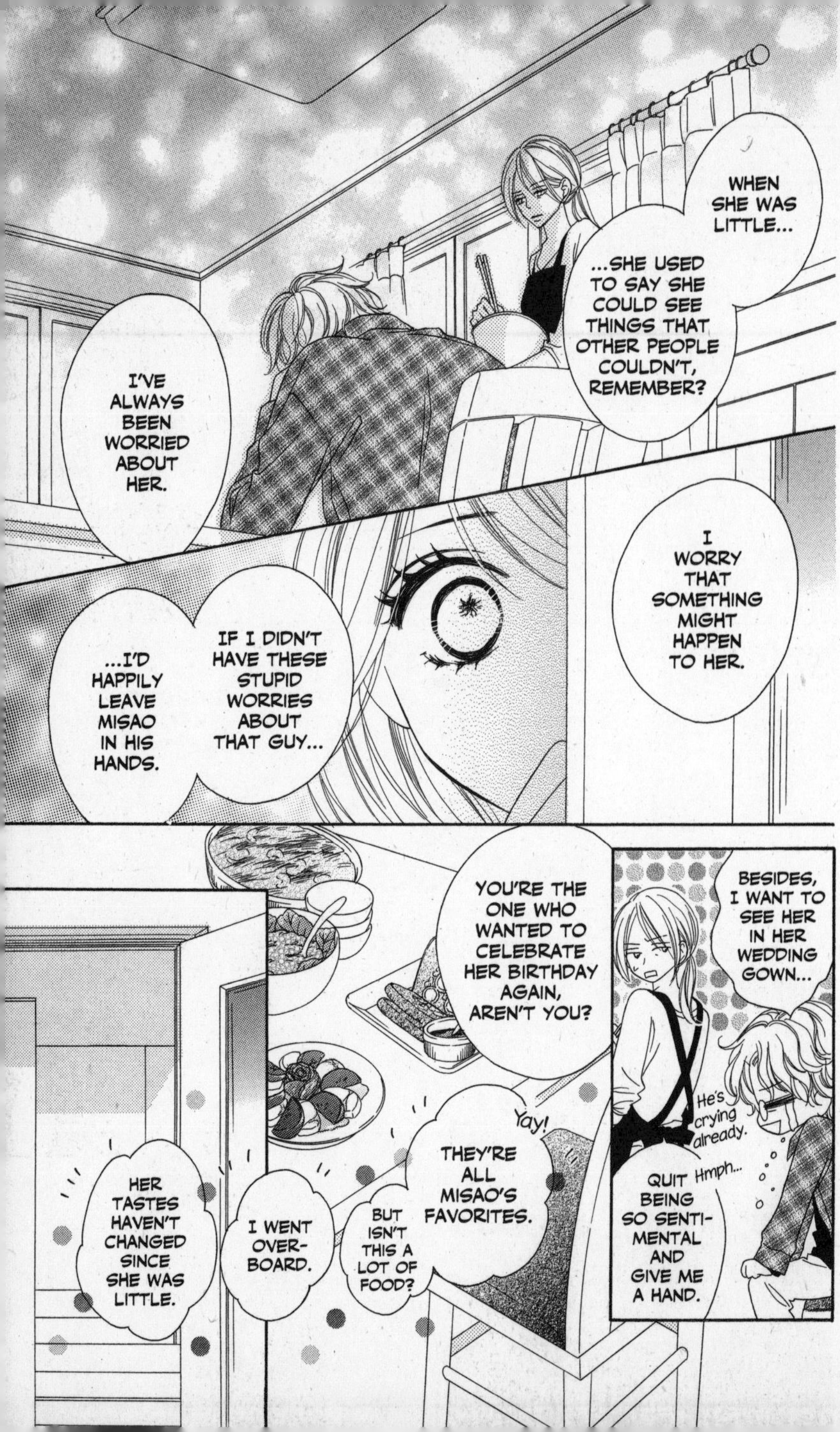
WHEN SHE WAS LITTLE...
...SHE USED TO SAY SHE COULD SEE THINGS THAT OTHER PEOPLE COULDN'T, REMEMBER?
I'VE ALWAYS BEEN WORRIED ABOUT HER.
I WORRY THAT SOMETHING MIGHT HAPPEN TO HER.
IF I DIDN'T HAVE THESE STUPID WORRIES ABOUT THAT GUY...
...I'D HAPPILY LEAVE MISAO IN HIS HANDS.
BESIDES, I WANT TO SEE HER IN HER WEDDING GOWN...
He's crying already.
Hmph...
QUIT BEING SO SENTI-MENTAL AND GIVE ME A HAND.
YOU'RE THE ONE WHO WANTED TO CELEBRATE HER BIRTHDAY AGAIN, AREN'T YOU?
Yay!
THEY'RE ALL MISAO'S FAVORITES.
BUT ISN'T THIS A LOT OF FOOD?
I WENT OVER-BOARD.
HER TASTES HAVEN'T CHANGED SINCE SHE WAS LITTLE.

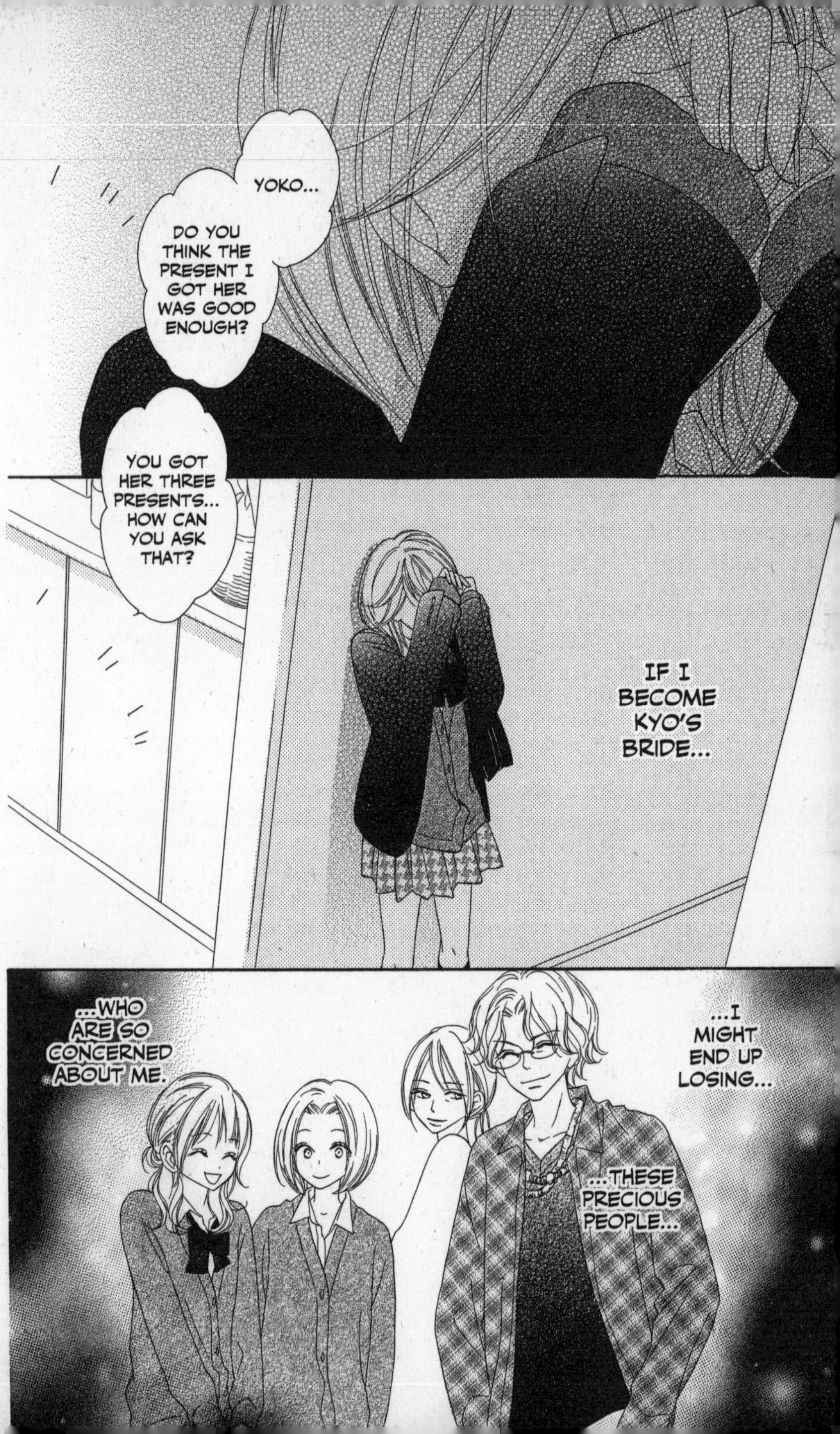
YOKO...
DO YOU THINK THE PRESENT I GOT HER WAS GOOD ENOUGH?
YOU GOT HER THREE PRESENTS... HOW CAN YOU ASK THAT?
IF I BECOME KYO'S BRIDE...
...I MIGHT END UP LOSING...
...THESE PRECIOUS PEOPLE...
...WHO ARE SO CONCERNED ABOUT ME.

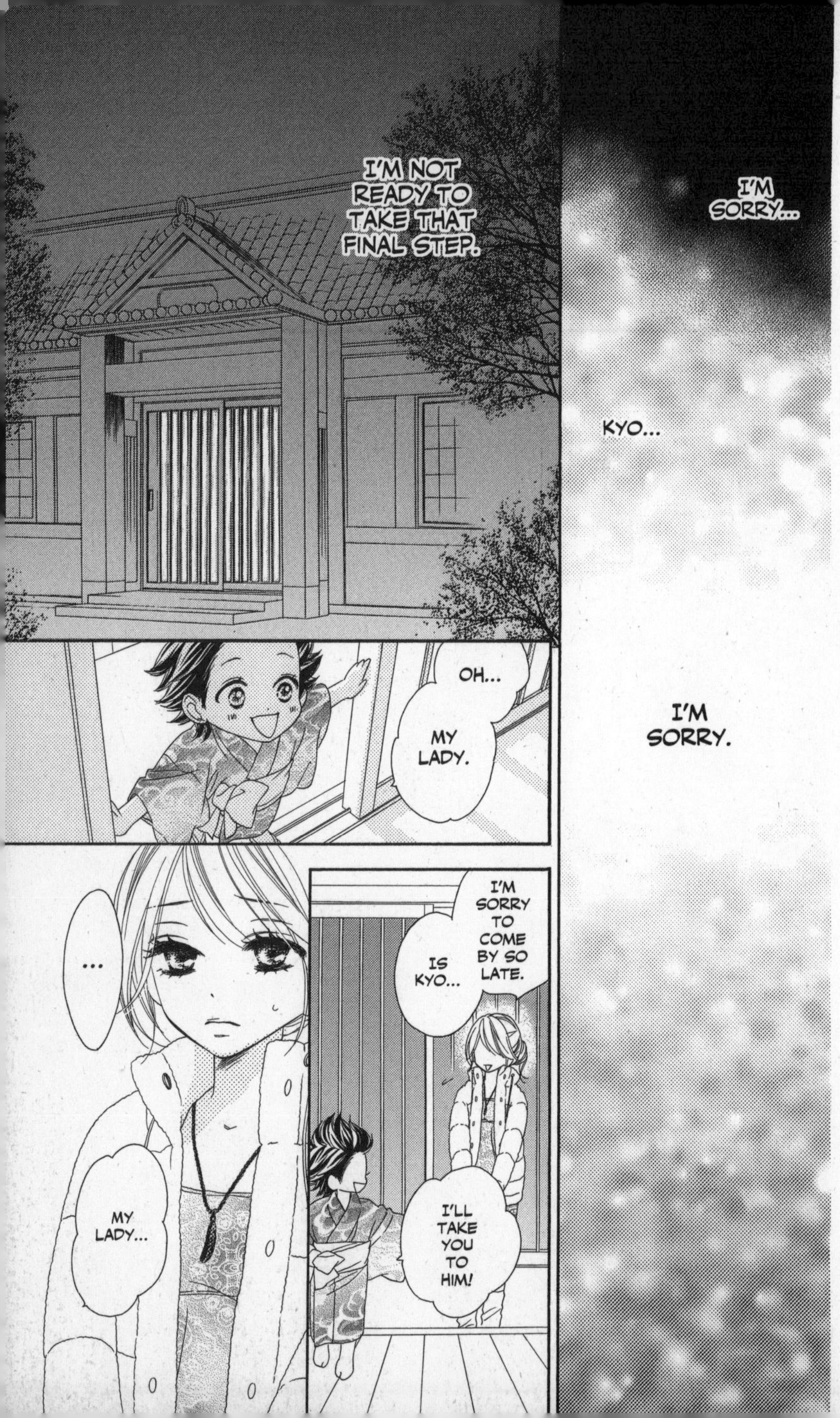
I'M SORRY...
KYO...
I'M SORRY.
I'M NOT READY TO TAKE THAT FINAL STEP.
OH...
MY LADY.
I'M SORRY TO COME BY SO LATE.
IS KYO...
I'LL TAKE YOU TO HIM!
...
MY LADY...

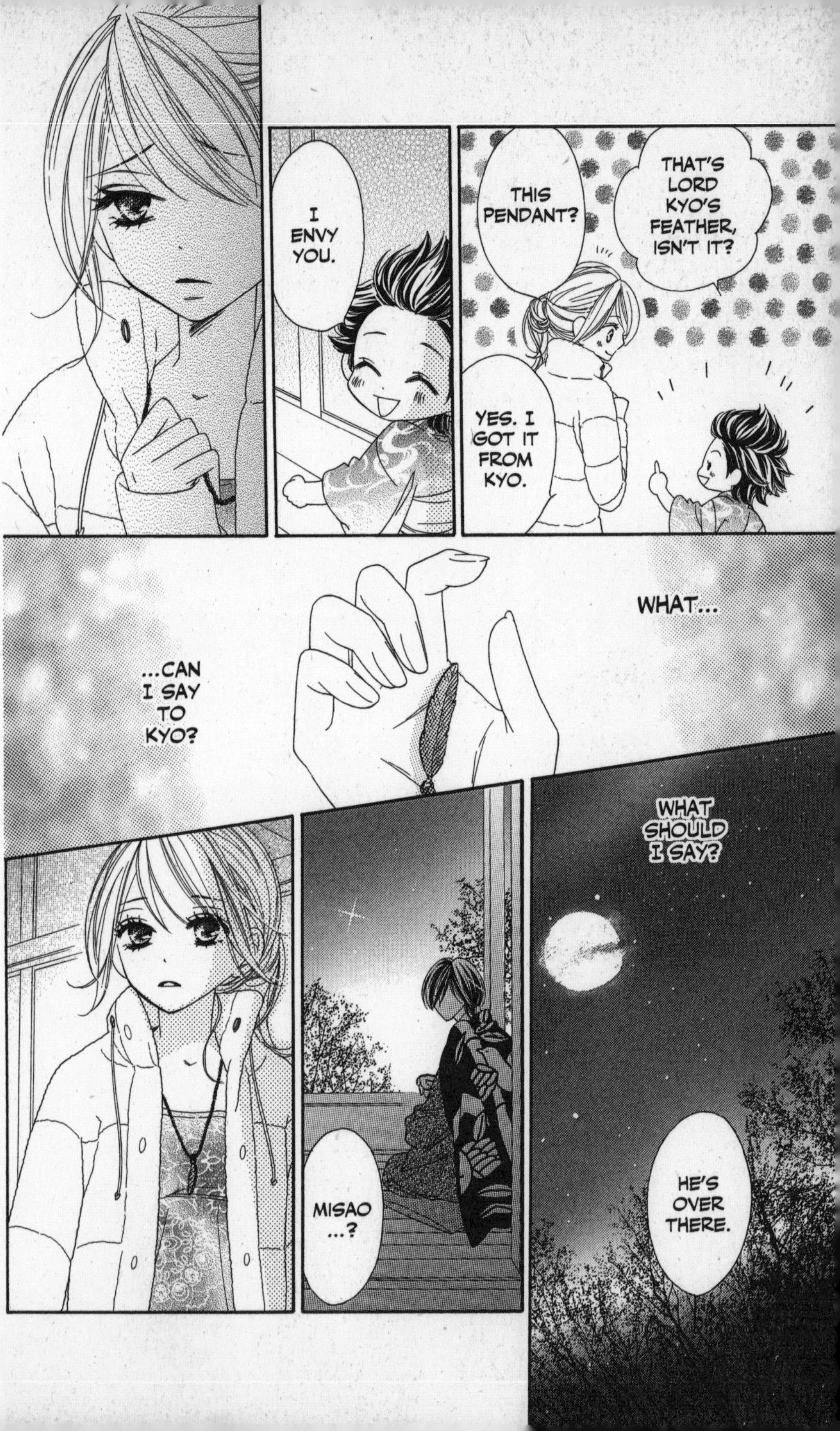
THAT'S LORD KYO'S FEATHER, ISN'T IT?
THIS PENDANT?
YES. I GOT IT FROM KYO.
I ENVY YOU.
WHAT...
...CAN I SAY TO KYO?
WHAT SHOULD I SAY?
HE'S OVER THERE.
MISAO ...?

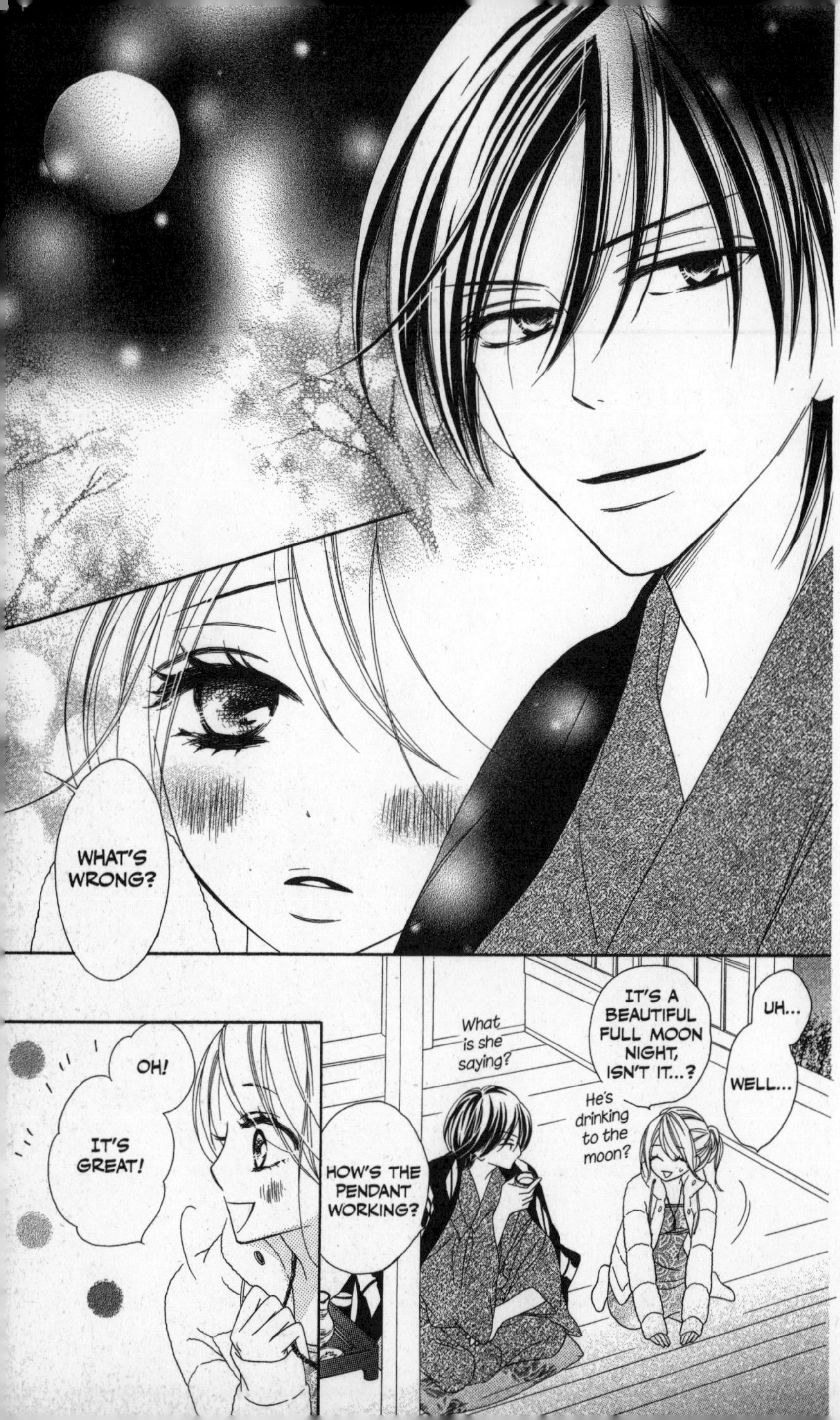
WHAT'S WRONG?
UH... WELL...
IT'S A BEAUTIFUL FULL MOON NIGHT, ISN'T IT...?
What is she saying?
He's drinking to the moon?
HOW'S THE PENDANT WORKING?
OH! IT'S GREAT!

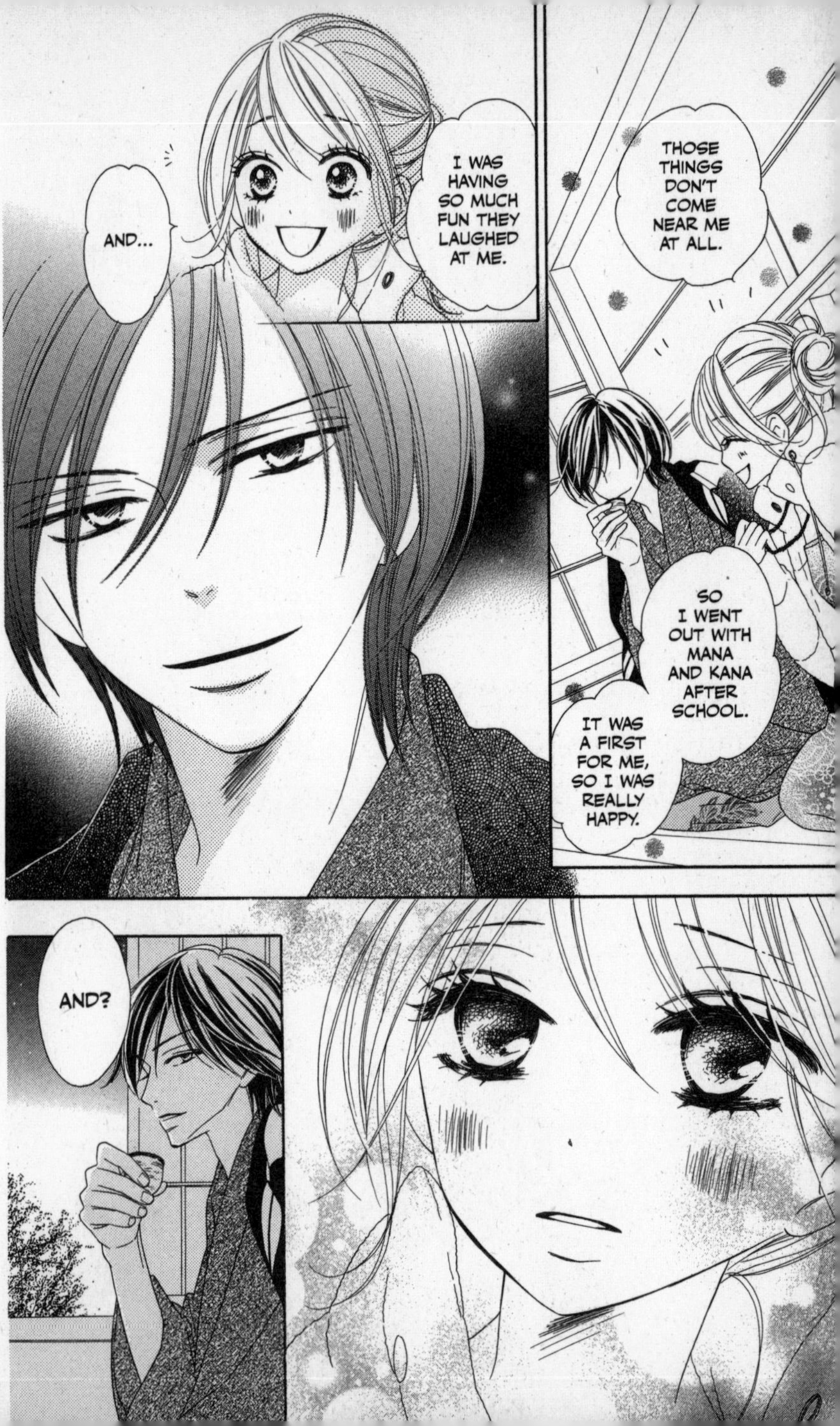
THOSE THINGS DON'T COME NEAR ME AT ALL.
SO I WENT OUT WITH MANA AND KANA AFTER SCHOOL.
IT WAS A FIRST FOR ME, SO I WAS REALLY HAPPY.
I WAS HAVING SO MUCH FUN THEY LAUGHED AT ME.
AND...
AND?

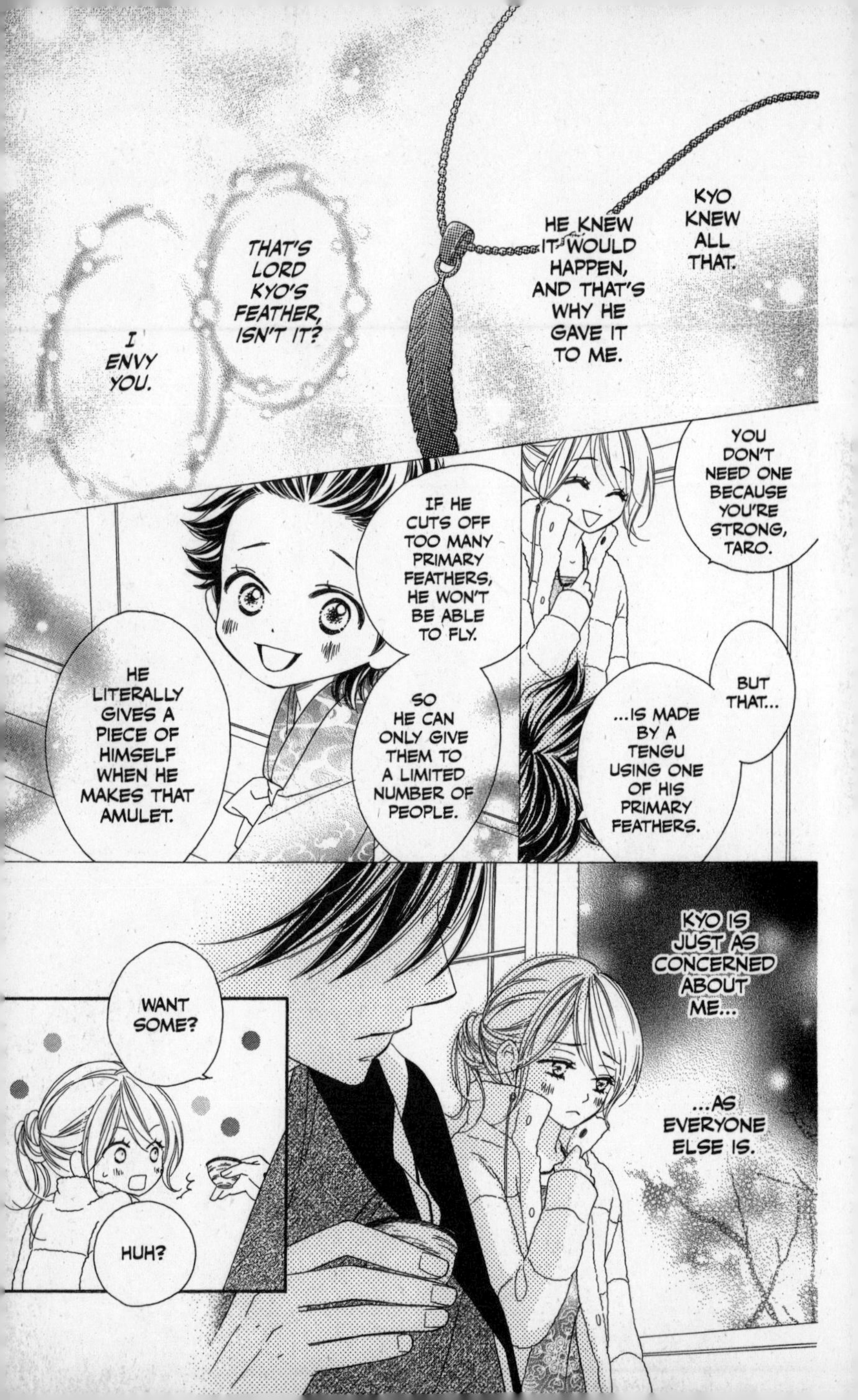
KYO KNEW ALL THAT.
HE KNEW IT WOULD HAPPEN, AND THAT'S WHY HE GAVE IT TO ME.
THAT'S LORD KYO'S FEATHER, ISN'T IT?
I ENVY YOU.
YOU DON'T NEED ONE BECAUSE YOU'RE STRONG, TARO.
BUT THAT...
...IS MADE BY A TENGU USING ONE OF HIS PRIMARY FEATHERS.
IF HE CUTS OFF TOO MANY PRIMARY FEATHERS, HE WON'T BE ABLE TO FLY.
SO HE CAN ONLY GIVE THEM TO A LIMITED NUMBER OF PEOPLE.
HE LITERALLY GIVES A PIECE OF HIMSELF WHEN HE MAKES THAT AMULET.
KYO IS JUST AS CONCERNED ABOUT ME...
...AS EVERYONE ELSE IS.
WANT SOME?
HUH?

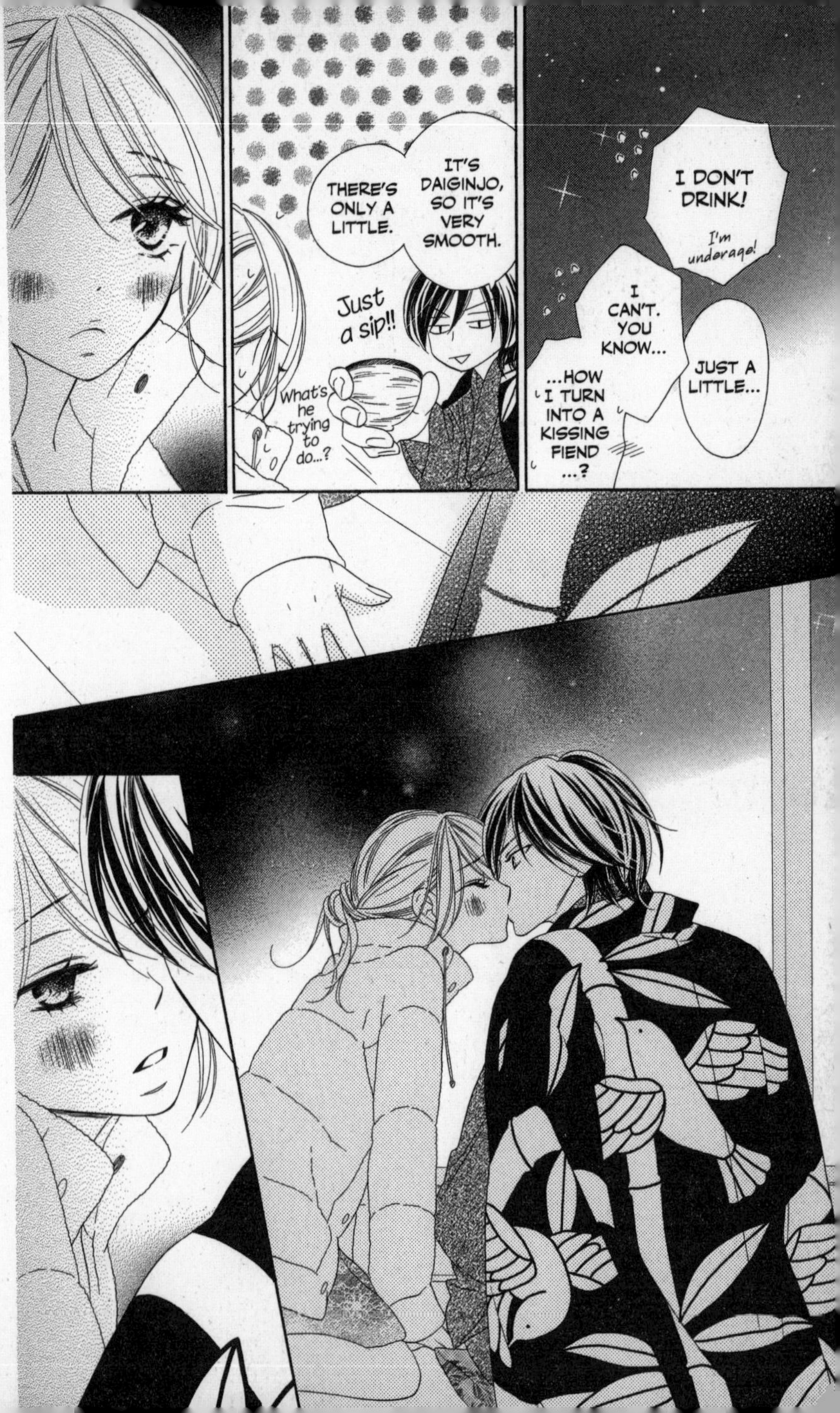
I DON'T DRINK!
I'm underage!
JUST A LITTLE...
I CAN'T. YOU KNOW...
...HOW I TURN INTO A KISSING FIEND ...?
IT'S DAIGINJO, SO IT'S VERY SMOOTH.
THERE'S ONLY A LITTLE.
Just a sip!!
What's he trying to do...?

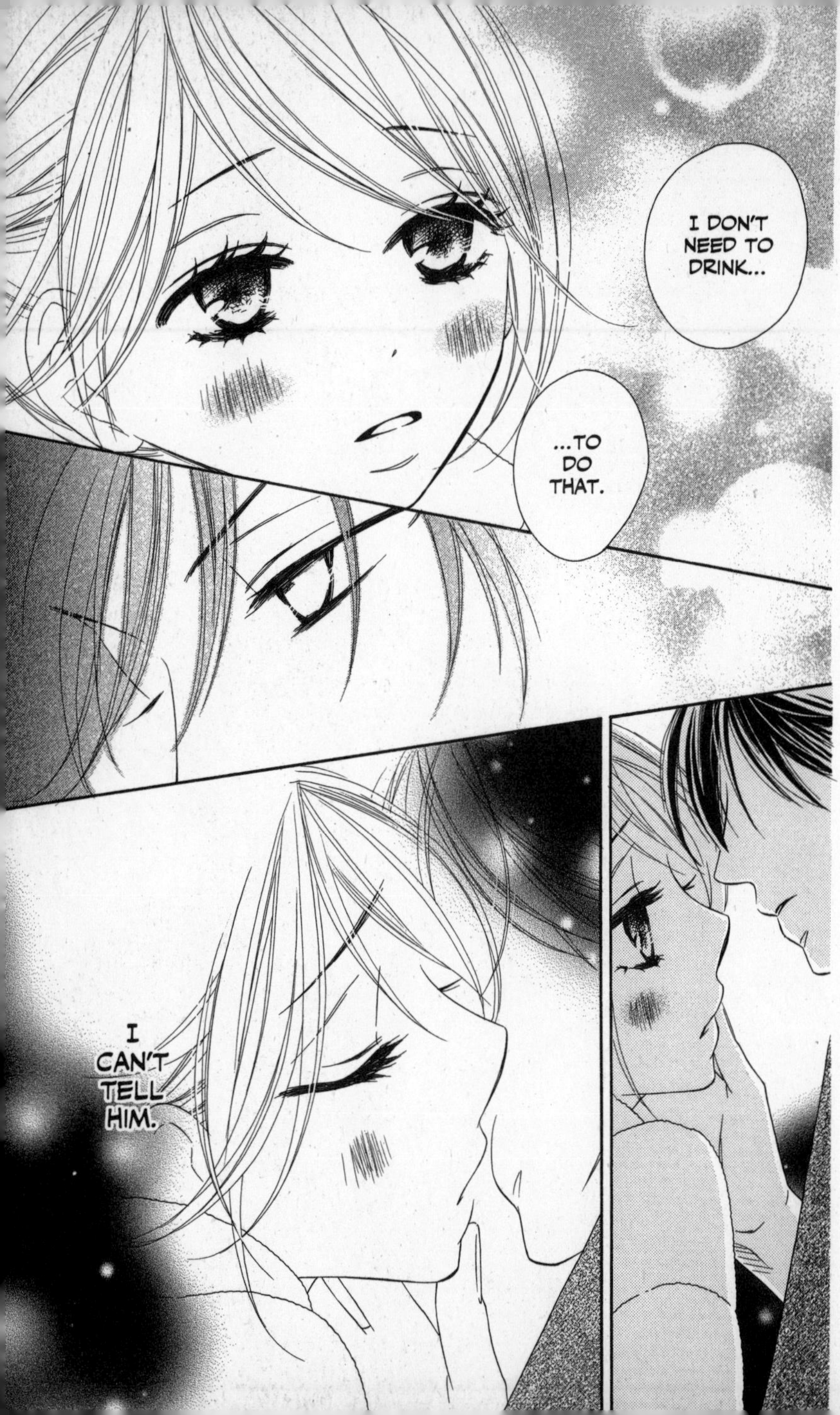
I DON'T NEED TO DRINK...
...TO DO THAT.
I CAN'T TELL HIM.

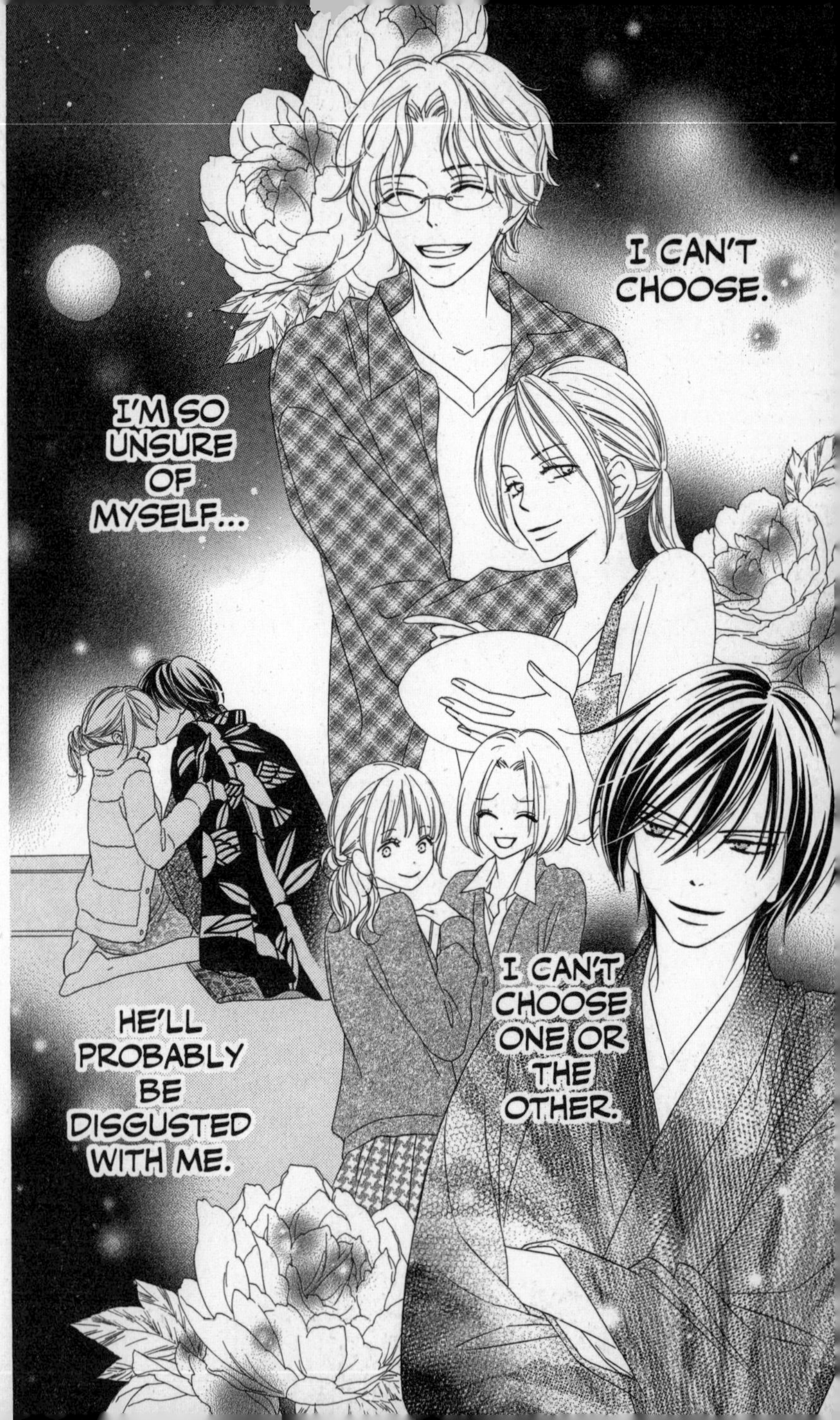
I CAN'T CHOOSE.
I'M SO UNSURE OF MYSELF...
I CAN'T CHOOSE ONE OR THE OTHER.
HE'LL PROBABLY BE DISGUSTED WITH ME.

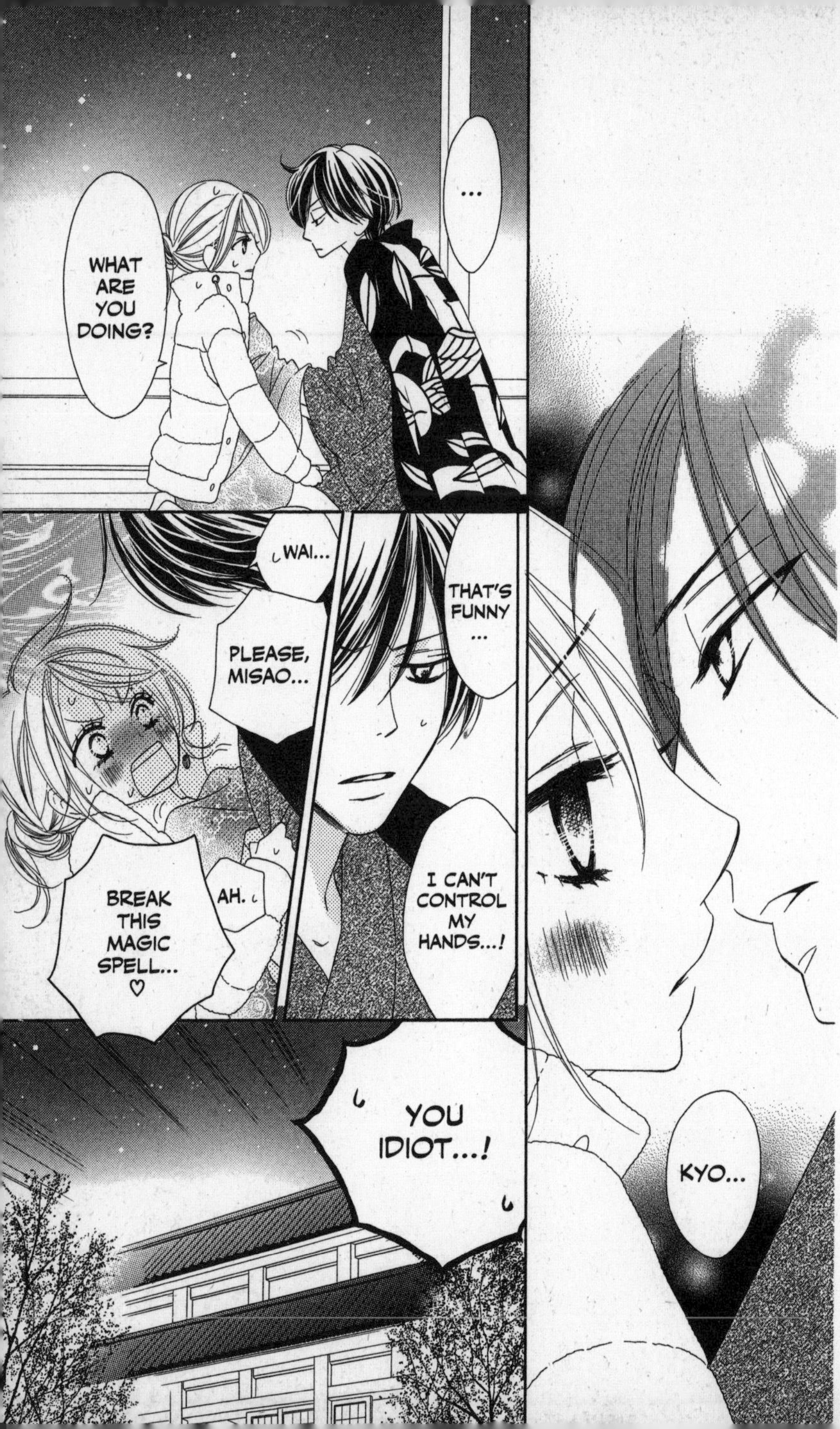
KYO...
...
WHAT ARE YOU DOING?
THAT'S FUNNY...
I CAN'T CONTROL MY HANDS...!
WAI...
PLEASE, MISAO...
AH.
BREAK THIS MAGIC SPELL... ♡
YOU IDIOT...!

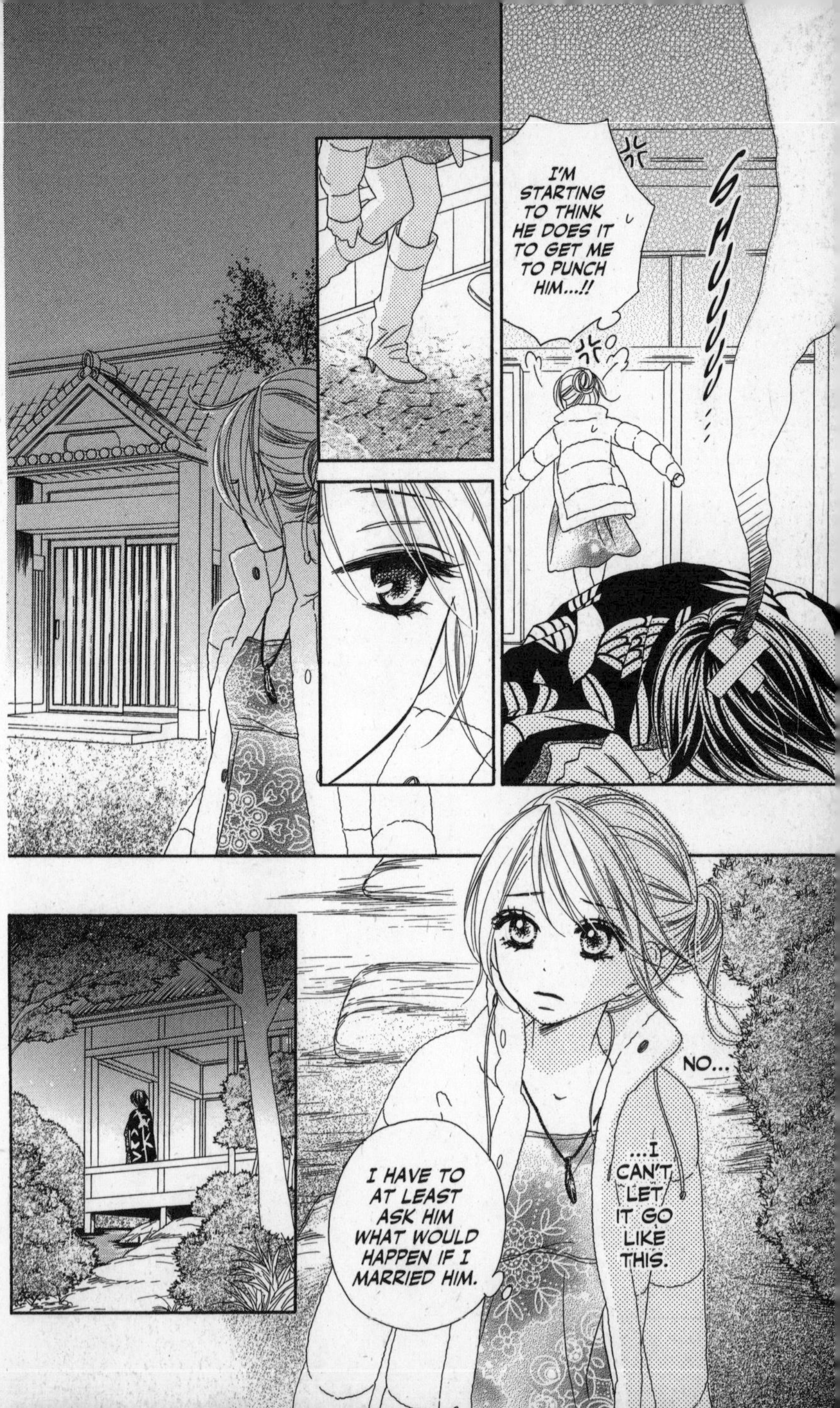
I'M STARTING TO THINK HE DOES IT TO GET ME TO PUNCH HIM...!!
NO...
...I CAN'T LET IT GO LIKE THIS.
I HAVE TO AT LEAST ASK HIM WHAT WOULD HAPPEN IF I MARRIED HIM.

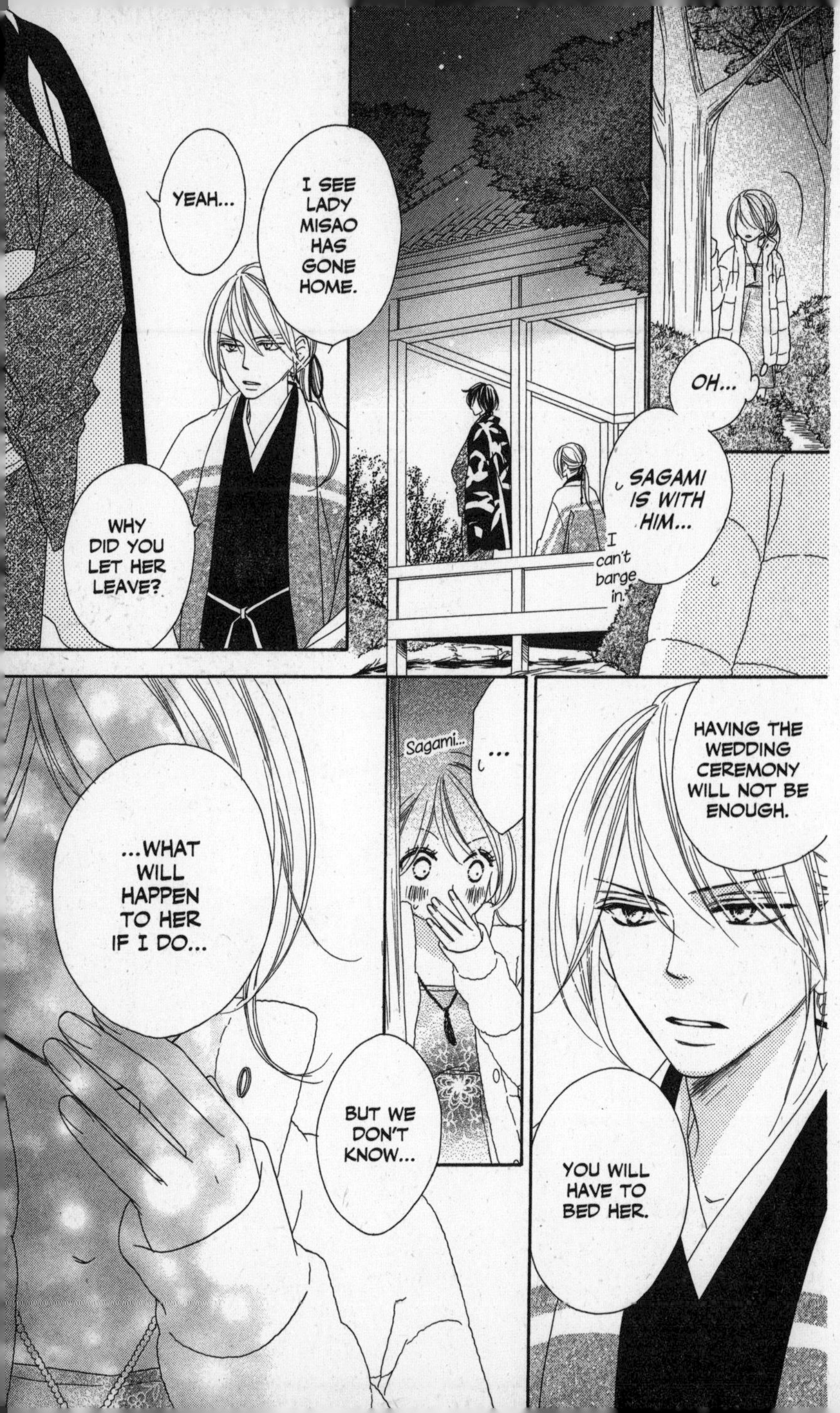
OH...
SAGAMI IS WITH HIM...
I can't barge in.
I SEE LADY MISAO HAS GONE HOME.
YEAH...
WHY DID YOU LET HER LEAVE?
HAVING THE WEDDING CEREMONY WILL NOT BE ENOUGH.
YOU WILL HAVE TO BED HER.
Sagami...
...
BUT WE DON'T KNOW...
...WHAT WILL HAPPEN TO HER IF I DO...

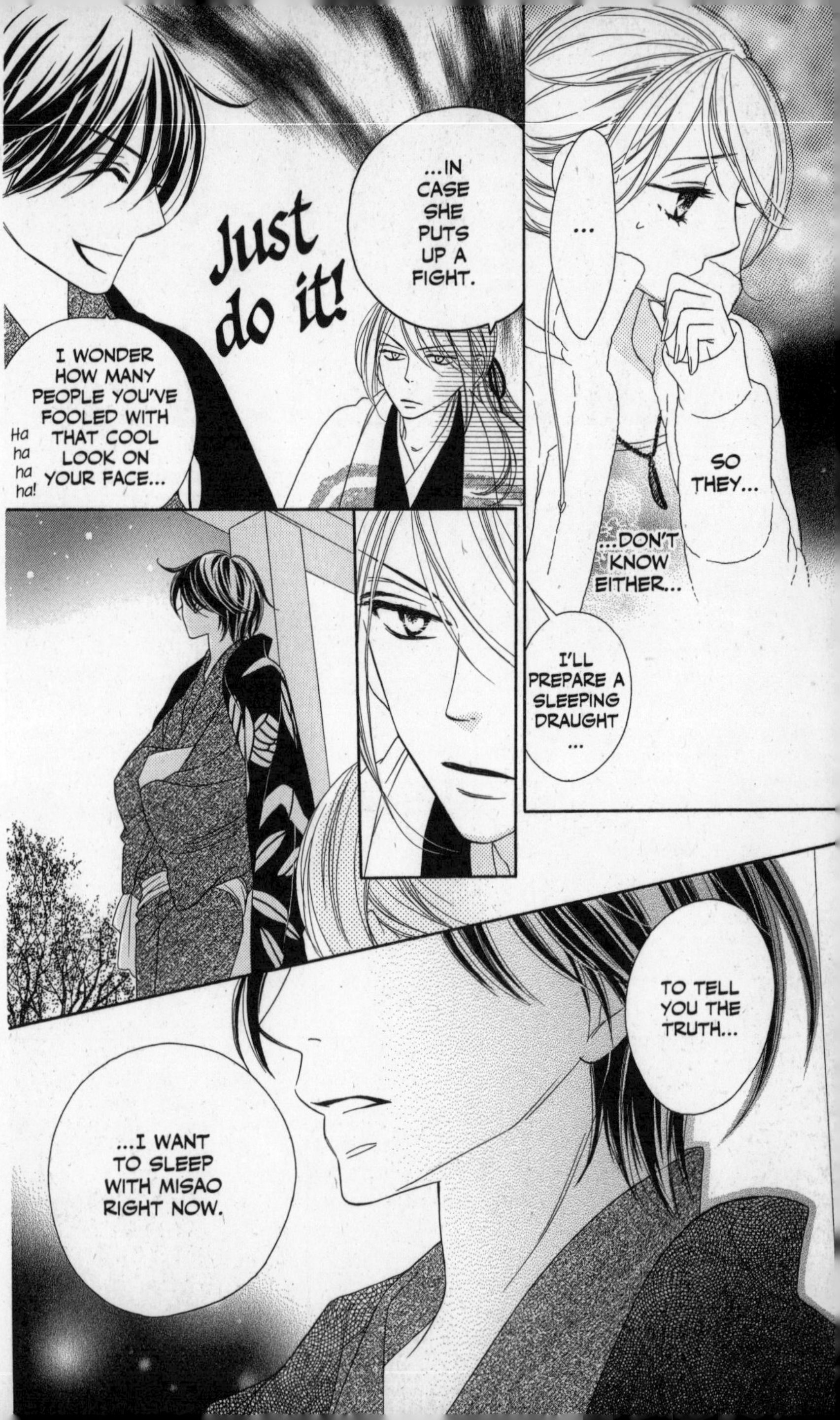
...
SO THEY...
...DON'T KNOW EITHER...
I'LL PREPARE A SLEEPING DRAUGHT ...
...IN CASE SHE PUTS UP A FIGHT.
Just do it!
I WONDER HOW MANY PEOPLE YOU'VE FOOLED WITH THAT COOL LOOK ON YOUR FACE...
Ha ha ha ha!
TO TELL YOU THE TRUTH...
...I WANT TO SLEEP WITH MISAO RIGHT NOW.

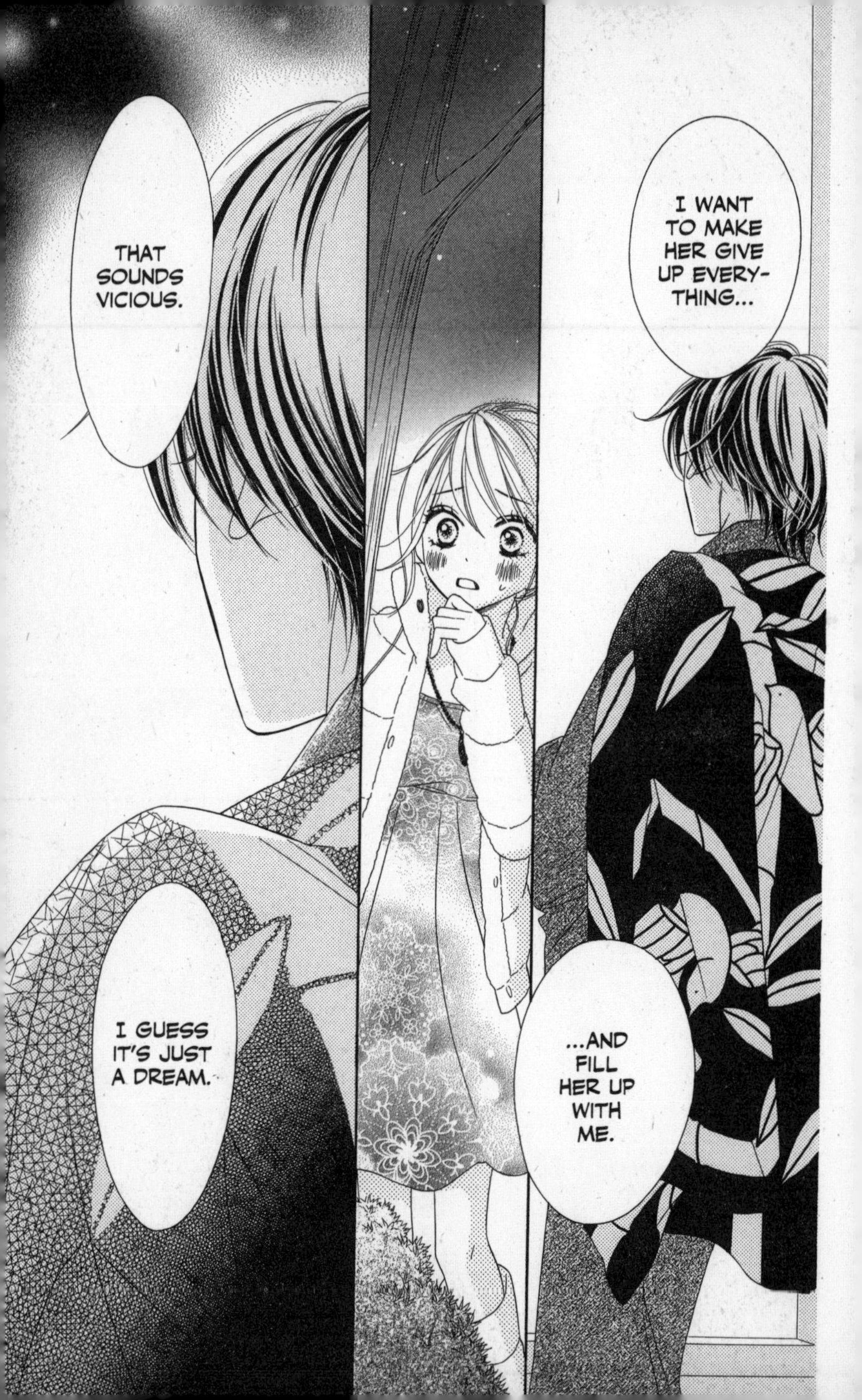
I WANT TO MAKE HER GIVE UP EVERY-THING...
...AND FILL HER UP WITH ME.
THAT SOUNDS VICIOUS.
I GUESS IT'S JUST A DREAM.

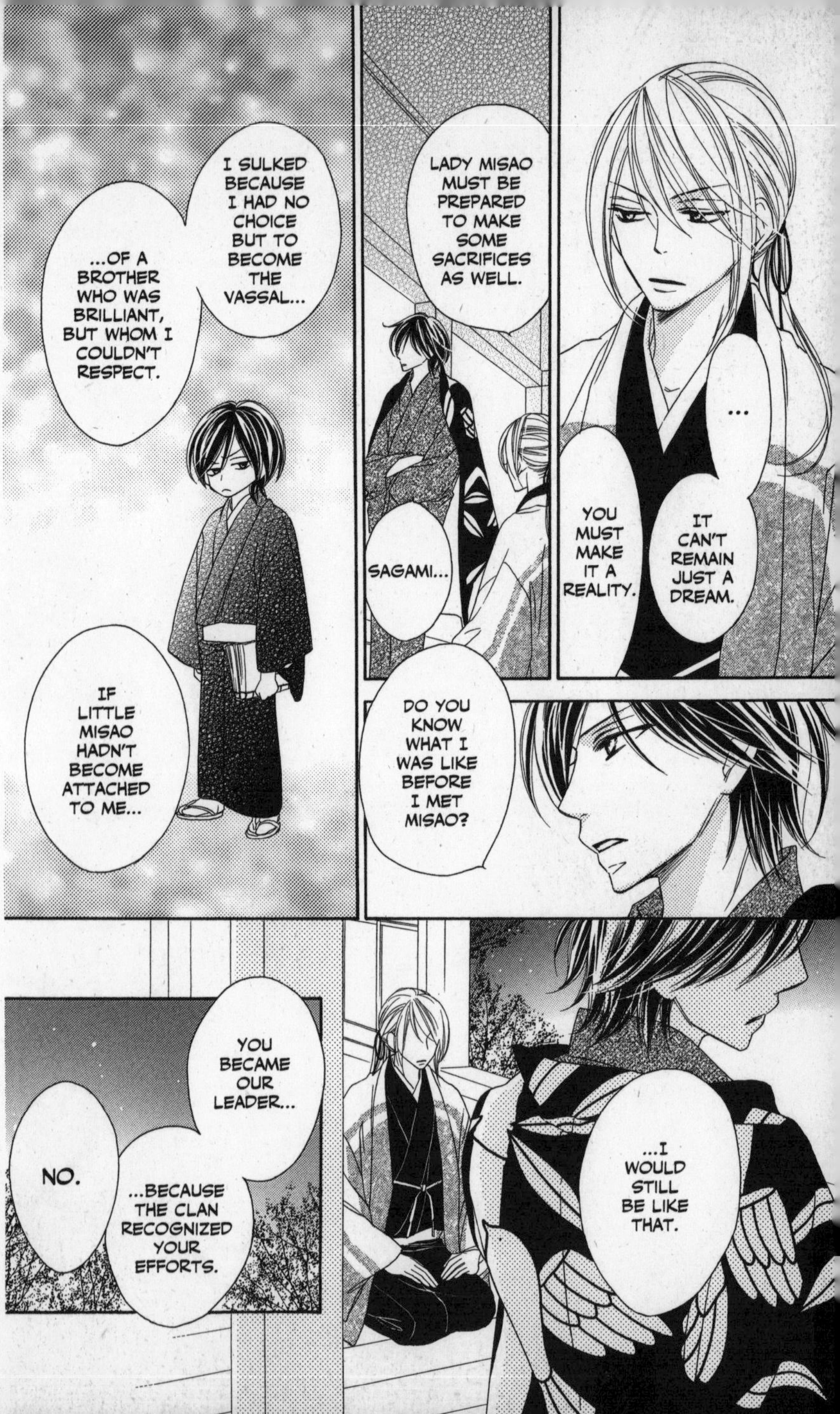
...
IT CAN'T REMAIN JUST A DREAM.
YOU MUST MAKE IT A REALITY.
LADY MISAO MUST BE PREPARED TO MAKE SOME SACRIFICES AS WELL.
SAGAMI...
DO YOU KNOW WHAT I WAS LIKE BEFORE I MET MISAO?
I SULKED BECAUSE I HAD NO CHOICE BUT TO BECOME THE VASSAL...
...OF A BROTHER WHO WAS BRILLIANT, BUT WHOM I COULDN'T RESPECT.
IF LITTLE MISAO HADN'T BECOME ATTACHED TO ME...
...I WOULD STILL BE LIKE THAT.
YOU BECAME OUR LEADER...
...BECAUSE THE CLAN RECOGNIZED YOUR EFFORTS.
NO.

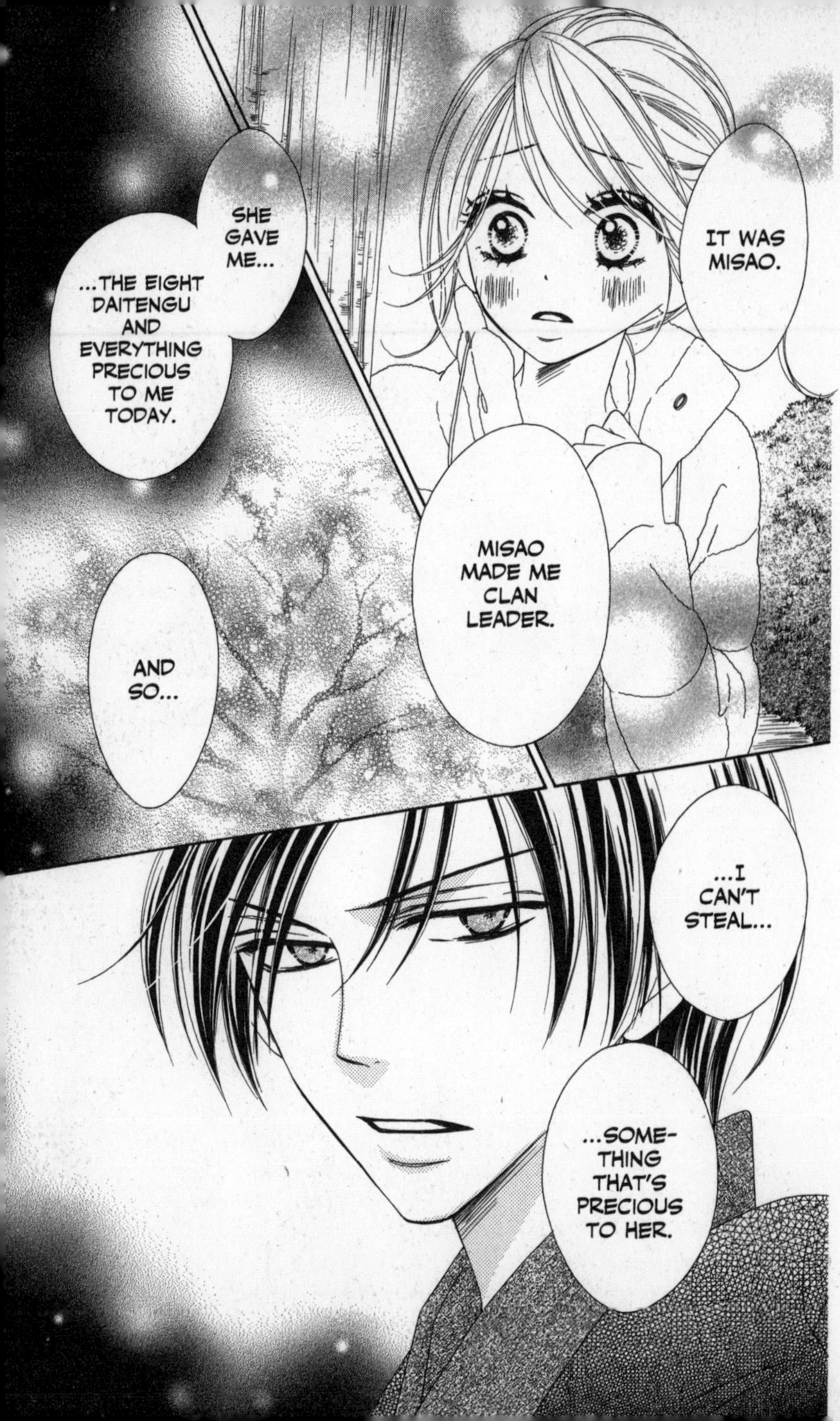
IT WAS MISAO.
MISAO MADE ME CLAN LEADER.
SHE GAVE ME...
...THE EIGHT DAITENGU AND EVERYTHING PRECIOUS TO ME TODAY.
AND SO...
...I CAN'T STEAL...
...SOME-THING THAT'S PRECIOUS TO HER.

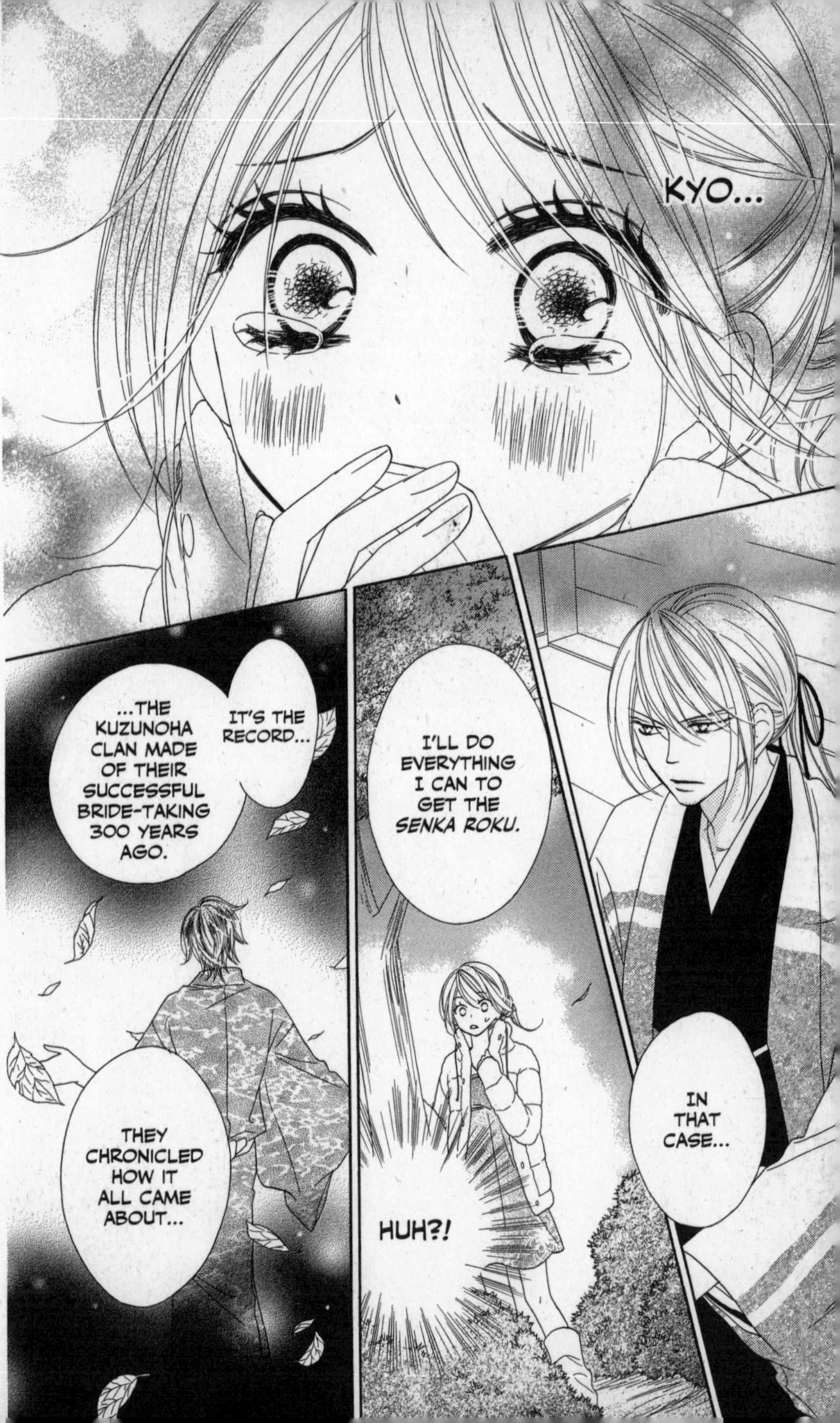
KYO...
IN THAT CASE...
I'LL DO EVERYTHING I CAN TO GET THE *SENKA ROKU.*
HUH?!
IT'S THE RECORD...
...THE KUZUNOHA CLAN MADE OF THEIR SUCCESSFUL BRIDE-TAKING 300 YEARS AGO.
THEY CHRONICLED HOW IT ALL CAME ABOUT...

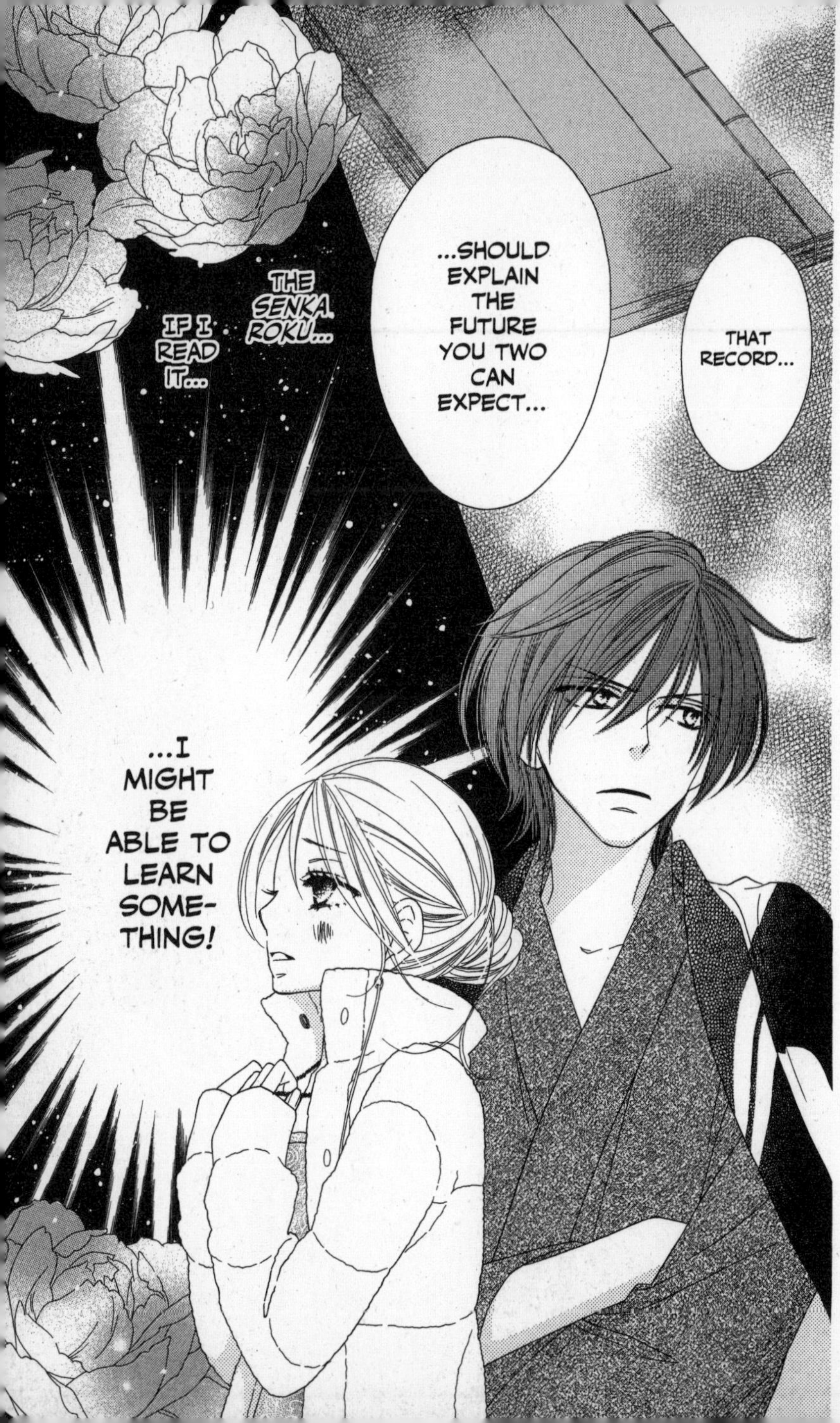
THAT RECORD...
...SHOULD EXPLAIN THE FUTURE YOU TWO CAN EXPECT...
THE SENKA ROKU...
IF I READ IT...
...I MIGHT BE ABLE TO LEARN SOME-THING!

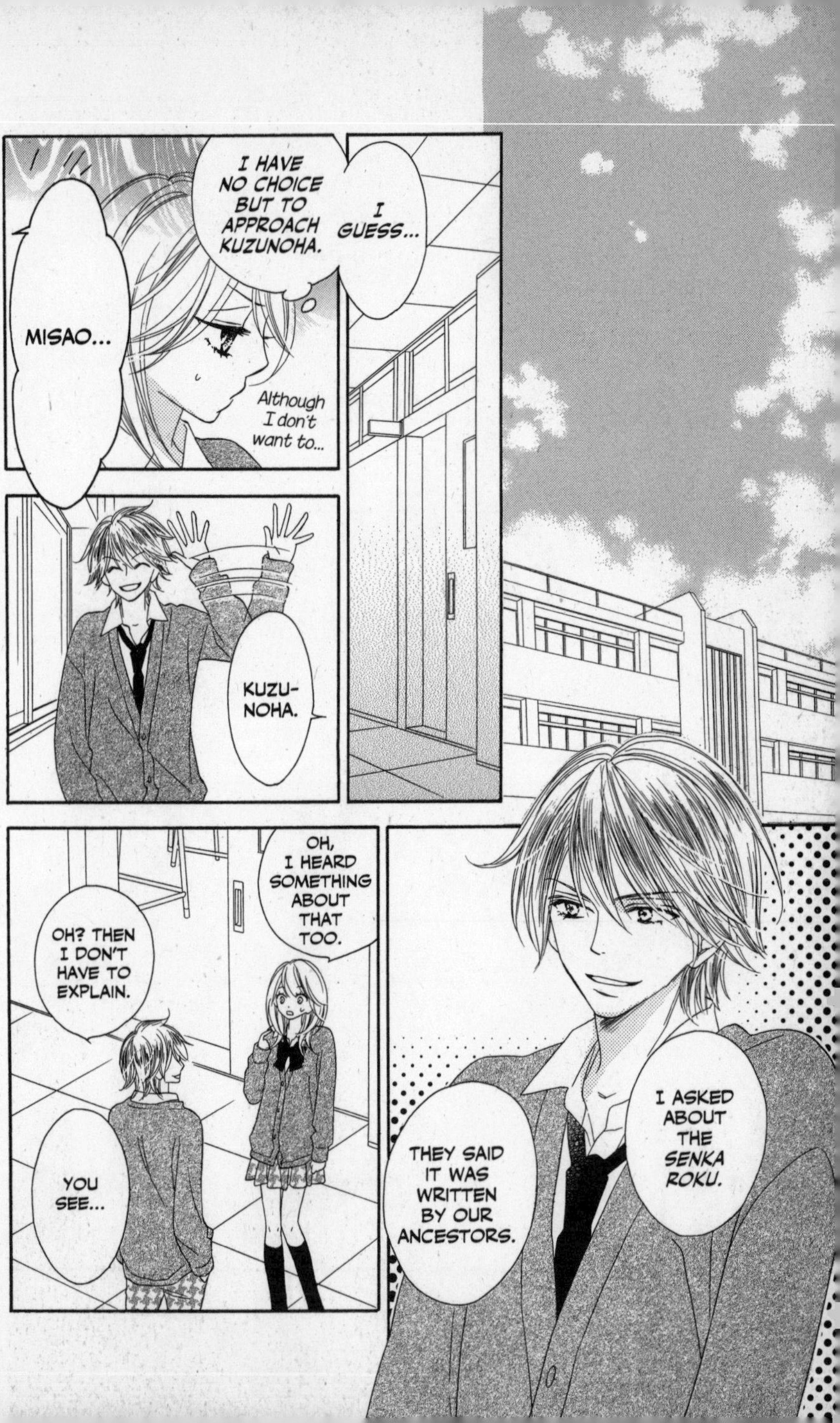
I HAVE NO CHOICE BUT TO APPROACH KUZUNOHA.
I GUESS...
Although I don't want to...
MISAO...
KUZUNOHA.
I ASKED ABOUT THE SENKA ROKU.
THEY SAID IT WAS WRITTEN BY OUR ANCESTORS.
OH, I HEARD SOMETHING ABOUT THAT TOO.
OH? THEN I DON'T HAVE TO EXPLAIN.
YOU SEE...

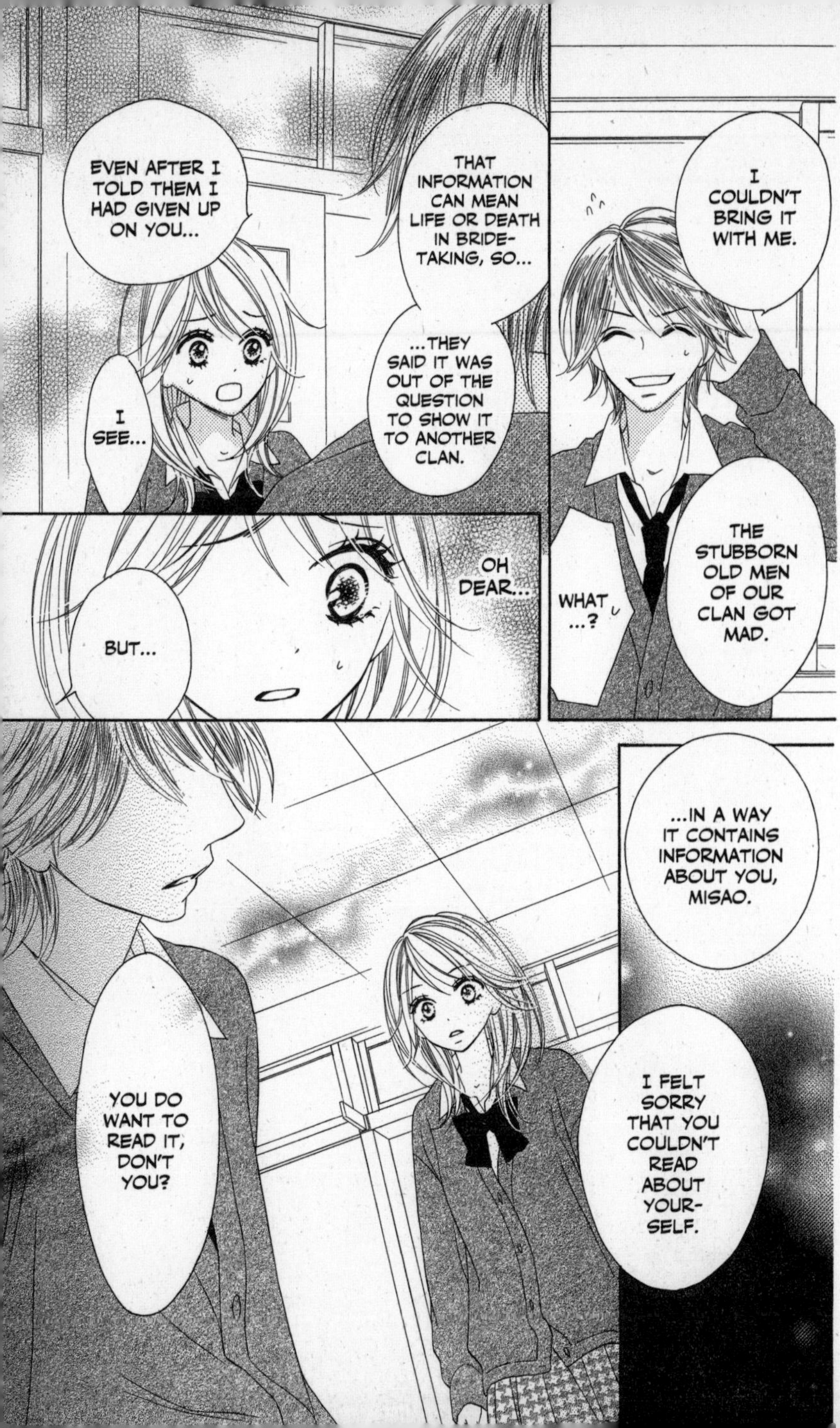
I COULDN'T BRING IT WITH ME.
WHAT ...?
THE STUBBORN OLD MEN OF OUR CLAN GOT MAD.
THAT INFORMATION CAN MEAN LIFE OR DEATH IN BRIDE-TAKING, SO...
...THEY SAID IT WAS OUT OF THE QUESTION TO SHOW IT TO ANOTHER CLAN.
EVEN AFTER I TOLD THEM I HAD GIVEN UP ON YOU...
I SEE...
OH DEAR...
BUT...
...IN A WAY IT CONTAINS INFORMATION ABOUT YOU, MISAO.
I FELT SORRY THAT YOU COULDN'T READ ABOUT YOUR-SELF.
YOU DO WANT TO READ IT, DON'T YOU?

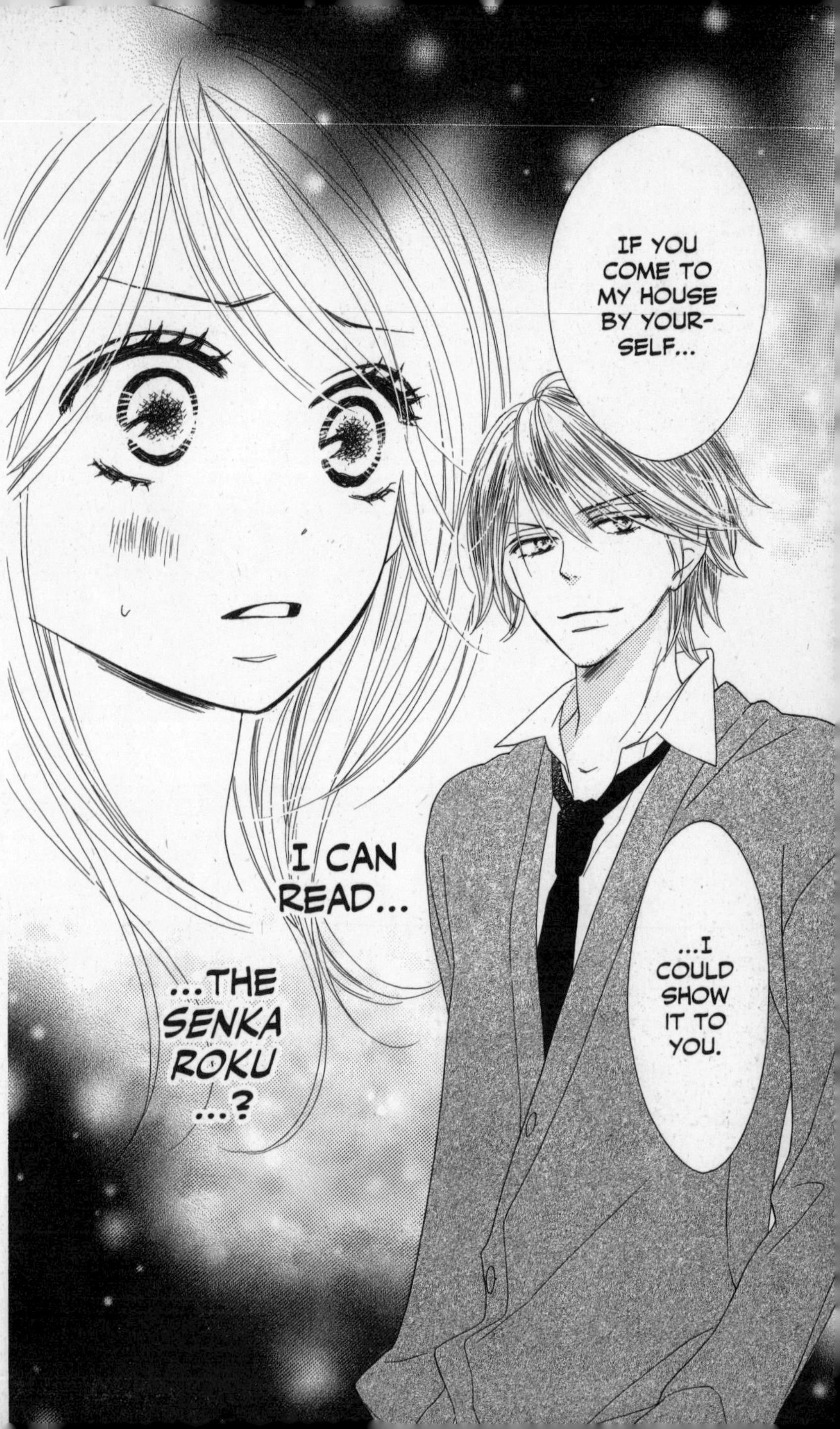
IF YOU COME TO MY HOUSE BY YOUR-SELF...
...I COULD SHOW IT TO YOU.
I CAN READ...
...THE SENKA ROKU ...?

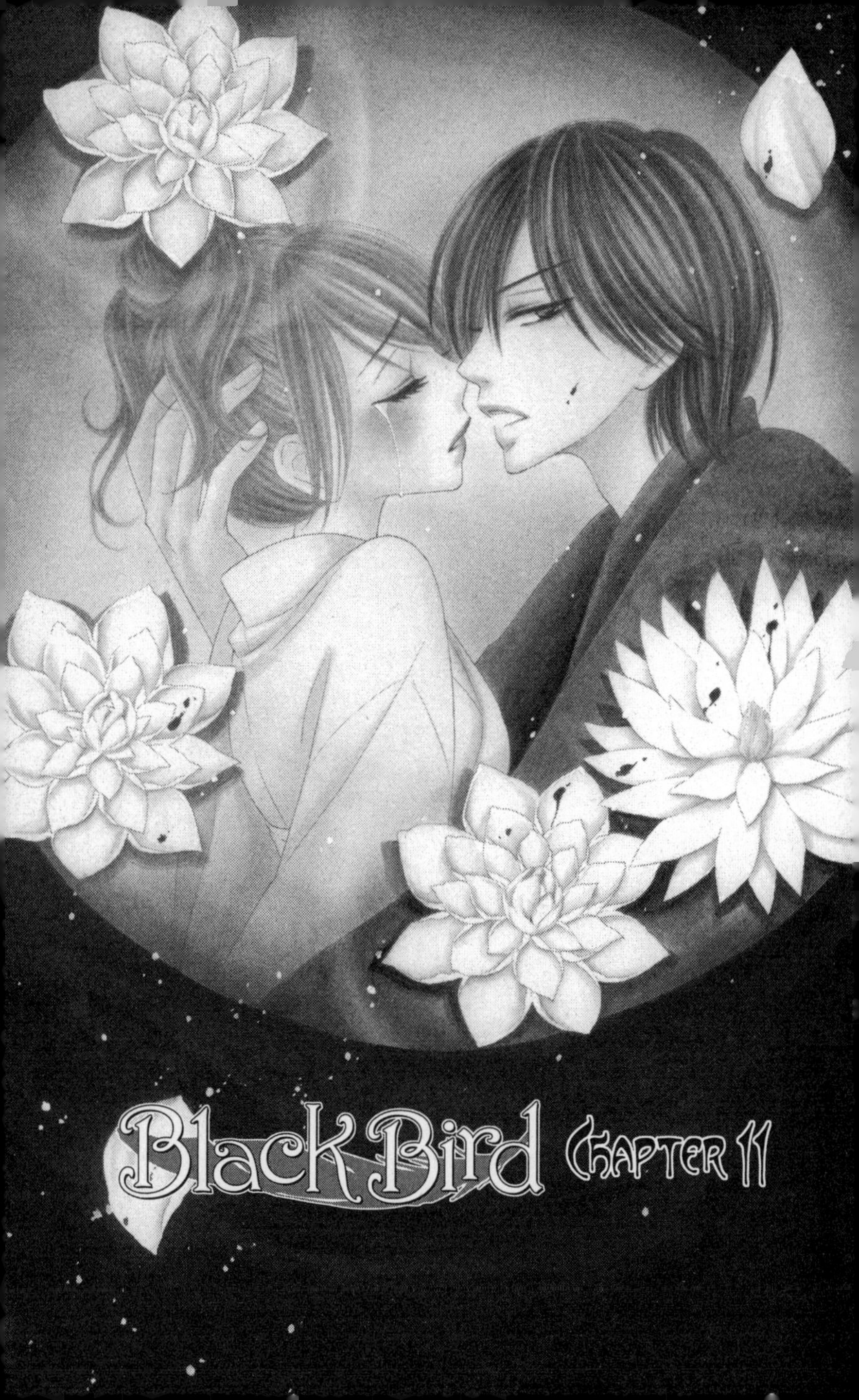
Black Bird
Chapter 11

I had a *Black Bird* fan page called "Peach Tengu Mansion" for *Betsucomi*

In one section, I do drawings requested by the readers. It seems to be a very popular section. ~~I couldn't quit even if I wanted to.~~ I want to continue to do my best to keep everyone happy!

I get so many unexpected requests that it's a lot of fun.

This ↓ is number one: "Tengu Surgical Wing."

The Black Tower
HEH HEH HEH
Shall I slice you up...?
Eeek... This is sexual harassment!!
It's cancer. The patient hasn't long to live.

Lab coats! Scrubs! I love it...♥
I love how Kyo is dressed (surgical scrubs under his lab coat).

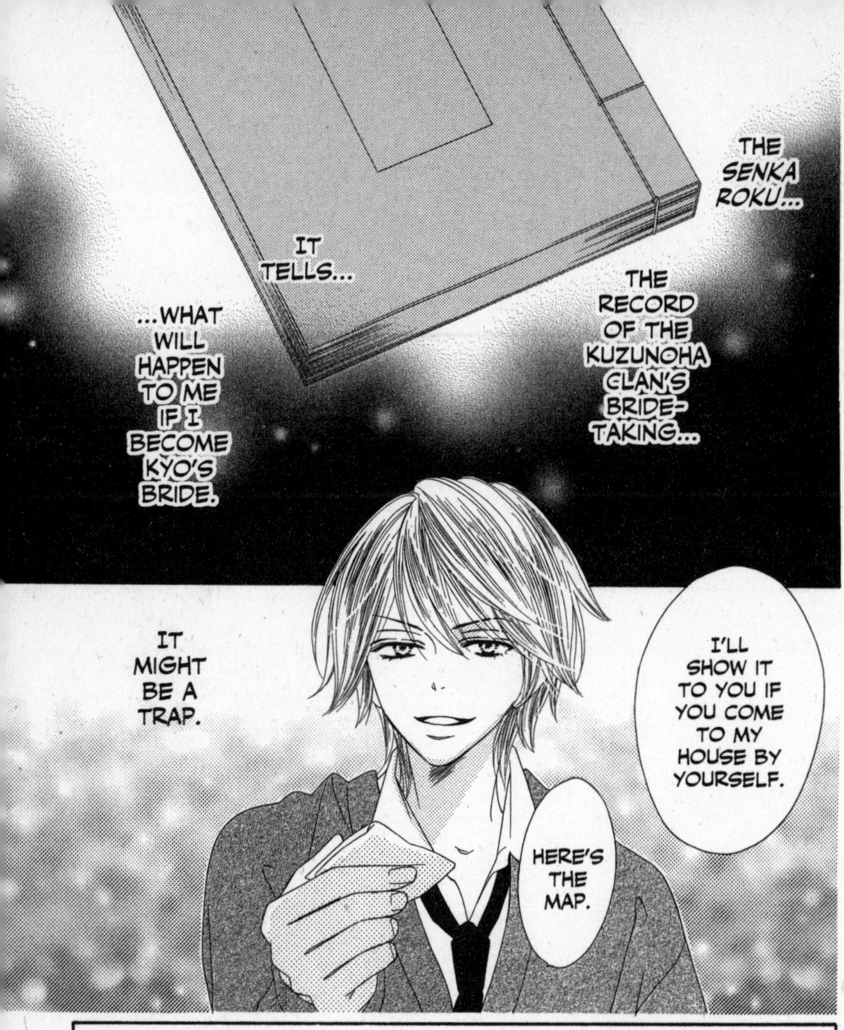
THE SENKA ROKU...
THE RECORD OF THE KUZUNOHA CLAN'S BRIDE-TAKING...
IT TELLS...
...WHAT WILL HAPPEN TO ME IF I BECOME KYO'S BRIDE.
I'LL SHOW IT TO YOU IF YOU COME TO MY HOUSE BY YOURSELF.
HERE'S THE MAP.
IT MIGHT BE A TRAP.

I have a feeling the person who looks forward to the Fan Page the most is me. I'd be happy if people who prefer the graphic novel format look at this page. Plus, you can only see color pages in a magazine. Please, by all means, pick up and read a *Betsucomi* magazine.♥

And please send in your requests.♥♥

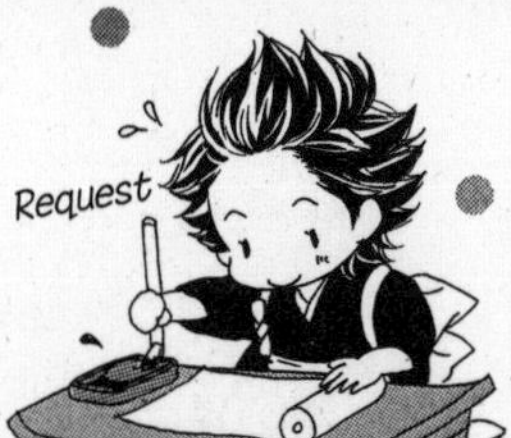
Request

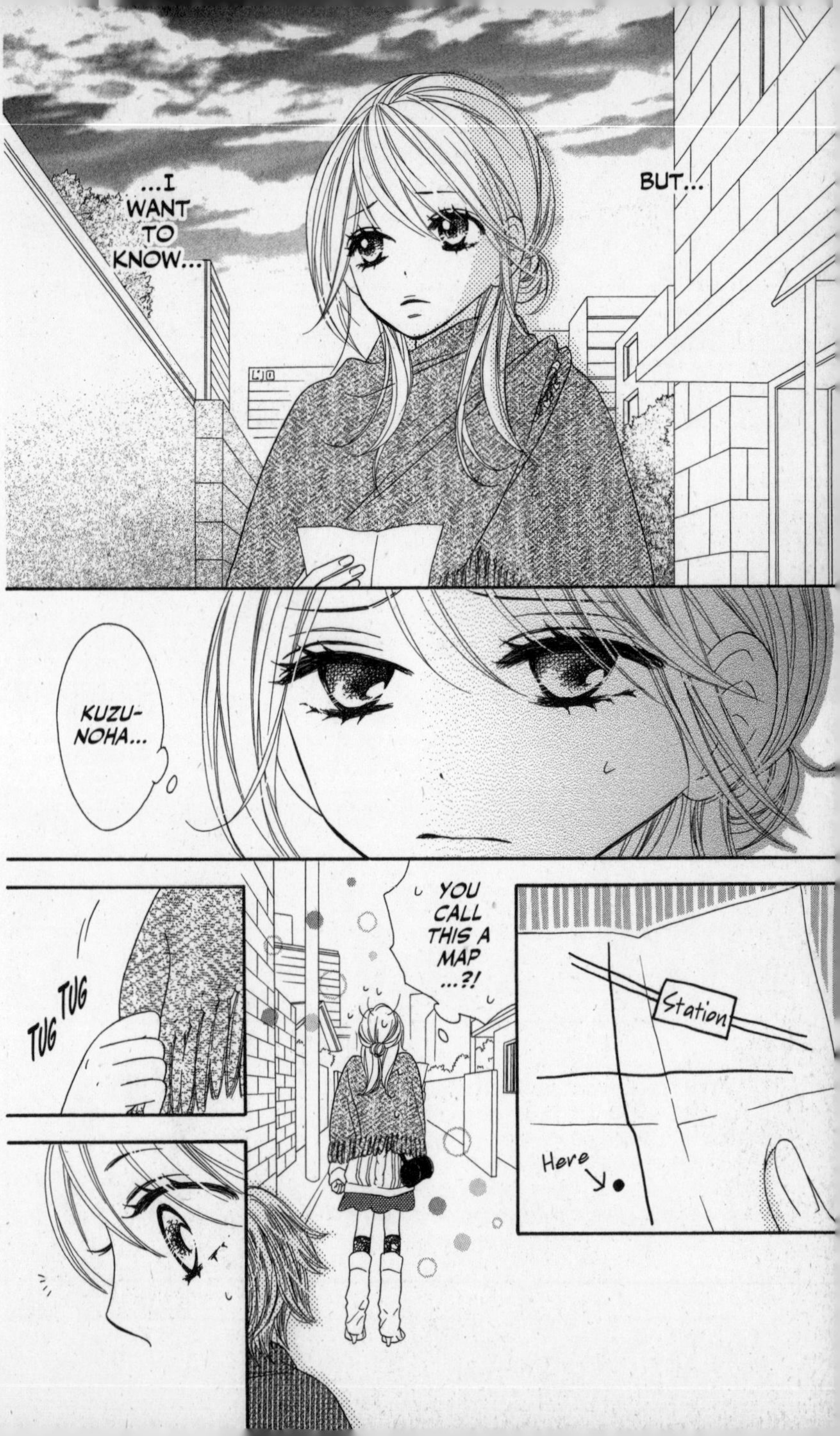
BUT...
...I WANT TO KNOW...
KUZU-NOHA...
Station
Here
YOU CALL THIS A MAP ...?!
TUG TUG

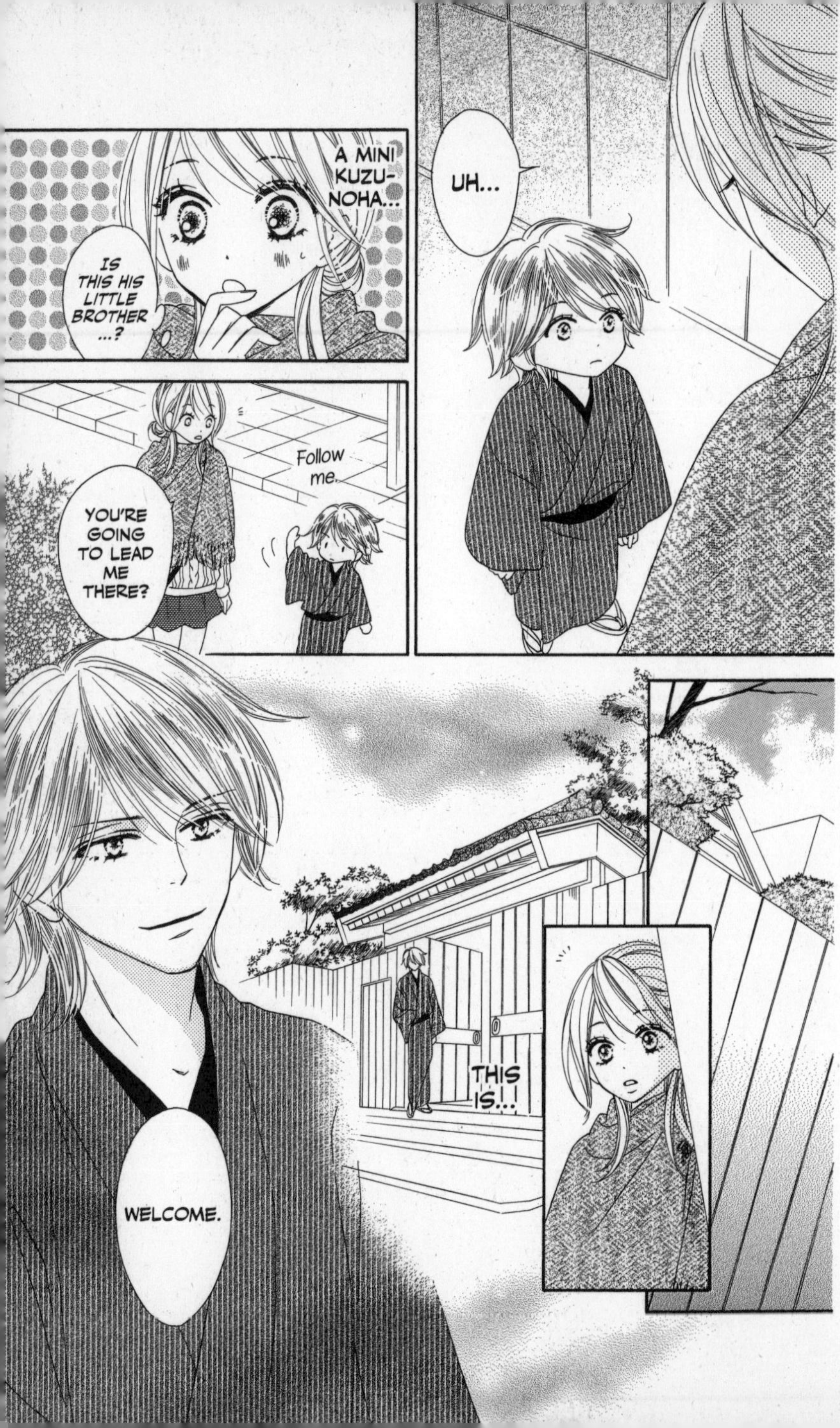

UH...
A MINI KUZUNOHA...
IS THIS HIS LITTLE BROTHER ...?
Follow me.
YOU'RE GOING TO LEAD ME THERE?
THIS IS...
WELCOME.

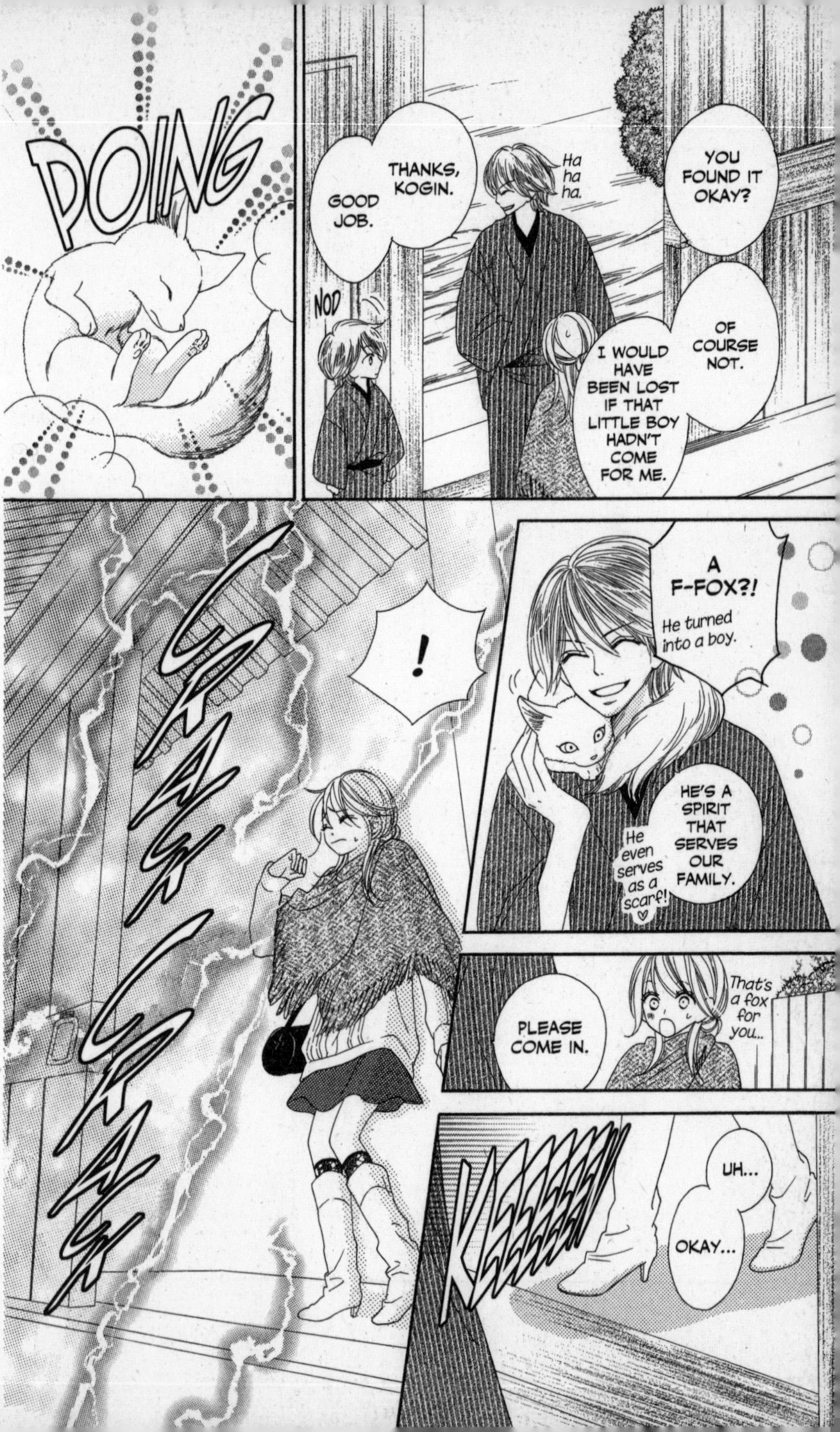
YOU FOUND IT OKAY?
Ha ha ha.
OF COURSE NOT.
I WOULD HAVE BEEN LOST IF THAT LITTLE BOY HADN'T COME FOR ME.
THANKS, KOGIN.
GOOD JOB.
NOD
POING
A F-FOX?!
He turned into a boy.
HE'S A SPIRIT THAT SERVES OUR FAMILY.
He even serves as a scarf! ♥
That's a fox for you...
PLEASE COME IN.
UH...
OKAY...
KSSSSSH
!
CRAAASH CRAAASH

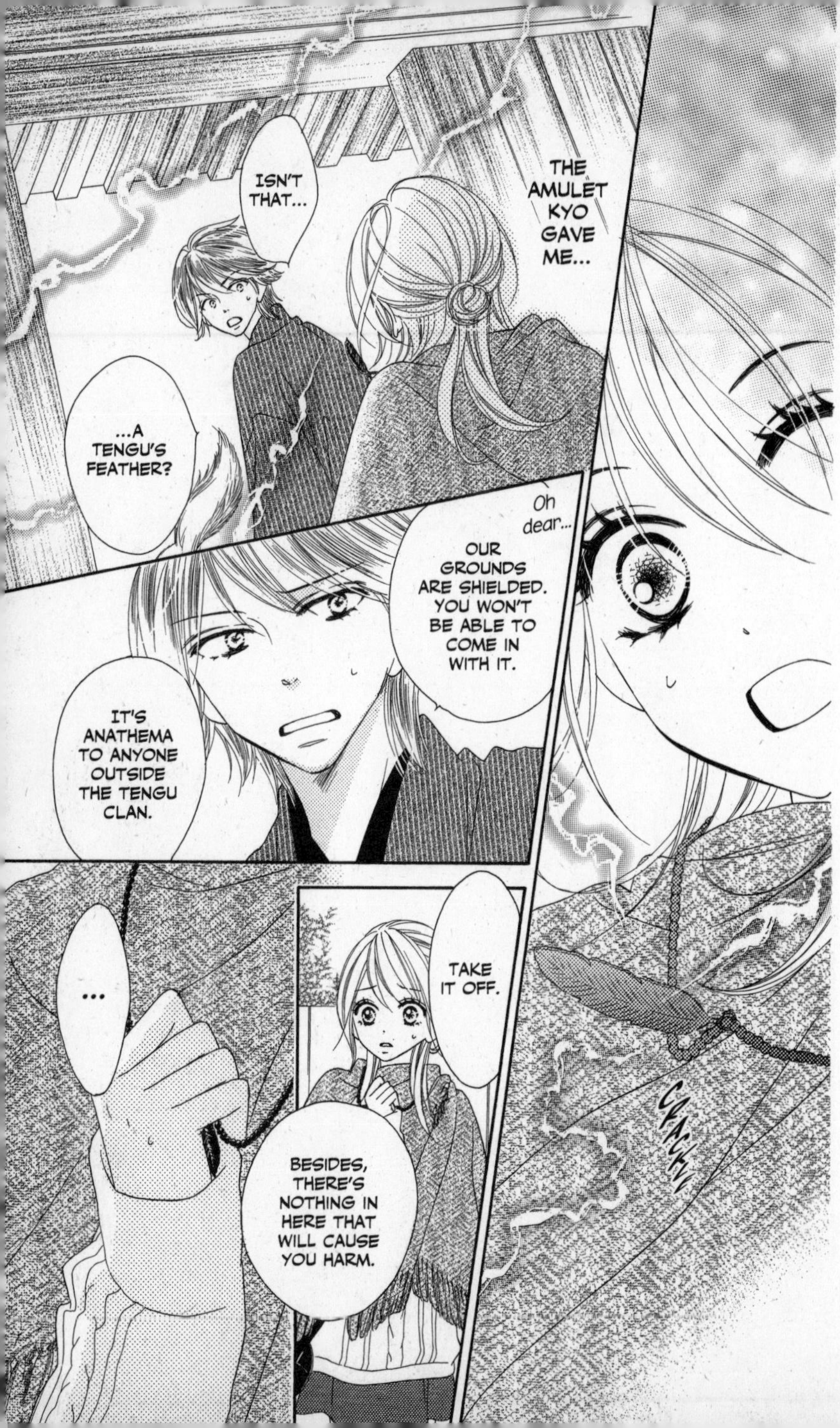
THE AMULET KYO GAVE ME...
ISN'T THAT...
...A TENGU'S FEATHER?
Oh dear...
OUR GROUNDS ARE SHIELDED. YOU WON'T BE ABLE TO COME IN WITH IT.
IT'S ANATHEMA TO ANYONE OUTSIDE THE TENGU CLAN.
CRACK
TAKE IT OFF.
BESIDES, THERE'S NOTHING IN HERE THAT WILL CAUSE YOU HARM.
...

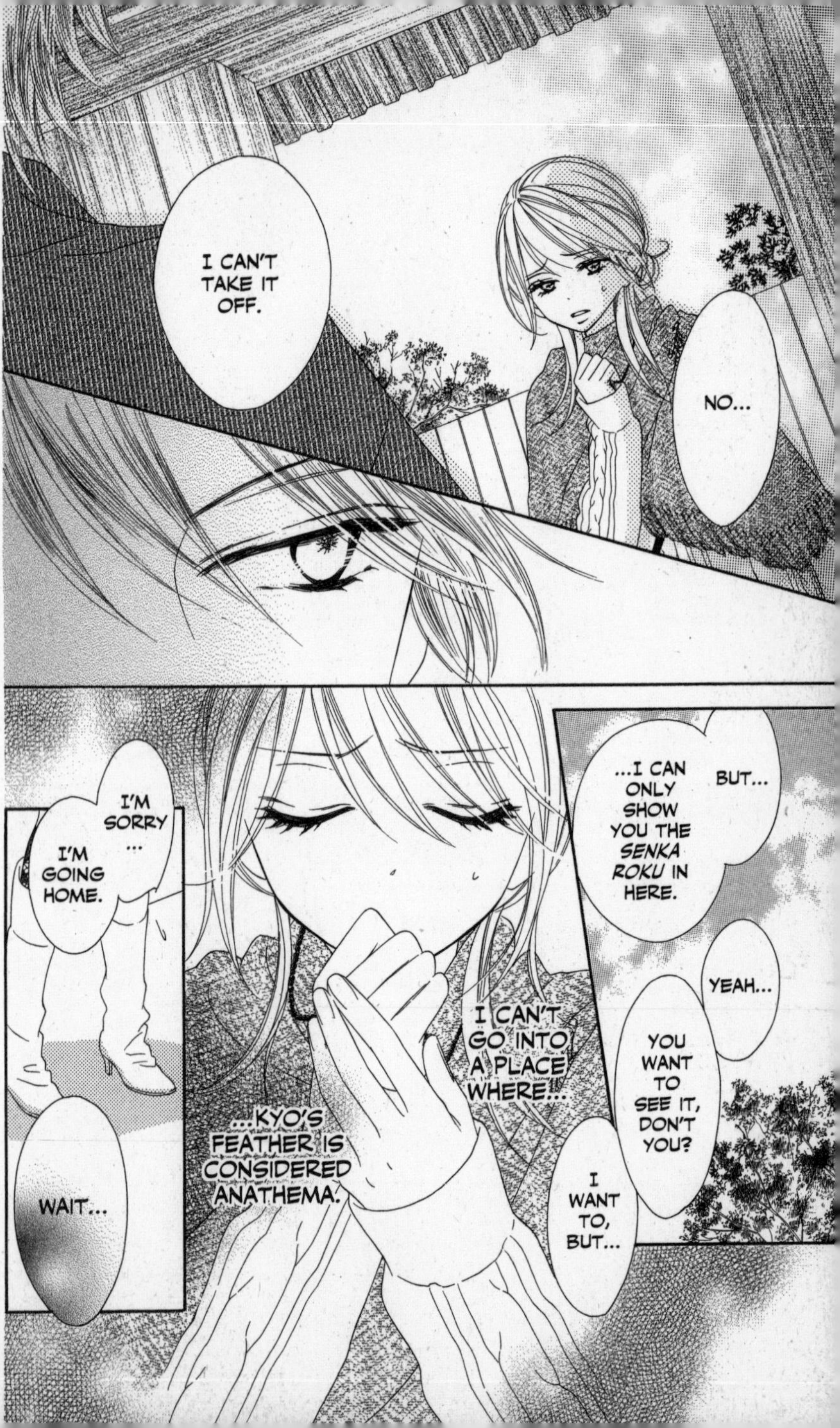
I CAN'T TAKE IT OFF.
NO...
BUT...
...I CAN ONLY SHOW YOU THE *SENKA ROKU* IN HERE.
YOU WANT TO SEE IT, DON'T YOU?
YEAH...
I WANT TO, BUT...
I CAN'T GO INTO A PLACE WHERE...
...KYO'S FEATHER IS CONSIDERED ANATHEMA.
I'M SORRY...
I'M GOING HOME.
WAIT...

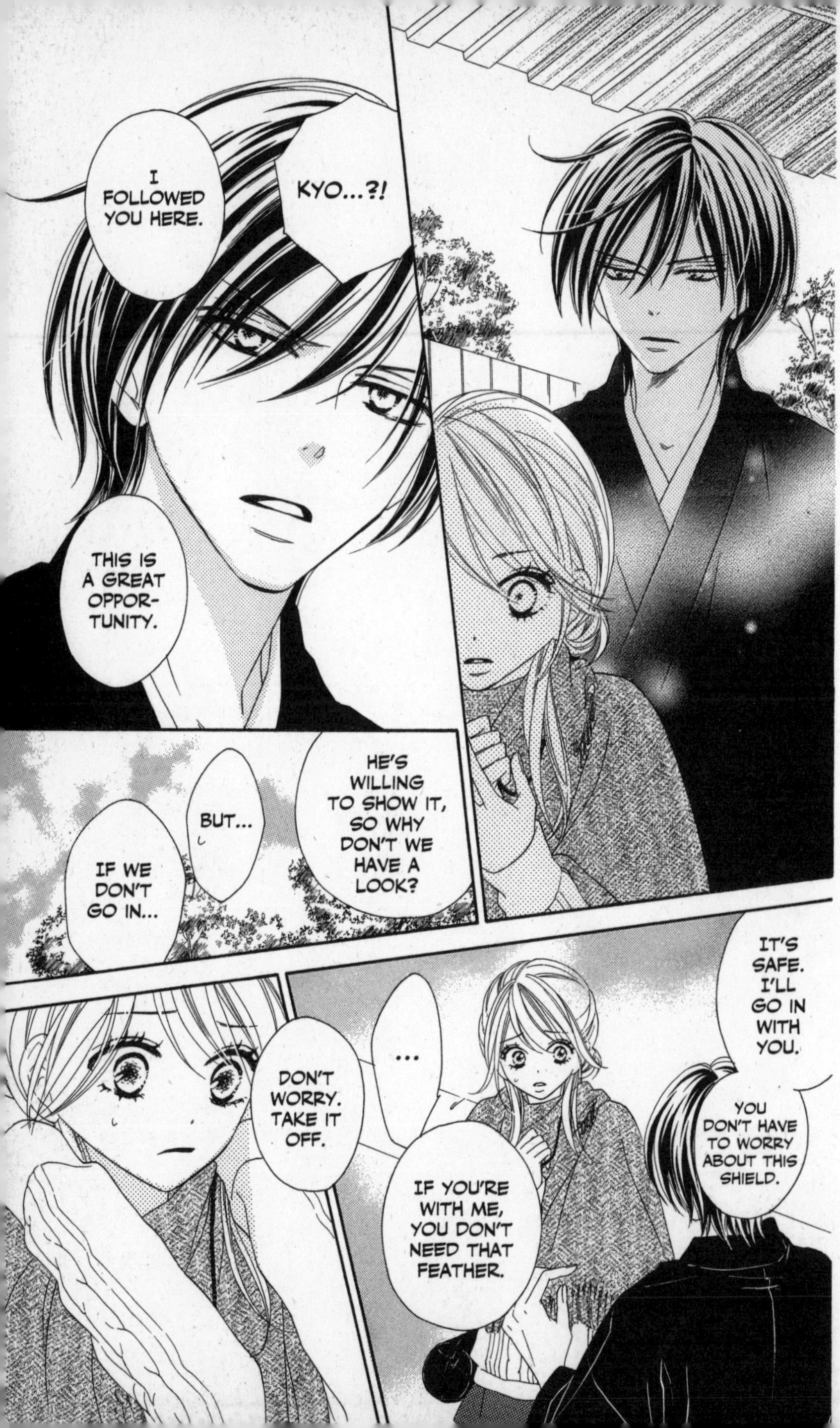

KYO...?!
I FOLLOWED YOU HERE.
THIS IS A GREAT OPPORTUNITY.
HE'S WILLING TO SHOW IT, SO WHY DON'T WE HAVE A LOOK?
BUT...
IF WE DON'T GO IN...
IT'S SAFE. I'LL GO IN WITH YOU.
YOU DON'T HAVE TO WORRY ABOUT THIS SHIELD.
...
IF YOU'RE WITH ME, YOU DON'T NEED THAT FEATHER.
DON'T WORRY. TAKE IT OFF.

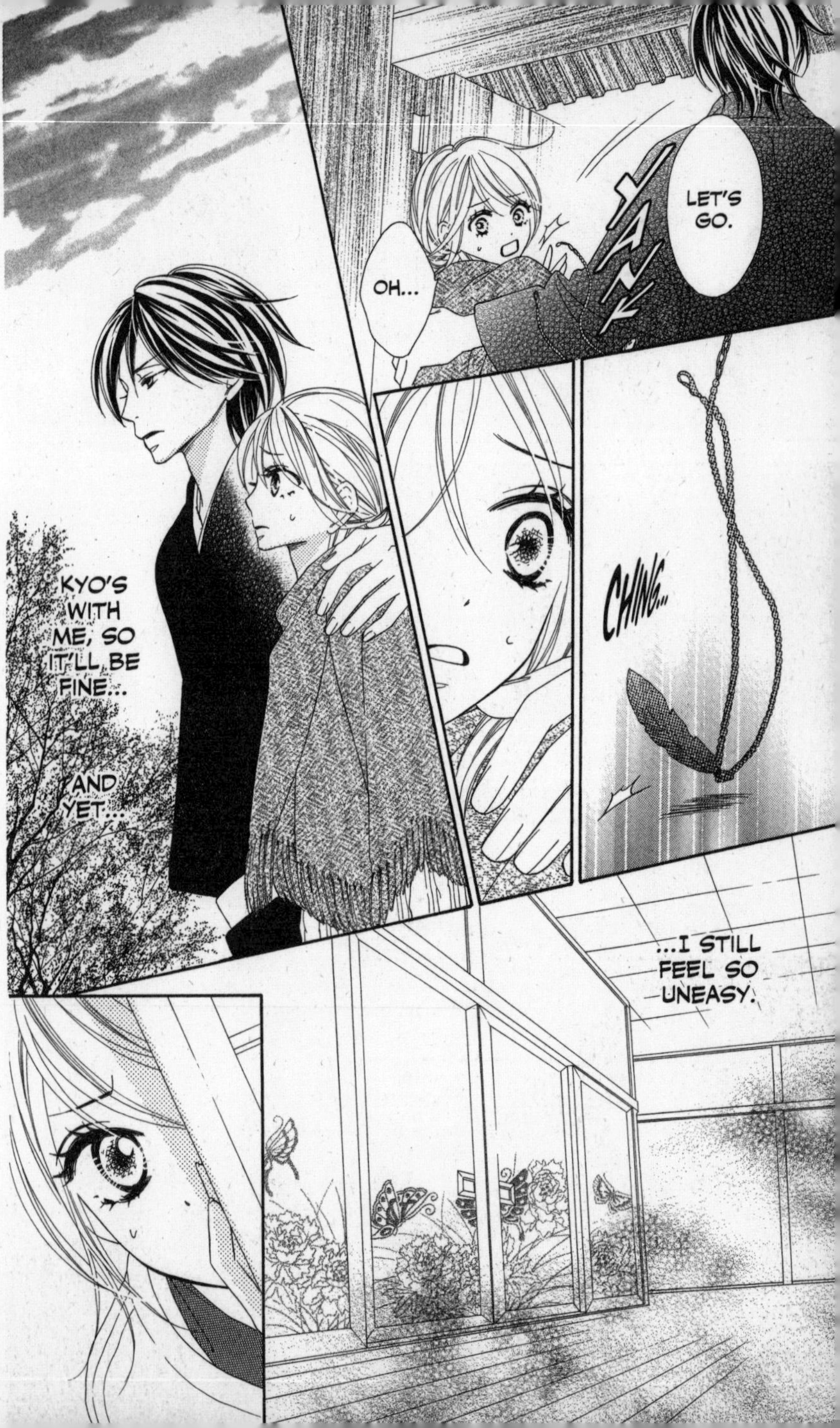
LET'S GO.
YANK
OH...
CHING...
KYO'S WITH ME, SO IT'LL BE FINE...
AND YET...
...I STILL FEEL SO UNEASY.

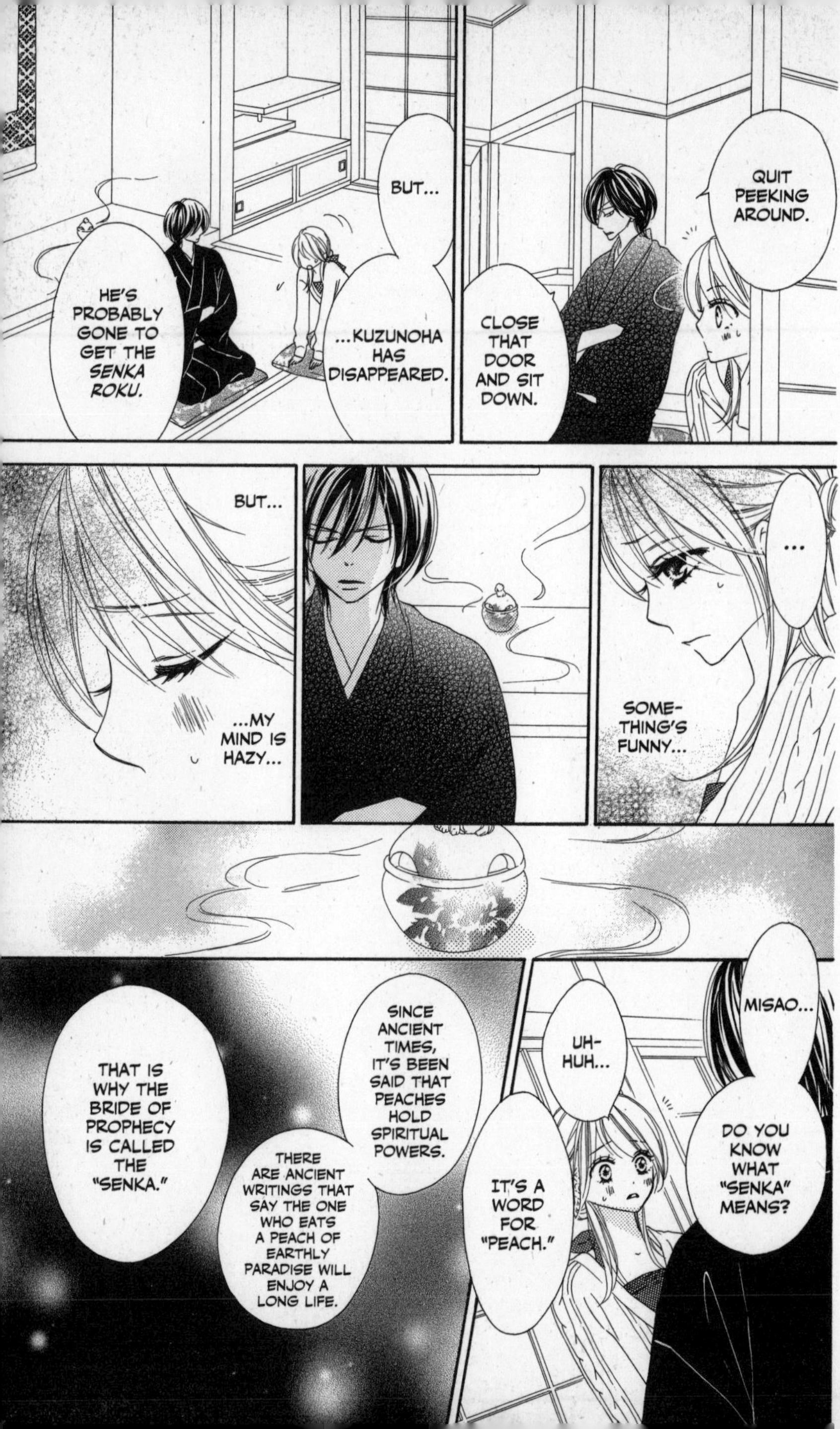
QUIT PEEKING AROUND.
CLOSE THAT DOOR AND SIT DOWN.
BUT...
...KUZUNOHA HAS DISAPPEARED.
HE'S PROBABLY GONE TO GET THE SENKA ROKU.
...
SOME-THING'S FUNNY...
BUT...
...MY MIND IS HAZY...
MISAO...
DO YOU KNOW WHAT "SENKA" MEANS?
UH-HUH...
IT'S A WORD FOR "PEACH."
SINCE ANCIENT TIMES, IT'S BEEN SAID THAT PEACHES HOLD SPIRITUAL POWERS.
THERE ARE ANCIENT WRITINGS THAT SAY THE ONE WHO EATS A PEACH OF EARTHLY PARADISE WILL ENJOY A LONG LIFE.
THAT IS WHY THE BRIDE OF PROPHECY IS CALLED THE "SENKA."

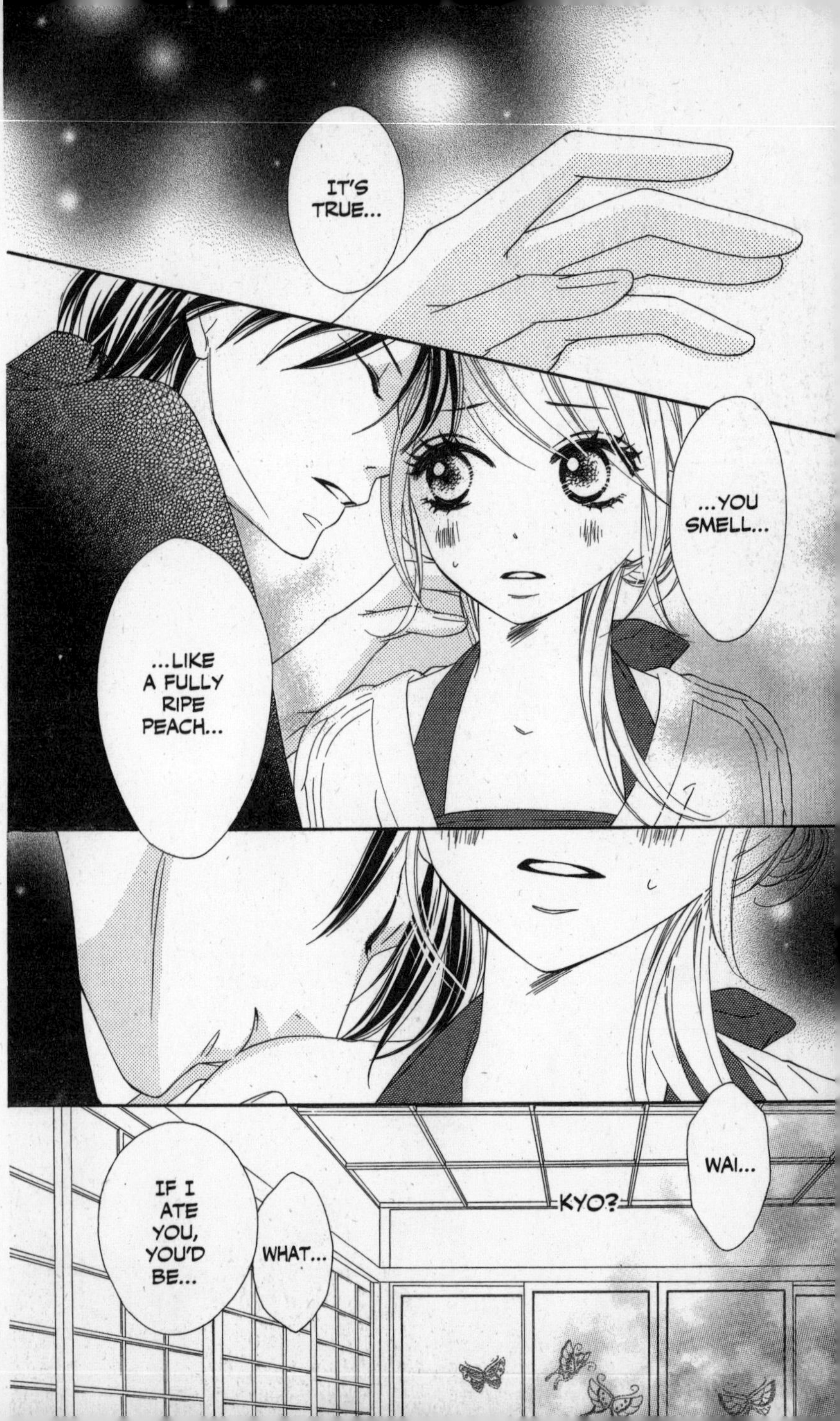
IT'S TRUE...
...YOU SMELL...
...LIKE A FULLY RIPE PEACH...
WAI...
KYO?
WHAT...
IF I ATE YOU, YOU'D BE...

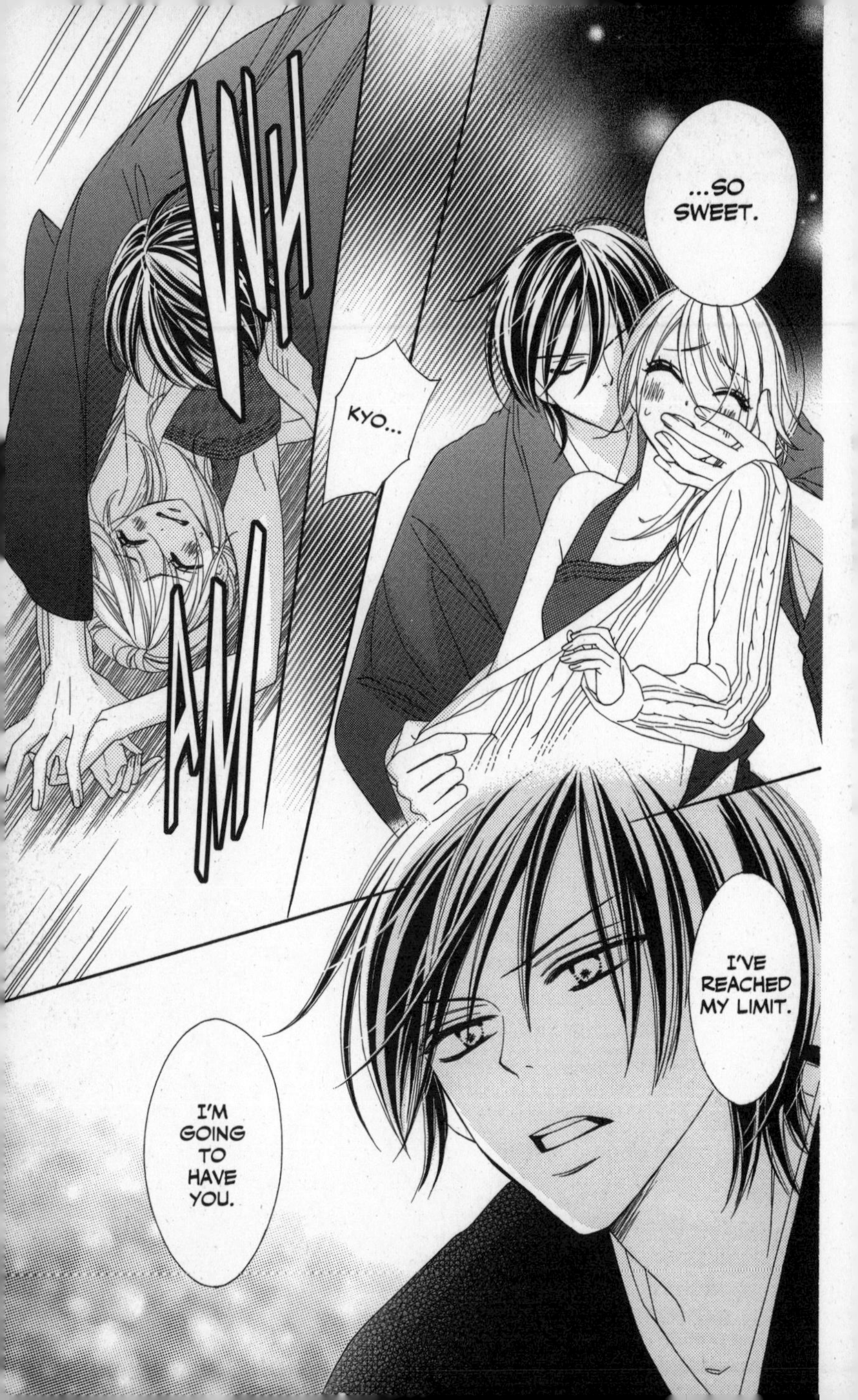
...SO SWEET.
KYO...
I'VE REACHED MY LIMIT.
I'M GOING TO HAVE YOU.

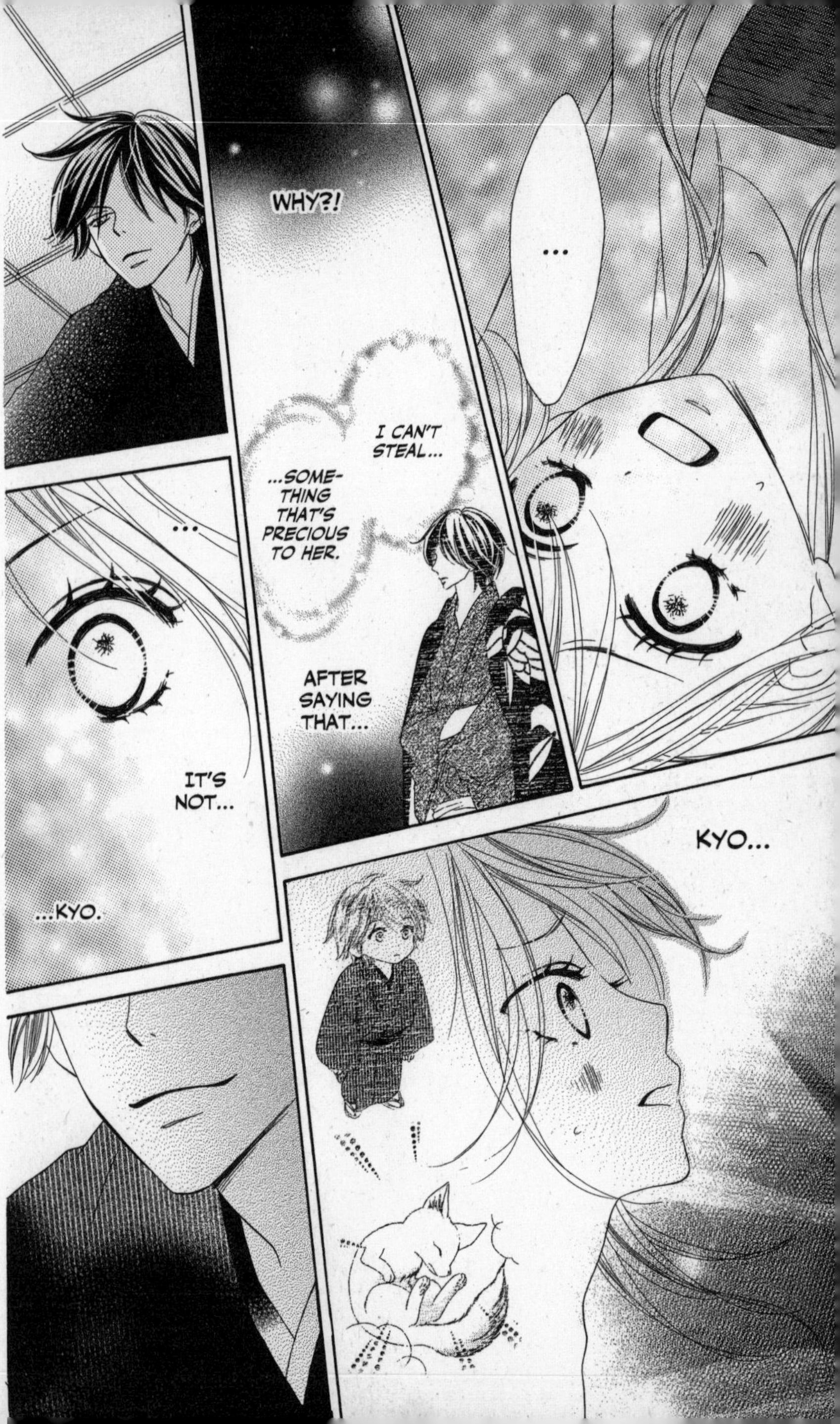
...
WHY?!
I CAN'T STEAL...
...SOME-THING THAT'S PRECIOUS TO HER.
AFTER SAYING THAT...
...
IT'S NOT...
...KYO.
KYO...

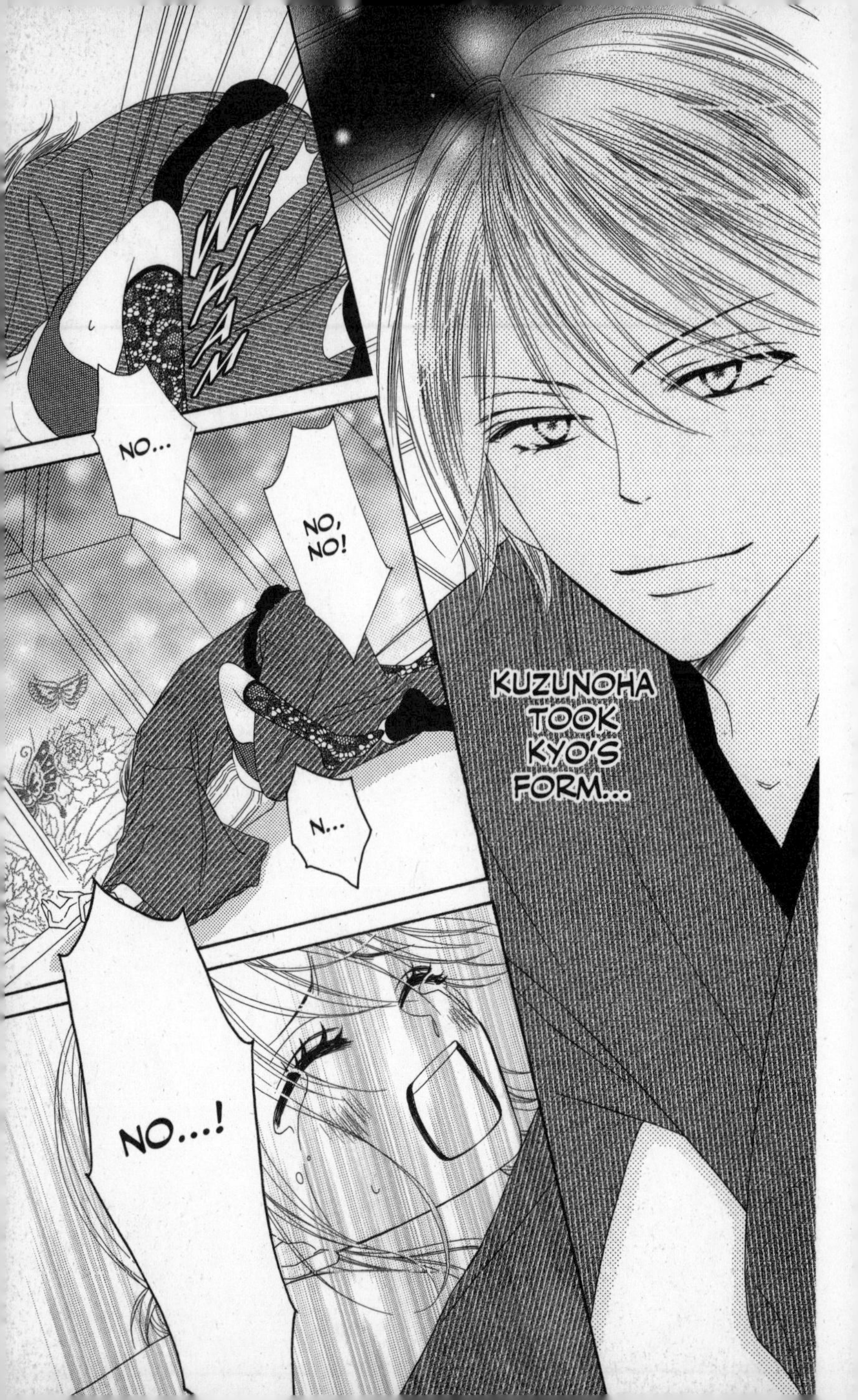
KUZUNOHA TOOK KYO'S FORM...
WHAM
NO...
NO, NO!
N...
NO...!

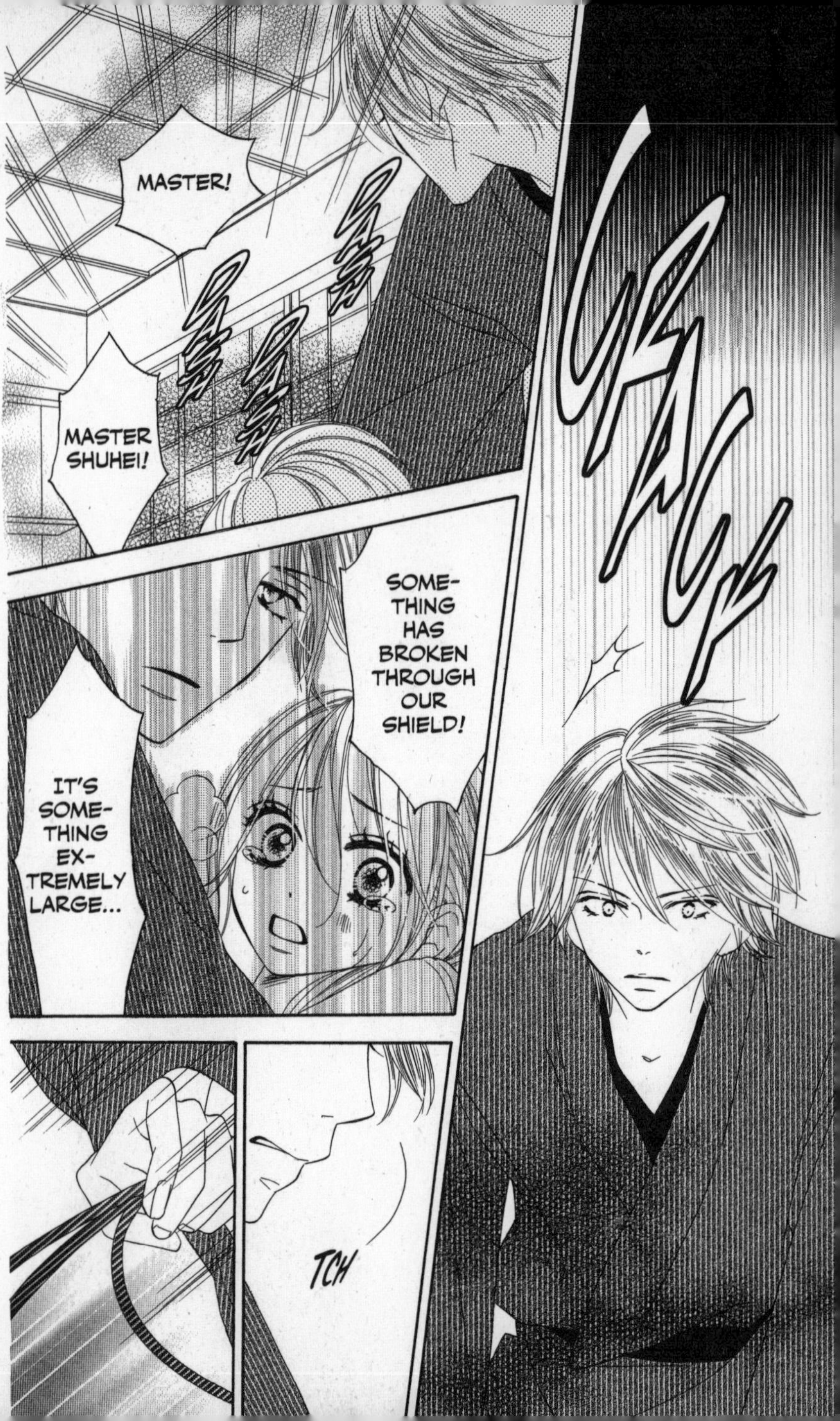
MASTER!
MASTER SHUHEI!
SOME-THING HAS BROKEN THROUGH OUR SHIELD!
IT'S SOME-THING EX-TREMELY LARGE...
TCH

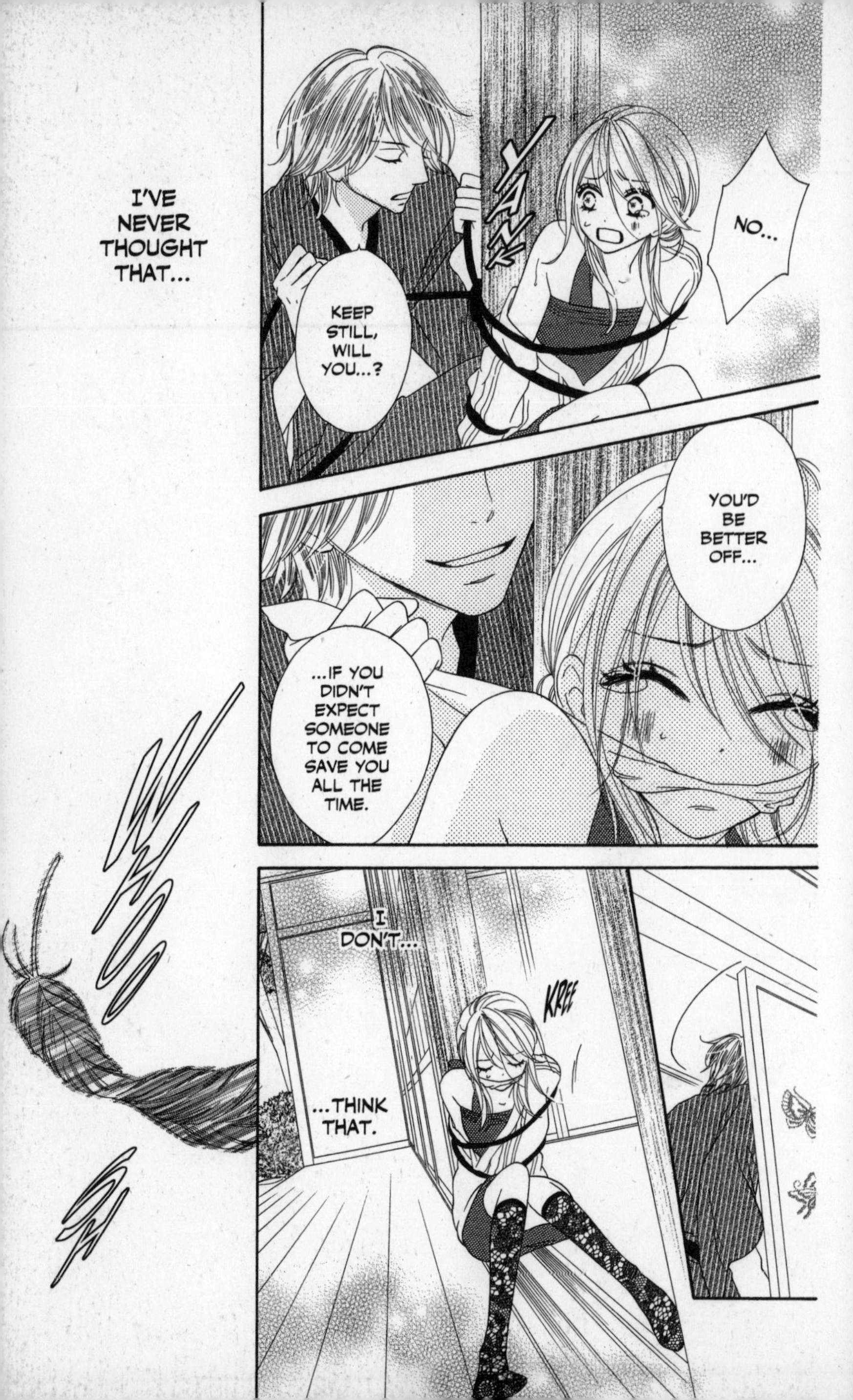
NO...
YANK
KEEP STILL, WILL YOU...?
YOU'D BE BETTER OFF...
...IF YOU DIDN'T EXPECT SOMEONE TO COME SAVE YOU ALL THE TIME.
I DON'T...
KREE
...THINK THAT.
I'VE NEVER THOUGHT THAT...

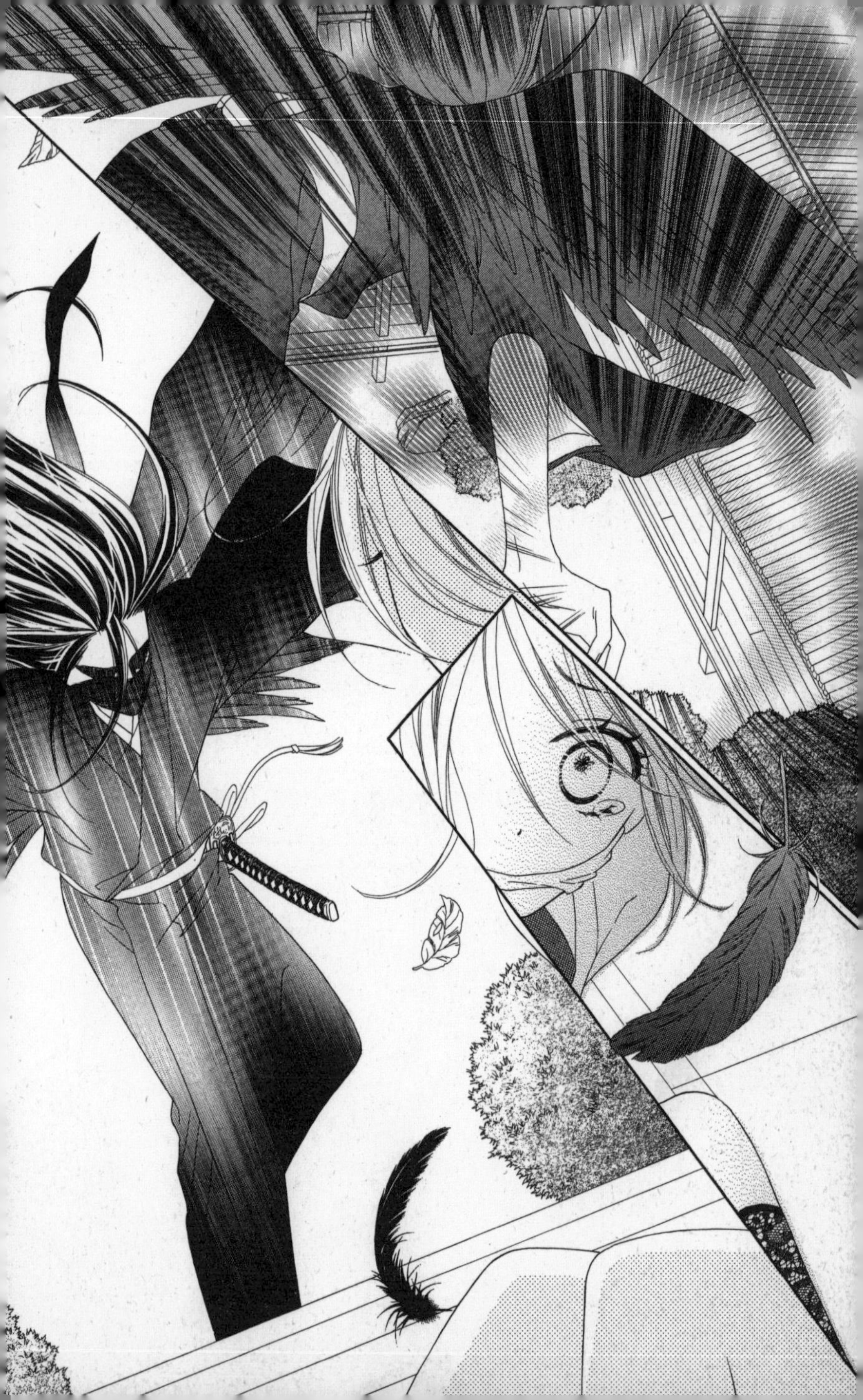

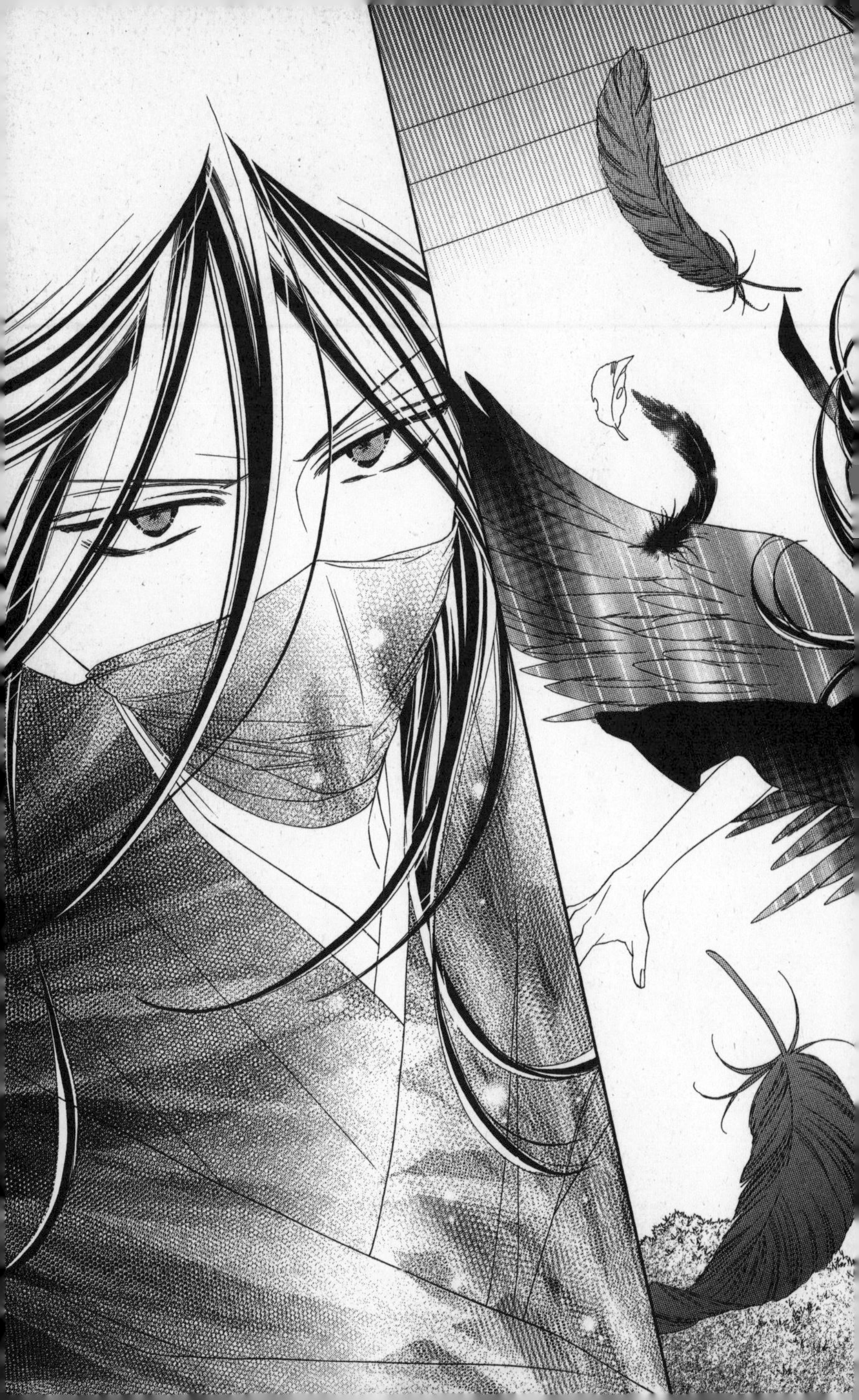

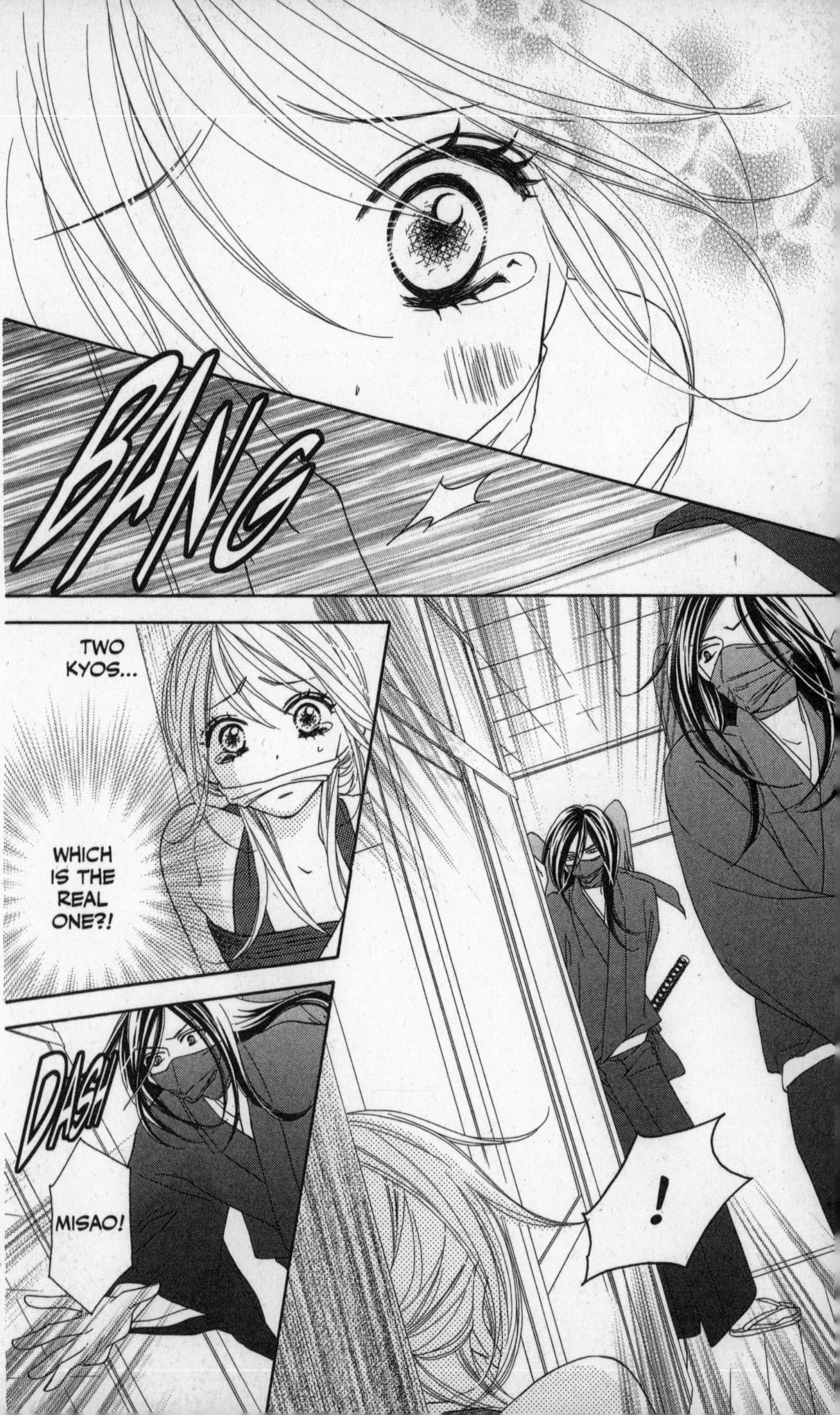
BANG
!
TWO KYOS...
WHICH IS THE REAL ONE?!
DASH
MISAO!

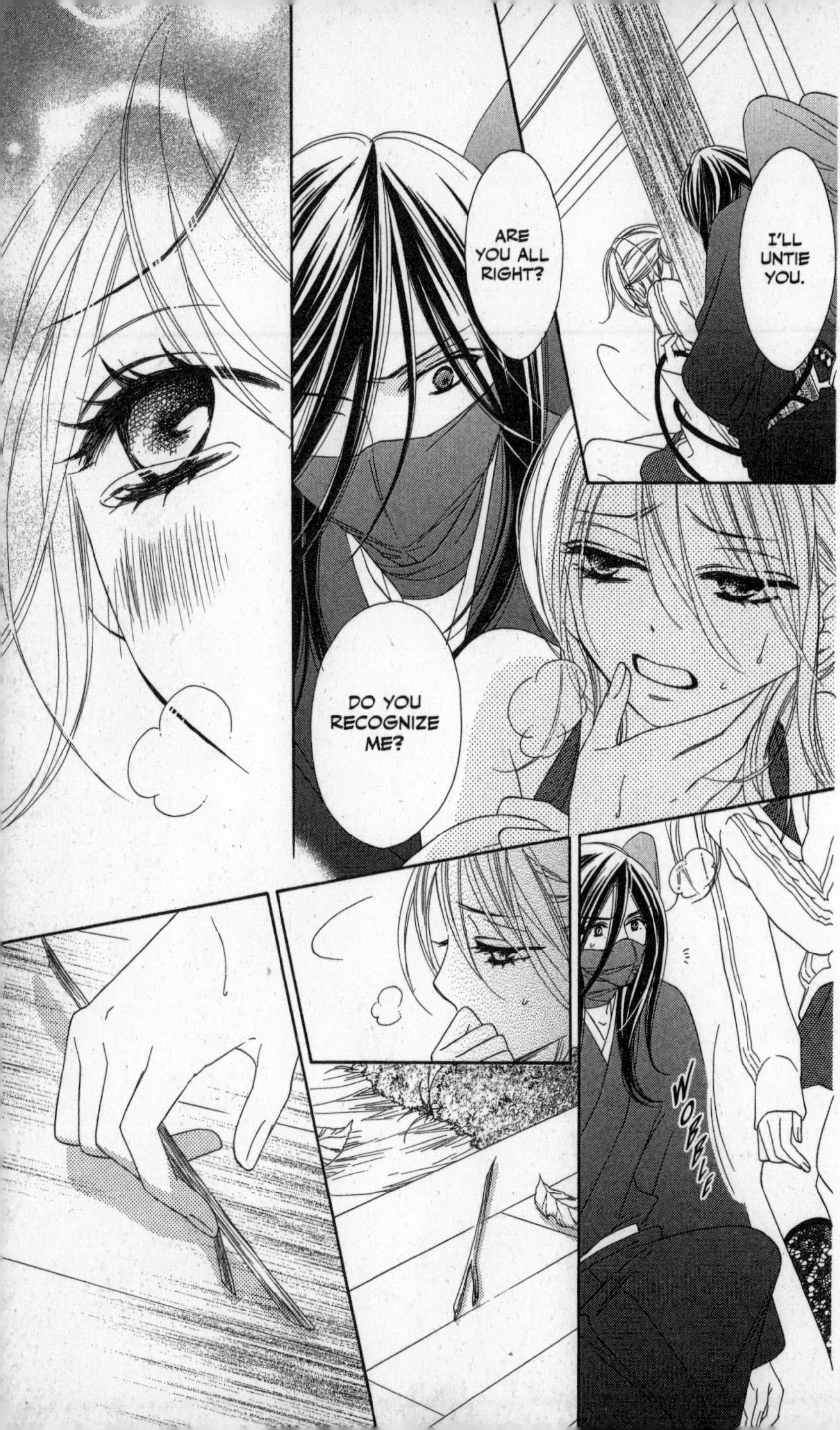
I'LL UNTIE YOU.
ARE YOU ALL RIGHT?
DO YOU RECOGNIZE ME?
WOBBLLL

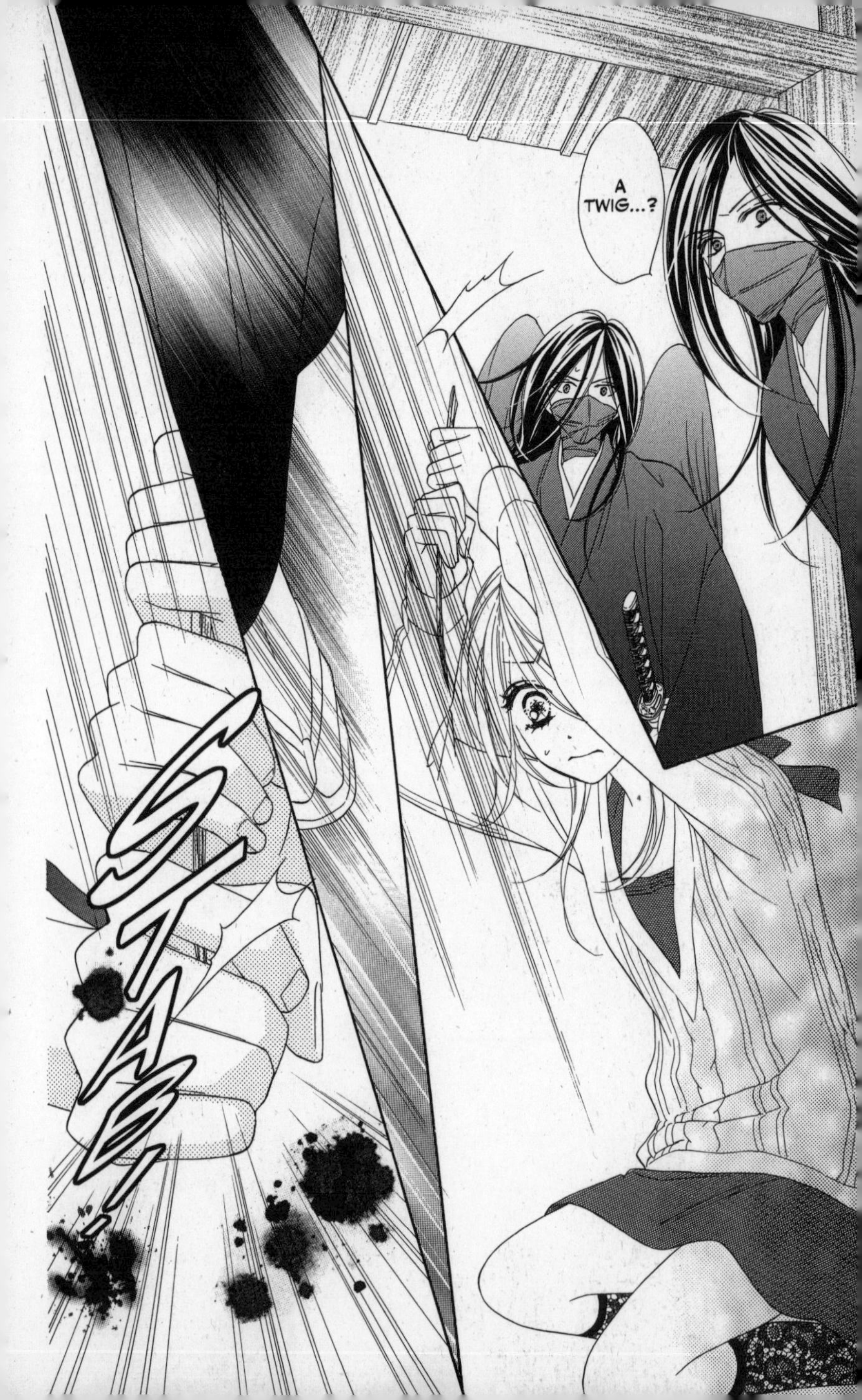
A TWIG...?
SHAAA!

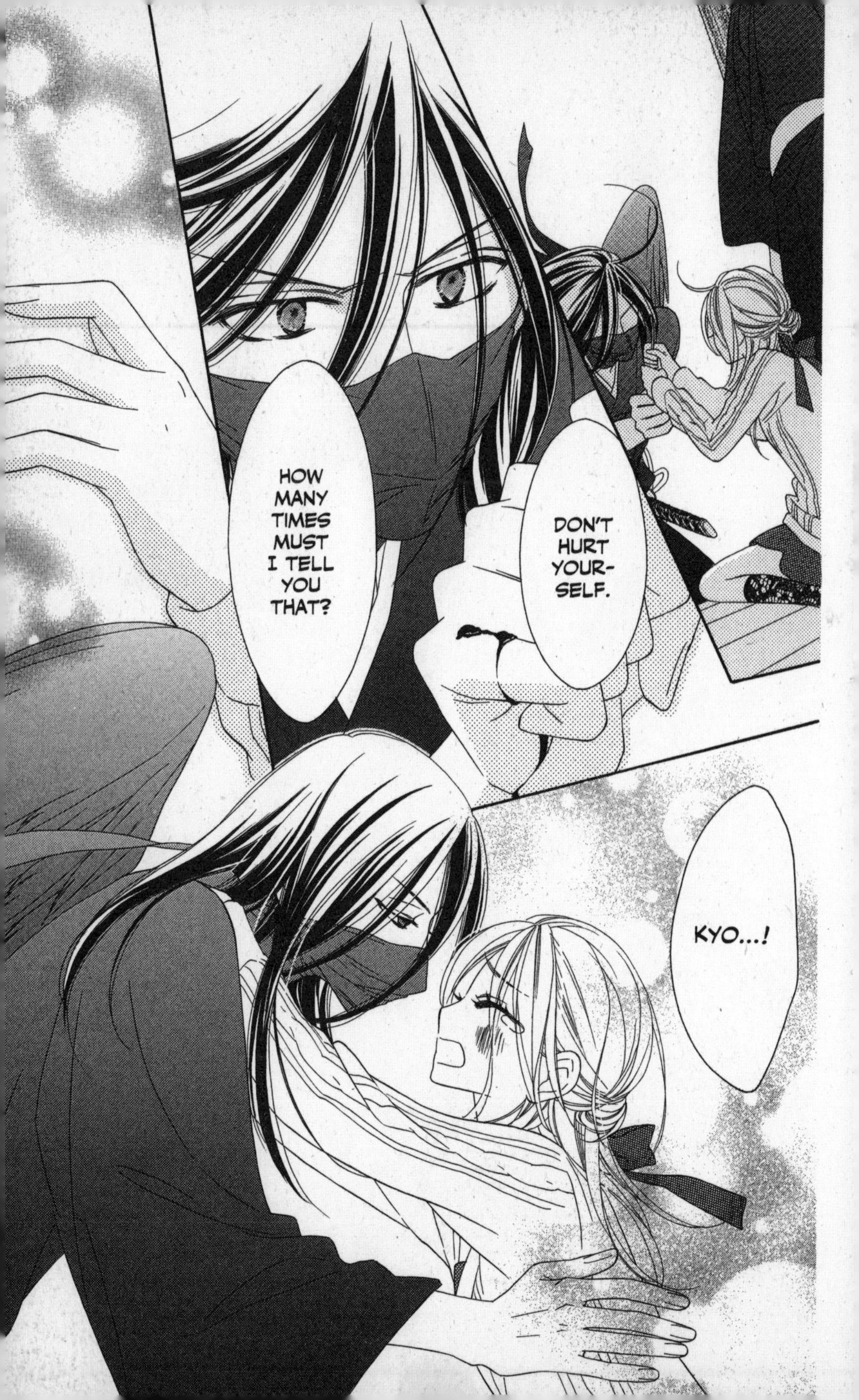
DON'T HURT YOUR-SELF.
HOW MANY TIMES MUST I TELL YOU THAT?
KYO...!

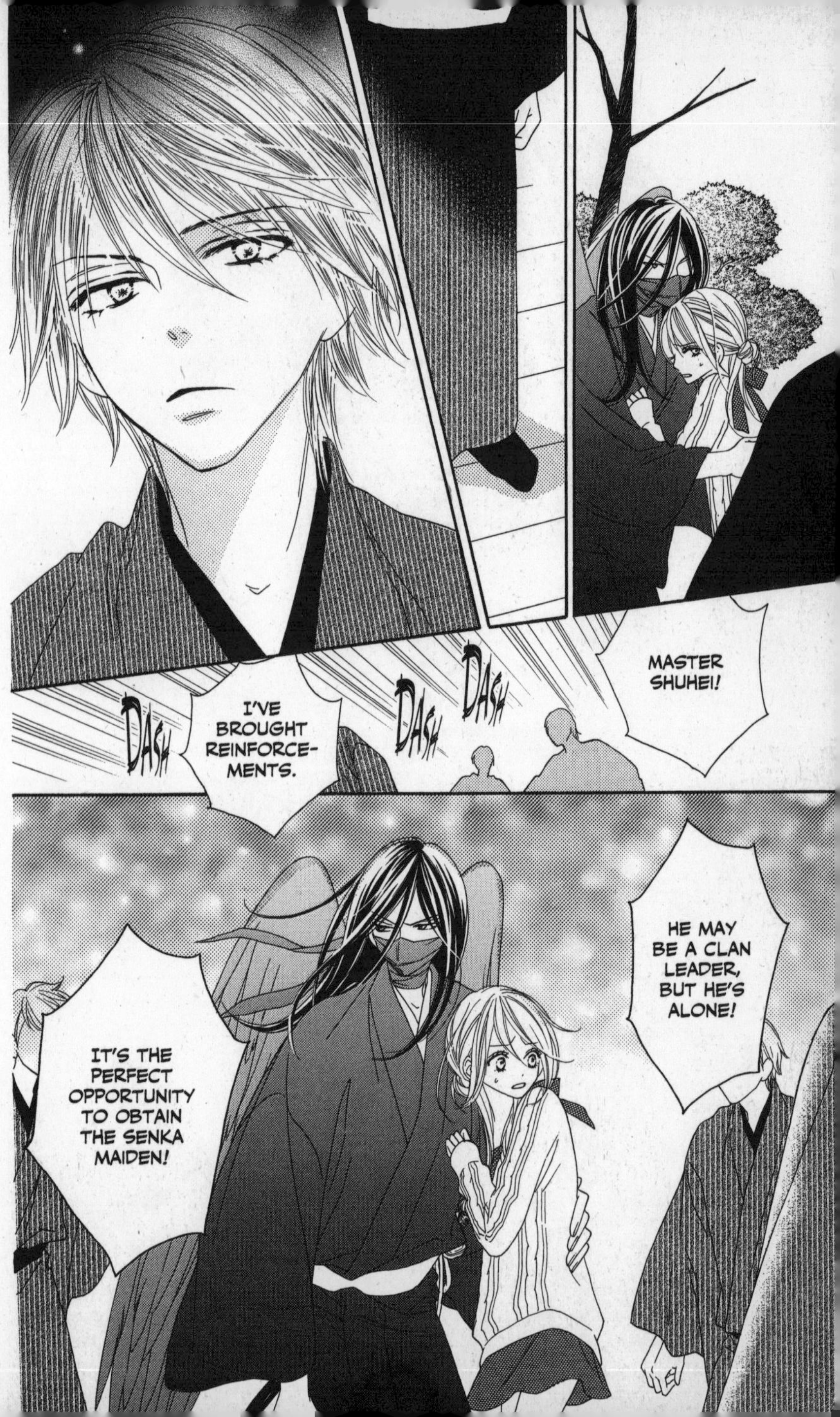
MASTER SHUHEI!
DASH
DASH
DASH
I'VE BROUGHT REINFORCEMENTS.
HE MAY BE A CLAN LEADER, BUT HE'S ALONE!
IT'S THE PERFECT OPPORTUNITY TO OBTAIN THE SENKA MAIDEN!

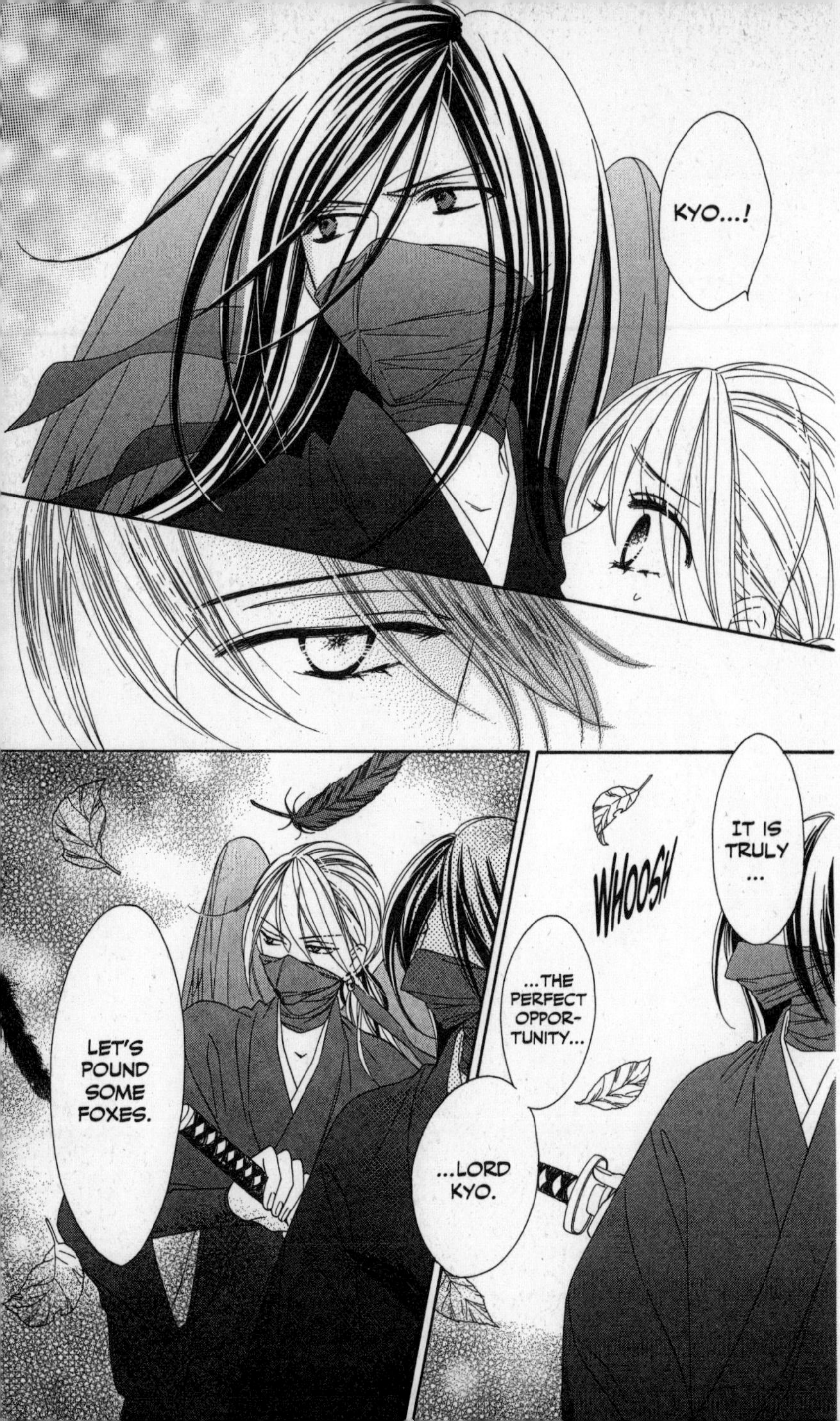
KYO...!
IT IS TRULY ...
WHOOSH
...THE PERFECT OPPORTUNITY...
...LORD KYO.
LET'S POUND SOME FOXES.

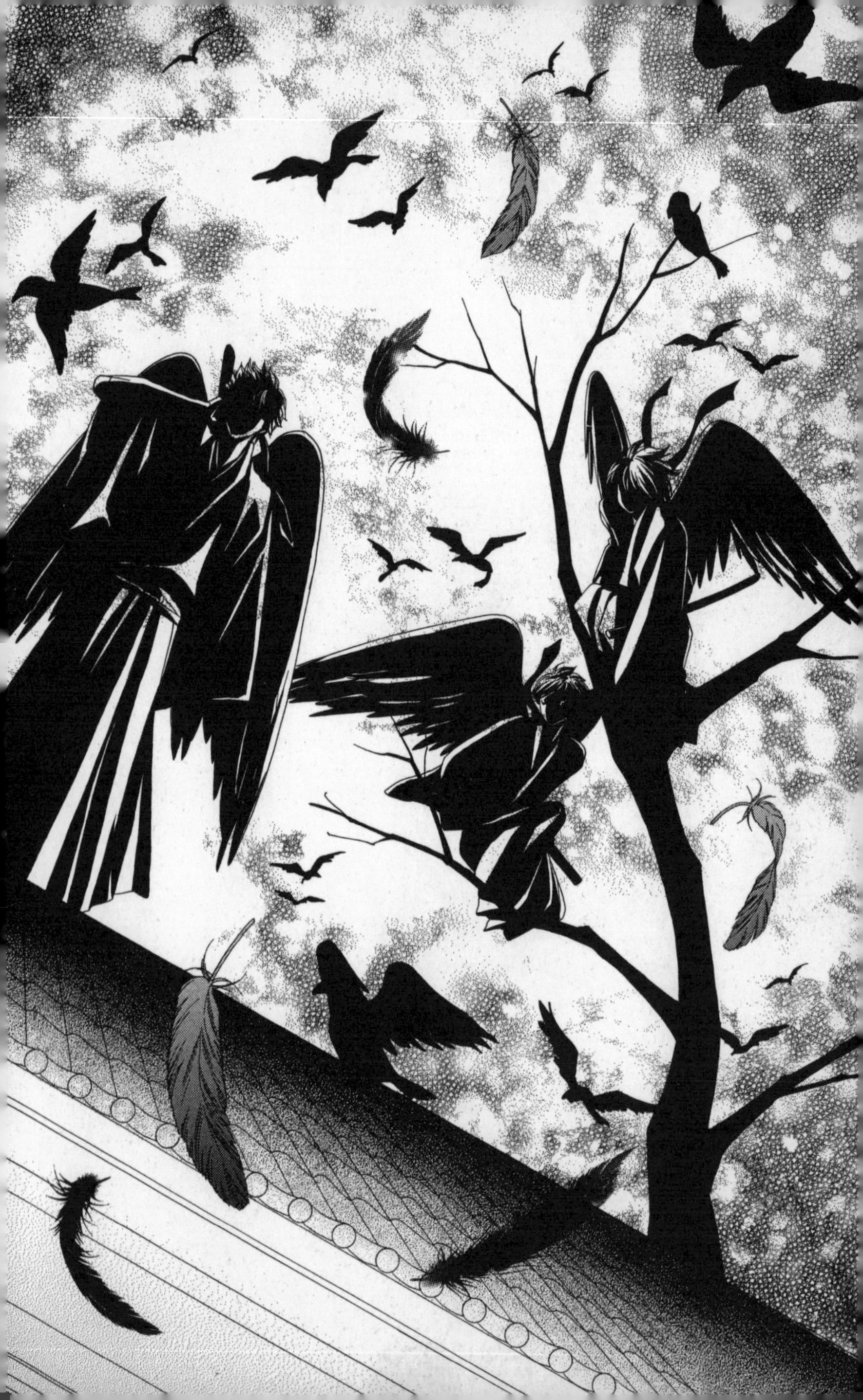

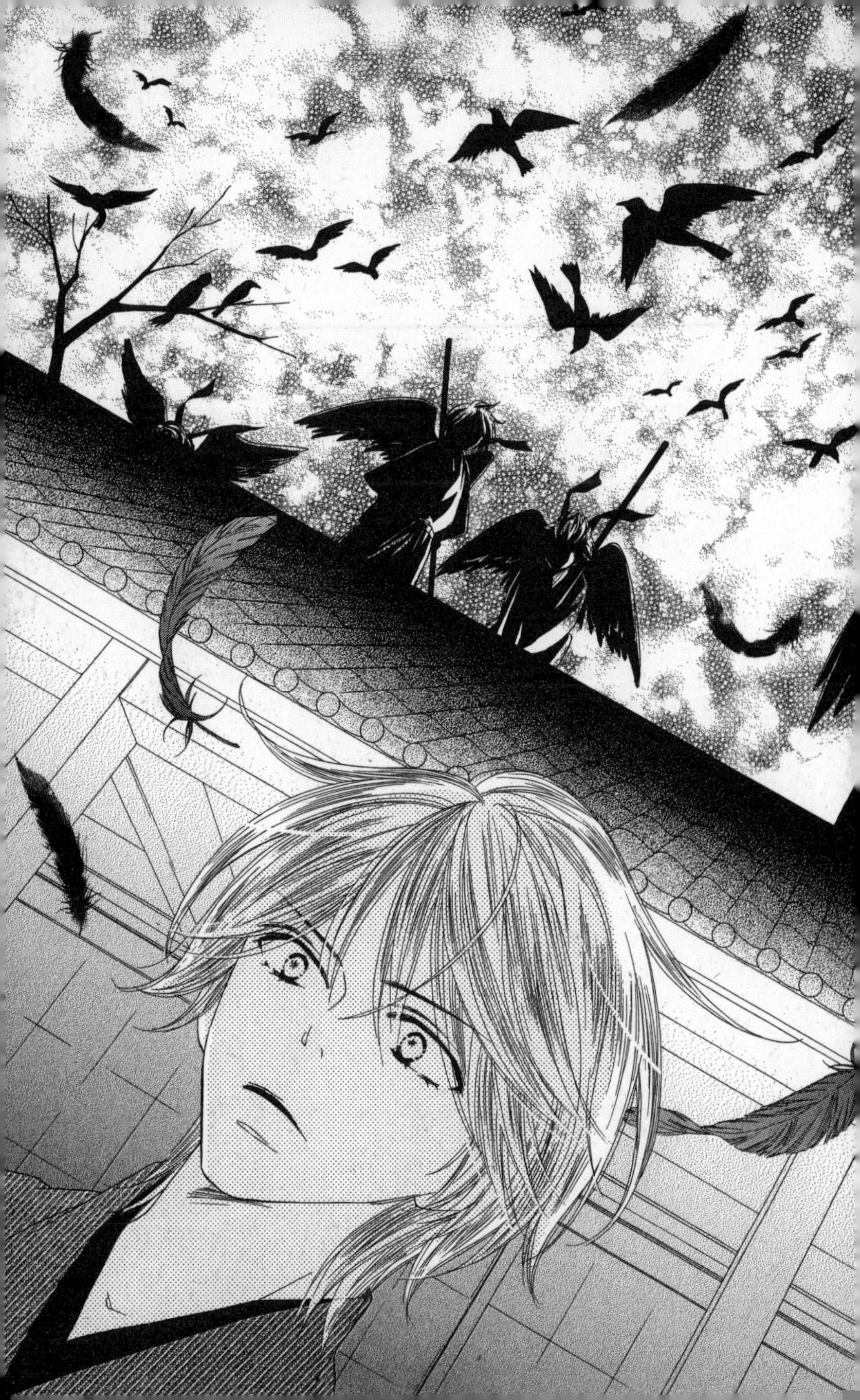

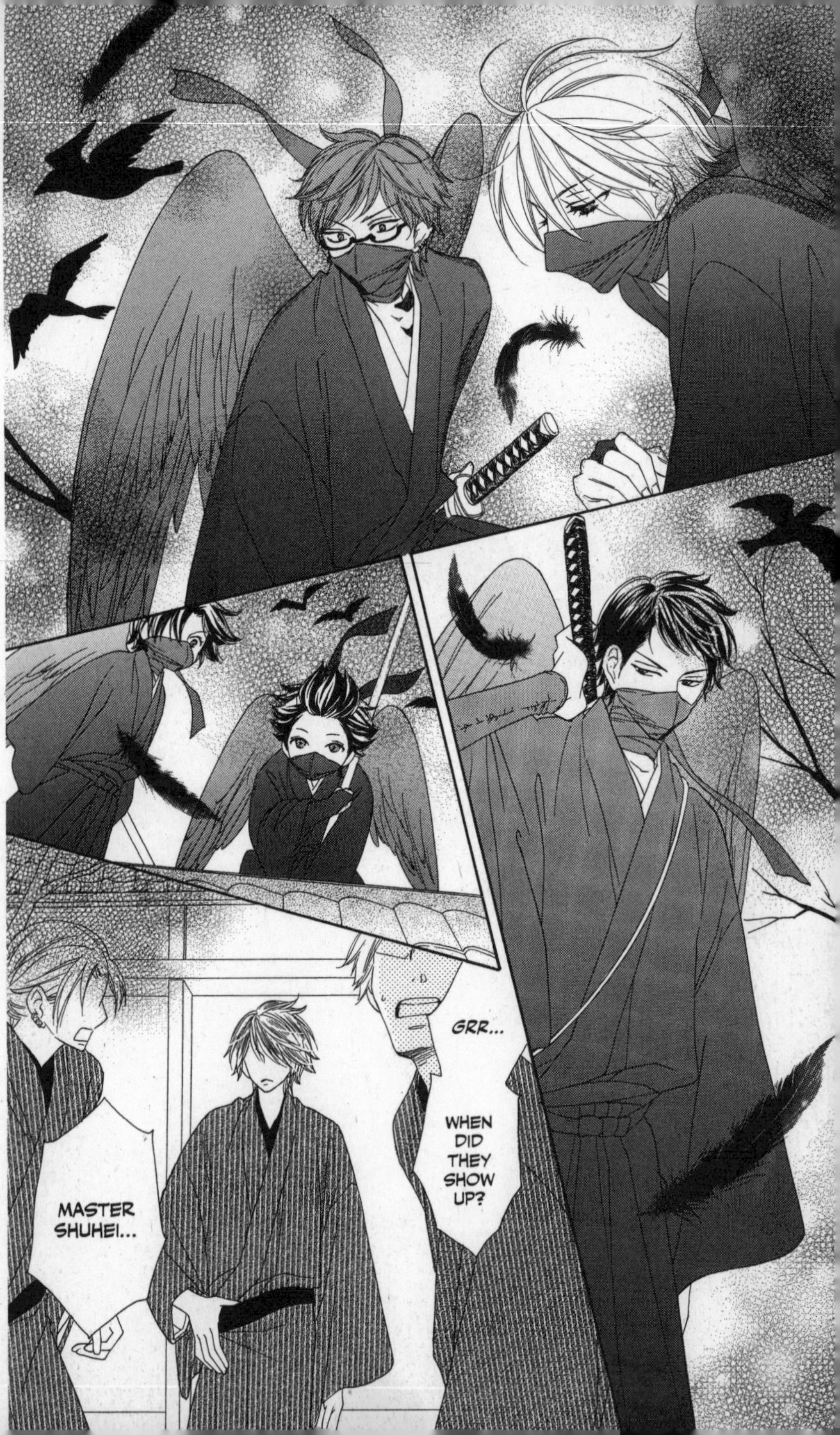
GRR...
WHEN DID THEY SHOW UP?
MASTER SHUHEI...

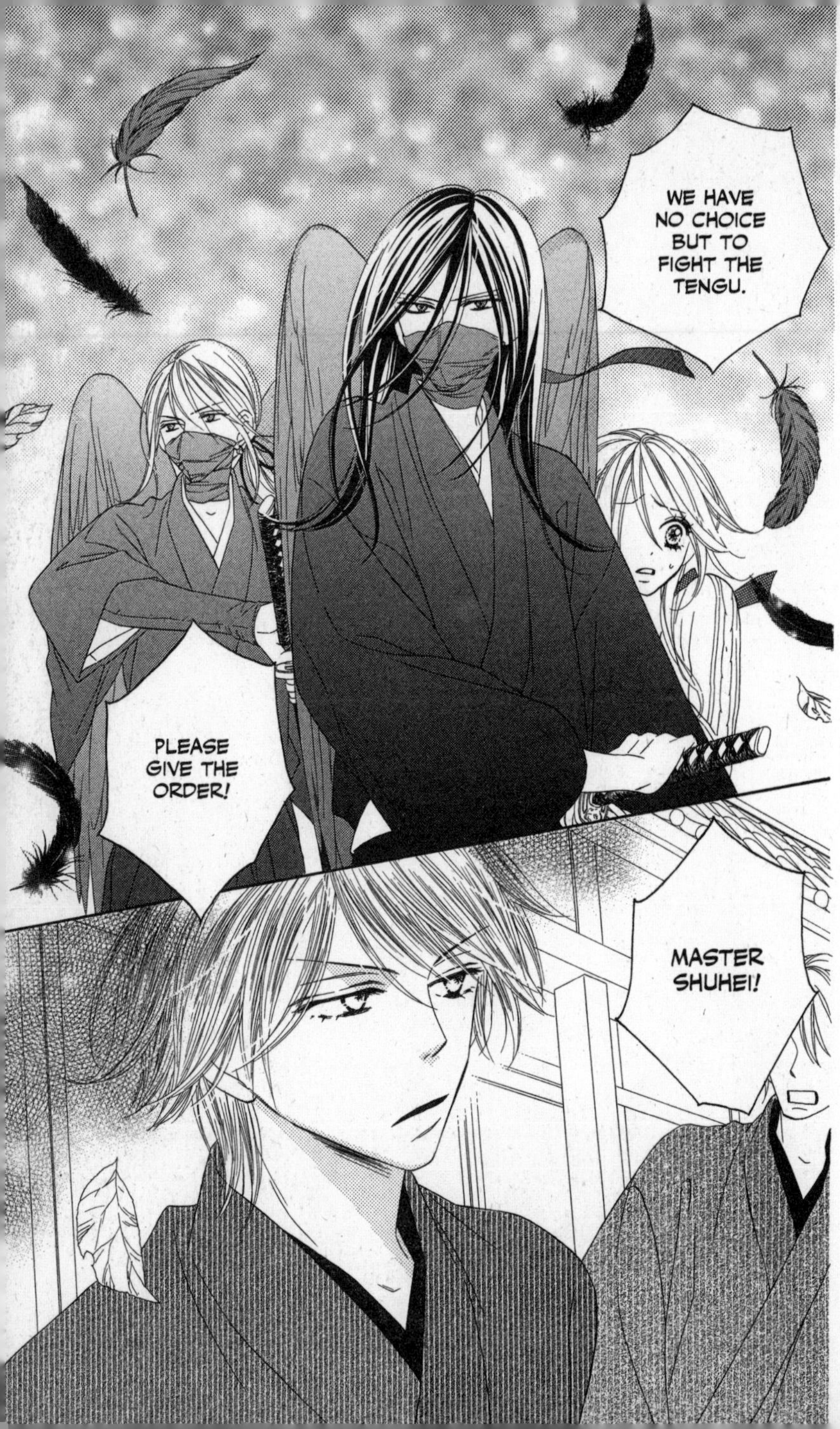
WE HAVE NO CHOICE BUT TO FIGHT THE TENGU.
PLEASE GIVE THE ORDER!
MASTER SHUHEI!

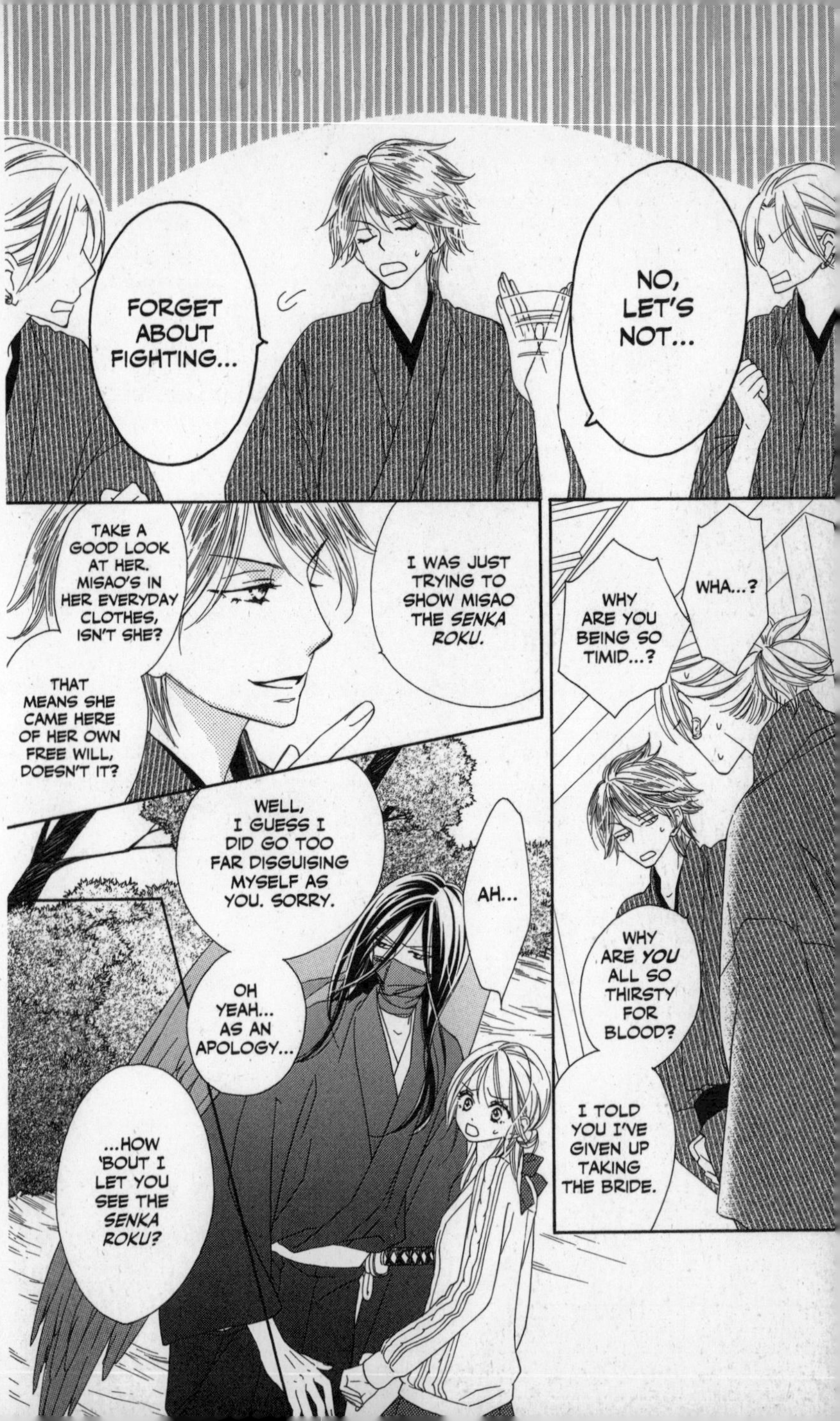
NO, LET'S NOT...
FORGET ABOUT FIGHTING...
WHA...?
WHY ARE YOU BEING SO TIMID...?
WHY ARE *YOU* ALL SO THIRSTY FOR BLOOD?
I TOLD YOU I'VE GIVEN UP TAKING THE BRIDE.
I WAS JUST TRYING TO SHOW MISAO THE *SENKA ROKU.*
TAKE A GOOD LOOK AT HER. MISAO'S IN HER EVERYDAY CLOTHES, ISN'T SHE?
THAT MEANS SHE CAME HERE OF HER OWN FREE WILL, DOESN'T IT?
AH...
WELL, I GUESS I DID GO TOO FAR DISGUISING MYSELF AS YOU. SORRY.
OH YEAH... AS AN APOLOGY...
...HOW 'BOUT I LET YOU SEE THE *SENKA ROKU?*

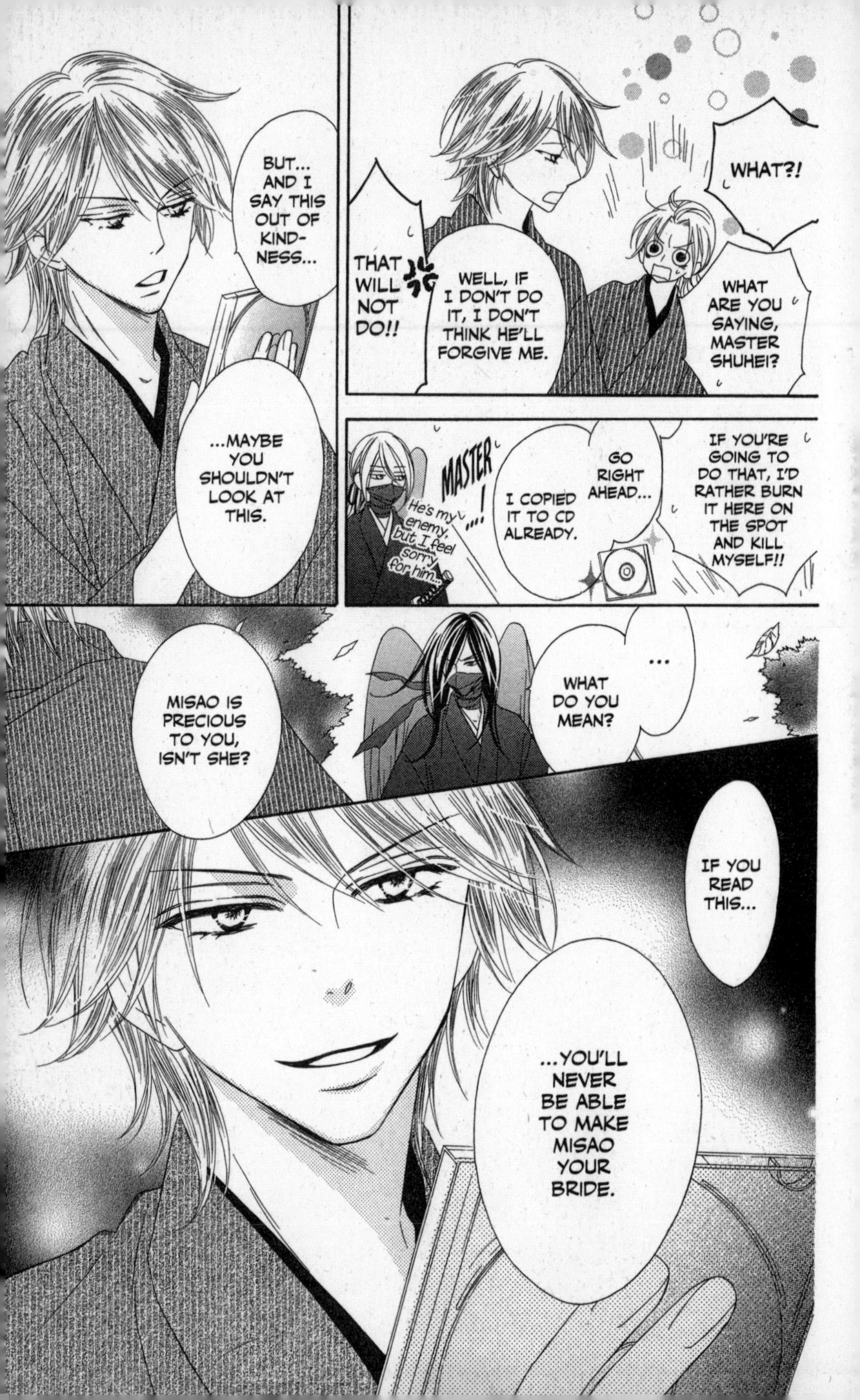
WHAT?!
WHAT ARE YOU SAYING, MASTER SHUHEI?
WELL, IF I DON'T DO IT, I DON'T THINK HE'LL FORGIVE ME.
THAT WILL NOT DO!!
IF YOU'RE GOING TO DO THAT, I'D RATHER BURN IT HERE ON THE SPOT AND KILL MYSELF!!
GO RIGHT AHEAD...
I COPIED IT TO CD ALREADY.
MASTER...!
He's my enemy, but I feel sorry for him...
BUT... AND I SAY THIS OUT OF KINDNESS...
...MAYBE YOU SHOULDN'T LOOK AT THIS.
...
WHAT DO YOU MEAN?
MISAO IS PRECIOUS TO YOU, ISN'T SHE?
IF YOU READ THIS...
...YOU'LL NEVER BE ABLE TO MAKE MISAO YOUR BRIDE.

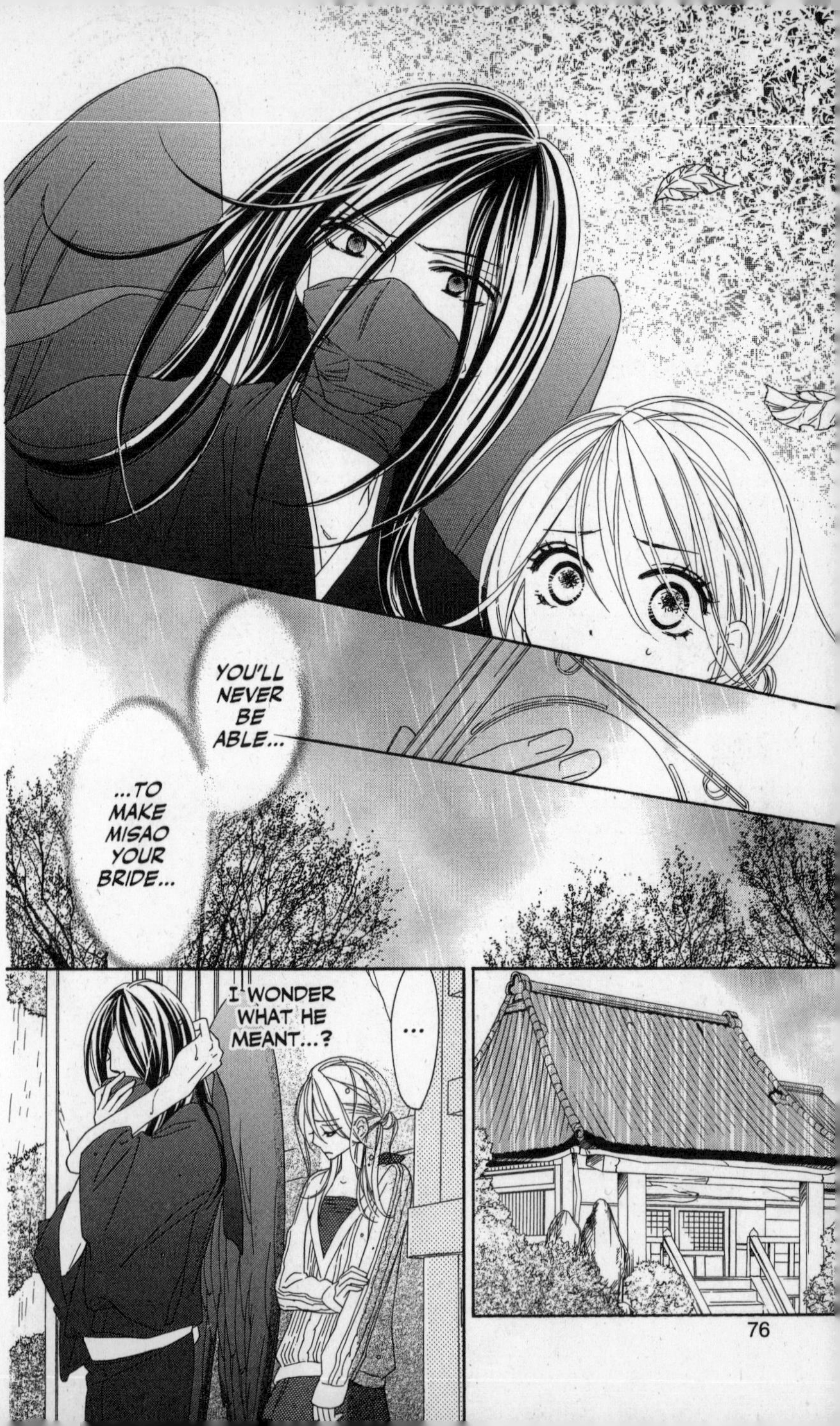
YOU'LL NEVER BE ABLE...
...TO MAKE MISAO YOUR BRIDE...
...
I WONDER WHAT HE MEANT...?

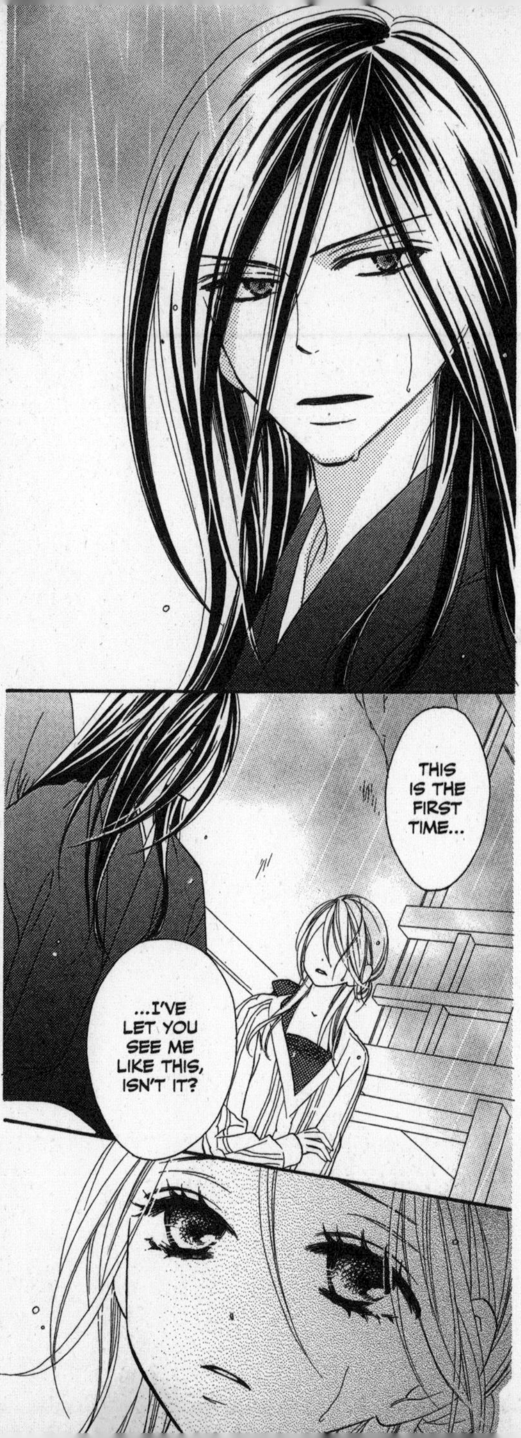
THIS IS THE FIRST TIME...
...I'VE LET YOU SEE ME LIKE THIS, ISN'T IT?

Introduction of Secondary Characters

• Two •

Misao's Parents

Yoshio (41) and Yoko (44)

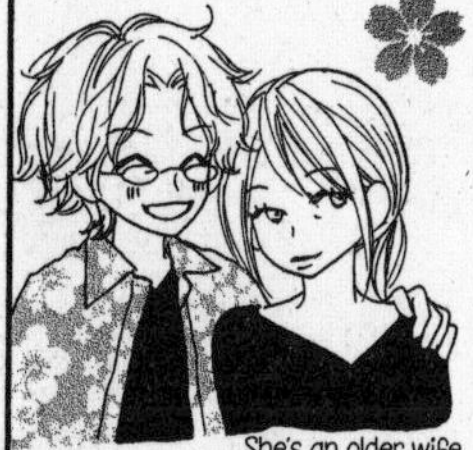

She's an older wife.

Yoko and Yoshio were in the same club in college. It took him years to persuade her to be with him. Although it has nothing to do with the story, I wonder why I set this background for them.

Yoko probably met Kyo when he was little. Yoshio's job will probably continue to have connections with this story... I think.

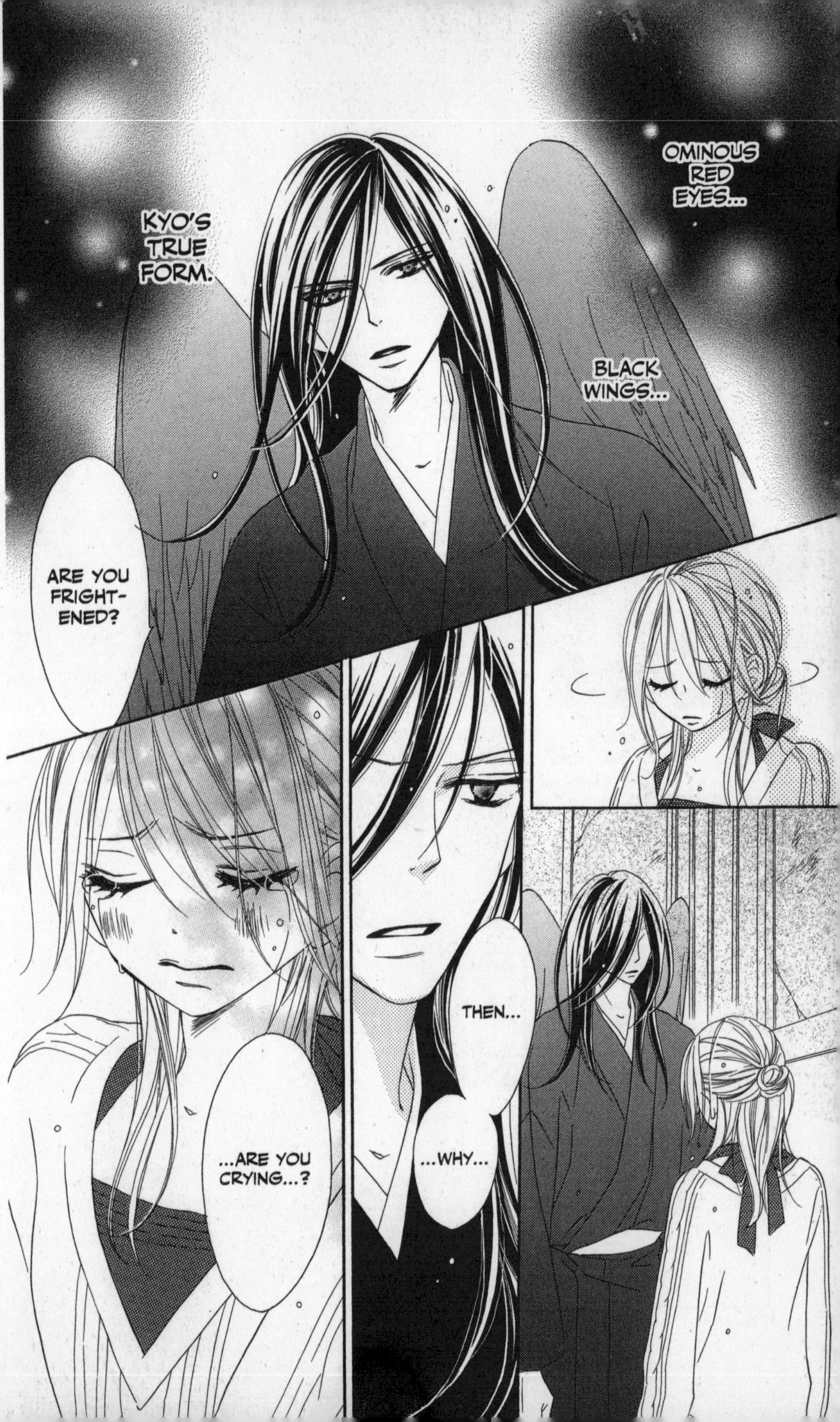
OMINOUS RED EYES...
BLACK WINGS...
KYO'S TRUE FORM.
ARE YOU FRIGHT-ENED?
THEN...
...WHY...
...ARE YOU CRYING...?

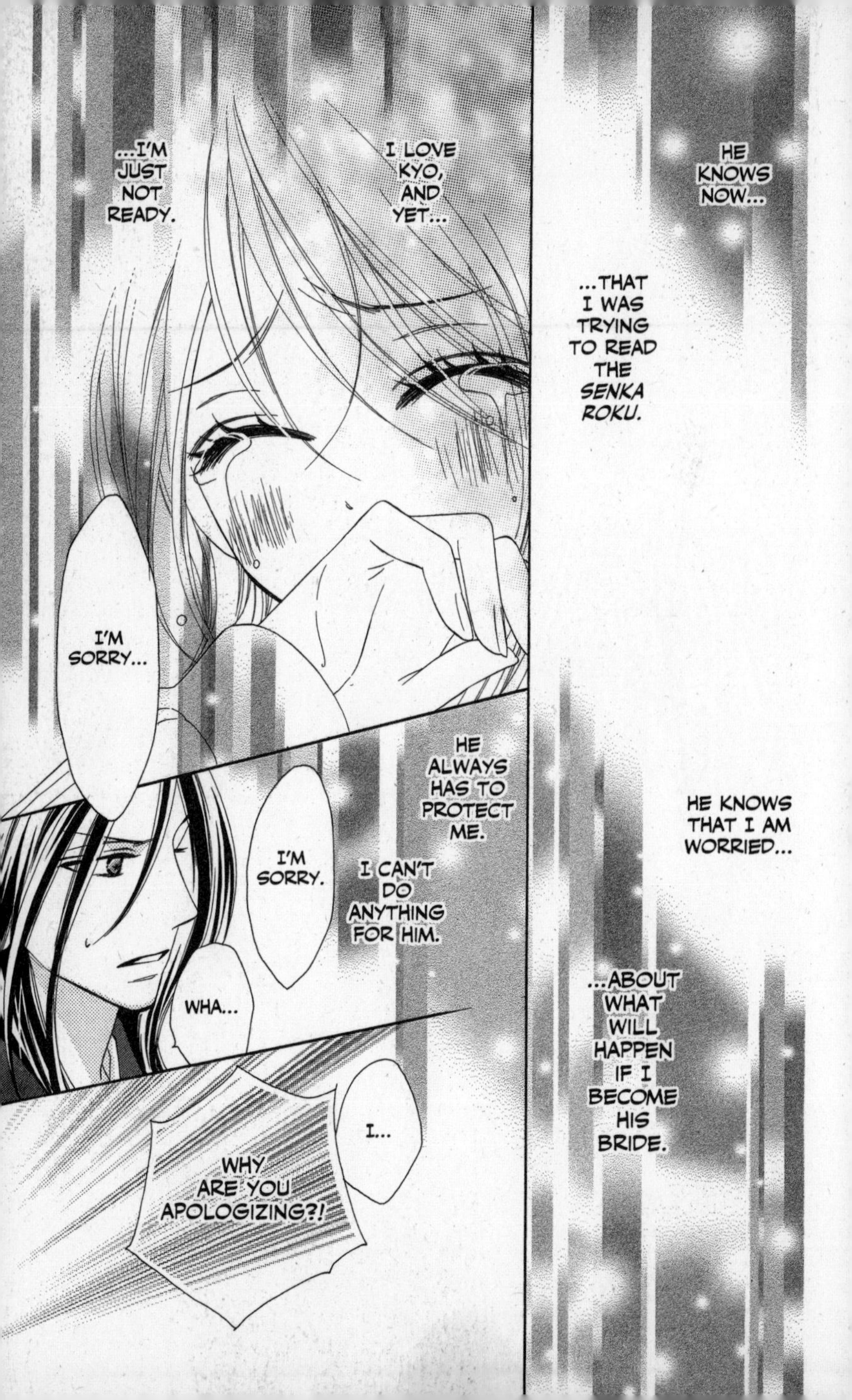
HE KNOWS NOW...
...THAT I WAS TRYING TO READ THE *SENKA ROKU.*
HE KNOWS THAT I AM WORRIED...
...ABOUT WHAT WILL HAPPEN IF I BECOME HIS BRIDE.
I LOVE KYO, AND YET...
...I'M JUST NOT READY.
I'M SORRY...
HE ALWAYS HAS TO PROTECT ME.
I CAN'T DO ANYTHING FOR HIM.
I'M SORRY.
WHA...
I...
WHY ARE YOU APOLOGIZING?!

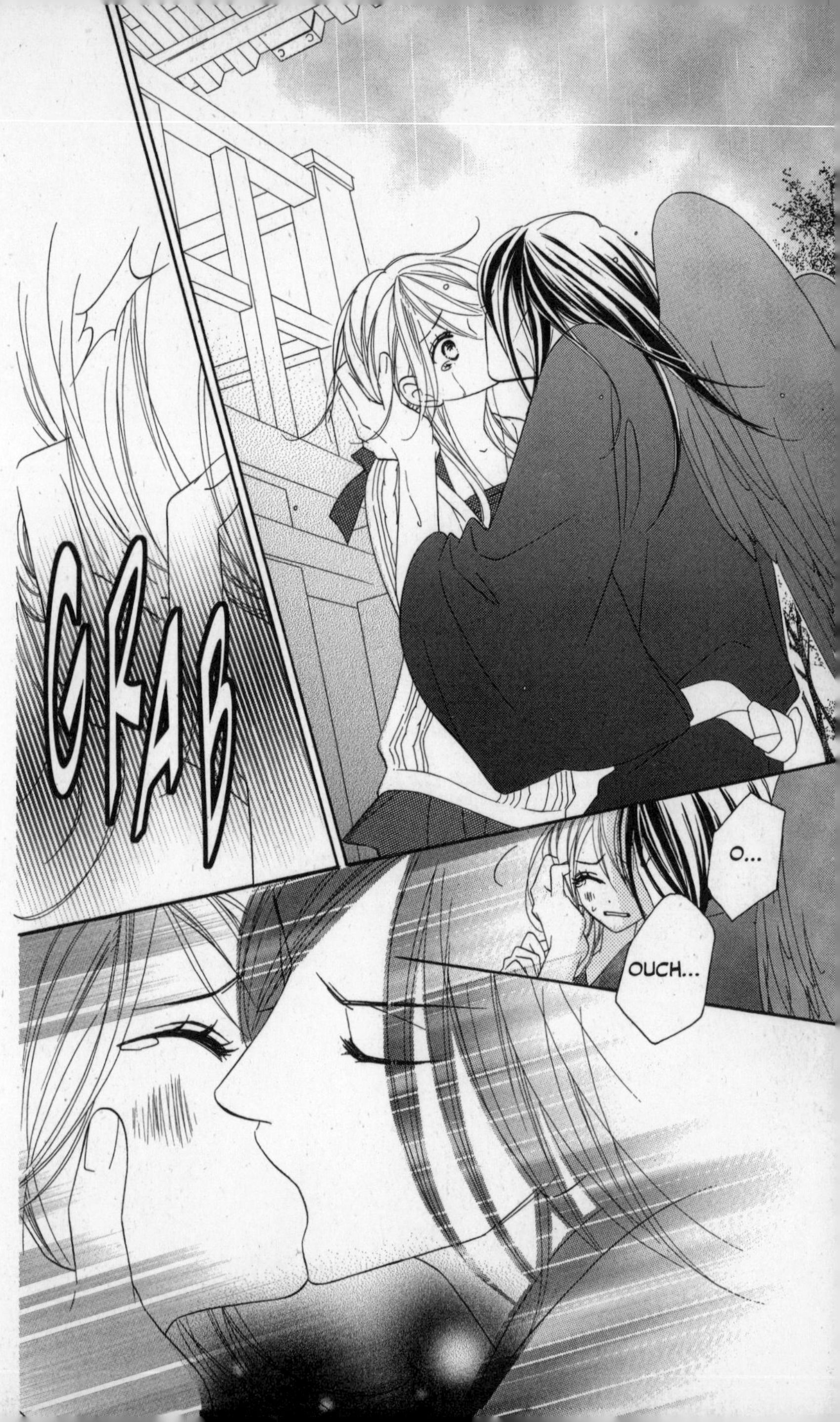
GRAB
O...
OUCH...

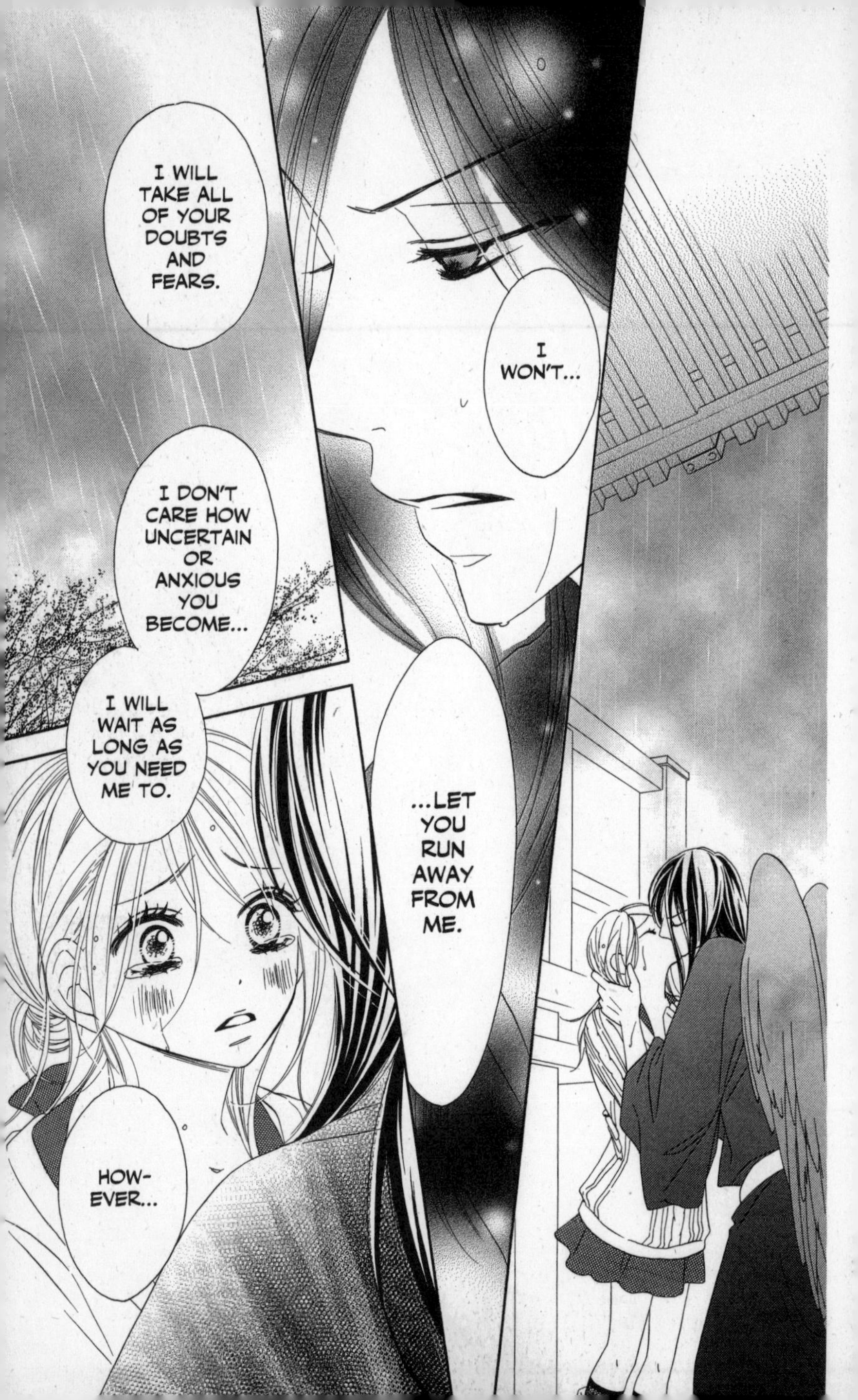
I WILL TAKE ALL OF YOUR DOUBTS AND FEARS.
I DON'T CARE HOW UNCERTAIN OR ANXIOUS YOU BECOME...
I WILL WAIT AS LONG AS YOU NEED ME TO.
HOW-EVER...
I WON'T...
...LET YOU RUN AWAY FROM ME.

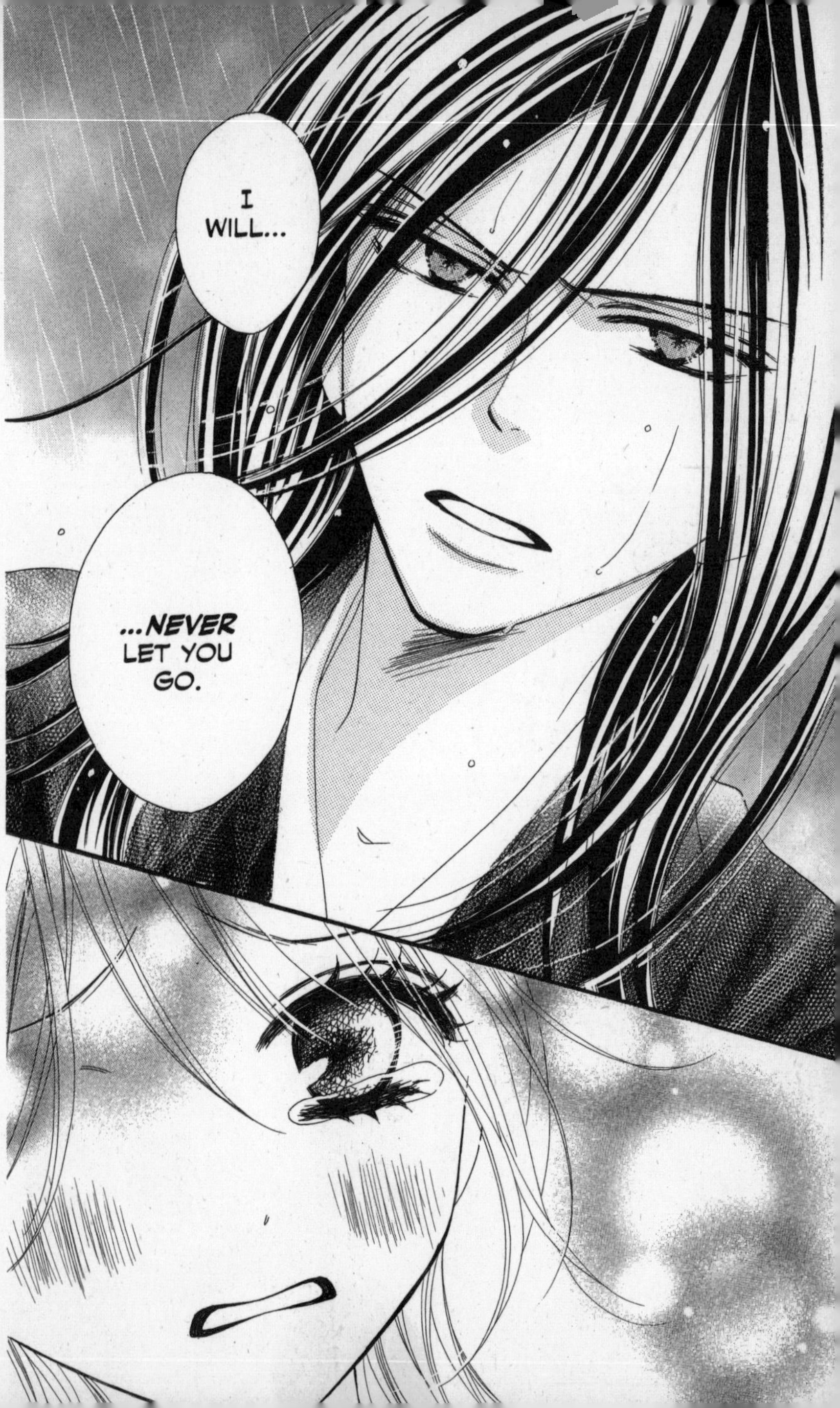
I WILL...
...NEVER LET YOU GO.

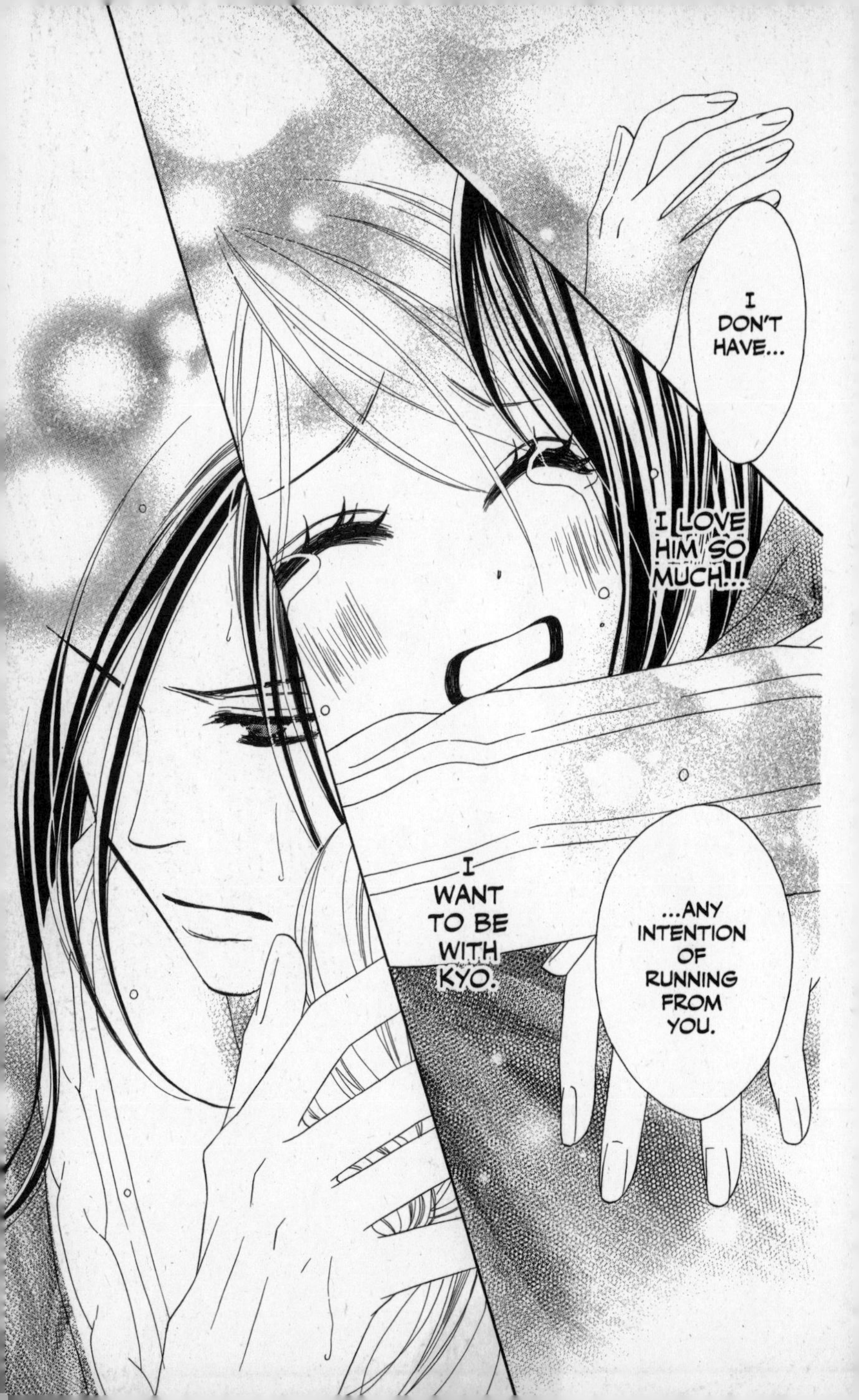
I DON'T HAVE...
I LOVE HIM SO MUCH...
...ANY INTENTION OF RUNNING FROM YOU.
I WANT TO BE WITH KYO.

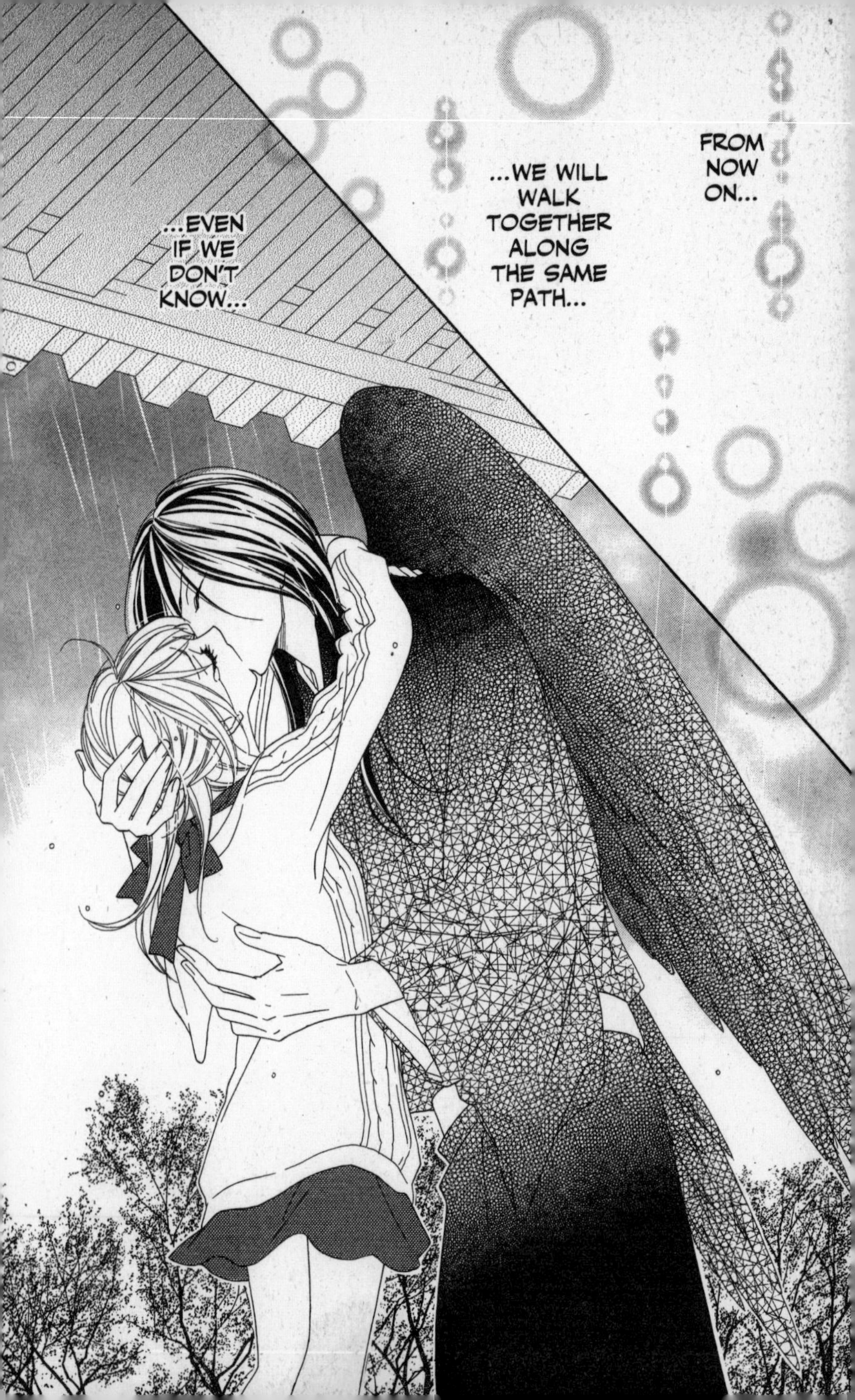
FROM NOW ON...
...WE WILL WALK TOGETHER ALONG THE SAME PATH...
...EVEN IF WE DON'T KNOW...

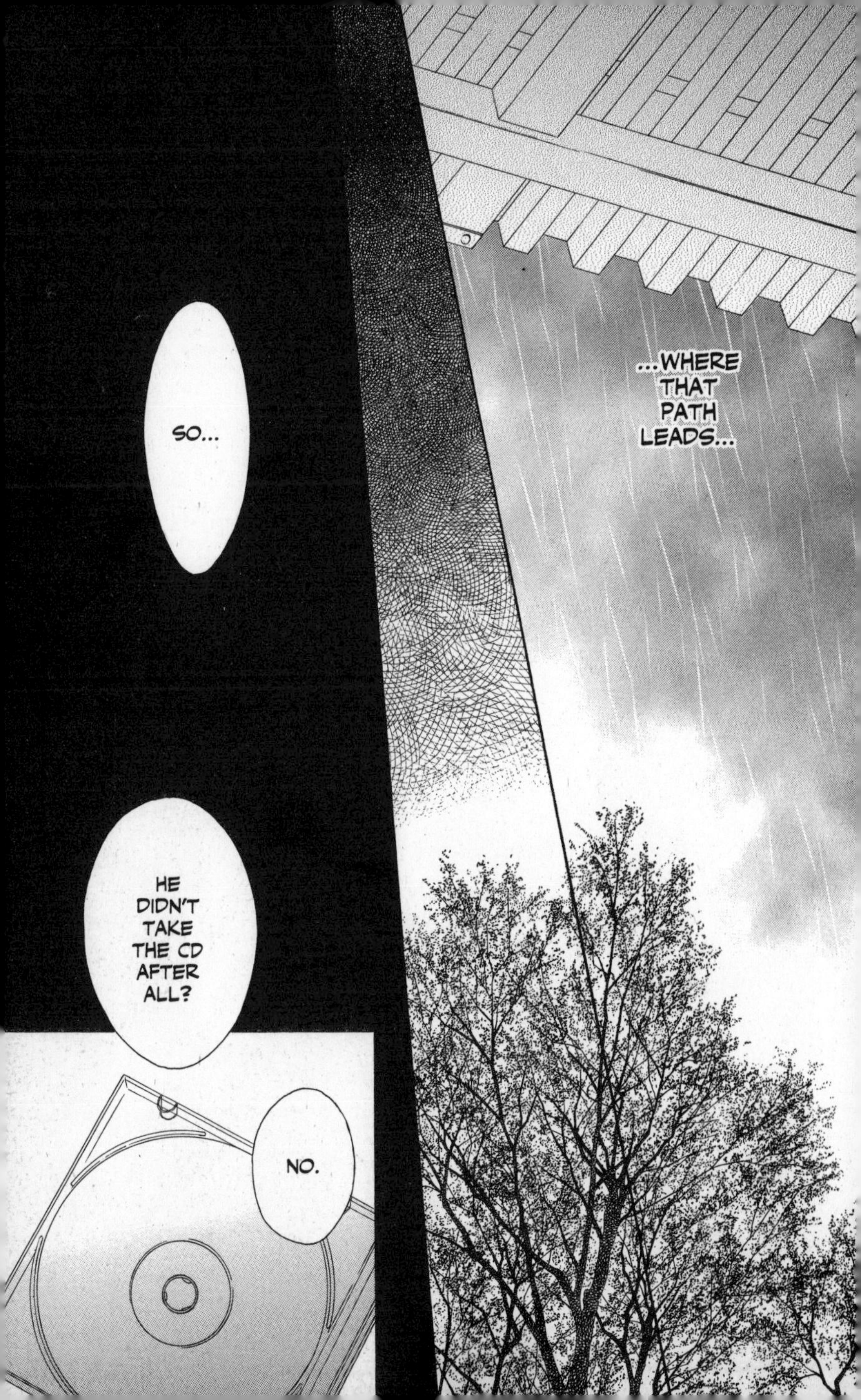
...WHERE THAT PATH LEADS...
SO...
HE DIDN'T TAKE THE CD AFTER ALL?
NO.

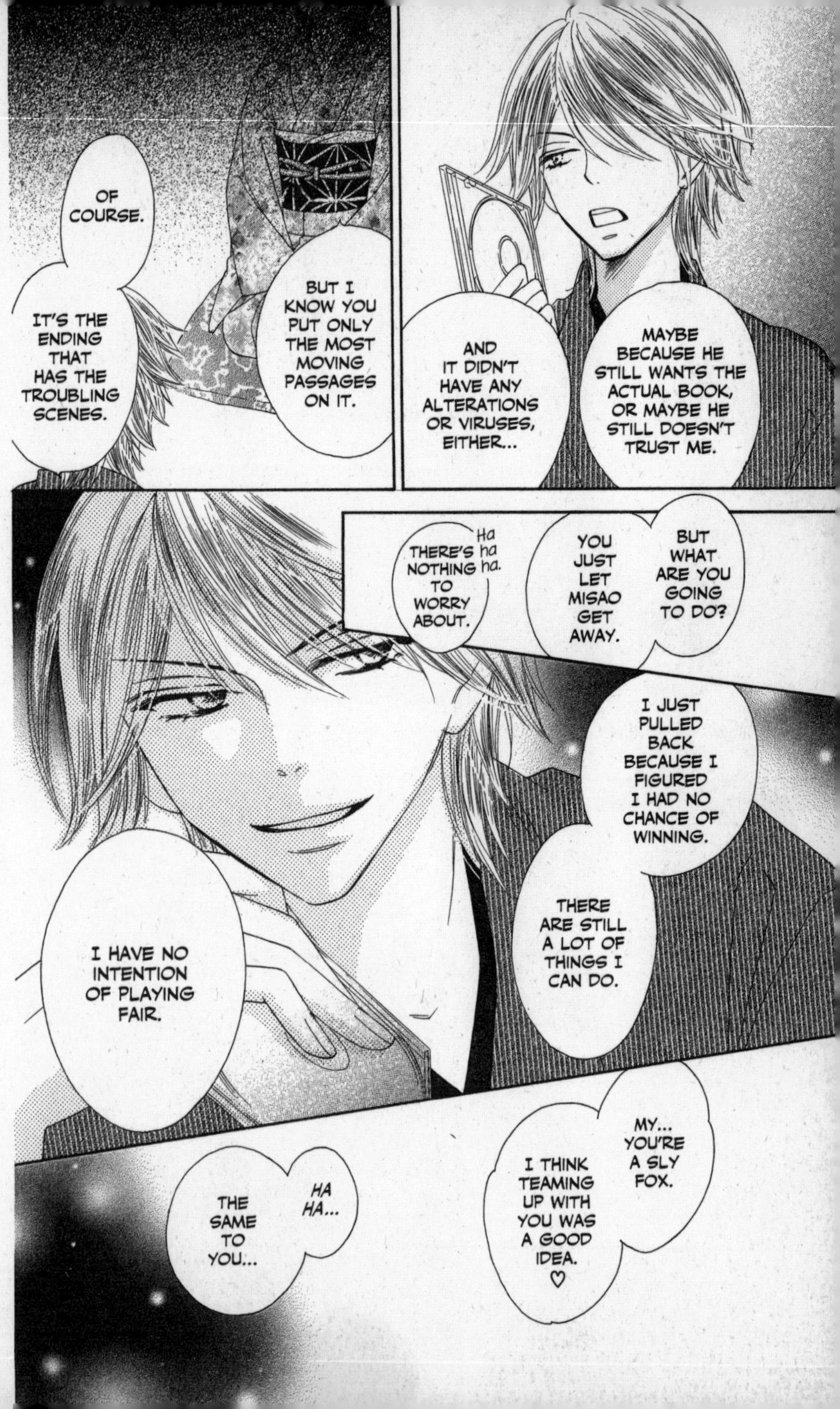
MAYBE BECAUSE HE STILL WANTS THE ACTUAL BOOK, OR MAYBE HE STILL DOESN'T TRUST ME.
AND IT DIDN'T HAVE ANY ALTERATIONS OR VIRUSES, EITHER...
BUT I KNOW YOU PUT ONLY THE MOST MOVING PASSAGES ON IT.
OF COURSE.
IT'S THE ENDING THAT HAS THE TROUBLING SCENES.
BUT WHAT ARE YOU GOING TO DO?
YOU JUST LET MISAO GET AWAY.
Ha ha ha.
THERE'S NOTHING TO WORRY ABOUT.
I JUST PULLED BACK BECAUSE I FIGURED I HAD NO CHANCE OF WINNING.
THERE ARE STILL A LOT OF THINGS I CAN DO.
I HAVE NO INTENTION OF PLAYING FAIR.
MY... YOU'RE A SLY FOX.
I THINK TEAMING UP WITH YOU WAS A GOOD IDEA. ♡
HA HA...
THE SAME TO YOU...

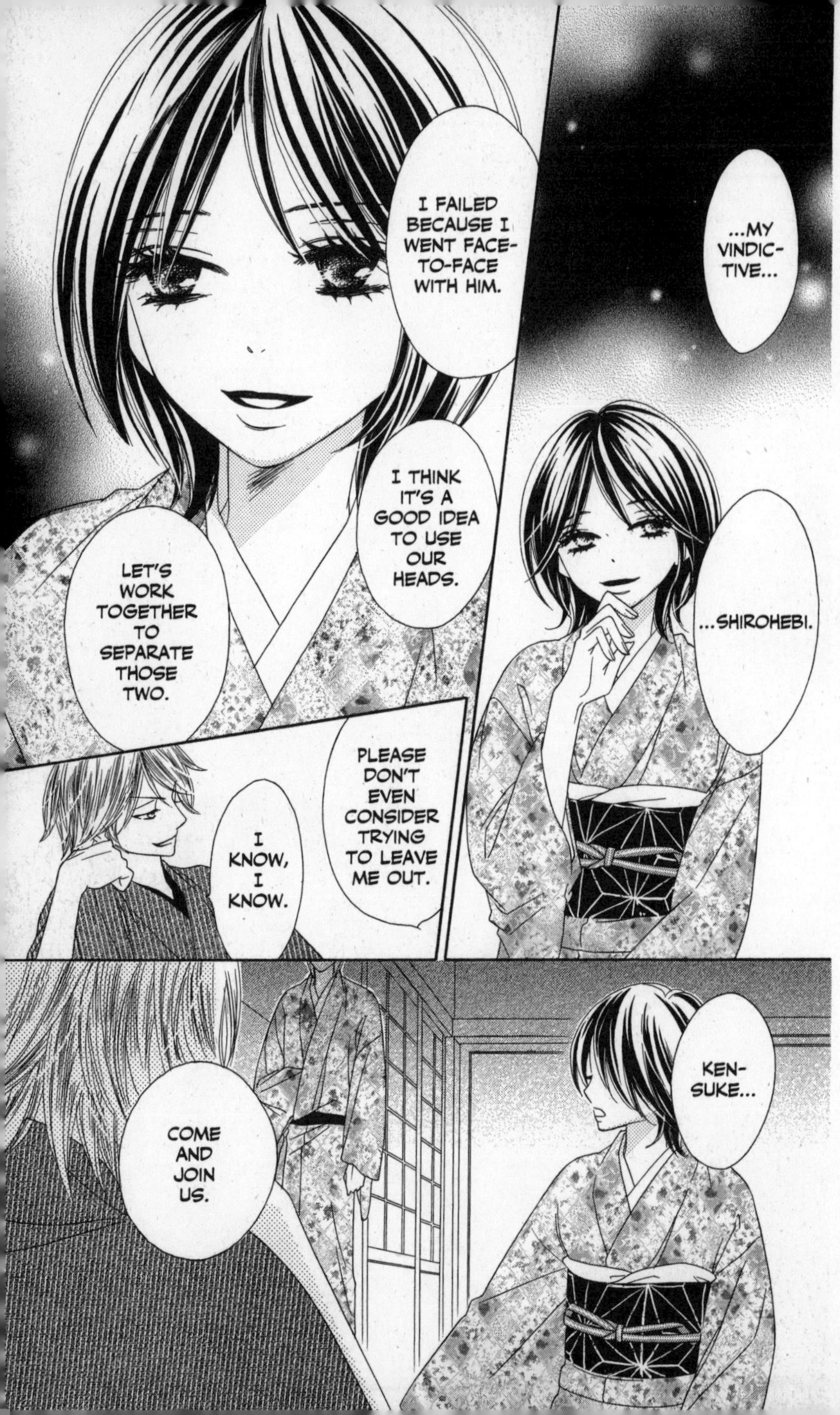
...MY VINDICTIVE...
...SHIROHEBI.
I FAILED BECAUSE I WENT FACE-TO-FACE WITH HIM.
I THINK IT'S A GOOD IDEA TO USE OUR HEADS.
LET'S WORK TOGETHER TO SEPARATE THOSE TWO.
PLEASE DON'T EVEN CONSIDER TRYING TO LEAVE ME OUT.
I KNOW, I KNOW.
KEN-SUKE...
COME AND JOIN US.

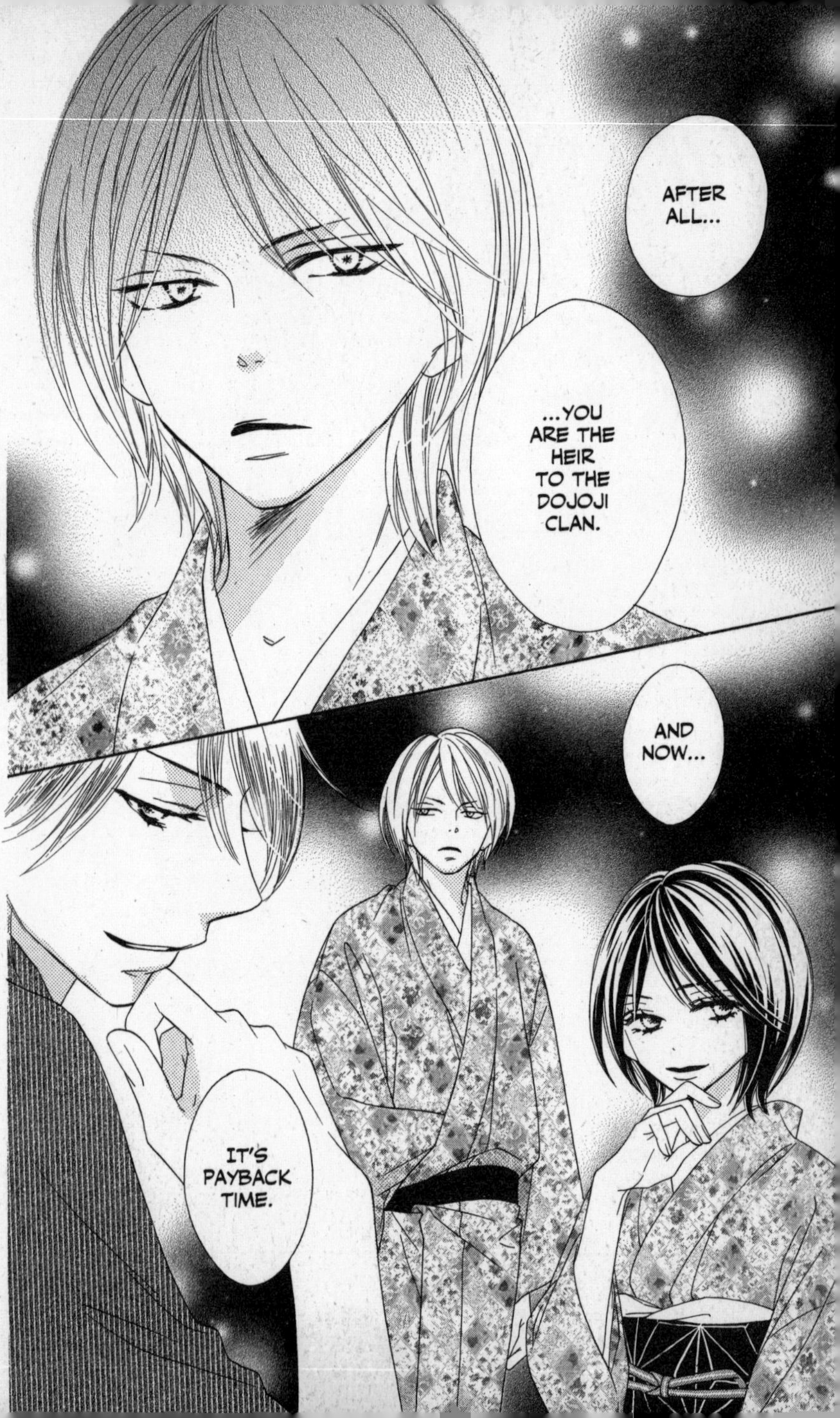
AFTER ALL...
...YOU ARE THE HEIR TO THE DOJOJI CLAN.
AND NOW...
IT'S PAYBACK TIME.

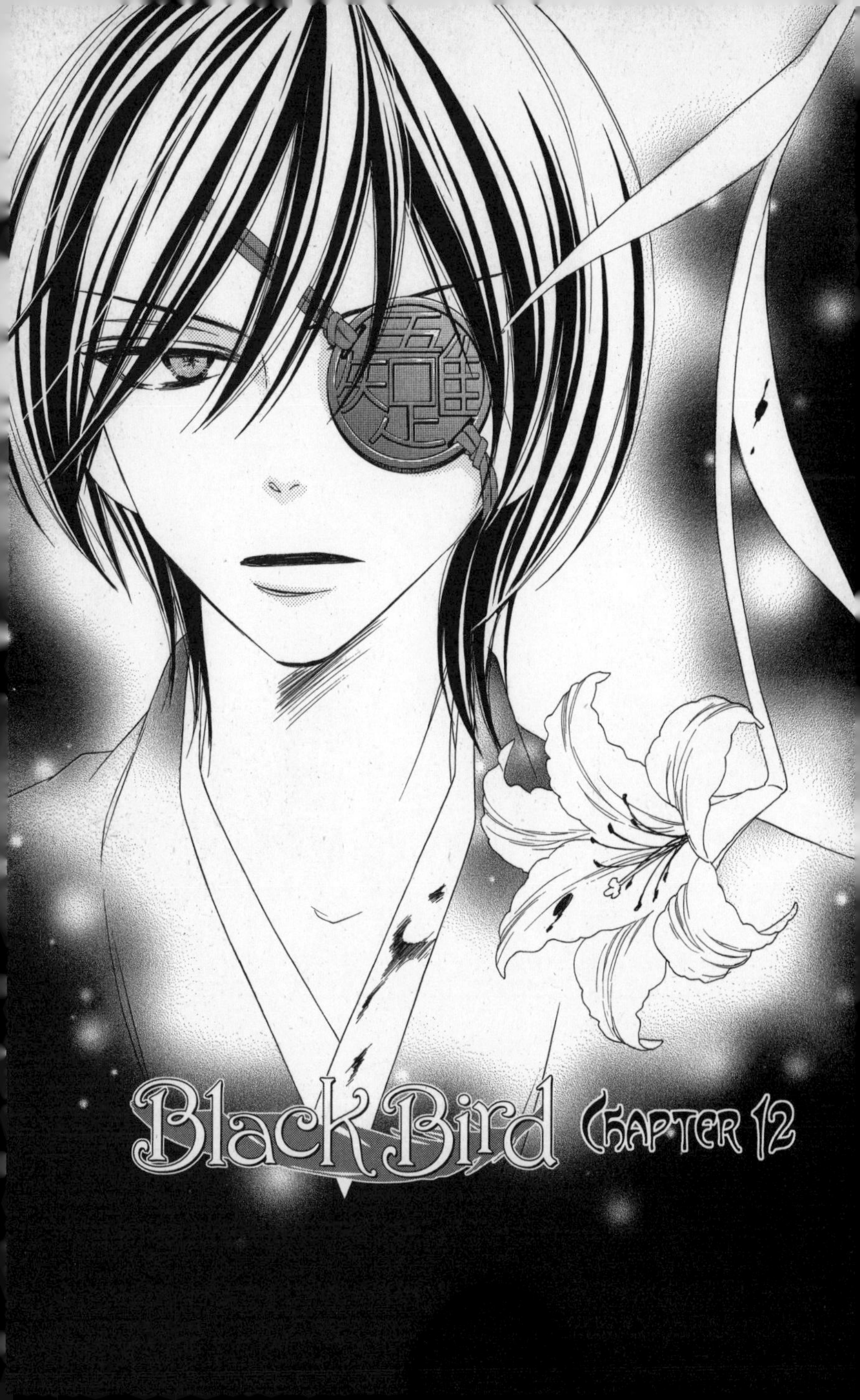
Black Bird
Chapter 12

MISAO IS PRECIOUS TO YOU, ISN'T SHE?

IF YOU READ THIS...

...YOU'LL NEVER BE ABLE TO MAKE MISAO YOUR BRIDE.

THOSE WORDS ARE LIKE THORNS PIERCING MY SIDE.

Satisfaction

On Kyo's eye patch on the previous page, the characters are copied from a stone basin (for washing hands in the garden) at Ryoanji Temple in Kyoto. The central character (口) forms part of four Chinese characters, clockwise from the top. Combined, they are 吾唯足ルヲ知ル and one simple translation is "I learn only to be contented."

Kyo still has a long way to go to realize this...

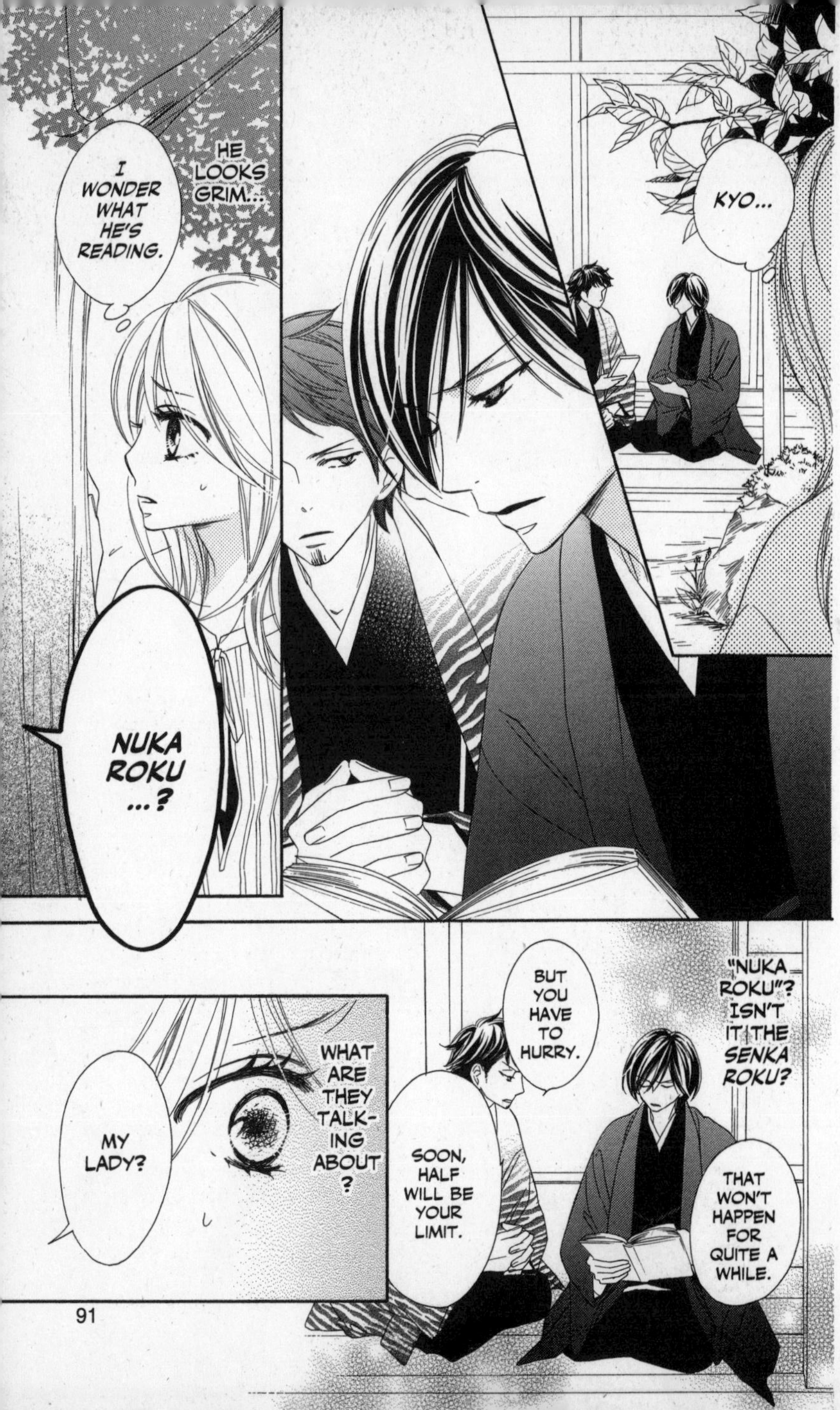
KYO...
HE LOOKS GRIM...
I WONDER WHAT HE'S READING.
NUKA ROKU ...?
"NUKA ROKU"? ISN'T IT THE SENKA ROKU?
BUT YOU HAVE TO HURRY.
THAT WON'T HAPPEN FOR QUITE A WHILE.
SOON, HALF WILL BE YOUR LIMIT.
WHAT ARE THEY TALK-ING ABOUT?
MY LADY?

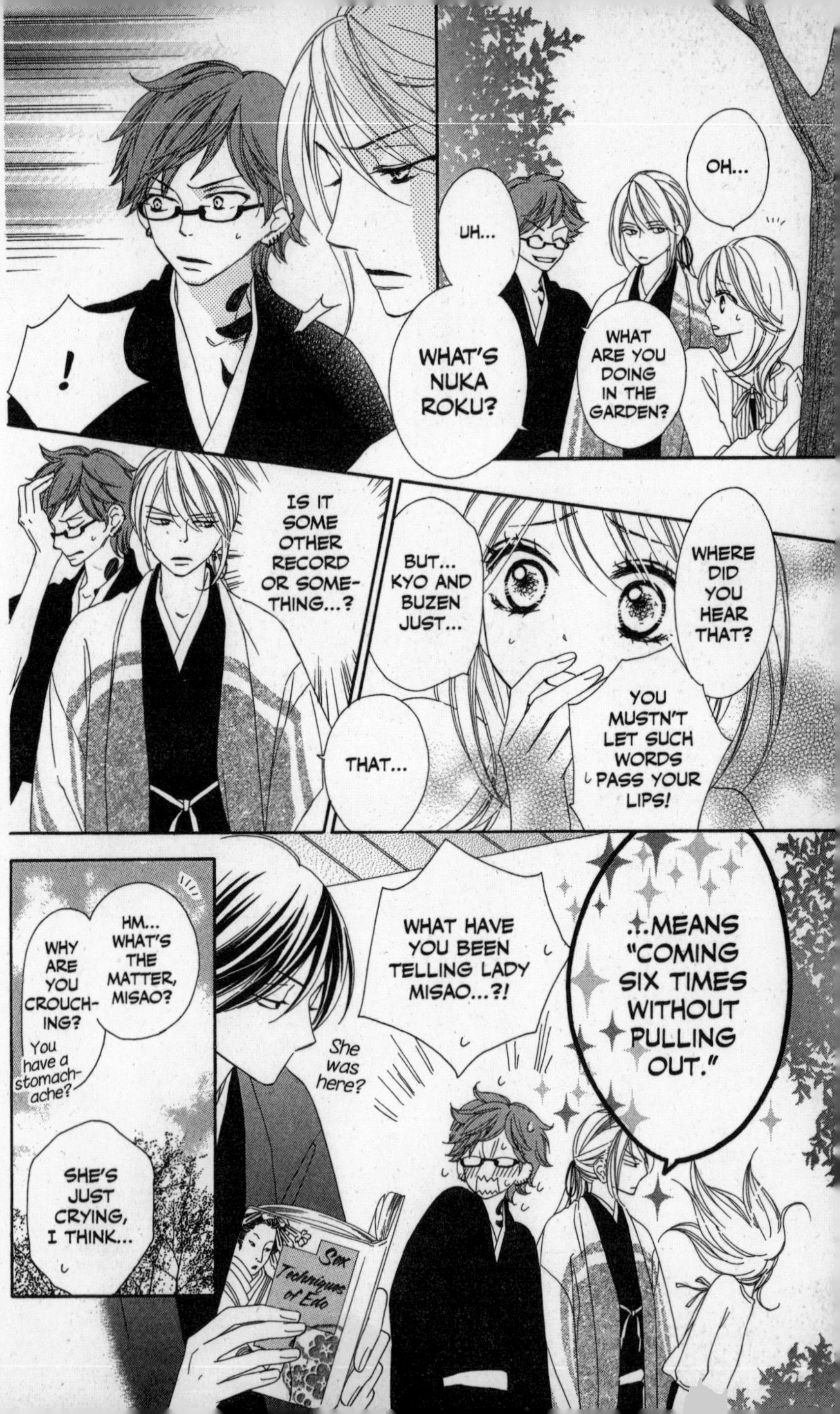
OH...
UH...
WHAT ARE YOU DOING IN THE GARDEN?
WHAT'S NUKA ROKU?
!
WHERE DID YOU HEAR THAT?
YOU MUSTN'T LET SUCH WORDS PASS YOUR LIPS!
BUT... KYO AND BUZEN JUST...
THAT...
IS IT SOME OTHER RECORD OR SOMETHING...?
...MEANS "COMING SIX TIMES WITHOUT PULLING OUT."
WHAT HAVE YOU BEEN TELLING LADY MISAO...?!
She was here?
Sex Techniques of Edo
HM... WHAT'S THE MATTER, MISAO?
WHY ARE YOU CROUCHING?
You have a stomachache?
SHE'S JUST CRYING, I THINK...

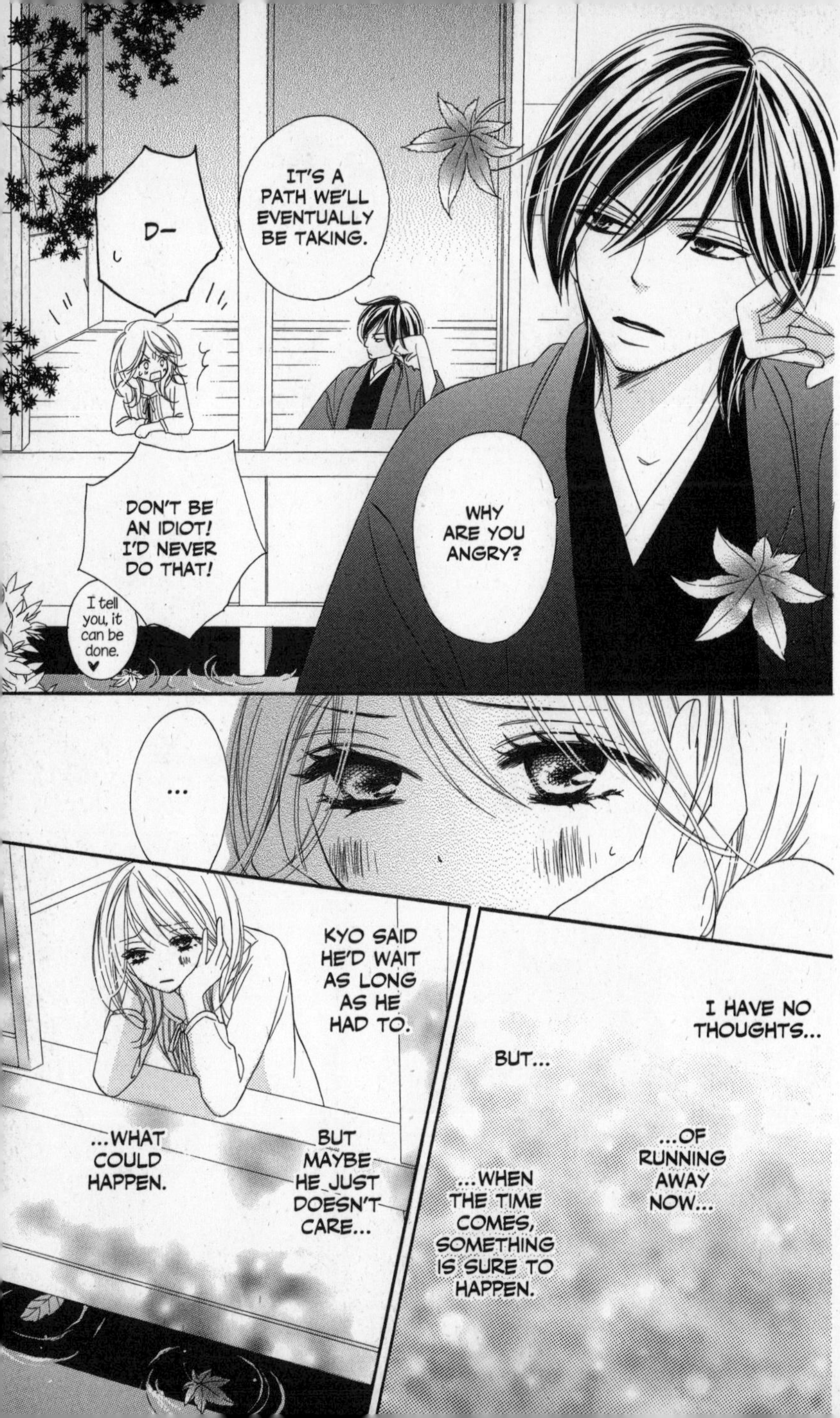
IT'S A PATH WE'LL EVENTUALLY BE TAKING.
D—
DON'T BE AN IDIOT! I'D NEVER DO THAT!
I tell you, it can be done. ♥
WHY ARE YOU ANGRY?
...
I HAVE NO THOUGHTS...
...OF RUNNING AWAY NOW...
BUT...
...WHEN THE TIME COMES, SOMETHING IS SURE TO HAPPEN.
KYO SAID HE'D WAIT AS LONG AS HE HAD TO.
BUT MAYBE HE JUST DOESN'T CARE...
...WHAT COULD HAPPEN.

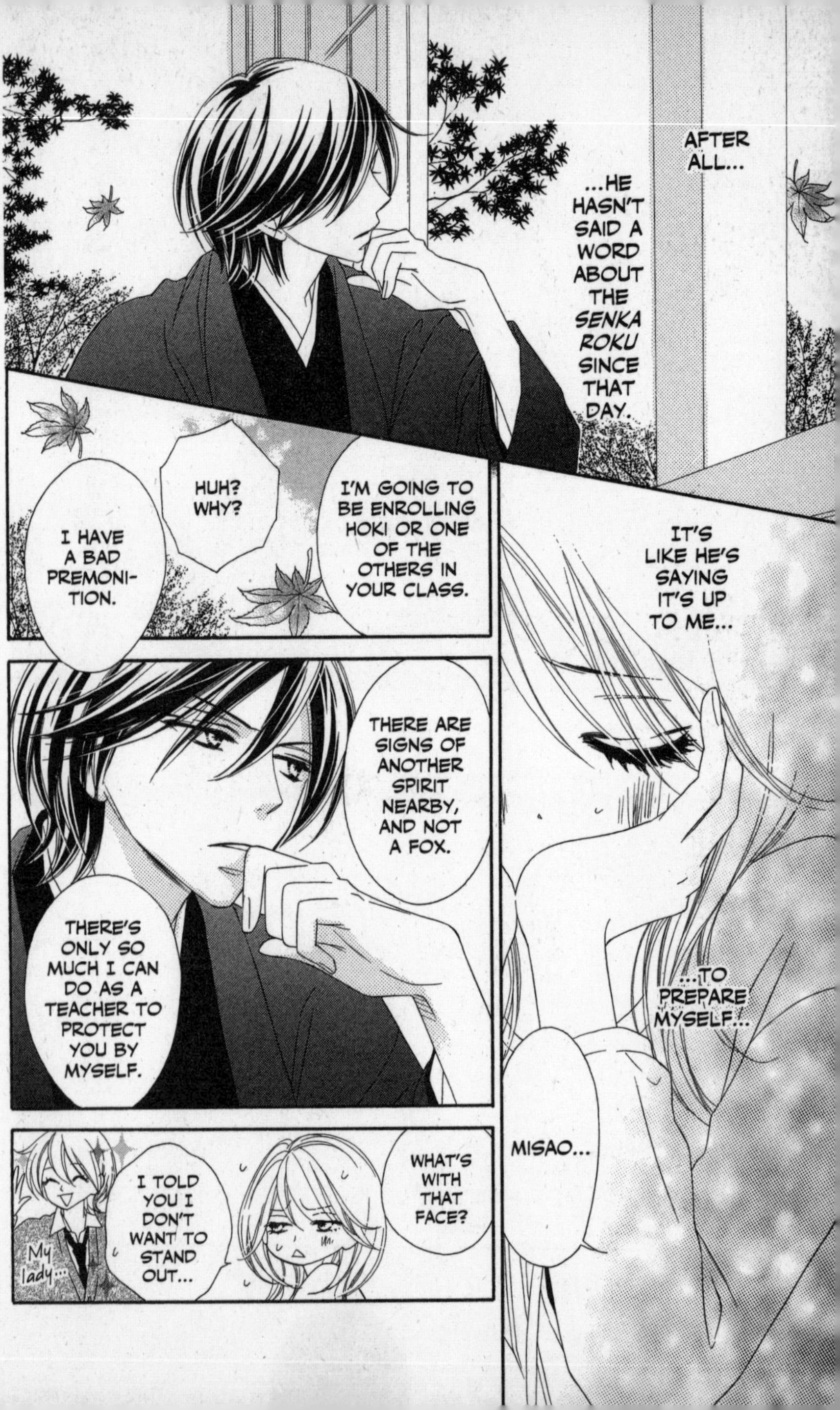
AFTER ALL...
...HE HASN'T SAID A WORD ABOUT THE SENKA ROKU SINCE THAT DAY.
IT'S LIKE HE'S SAYING IT'S UP TO ME...
...TO PREPARE MYSELF...
MISAO...
I'M GOING TO BE ENROLLING HOKI OR ONE OF THE OTHERS IN YOUR CLASS.
HUH? WHY?
I HAVE A BAD PREMONI-TION.
THERE ARE SIGNS OF ANOTHER SPIRIT NEARBY, AND NOT A FOX.
THERE'S ONLY SO MUCH I CAN DO AS A TEACHER TO PROTECT YOU BY MYSELF.
WHAT'S WITH THAT FACE?
I TOLD YOU I DON'T WANT TO STAND OUT...
My lady...

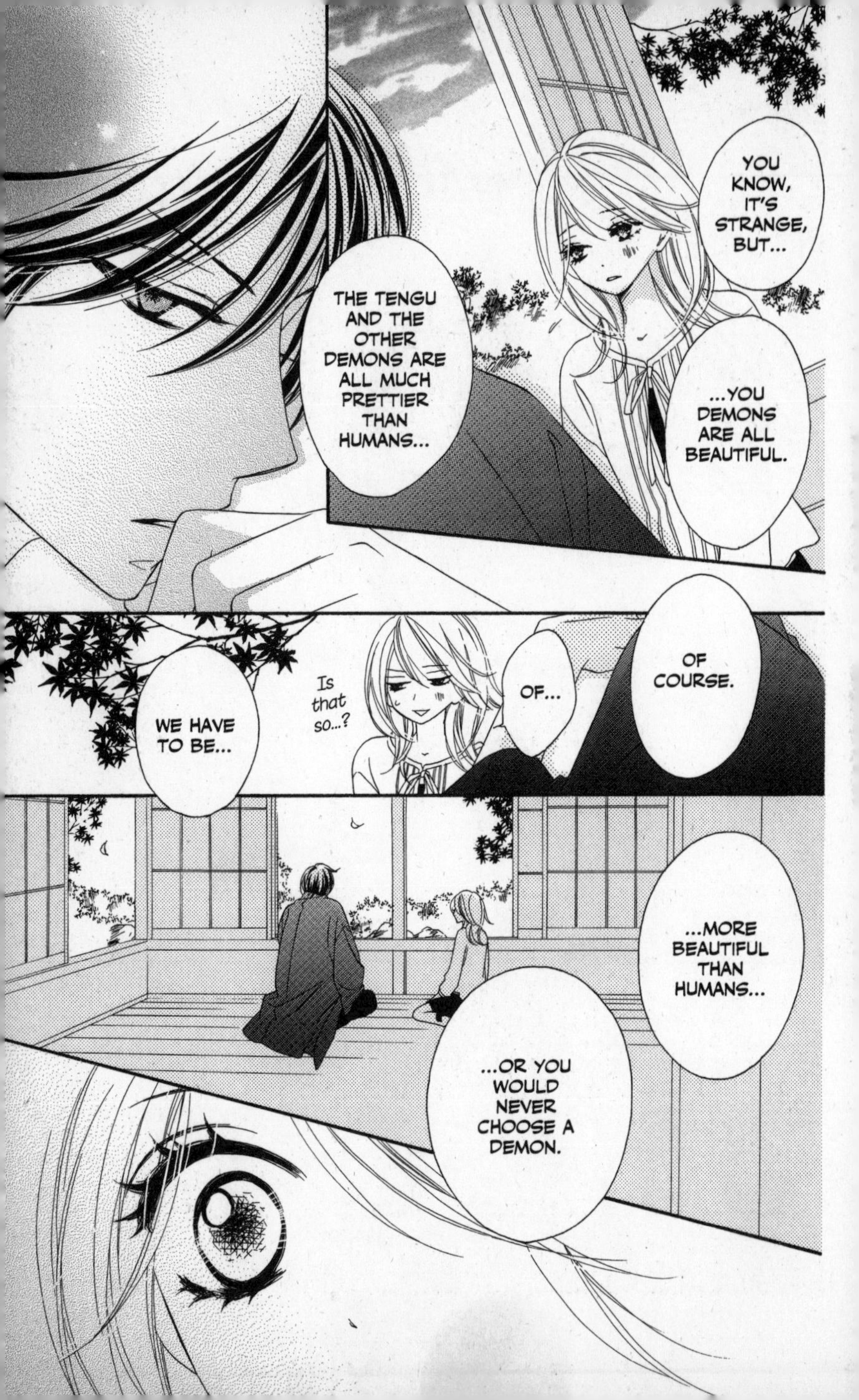
YOU KNOW, IT'S STRANGE, BUT...
THE TENGU AND THE OTHER DEMONS ARE ALL MUCH PRETTIER THAN HUMANS...
...YOU DEMONS ARE ALL BEAUTIFUL.
OF COURSE.
OF...
Is that so...?
WE HAVE TO BE...
...MORE BEAUTIFUL THAN HUMANS...
...OR YOU WOULD NEVER CHOOSE A DEMON.

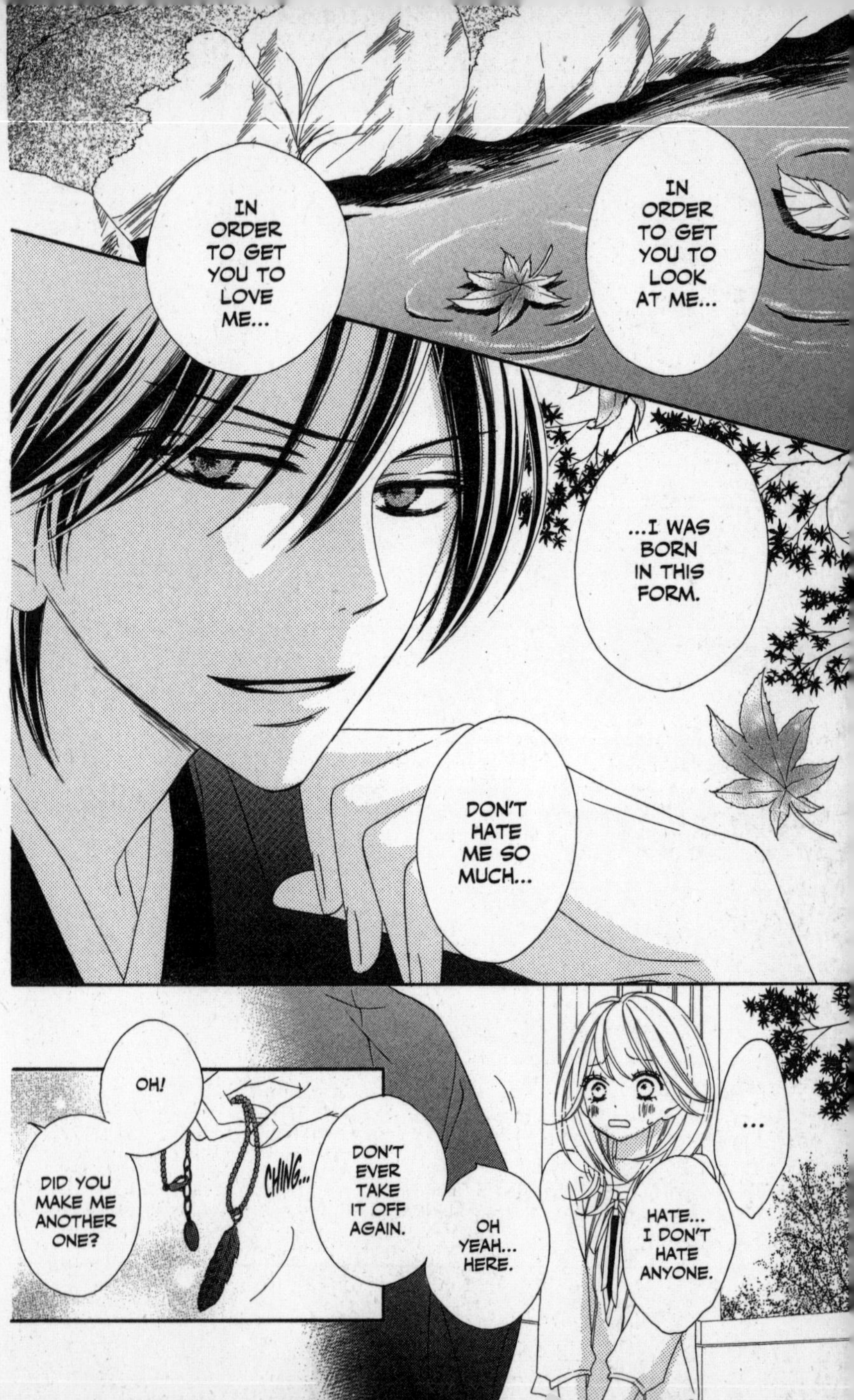
IN ORDER TO GET YOU TO LOOK AT ME...
IN ORDER TO GET YOU TO LOVE ME...
...I WAS BORN IN THIS FORM.
DON'T HATE ME SO MUCH...
...
HATE... I DON'T HATE ANYONE.
OH YEAH... HERE.
OH!
DID YOU MAKE ME ANOTHER ONE?
CHING...
DON'T EVER TAKE IT OFF AGAIN.

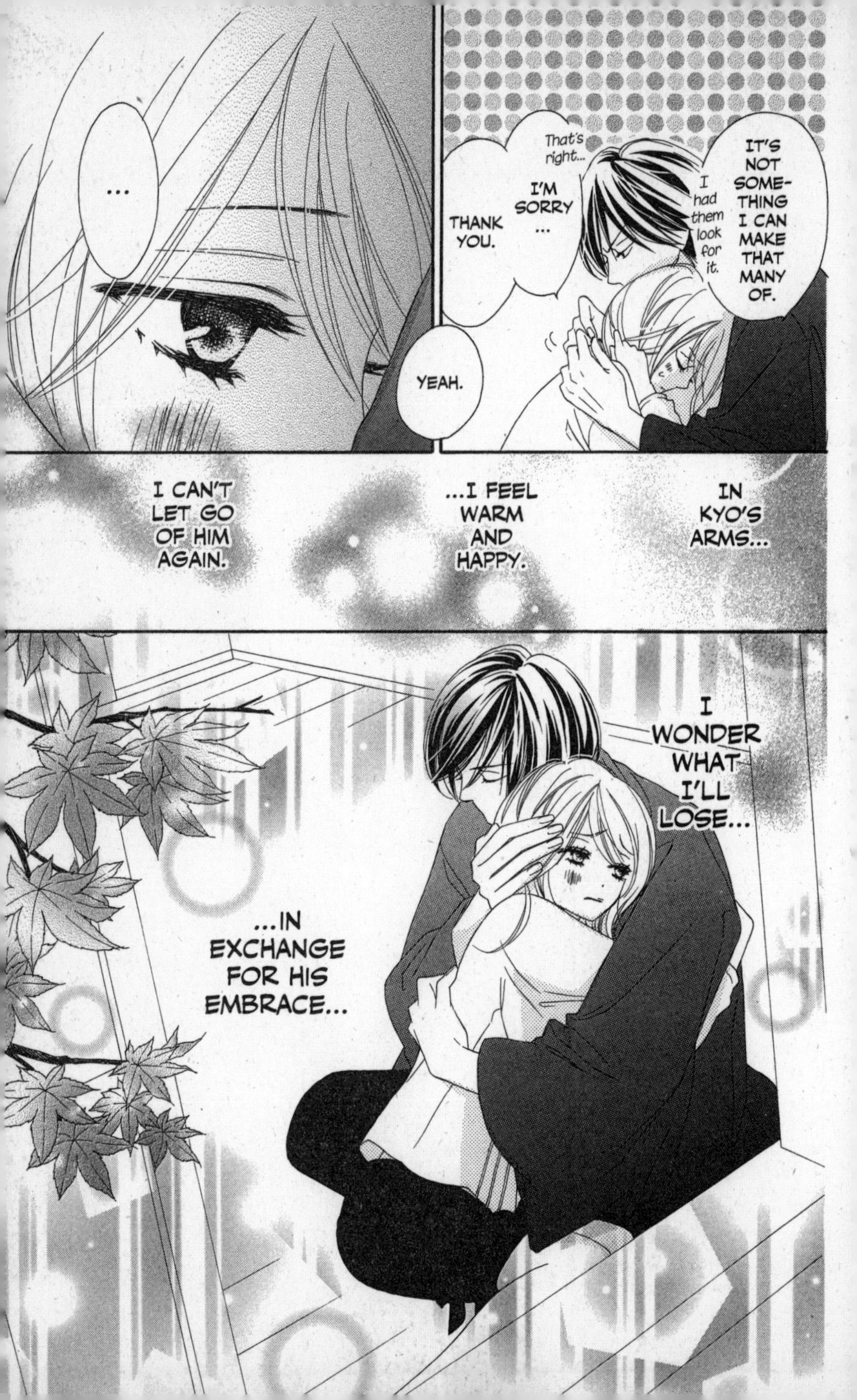
IT'S NOT SOME-THING I CAN MAKE THAT MANY OF.
I had them look for it.
That's right...
I'M SORRY...
THANK YOU.
YEAH.
...
IN KYO'S ARMS...
...I FEEL WARM AND HAPPY.
I CAN'T LET GO OF HIM AGAIN.
I WONDER WHAT I'LL LOSE...
...IN EXCHANGE FOR HIS EMBRACE...

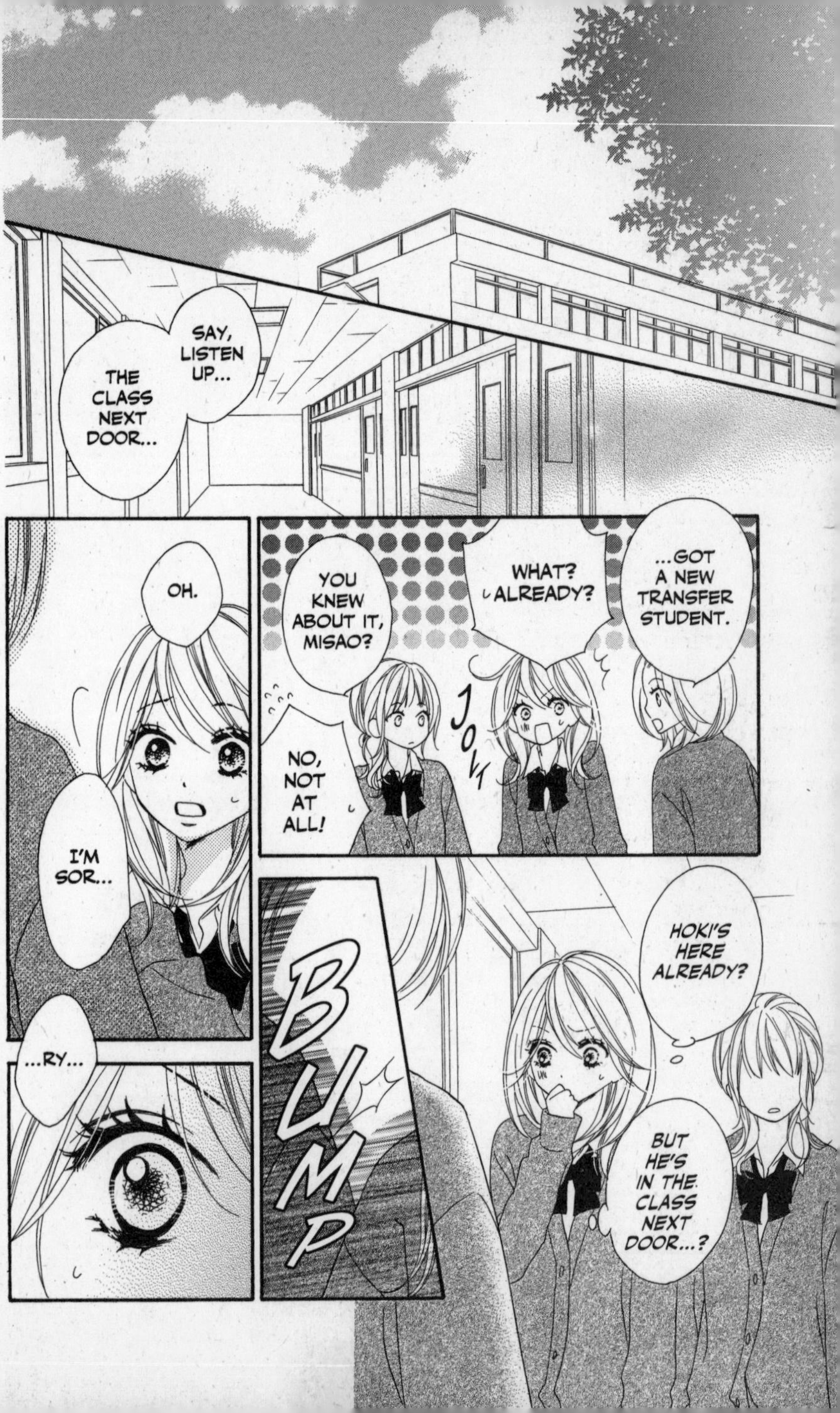
SAY, LISTEN UP...
THE CLASS NEXT DOOR...
...GOT A NEW TRANSFER STUDENT.
WHAT? ALREADY?
YOU KNEW ABOUT IT, MISAO?
NO, NOT AT ALL!
HOKI'S HERE ALREADY?
BUT HE'S IN THE CLASS NEXT DOOR...?
BUMP
OH.
I'M SOR...
...RY...

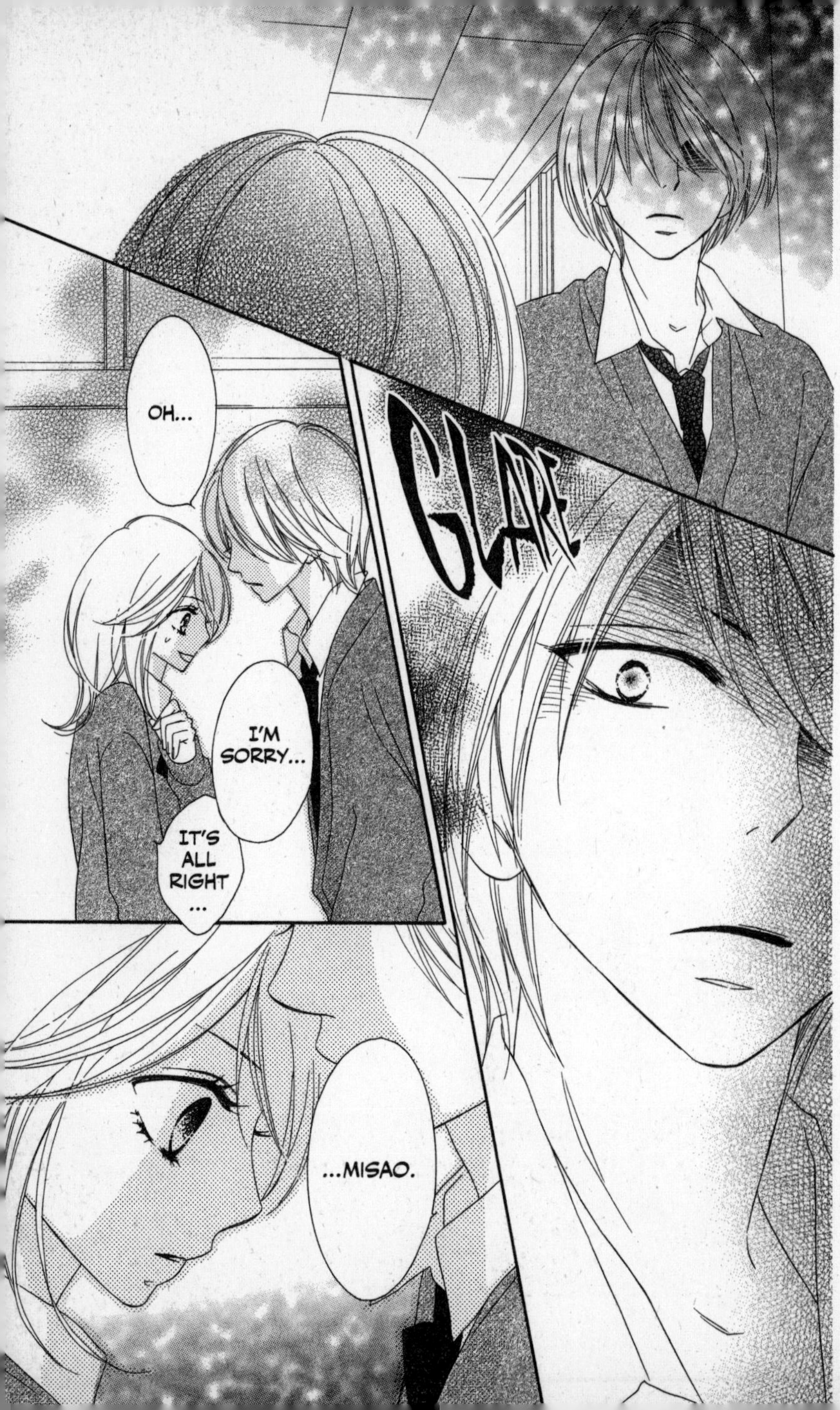
GLARE
OH...
I'M SORRY...
IT'S ALL RIGHT...
...MISAO.

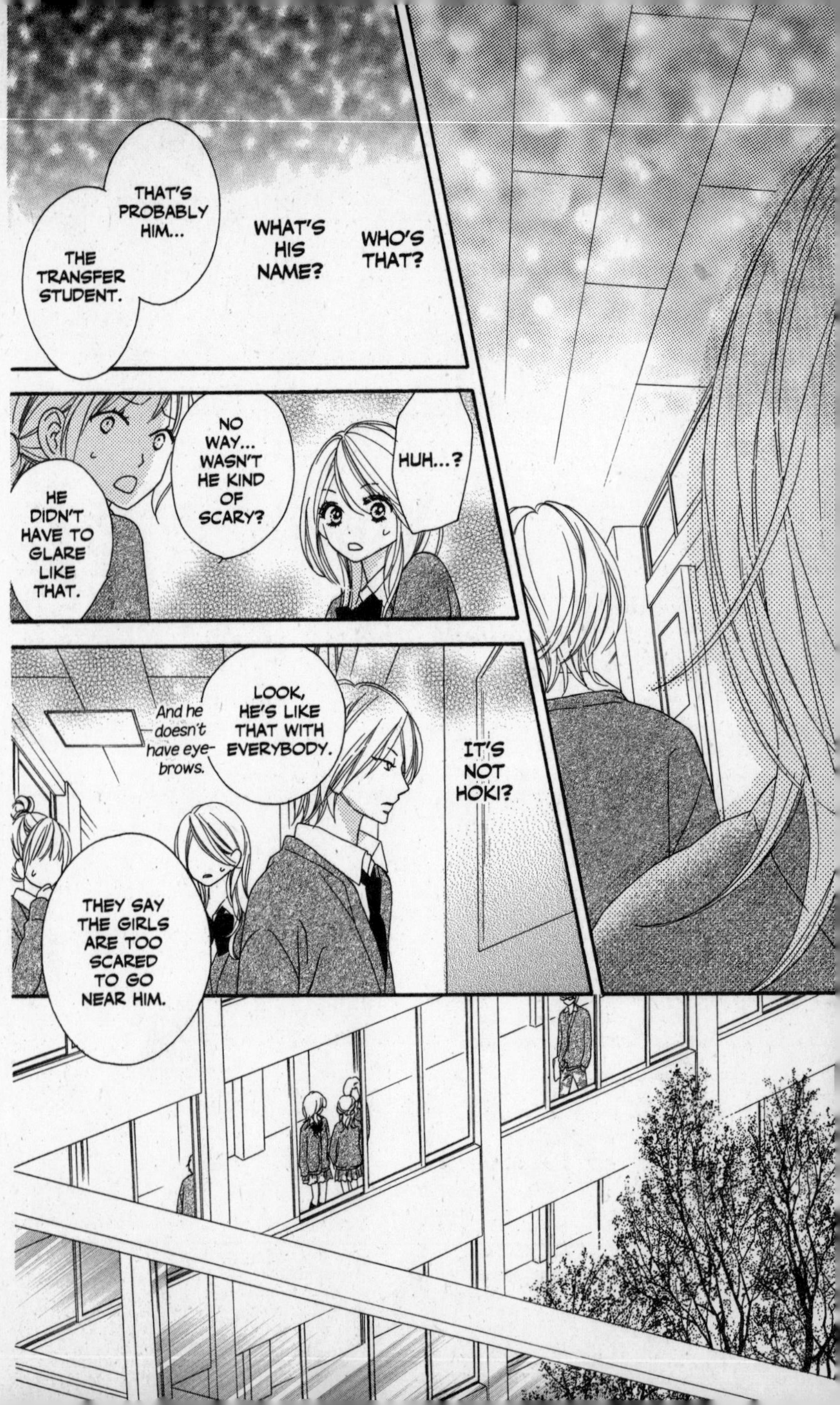
WHO'S THAT?
WHAT'S HIS NAME?
THAT'S PROBABLY HIM...
THE TRANSFER STUDENT.
HUH...?
NO WAY... WASN'T HE KIND OF SCARY?
HE DIDN'T HAVE TO GLARE LIKE THAT.
IT'S NOT HOKI?
LOOK, HE'S LIKE THAT WITH EVERYBODY.
And he doesn't have eye-brows.
THEY SAY THE GIRLS ARE TOO SCARED TO GO NEAR HIM.

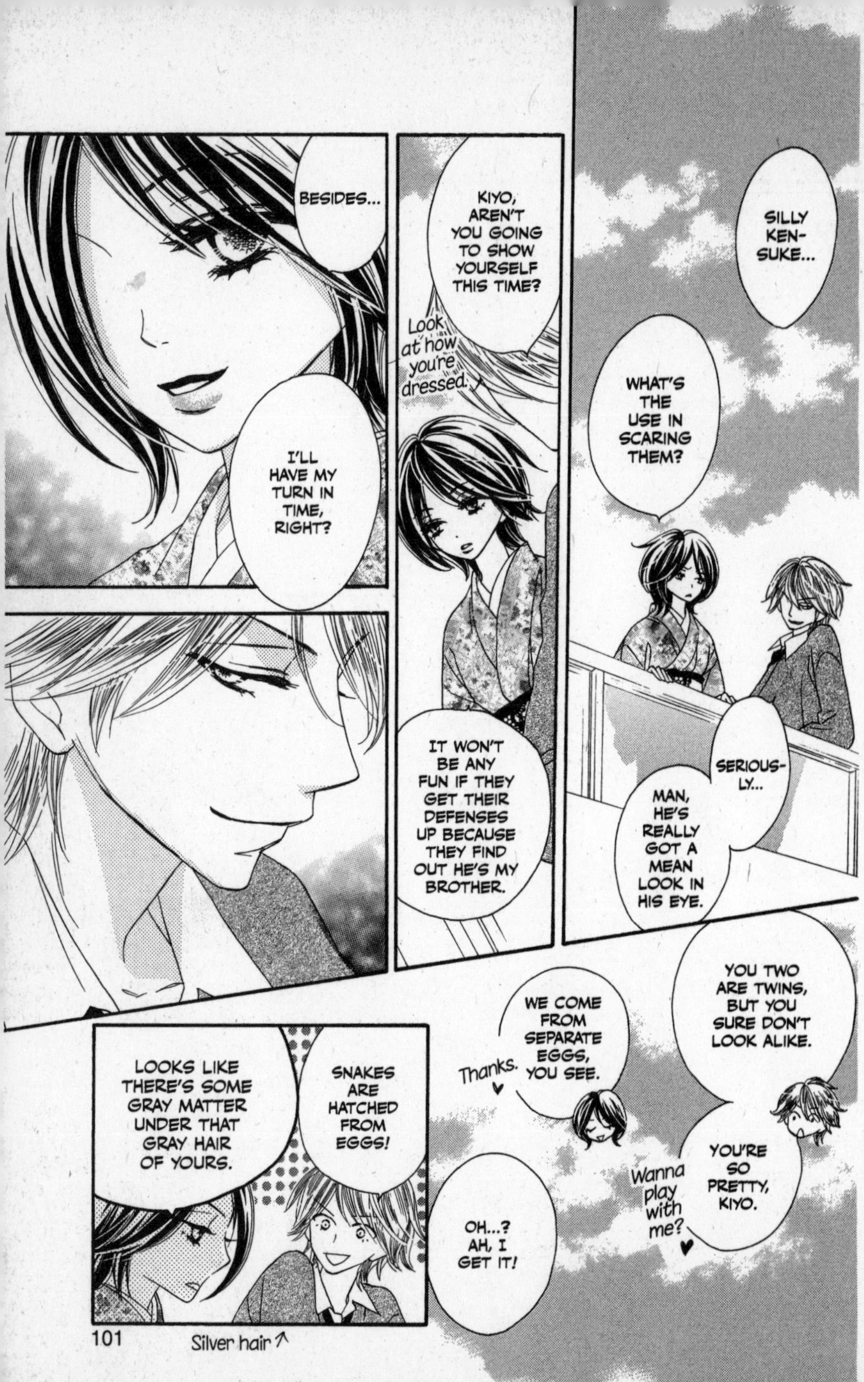
SILLY KEN-SUKE...
WHAT'S THE USE IN SCARING THEM?
SERIOUS-LY...
MAN, HE'S REALLY GOT A MEAN LOOK IN HIS EYE.
KIYO, AREN'T YOU GOING TO SHOW YOURSELF THIS TIME?
Look at how you're dressed.
IT WON'T BE ANY FUN IF THEY GET THEIR DEFENSES UP BECAUSE THEY FIND OUT HE'S MY BROTHER.
BESIDES...
I'LL HAVE MY TURN IN TIME, RIGHT?
YOU TWO ARE TWINS, BUT YOU SURE DON'T LOOK ALIKE.
WE COME FROM SEPARATE EGGS, YOU SEE.
Thanks.
YOU'RE SO PRETTY, KIYO.
Wanna play with me?
OH...? AH, I GET IT!
SNAKES ARE HATCHED FROM EGGS!
LOOKS LIKE THERE'S SOME GRAY MATTER UNDER THAT GRAY HAIR OF YOURS.
Silver hair

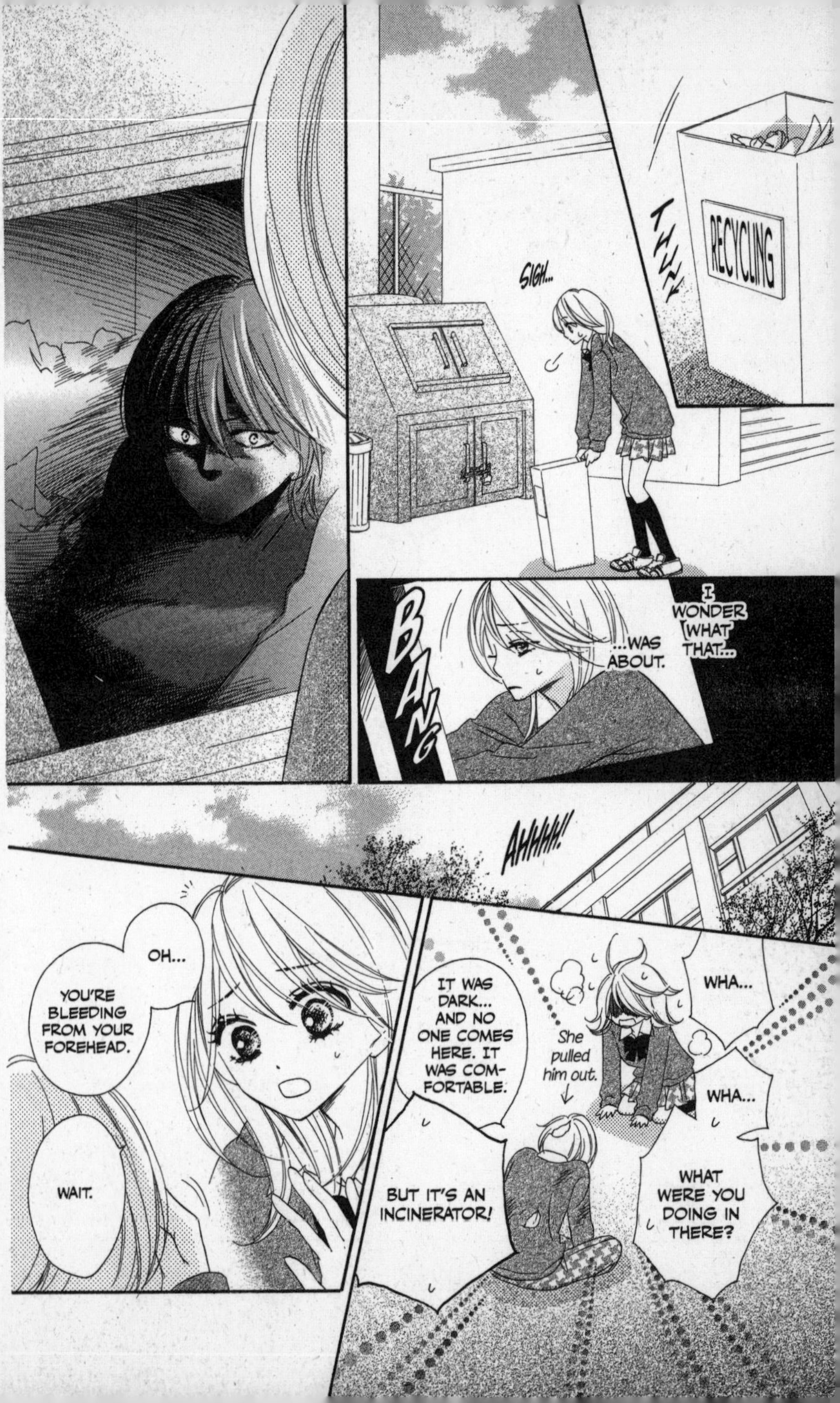
SIGH...
I WONDER WHAT THAT...
...WAS ABOUT.
BANG
AHHHH!
WHA...
WHA...
WHAT WERE YOU DOING IN THERE?
She pulled him out.
IT WAS DARK... AND NO ONE COMES HERE. IT WAS COMFORTABLE.
BUT IT'S AN INCINERATOR!
OH...
YOU'RE BLEEDING FROM YOUR FOREHEAD.
WAIT.
RECYCLING

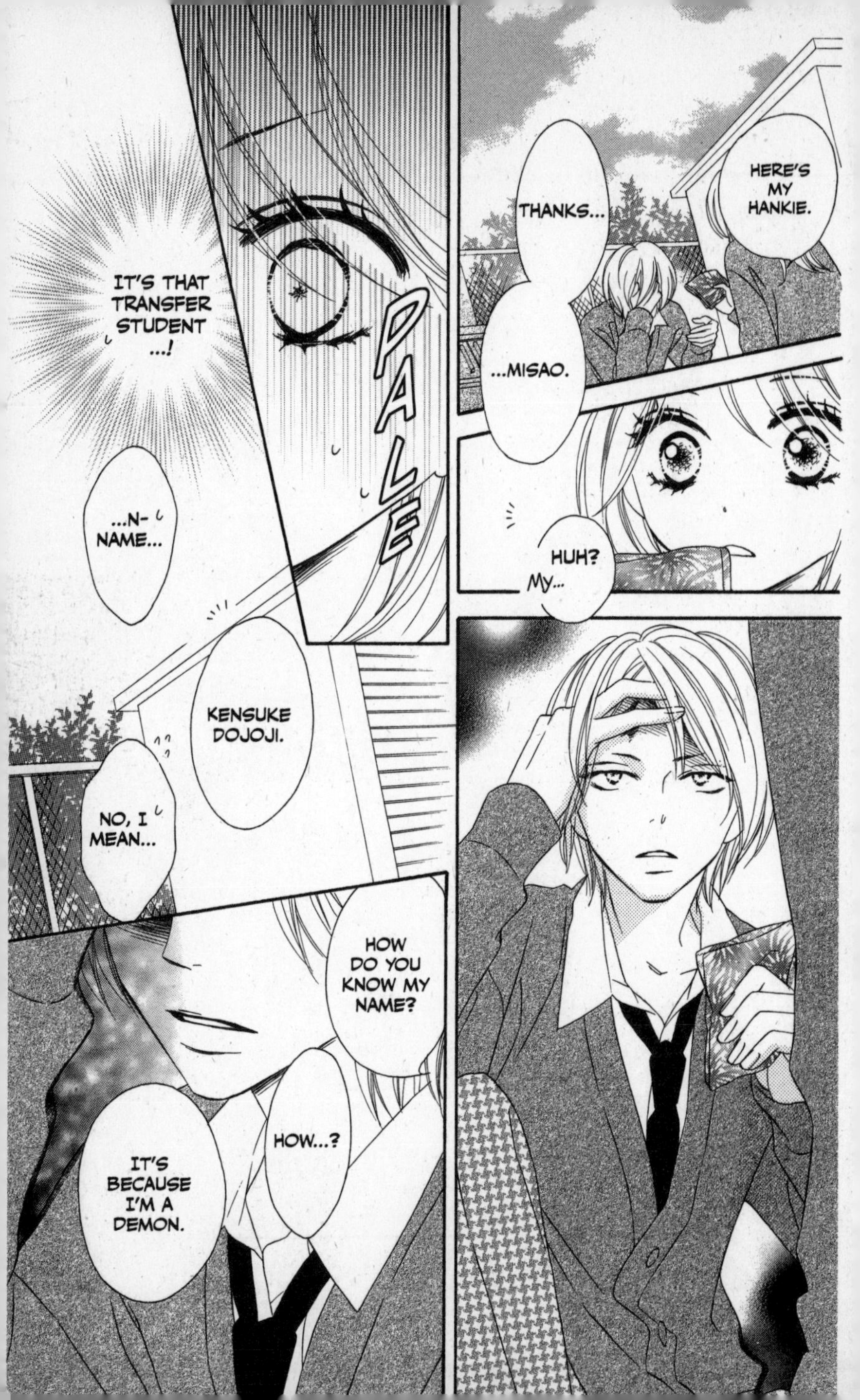
HERE'S MY HANKIE.
THANKS...
...MISAO.
HUH? My...
PALE
IT'S THAT TRANSFER STUDENT ...!
...N-NAME...
KENSUKE DOJOJI.
NO, I MEAN...
HOW DO YOU KNOW MY NAME?
HOW...?
IT'S BECAUSE I'M A DEMON.

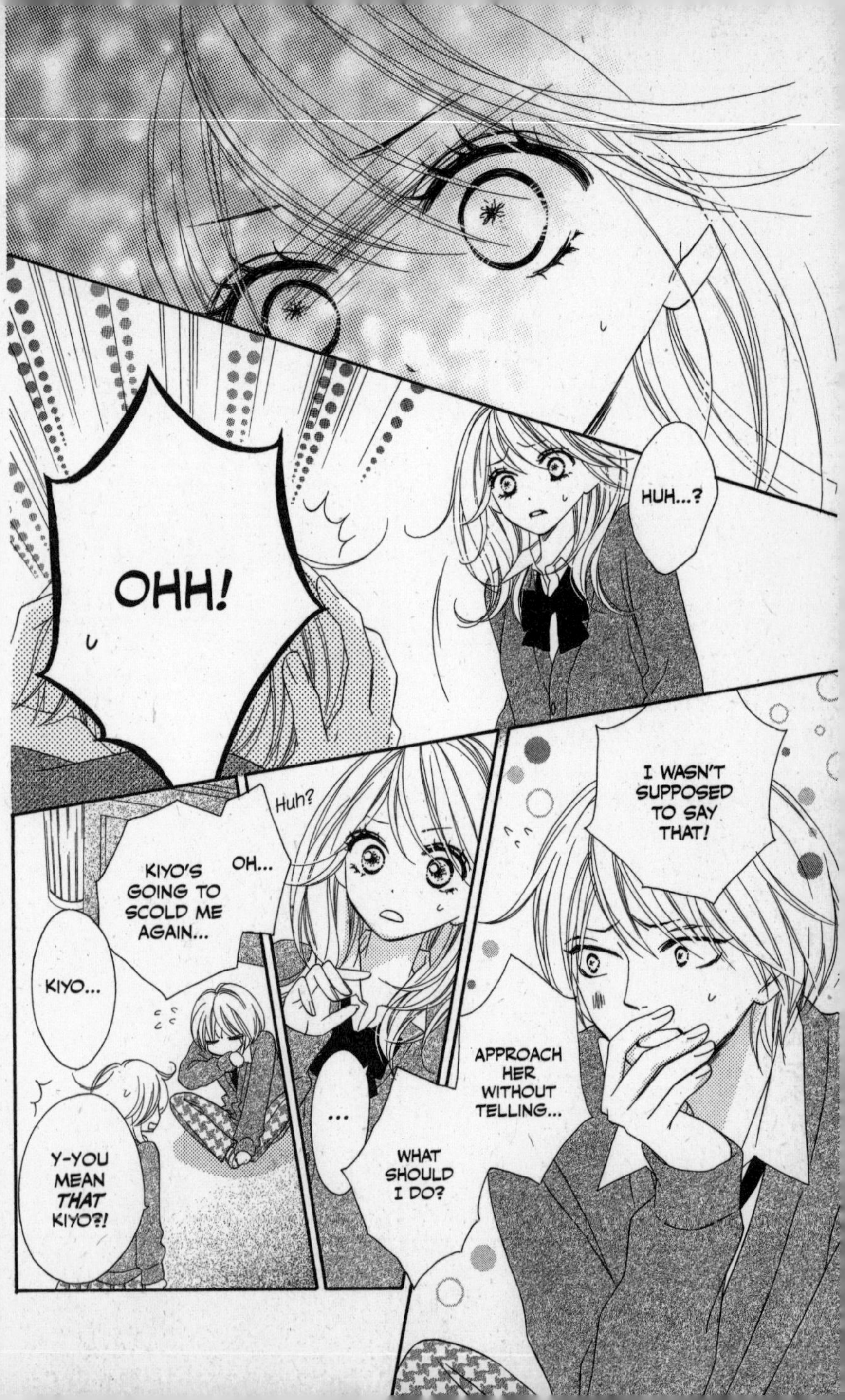
HUH...?
OHH!
I WASN'T SUPPOSED TO SAY THAT!
APPROACH HER WITHOUT TELLING...
WHAT SHOULD I DO?
Huh?
...
OH...
KIYO'S GOING TO SCOLD ME AGAIN...
KIYO...
Y-YOU MEAN *THAT* KIYO?!

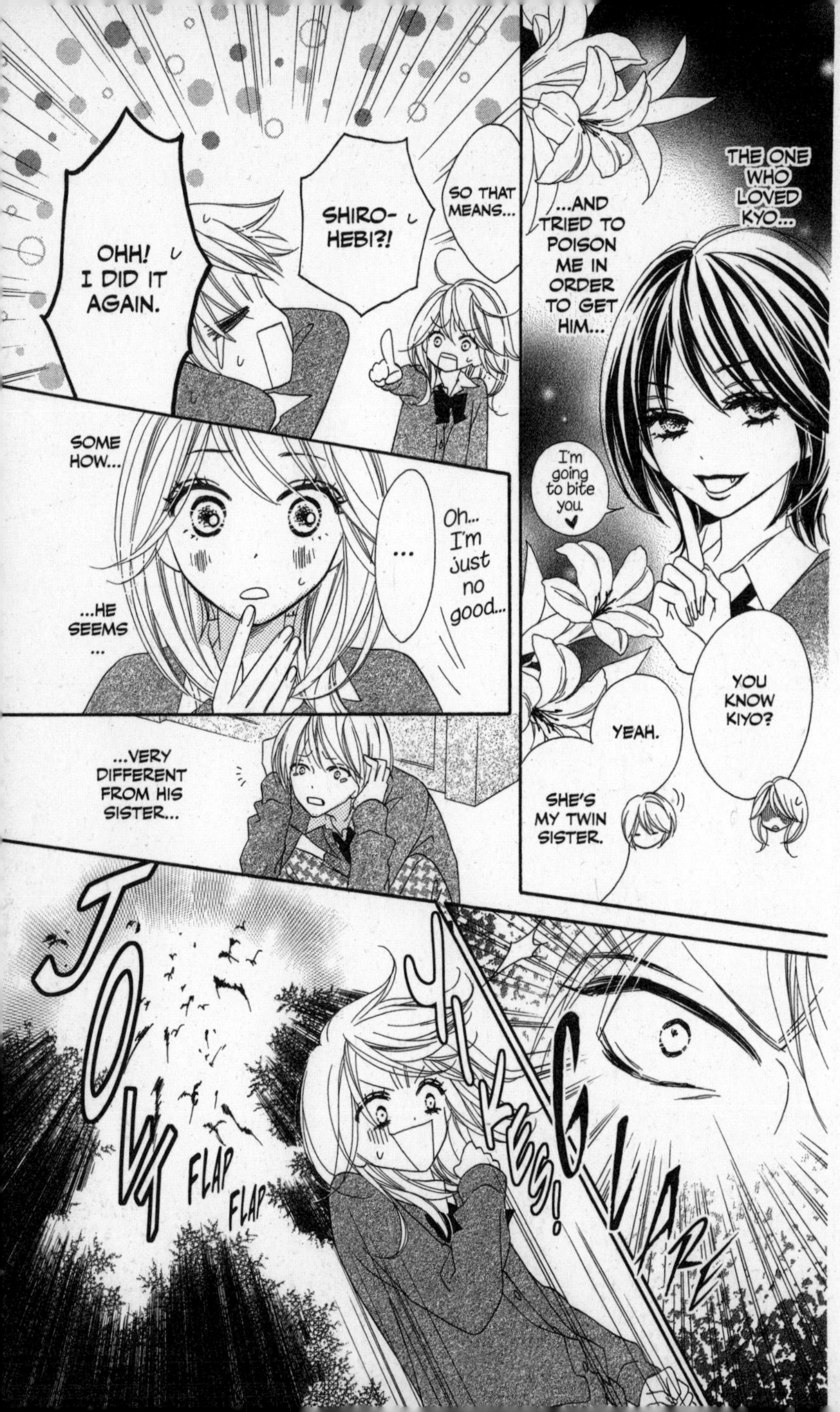
THE ONE WHO LOVED KYO...
...AND TRIED TO POISON ME IN ORDER TO GET HIM...
I'm going to bite you. ♥
YOU KNOW KIYO?
YEAH.
SHE'S MY TWIN SISTER.
SO THAT MEANS...
SHIRO-HEBI?!
OHH! I DID IT AGAIN.
Oh... I'm just no good...
...
SOME HOW...
...HE SEEMS ...
...VERY DIFFERENT FROM HIS SISTER...
GLARE
YIKES!
JOLT
FLAP
FLAP

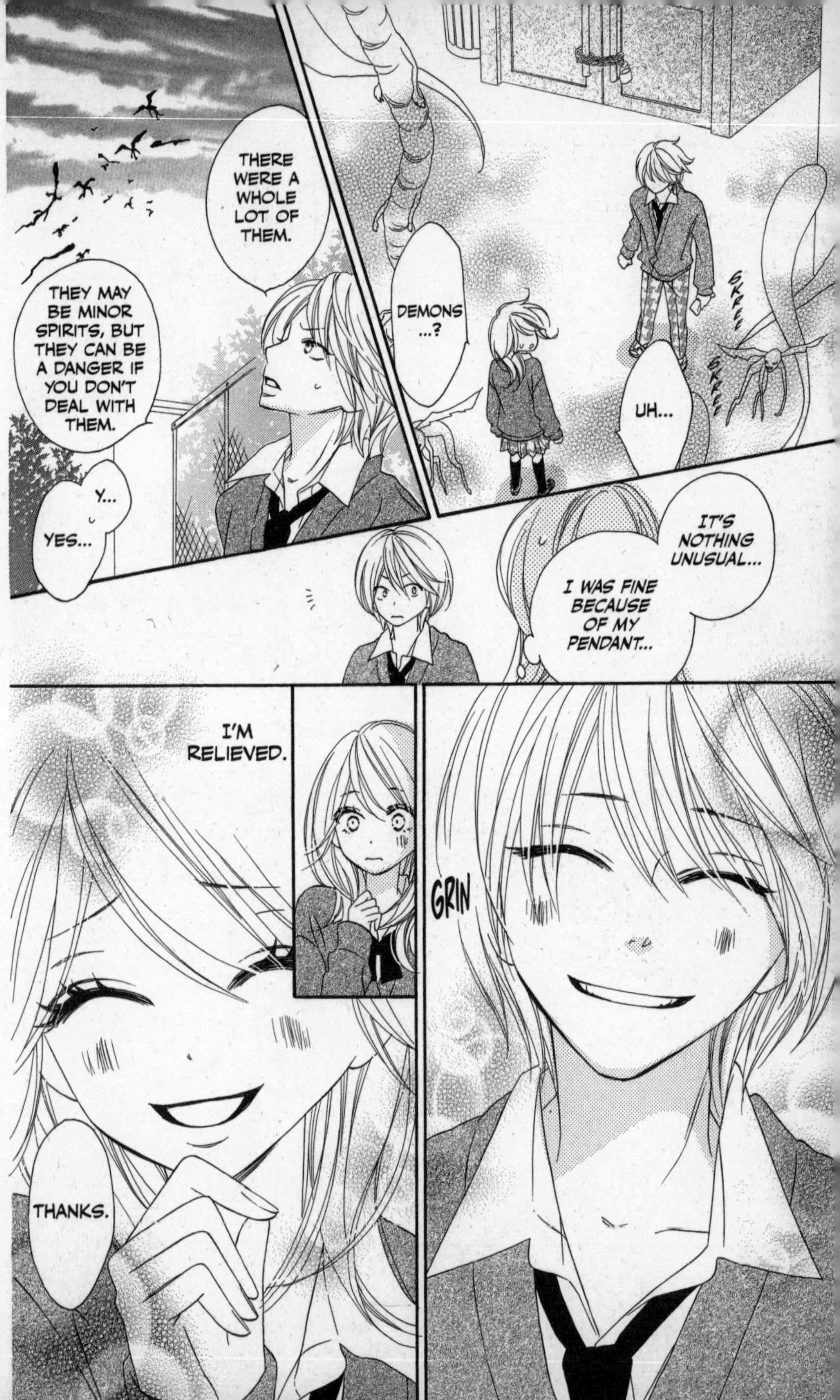
SKREE
SKREE
DEMONS ...?
UH...
THERE WERE A WHOLE LOT OF THEM.
THEY MAY BE MINOR SPIRITS, BUT THEY CAN BE A DANGER IF YOU DON'T DEAL WITH THEM.
Y... YES...
IT'S NOTHING UNUSUAL...
I WAS FINE BECAUSE OF MY PENDANT...
GRIN
I'M RELIEVED.
THANKS.

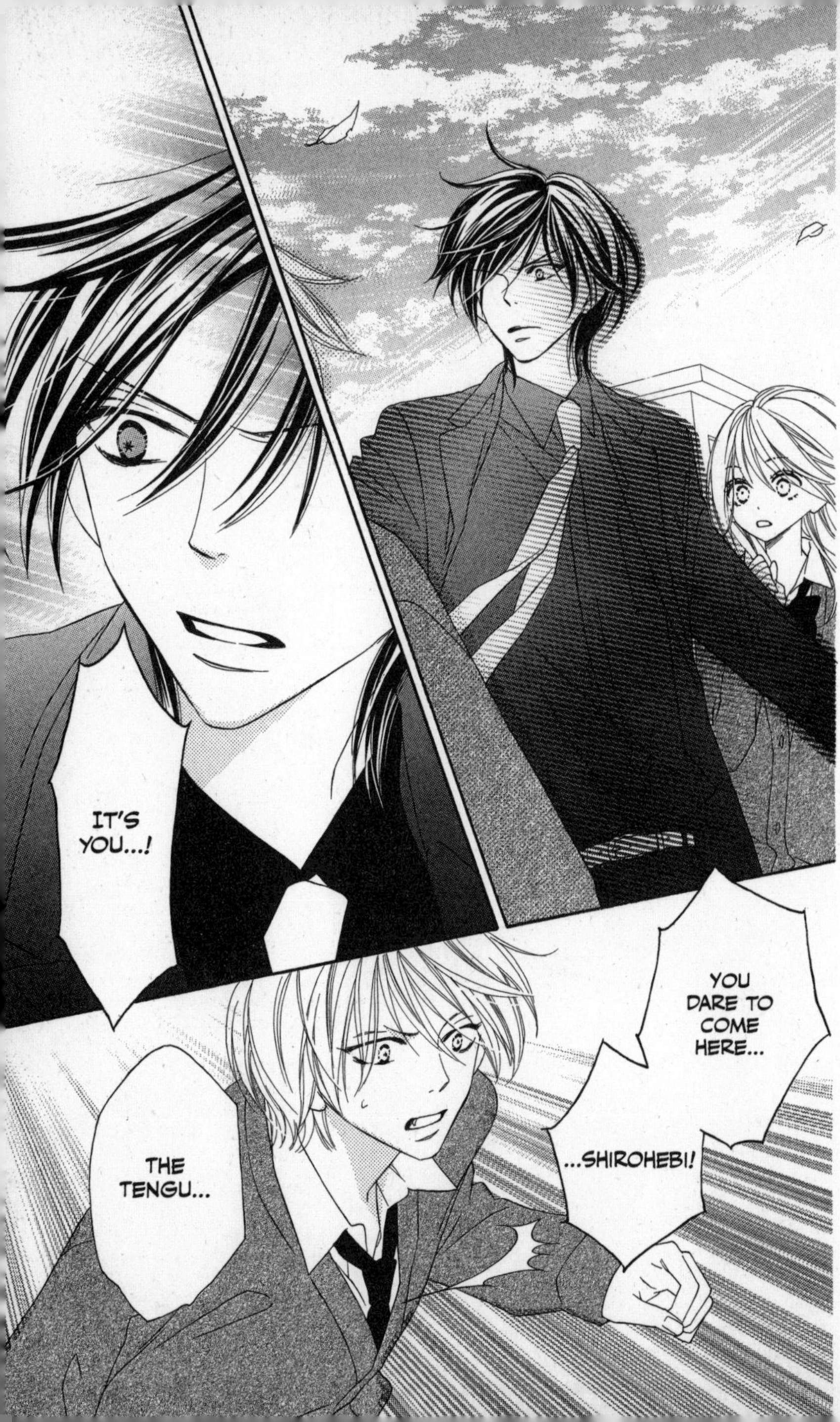
IT'S YOU...!
YOU DARE TO COME HERE...
...SHIROHEBI!
THE TENGU...

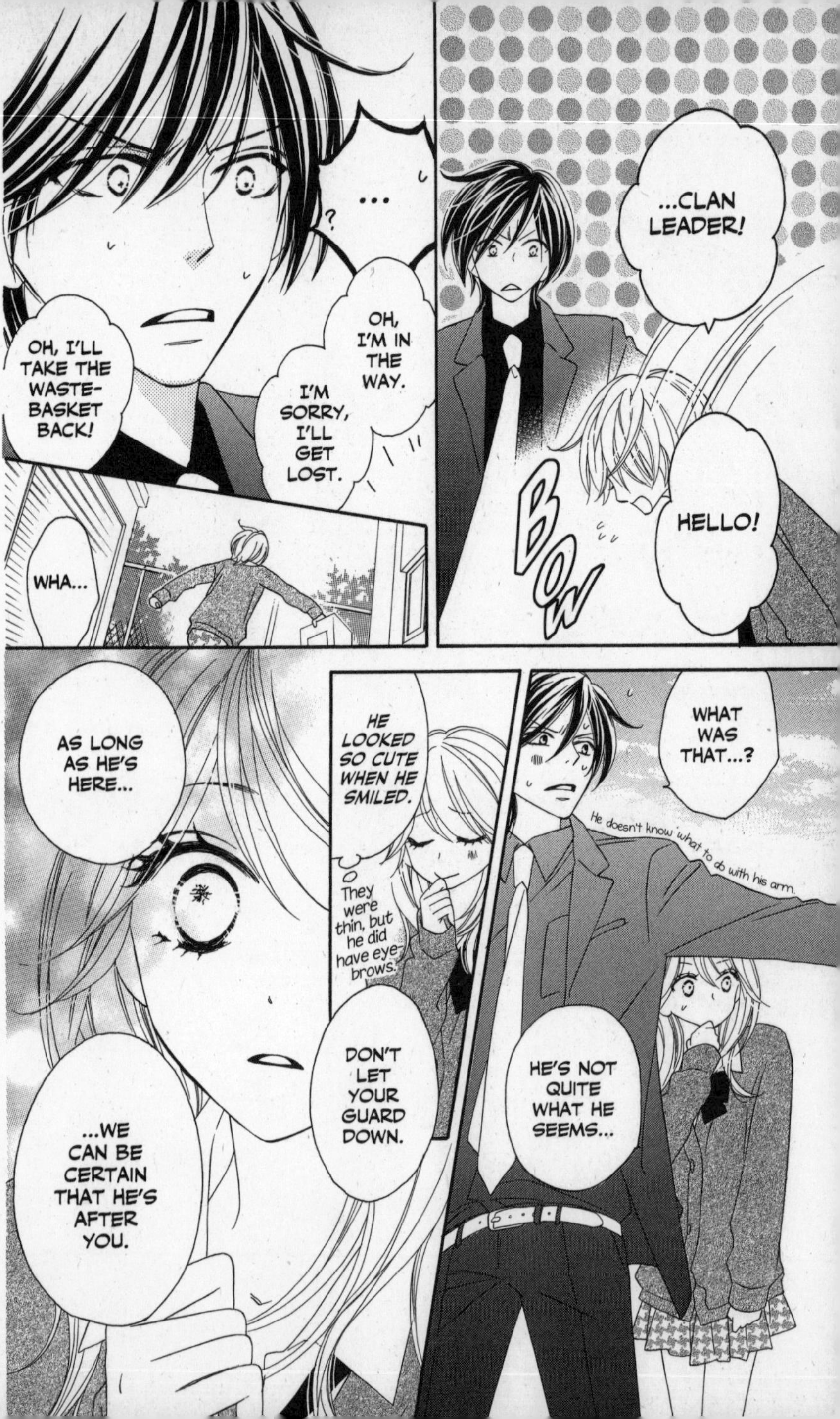
...CLAN LEADER!
HELLO!
BOW
...
?
OH, I'M IN THE WAY.
I'M SORRY, I'LL GET LOST.
OH, I'LL TAKE THE WASTE-BASKET BACK!
WHA...
WHAT WAS THAT...?
He doesn't know what to do with his arm.
HE'S NOT QUITE WHAT HE SEEMS...
HE LOOKED SO CUTE WHEN HE SMILED.
They were thin, but he did have eye-brows.
DON'T LET YOUR GUARD DOWN.
AS LONG AS HE'S HERE...
...WE CAN BE CERTAIN THAT HE'S AFTER YOU.

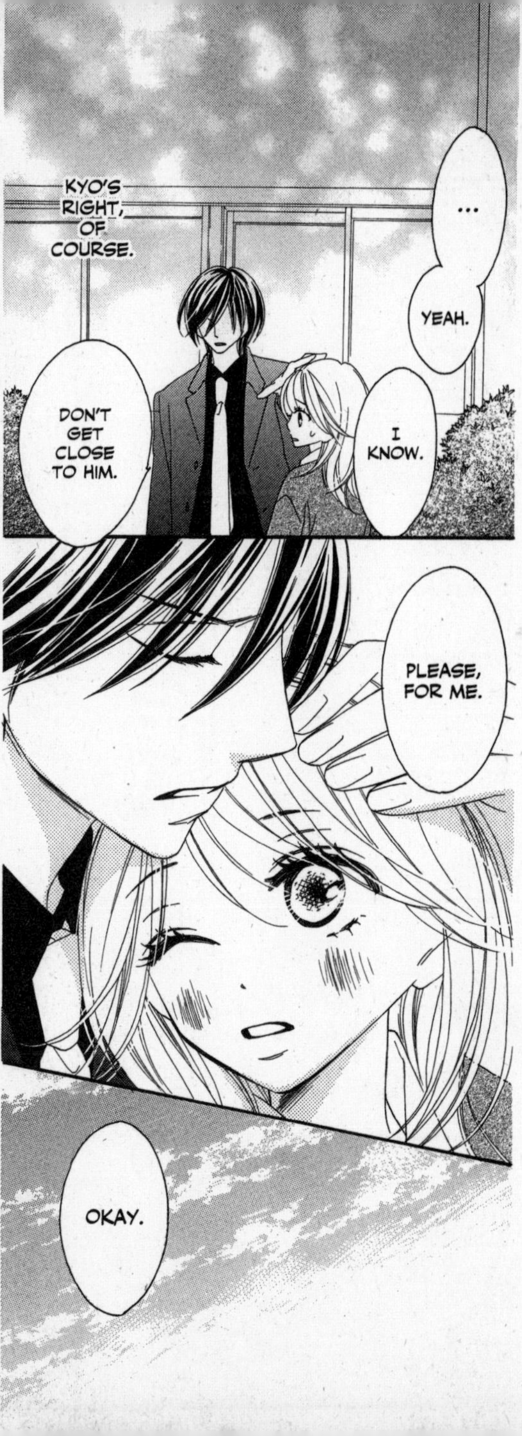
...
KYO'S RIGHT, OF COURSE.
YEAH.
DON'T GET CLOSE TO HIM.
I KNOW.
PLEASE, FOR ME.
OKAY.

Introduction of Secondary Characters

• Three •

Kiyo Dojoji

age: 16 height: 155 cm

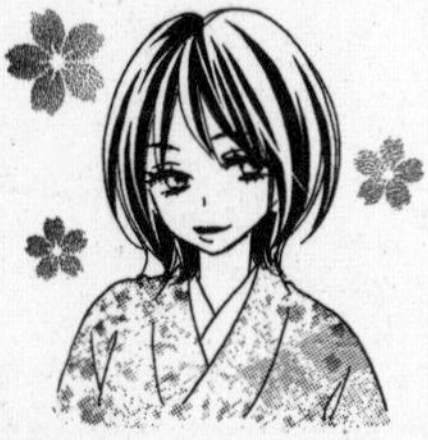

There is almost no name more appropriate to a snake! Of course, the name "Dojoji" comes from the legend. (The priest Anchin falls in love with Princess Kiyo who is really a serpent. When Princess Kiyo realizes that Anchin has had a change of heart, she chases him in the form of a serpent to Dojoji temple, where he is hiding inside a temple bell. She burns the bell and the priest inside.♥The story has become a Noh and Kabuki play.) I didn't think she would have a second appearance.

She seems more a match for Sojo than Kyo...

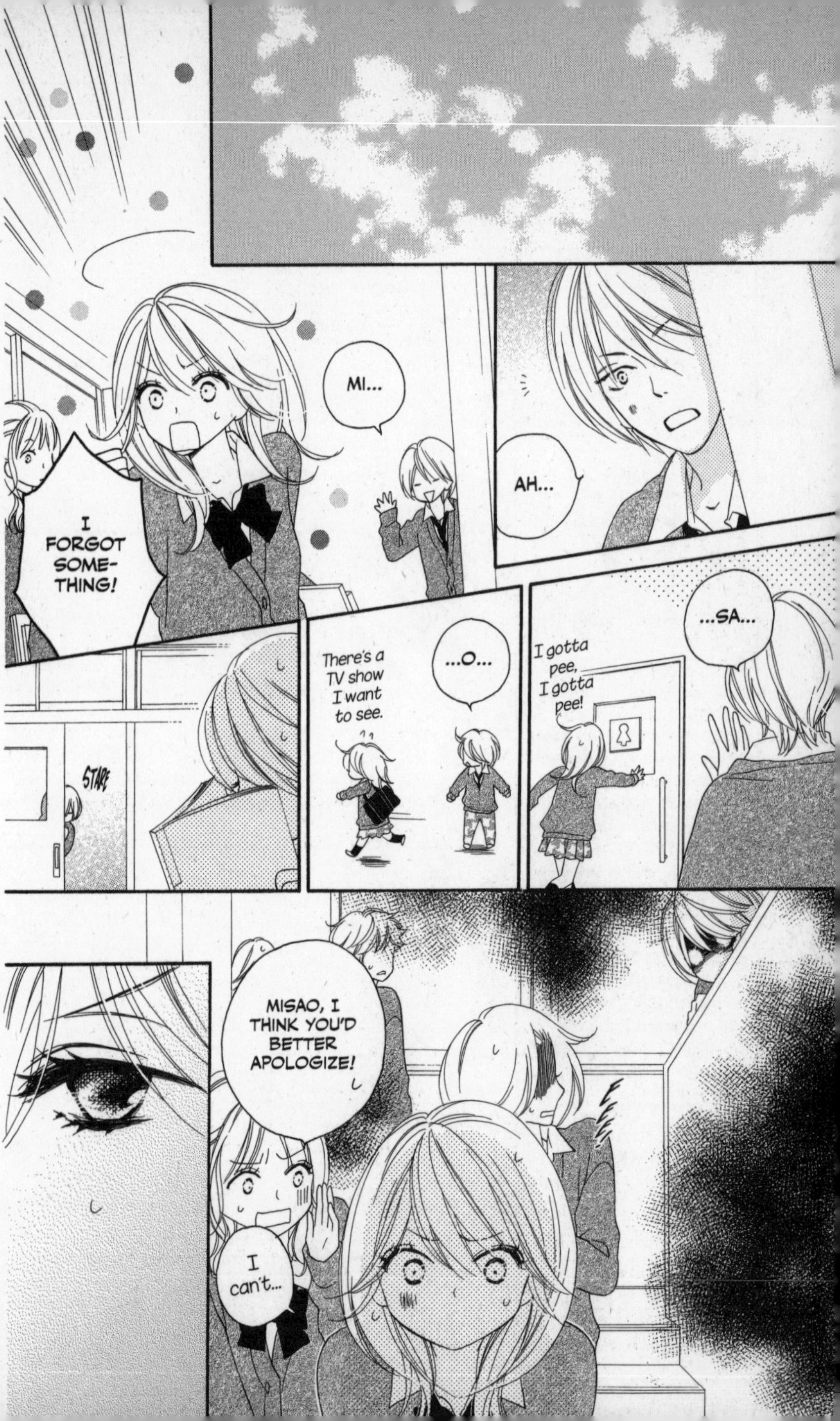
AH...
MI...
I FORGOT SOMETHING!
...SA...
I gotta pee, I gotta pee!
...O...
There's a TV show I want to see.
STARE
MISAO, I THINK YOU'D BETTER APOLOGIZE!
I can't...

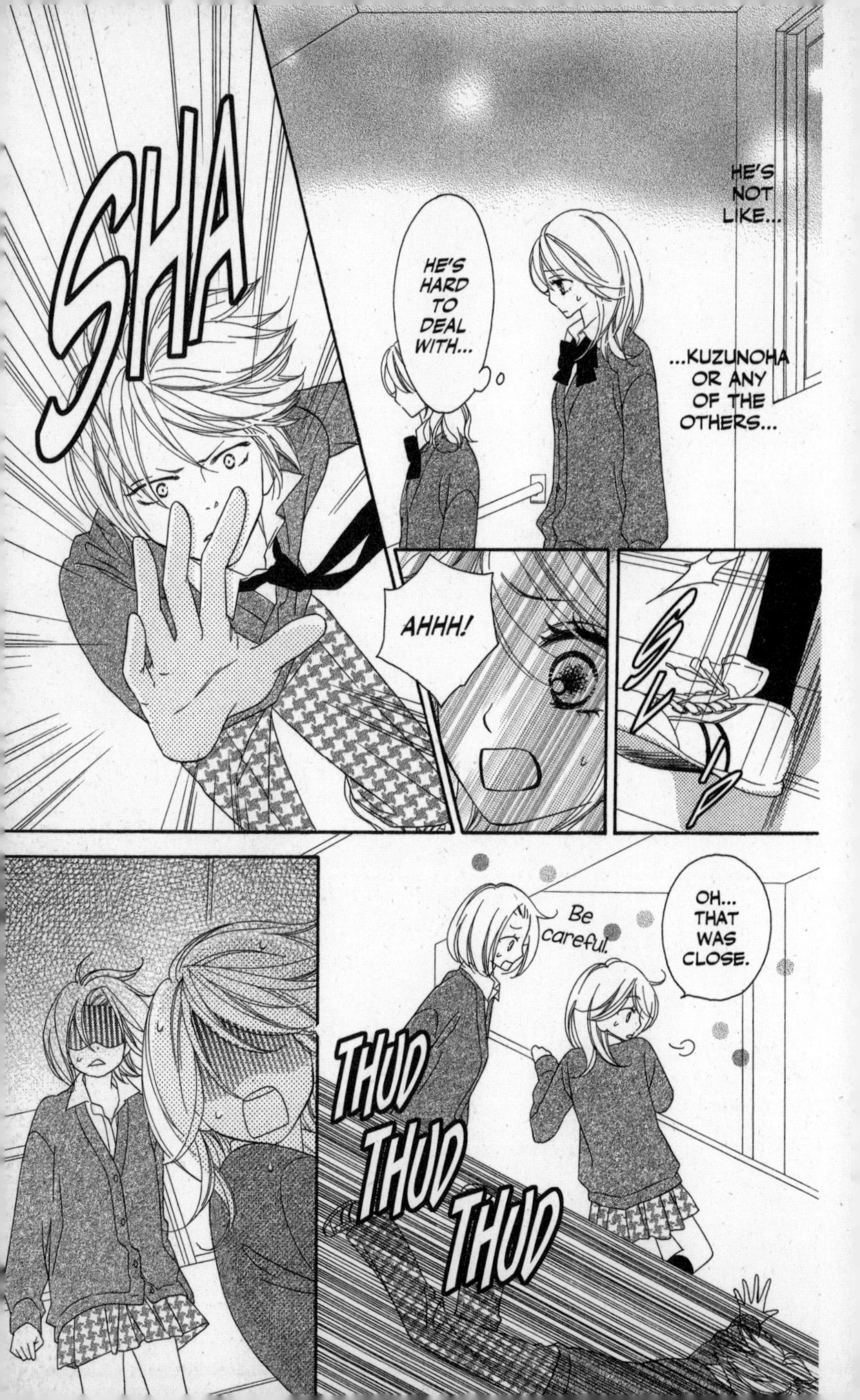
HE'S NOT LIKE...
...KUZUNOHA OR ANY OF THE OTHERS...
HE'S HARD TO DEAL WITH...
AHHH!
SHA
OH... THAT WAS CLOSE.
Be careful.
THUD THUD THUD

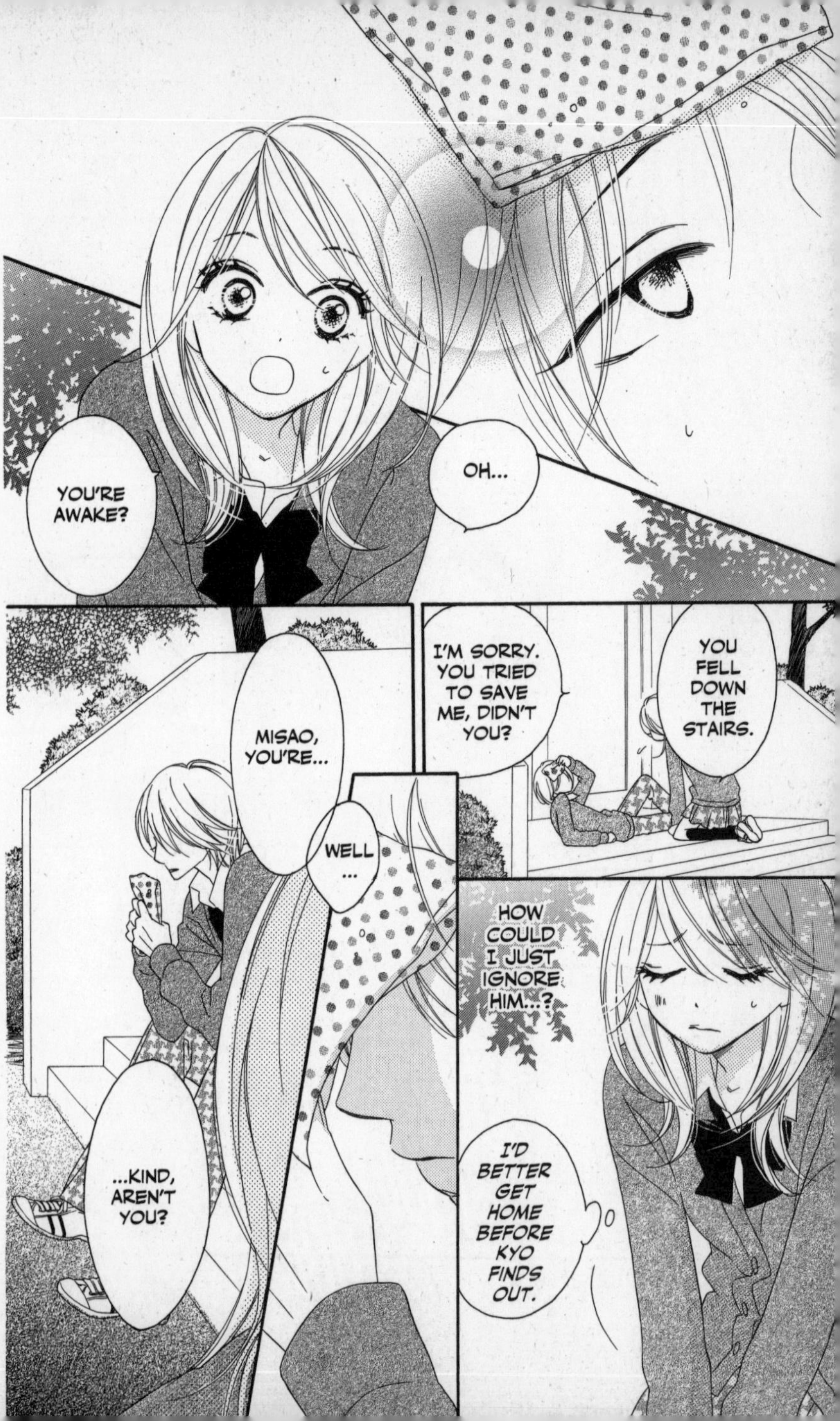
OH...
YOU'RE AWAKE?
YOU FELL DOWN THE STAIRS.
I'M SORRY. YOU TRIED TO SAVE ME, DIDN'T YOU?
HOW COULD I JUST IGNORE HIM...?
I'D BETTER GET HOME BEFORE KYO FINDS OUT.
MISAO, YOU'RE...
WELL...
...KIND, AREN'T YOU?

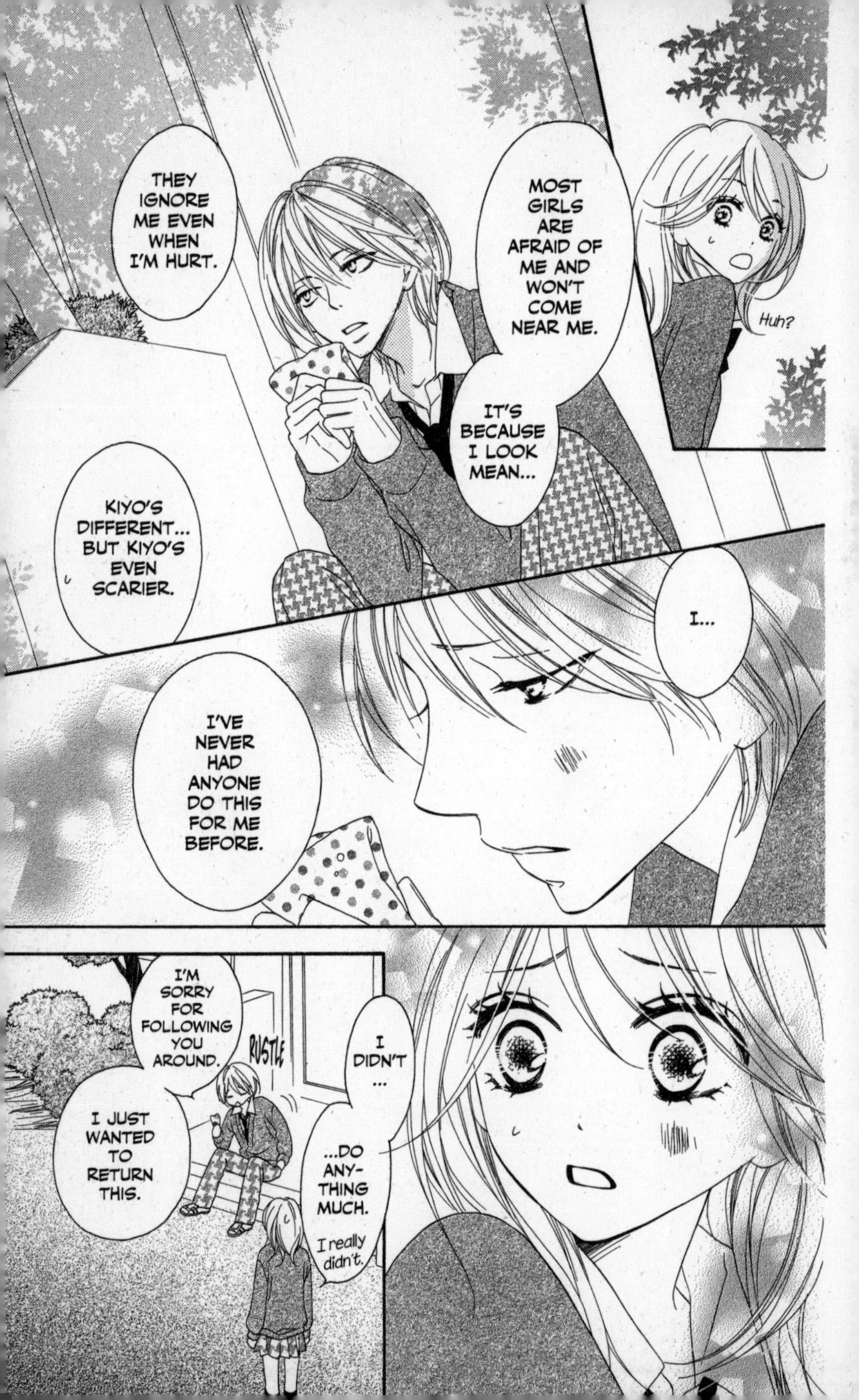
Huh?
MOST GIRLS ARE AFRAID OF ME AND WON'T COME NEAR ME.
THEY IGNORE ME EVEN WHEN I'M HURT.
IT'S BECAUSE I LOOK MEAN...
KIYO'S DIFFERENT... BUT KIYO'S EVEN SCARIER.
I...
I'VE NEVER HAD ANYONE DO THIS FOR ME BEFORE.
I DIDN'T ...
...DO ANY-THING MUCH.
I really didn't.
I'M SORRY FOR FOLLOWING YOU AROUND.
RUSTLE
I JUST WANTED TO RETURN THIS.

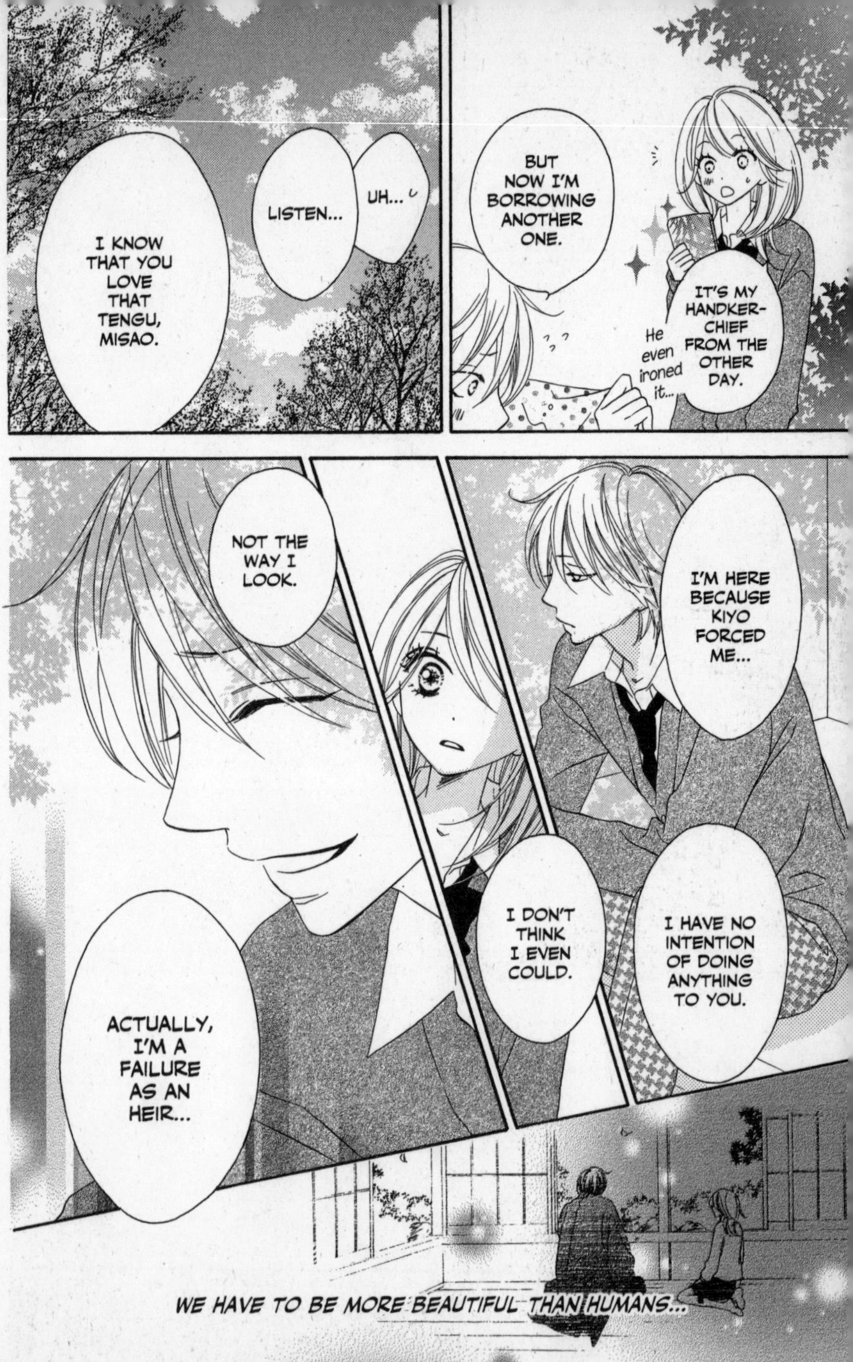
IT'S MY HANDKERCHIEF FROM THE OTHER DAY.
He even ironed it...
BUT NOW I'M BORROWING ANOTHER ONE.
UH...
LISTEN...
I KNOW THAT YOU LOVE THAT TENGU, MISAO.
I'M HERE BECAUSE KIYO FORCED ME...
I HAVE NO INTENTION OF DOING ANYTHING TO YOU.
I DON'T THINK I EVEN COULD.
NOT THE WAY I LOOK.
ACTUALLY, I'M A FAILURE AS AN HEIR...
WE HAVE TO BE MORE BEAUTIFUL THAN HUMANS...

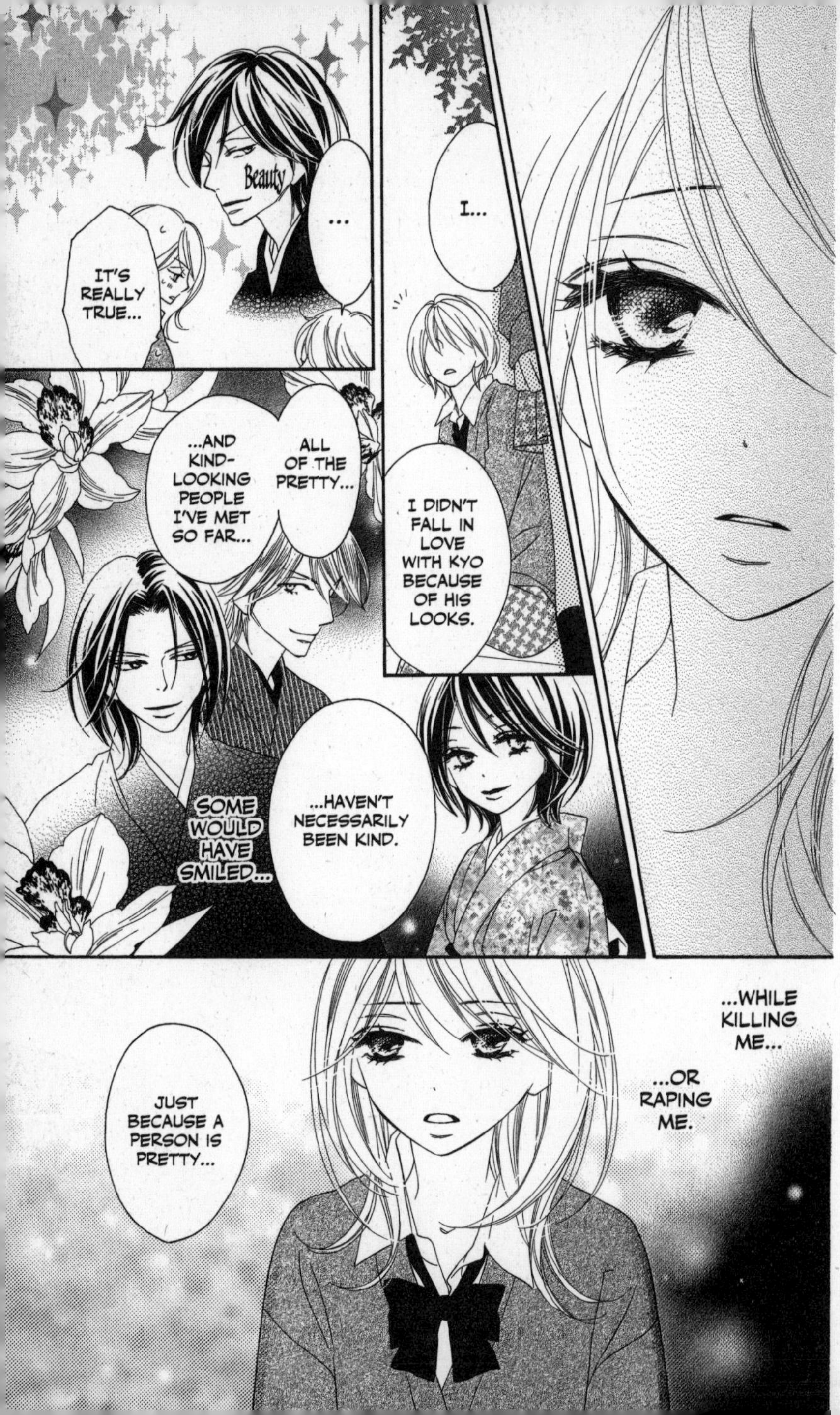

I...
I DIDN'T FALL IN LOVE WITH KYO BECAUSE OF HIS LOOKS.
Beauty
...
IT'S REALLY TRUE...
ALL OF THE PRETTY...
...AND KIND-LOOKING PEOPLE I'VE MET SO FAR...
...HAVEN'T NECESSARILY BEEN KIND.
SOME WOULD HAVE SMILED...
...WHILE KILLING ME...
...OR RAPING ME.
JUST BECAUSE A PERSON IS PRETTY...

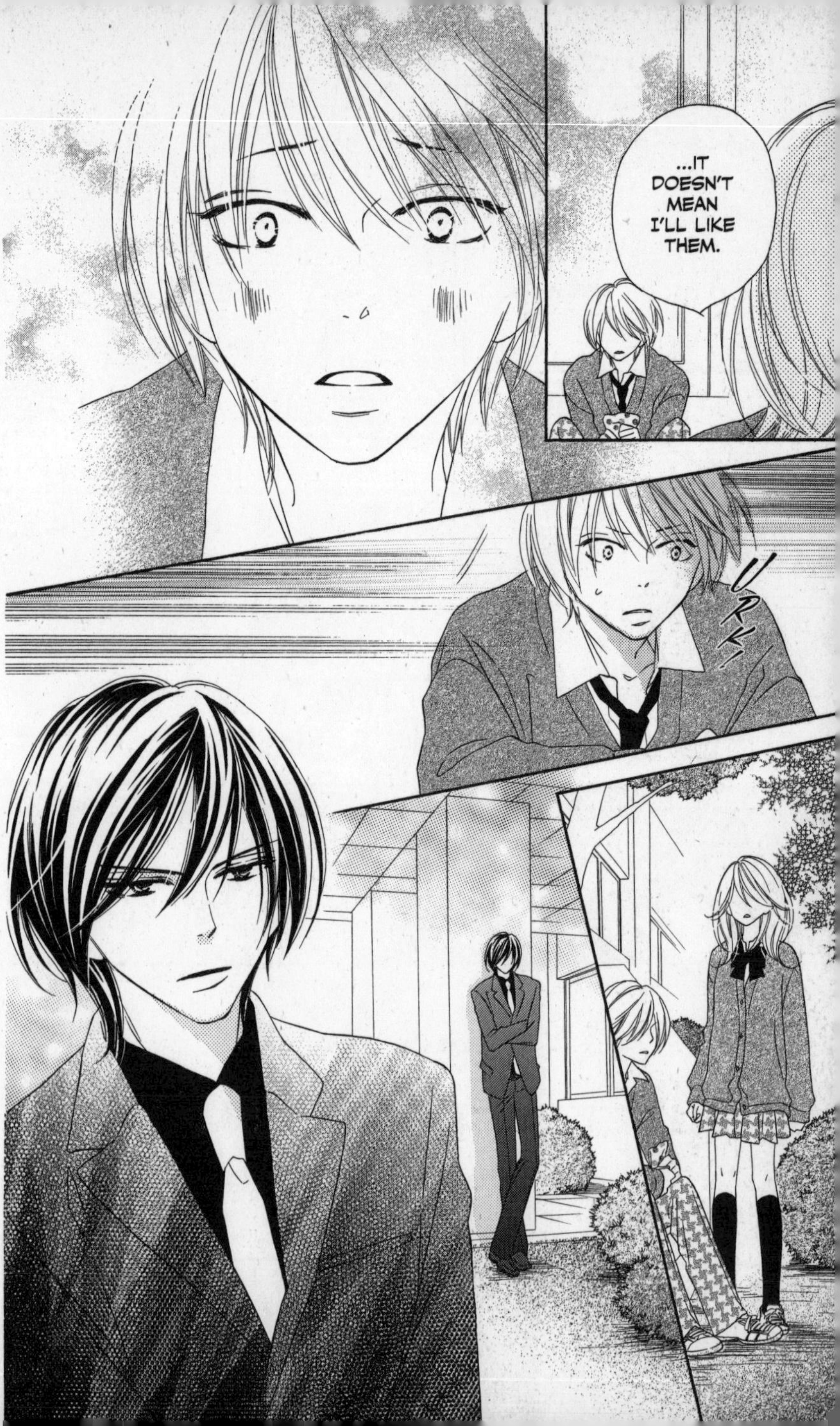
...IT DOESN'T MEAN I'LL LIKE THEM.
URK!

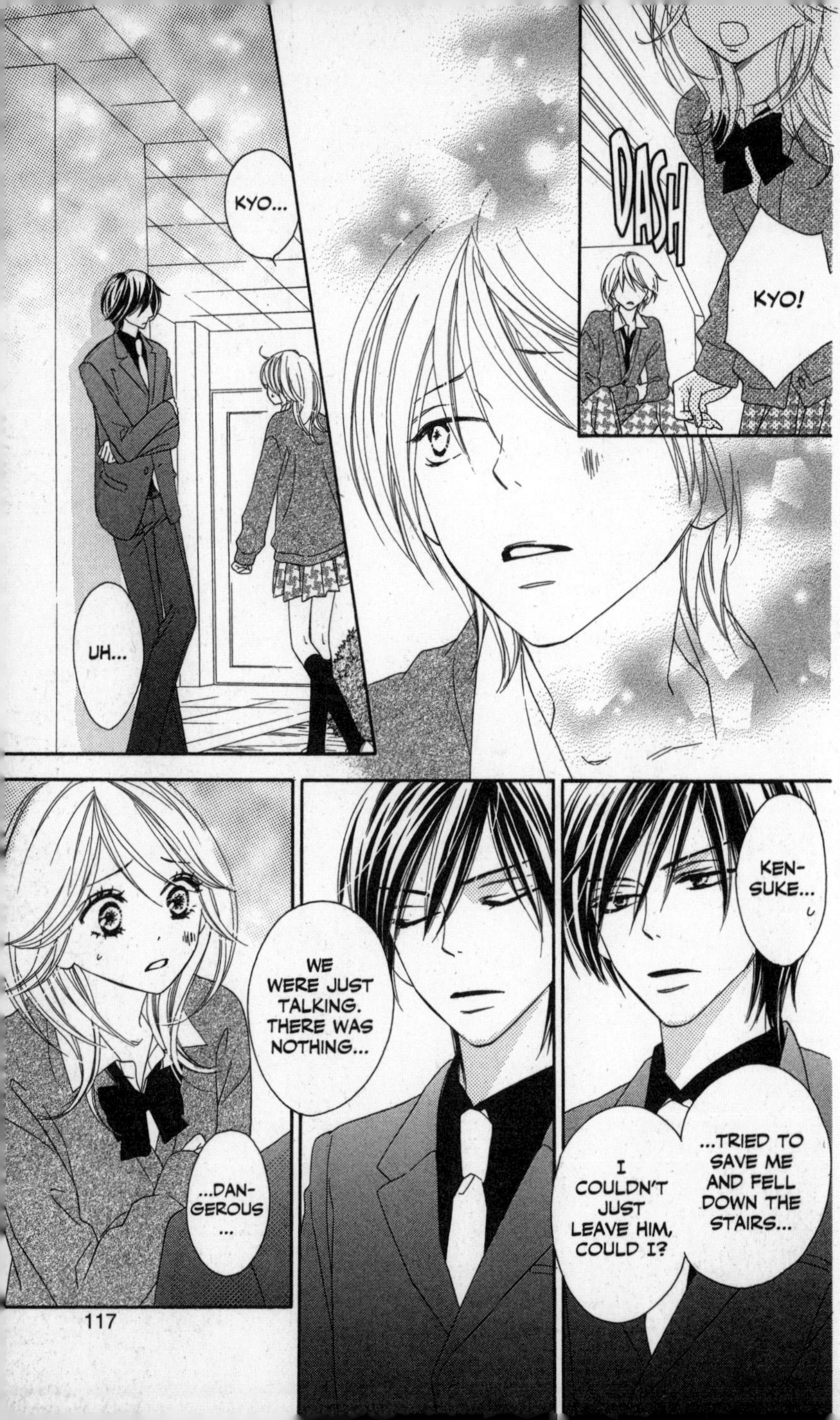
DASH
KYO!
KYO...
UH...
KEN-SUKE...
...TRIED TO SAVE ME AND FELL DOWN THE STAIRS...
I COULDN'T JUST LEAVE HIM, COULD I?
WE WERE JUST TALKING. THERE WAS NOTHING...
...DAN-GEROUS...

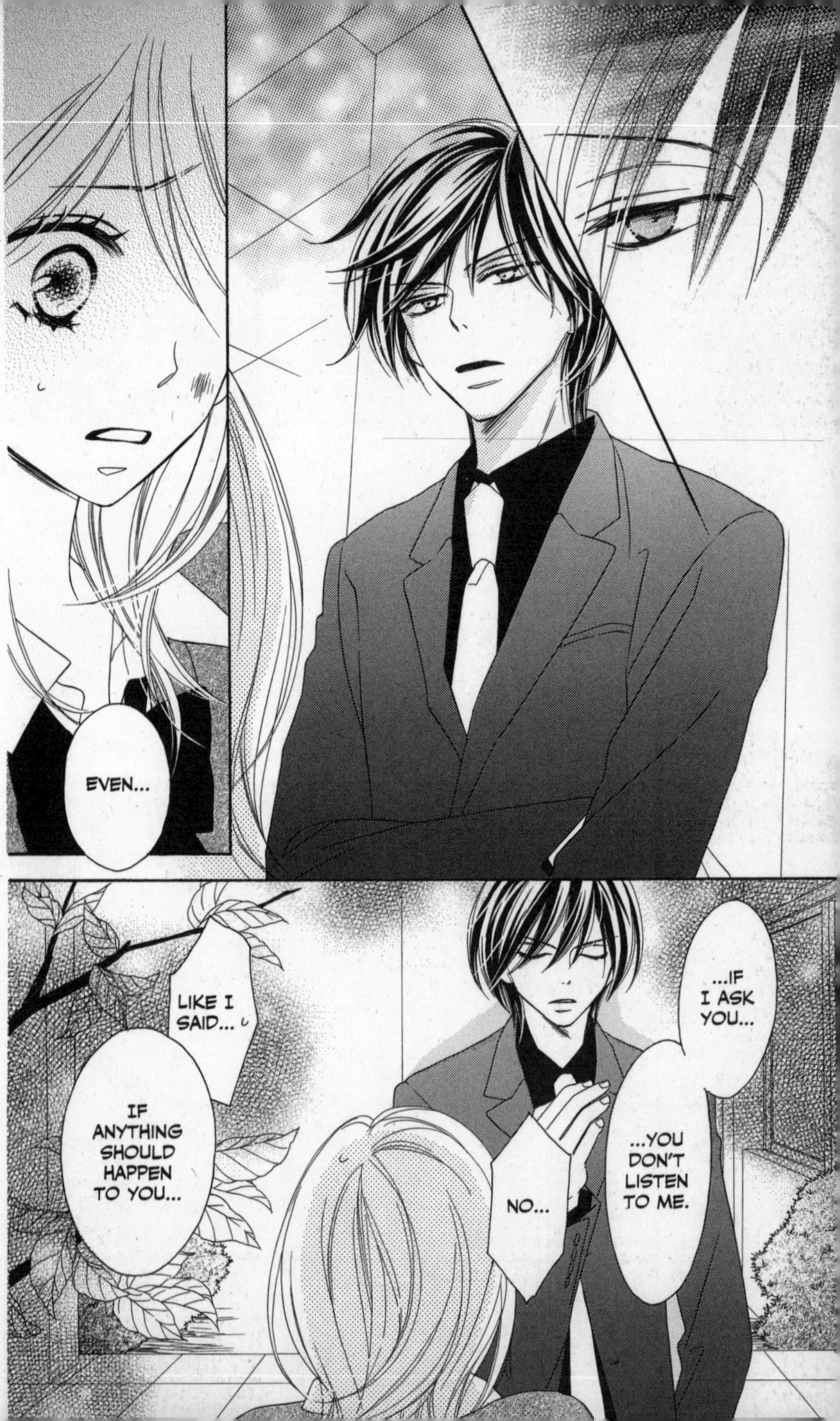
EVEN...
...IF I ASK YOU...
...YOU DON'T LISTEN TO ME.
NO...
LIKE I SAID...
IF ANYTHING SHOULD HAPPEN TO YOU...

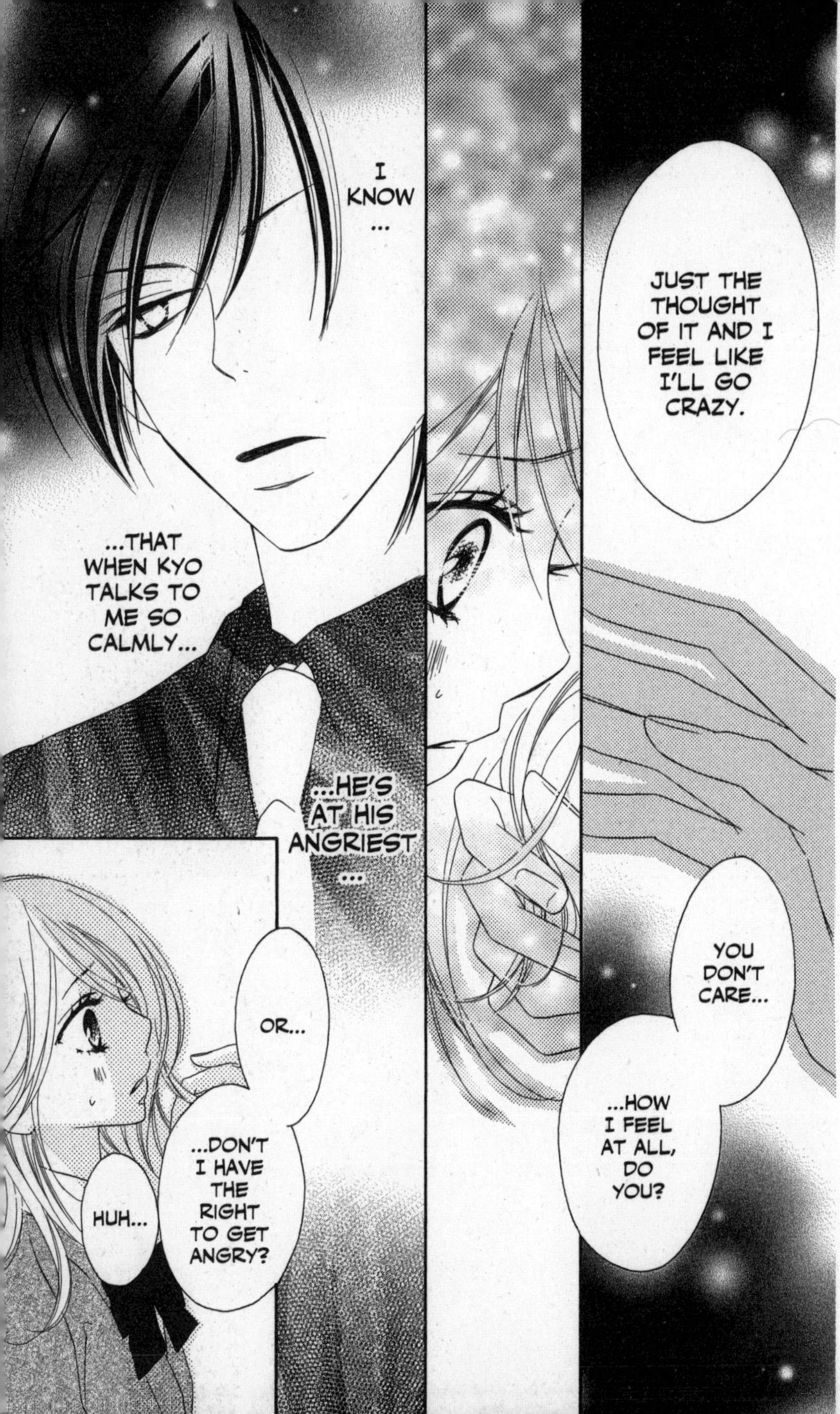
JUST THE THOUGHT OF IT AND I FEEL LIKE I'LL GO CRAZY.
YOU DON'T CARE...
...HOW I FEEL AT ALL, DO YOU?
I KNOW...
...THAT WHEN KYO TALKS TO ME SO CALMLY...
...HE'S AT HIS ANGRIEST...
OR...
...DON'T I HAVE THE RIGHT TO GET ANGRY?
HUH...

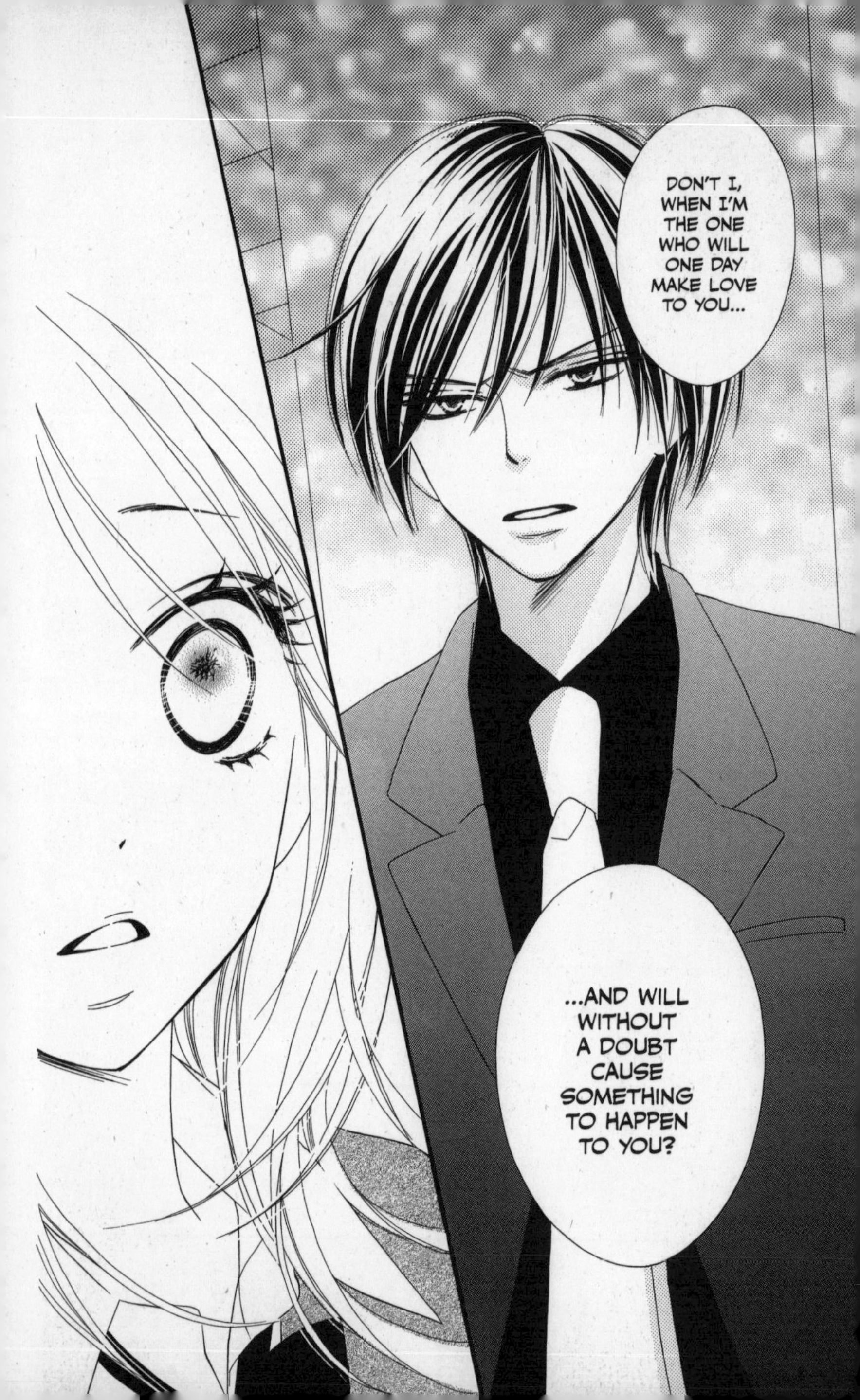
DON'T I, WHEN I'M THE ONE WHO WILL ONE DAY MAKE LOVE TO YOU...
...AND WILL WITHOUT A DOUBT CAUSE SOMETHING TO HAPPEN TO YOU?

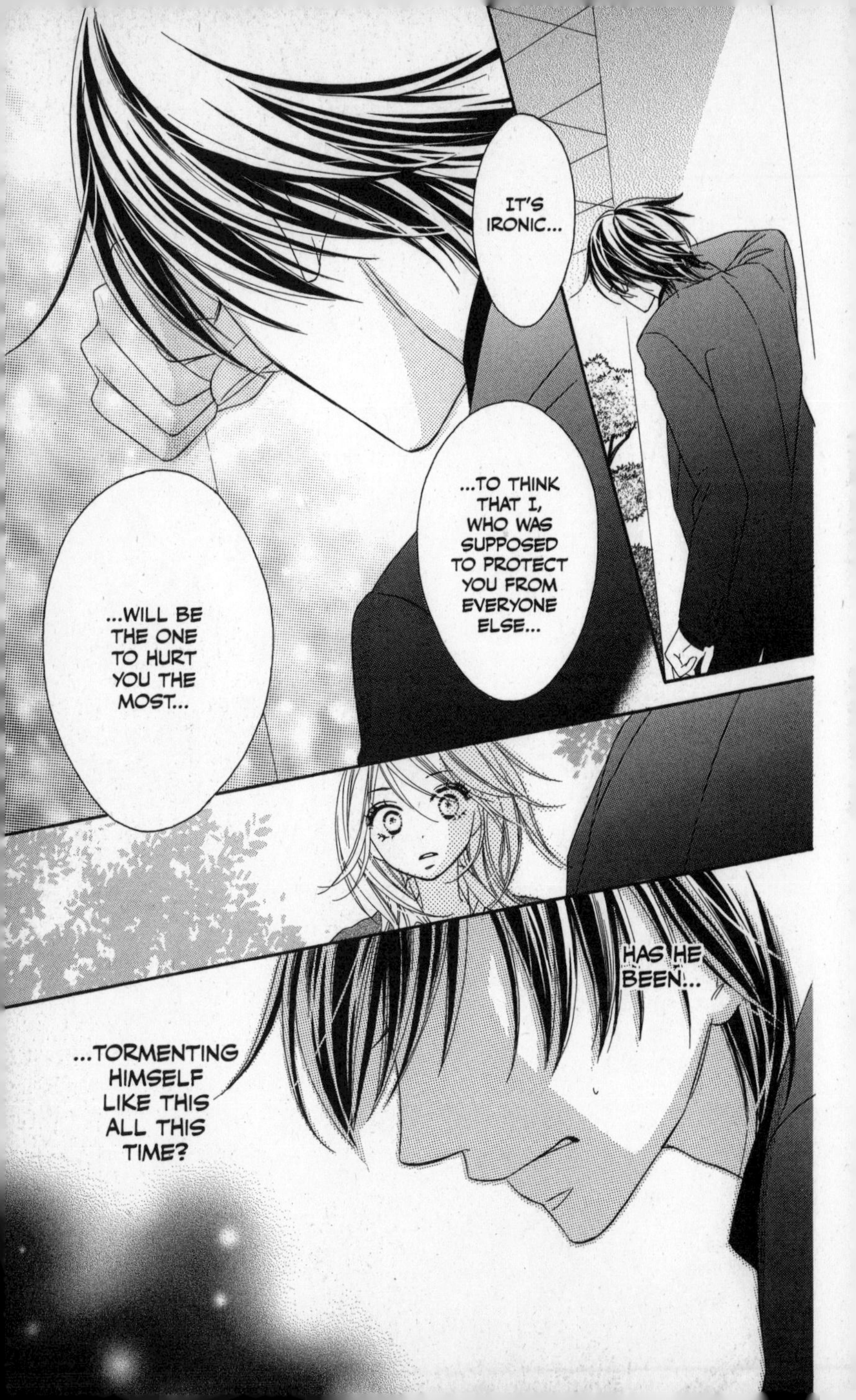
IT'S IRONIC...
...TO THINK THAT I, WHO WAS SUPPOSED TO PROTECT YOU FROM EVERYONE ELSE...
...WILL BE THE ONE TO HURT YOU THE MOST...
HAS HE BEEN...
...TORMENTING HIMSELF LIKE THIS ALL THIS TIME?

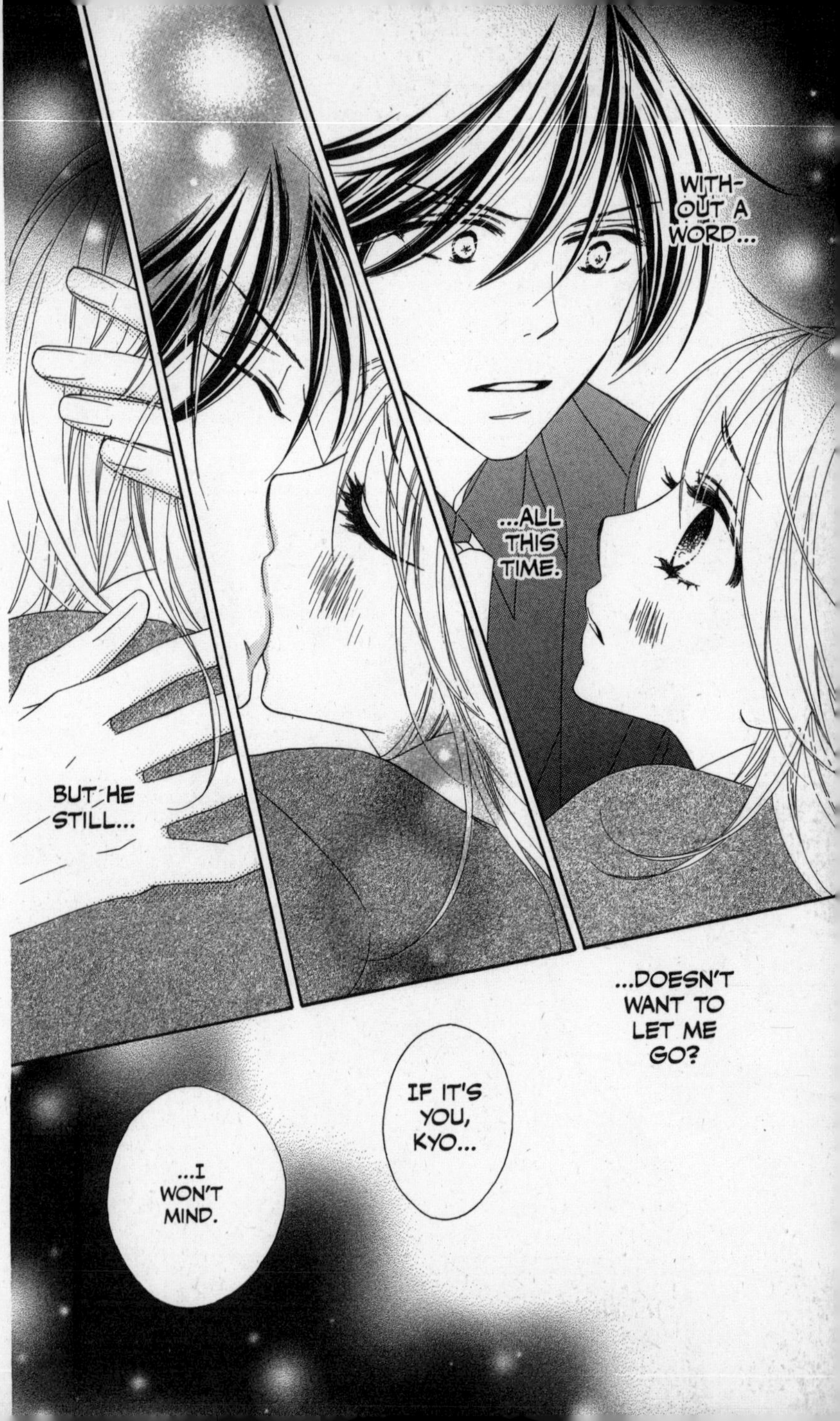
WITH-OUT A WORD...
...ALL THIS TIME.
BUT HE STILL...
...DOESN'T WANT TO LET ME GO?
IF IT'S YOU, KYO...
...I WON'T MIND.

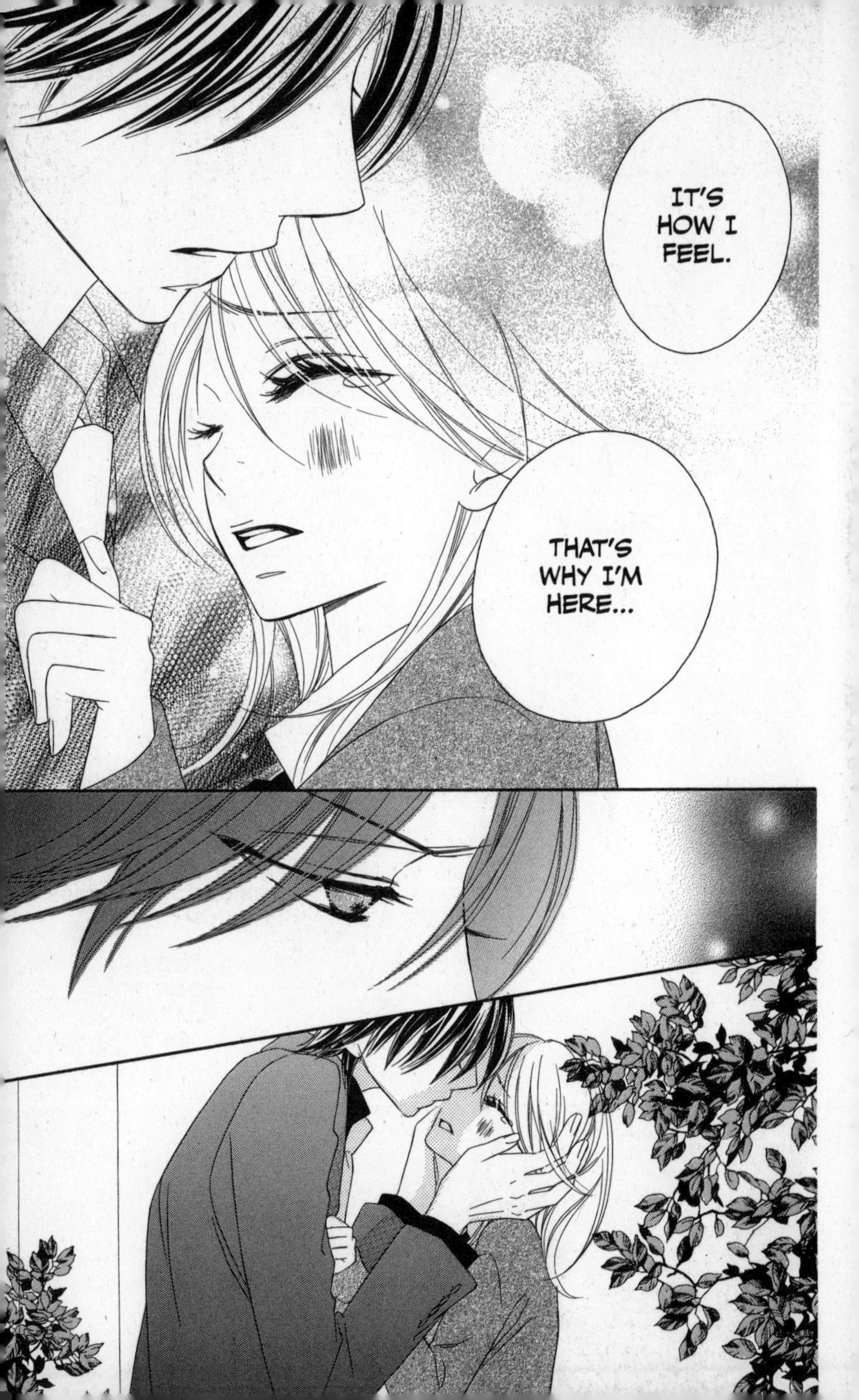
IT'S HOW I FEEL.
THAT'S WHY I'M HERE...

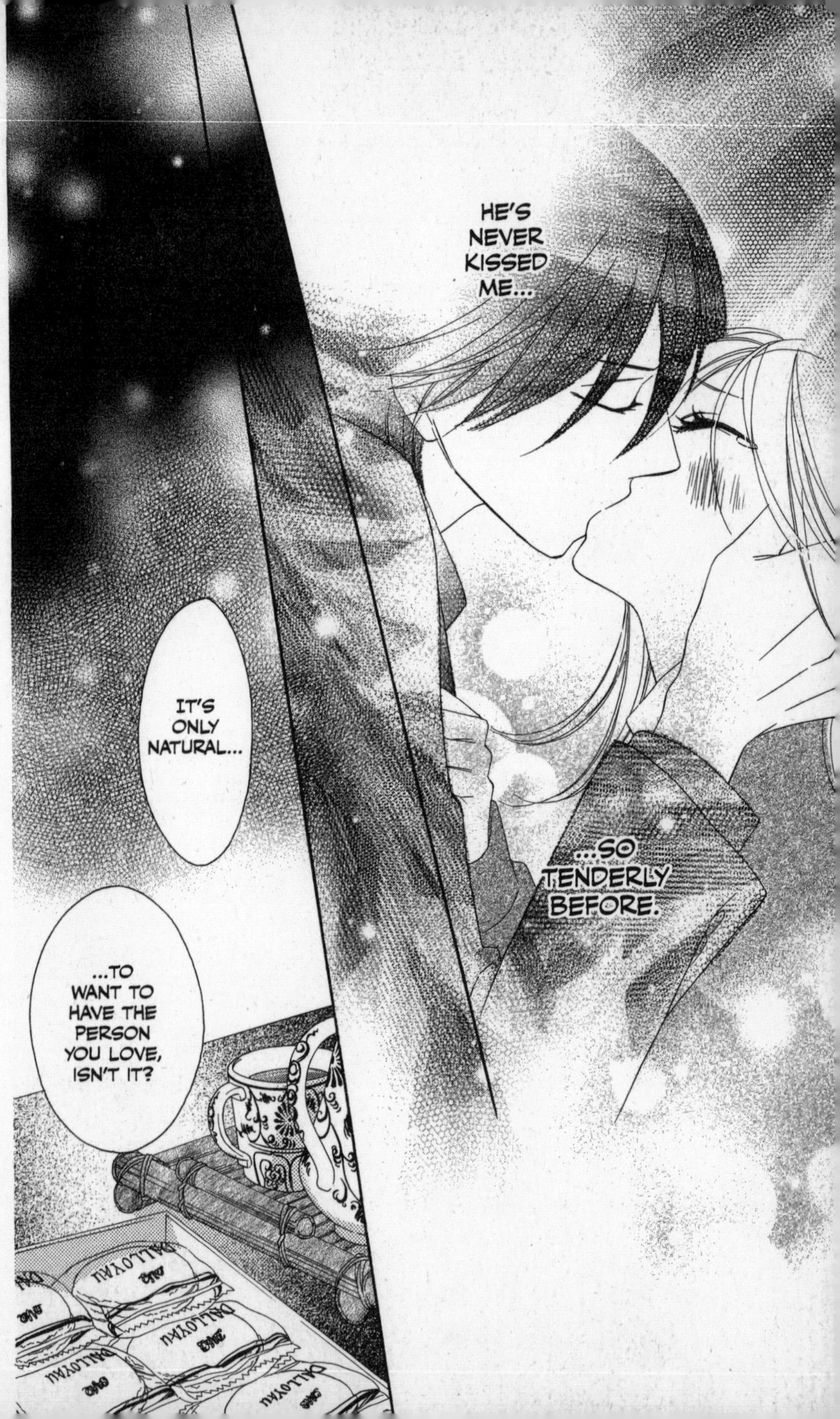
HE'S NEVER KISSED ME...
...SO TENDERLY BEFORE.
IT'S ONLY NATURAL...
...TO WANT TO HAVE THE PERSON YOU LOVE, ISN'T IT?

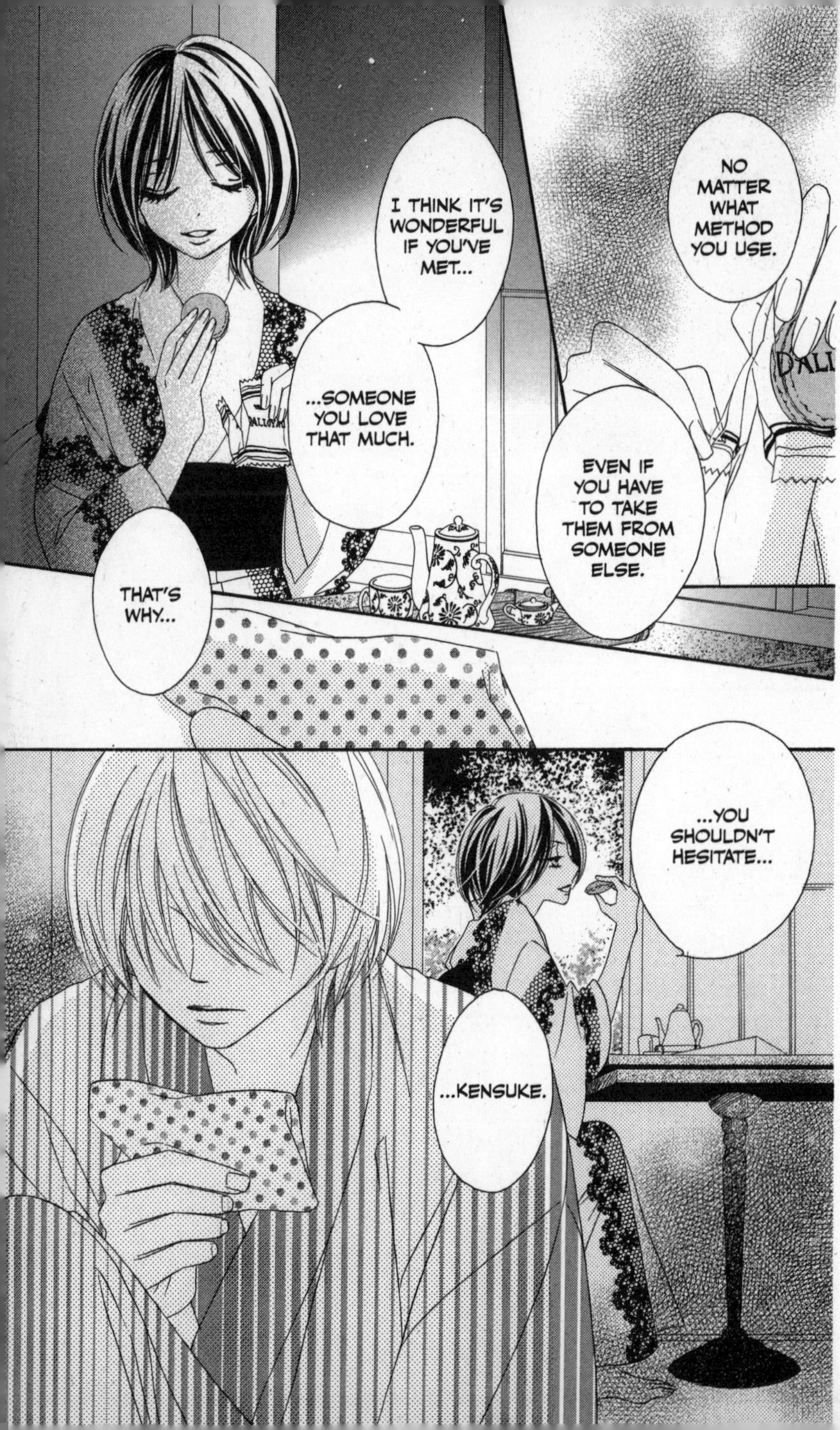
NO MATTER WHAT METHOD YOU USE.
EVEN IF YOU HAVE TO TAKE THEM FROM SOMEONE ELSE.
I THINK IT'S WONDERFUL IF YOU'VE MET...
...SOMEONE YOU LOVE THAT MUCH.
THAT'S WHY...
...YOU SHOULDN'T HESITATE...
...KENSUKE.

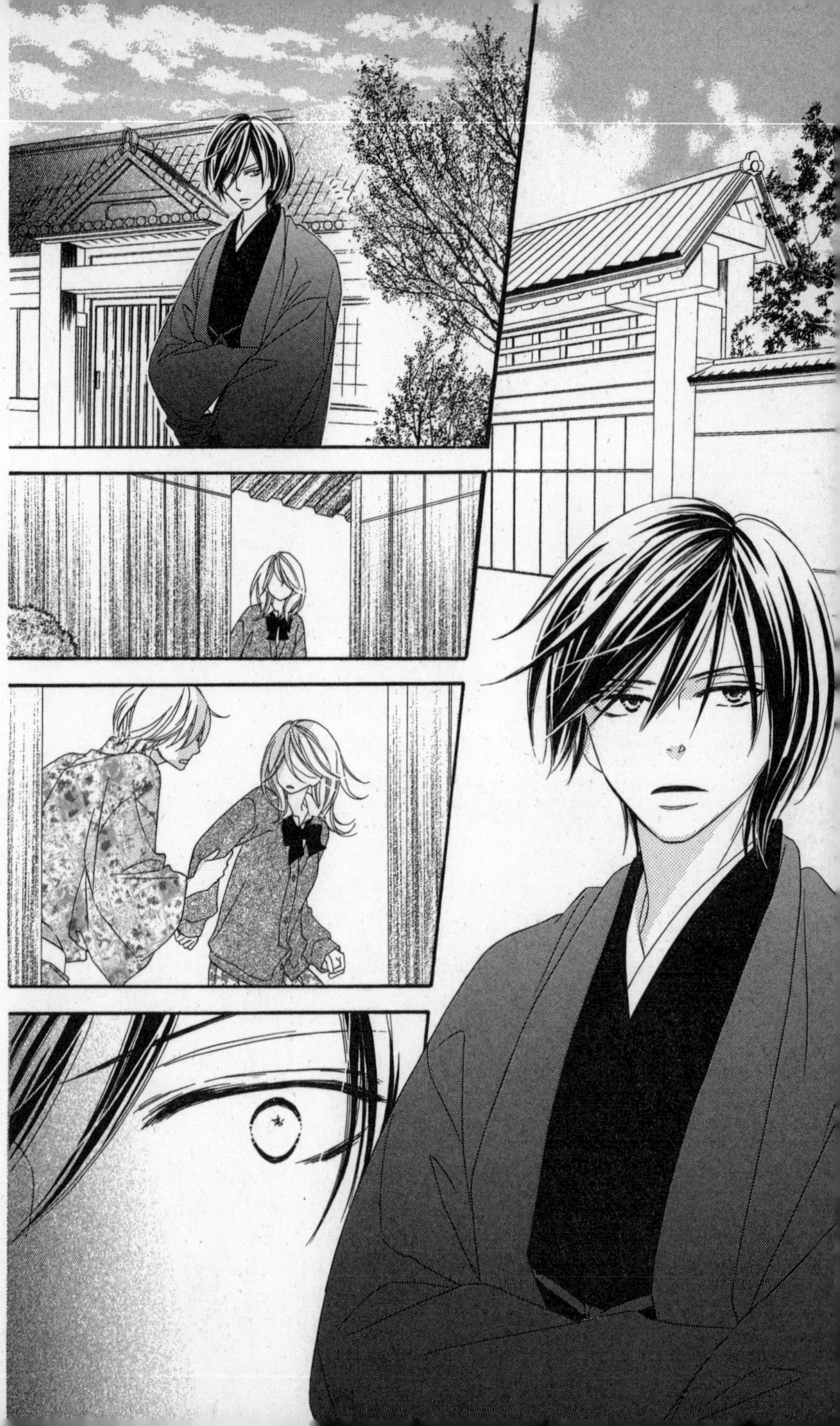

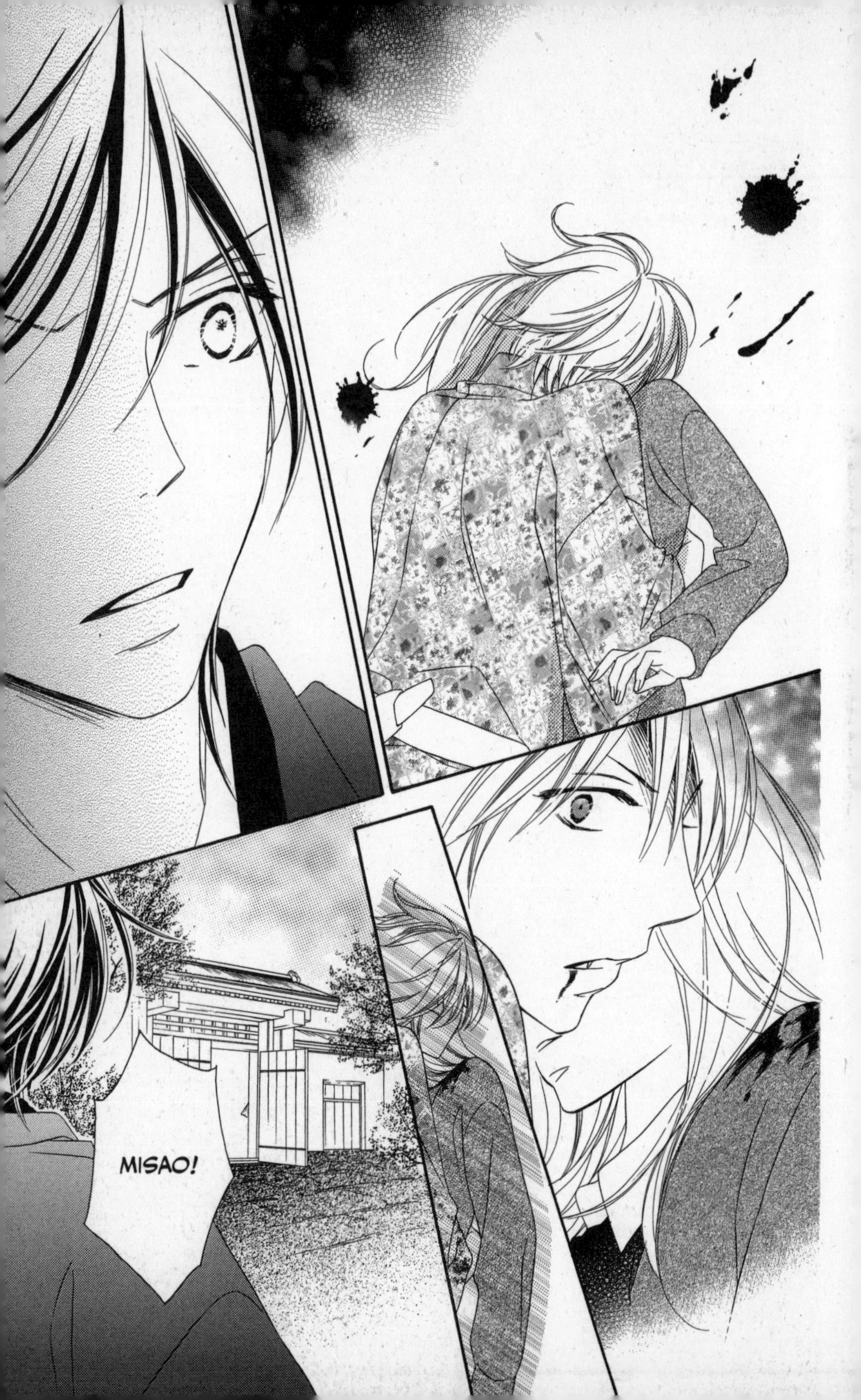
MISAO!

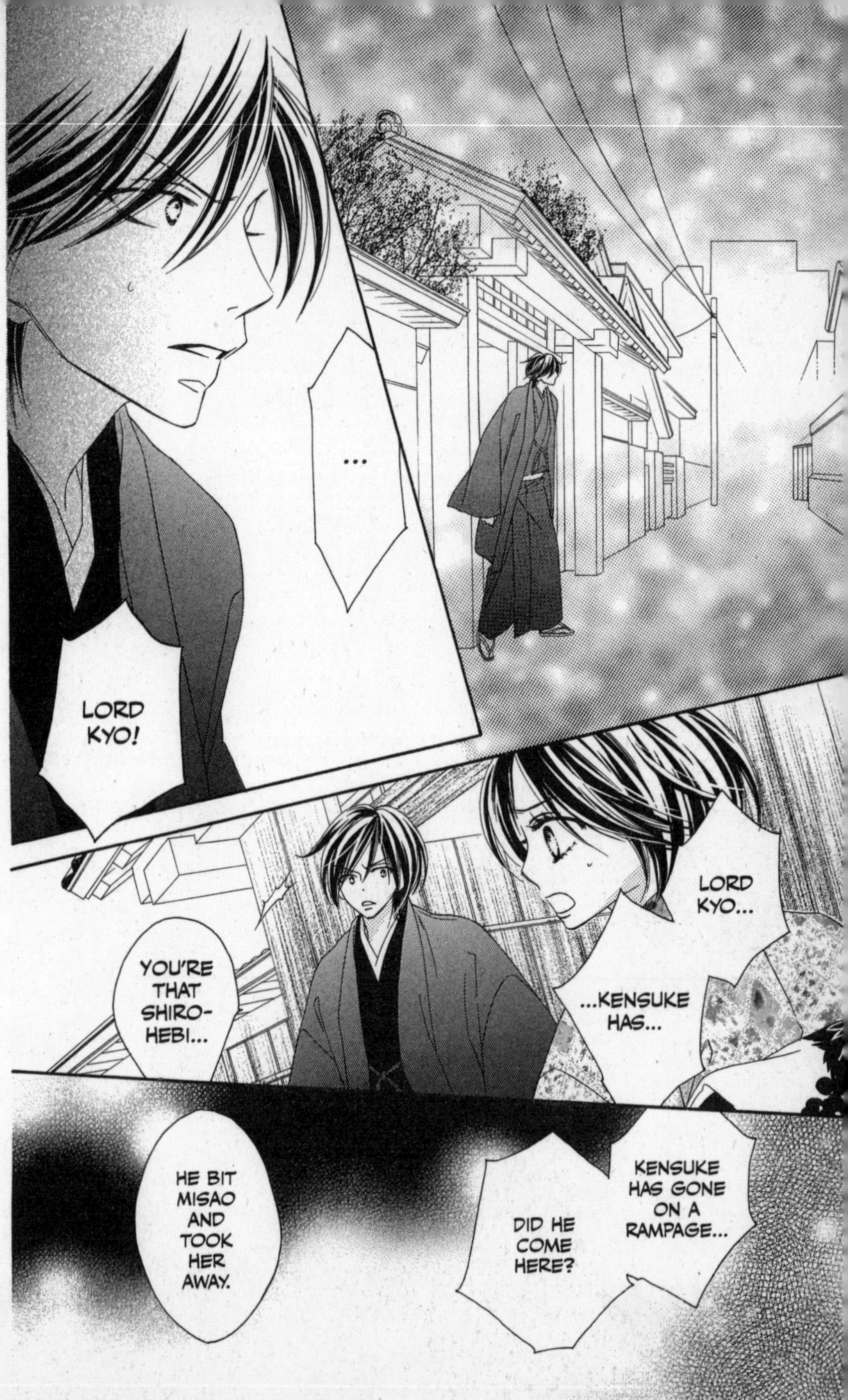
...
LORD KYO!
LORD KYO...
...KENSUKE HAS...
YOU'RE THAT SHIRO-HEBI...
KENSUKE HAS GONE ON A RAMPAGE...
DID HE COME HERE?
HE BIT MISAO AND TOOK HER AWAY.

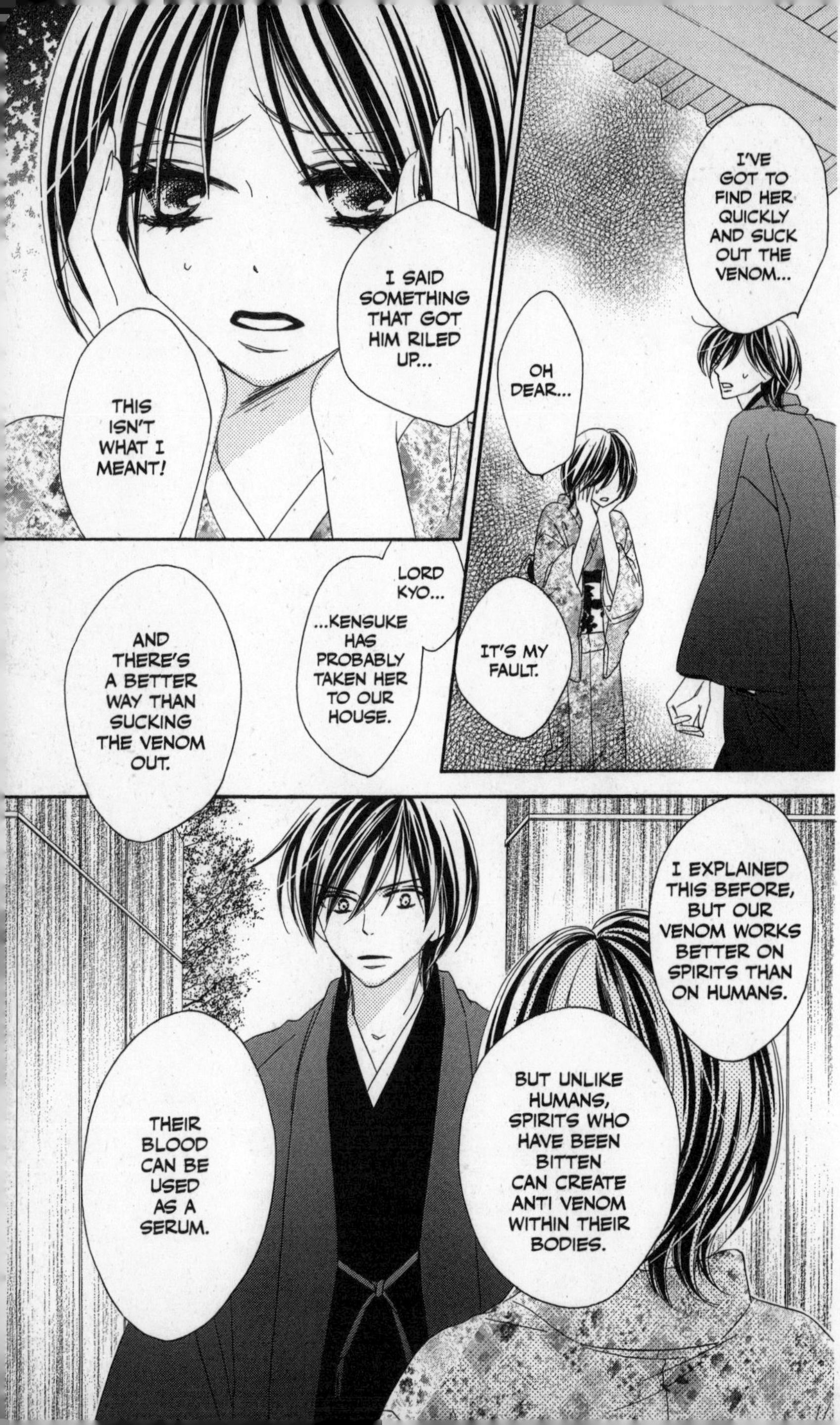
I'VE GOT TO FIND HER QUICKLY AND SUCK OUT THE VENOM...
OH DEAR...
IT'S MY FAULT.
I SAID SOMETHING THAT GOT HIM RILED UP...
THIS ISN'T WHAT I MEANT!
LORD KYO...
...KENSUKE HAS PROBABLY TAKEN HER TO OUR HOUSE.
AND THERE'S A BETTER WAY THAN SUCKING THE VENOM OUT.
I EXPLAINED THIS BEFORE, BUT OUR VENOM WORKS BETTER ON SPIRITS THAN ON HUMANS.
BUT UNLIKE HUMANS, SPIRITS WHO HAVE BEEN BITTEN CAN CREATE ANTI VENOM WITHIN THEIR BODIES.
THEIR BLOOD CAN BE USED AS A SERUM.

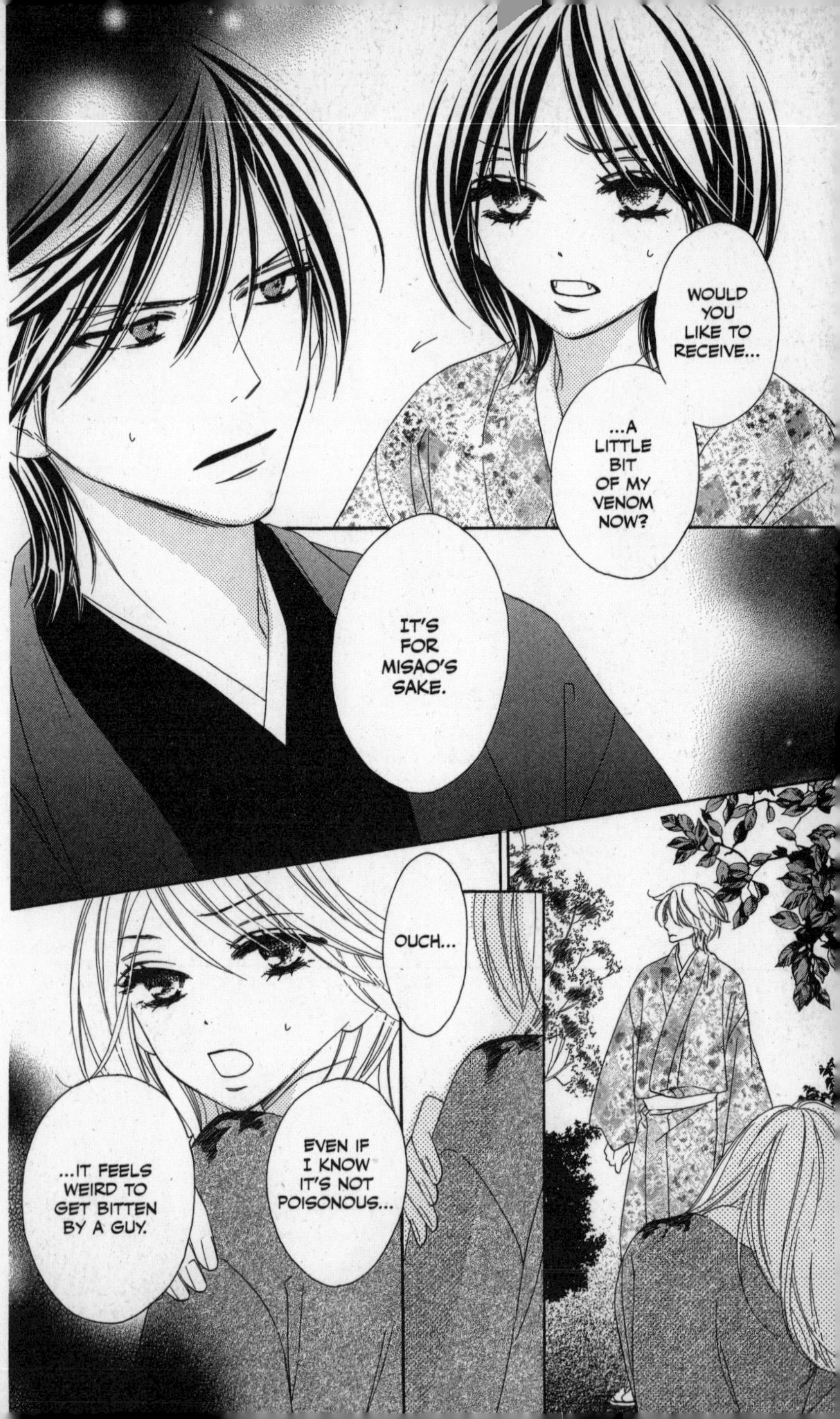
WOULD YOU LIKE TO RECEIVE...
...A LITTLE BIT OF MY VENOM NOW?
IT'S FOR MISAO'S SAKE.
OUCH...
EVEN IF I KNOW IT'S NOT POISONOUS...
...IT FEELS WEIRD TO GET BITTEN BY A GUY.

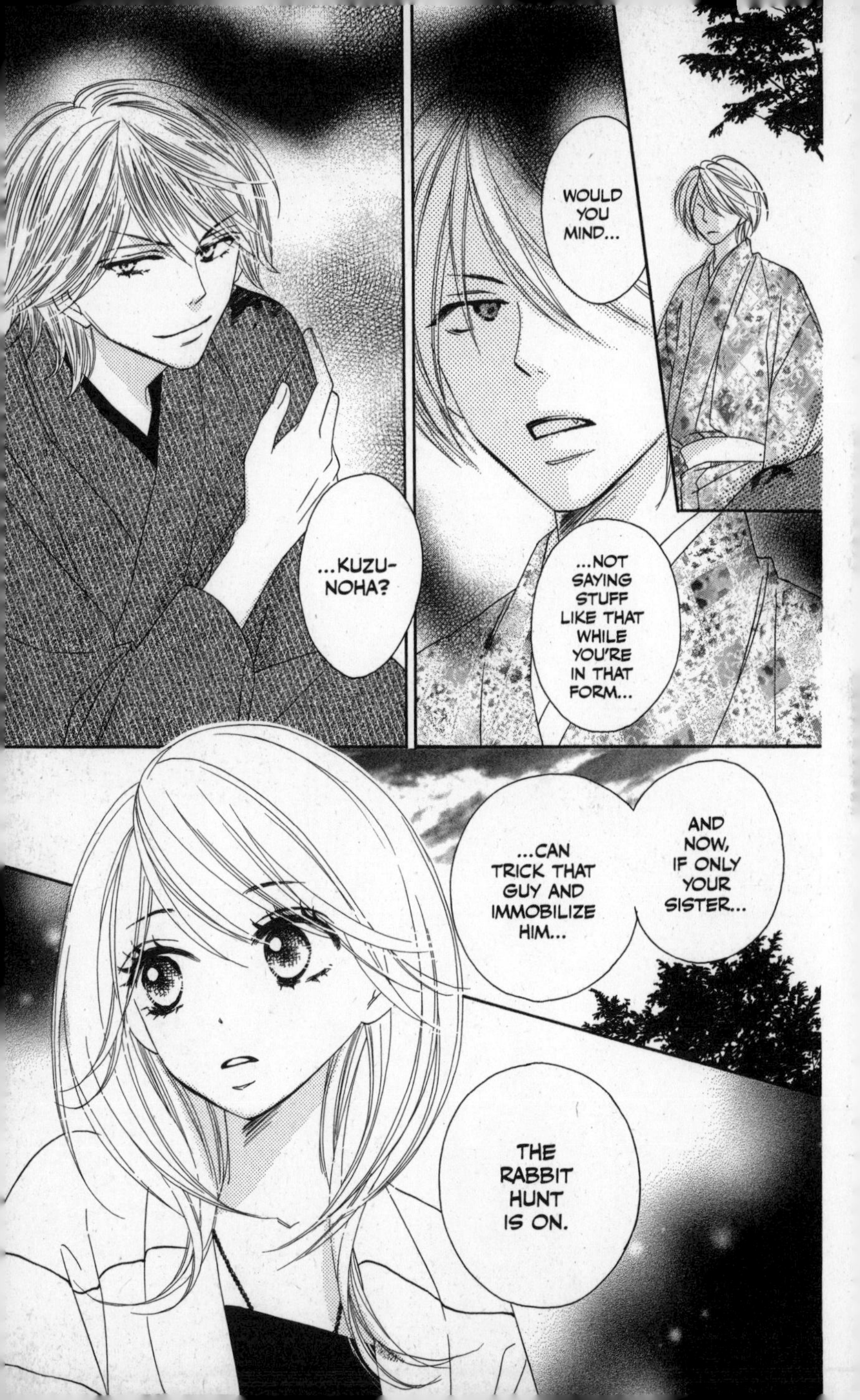
WOULD YOU MIND...
...NOT SAYING STUFF LIKE THAT WHILE YOU'RE IN THAT FORM...
...KUZU-NOHA?
AND NOW, IF ONLY YOUR SISTER...
...CAN TRICK THAT GUY AND IMMOBILIZE HIM...
THE RABBIT HUNT IS ON.

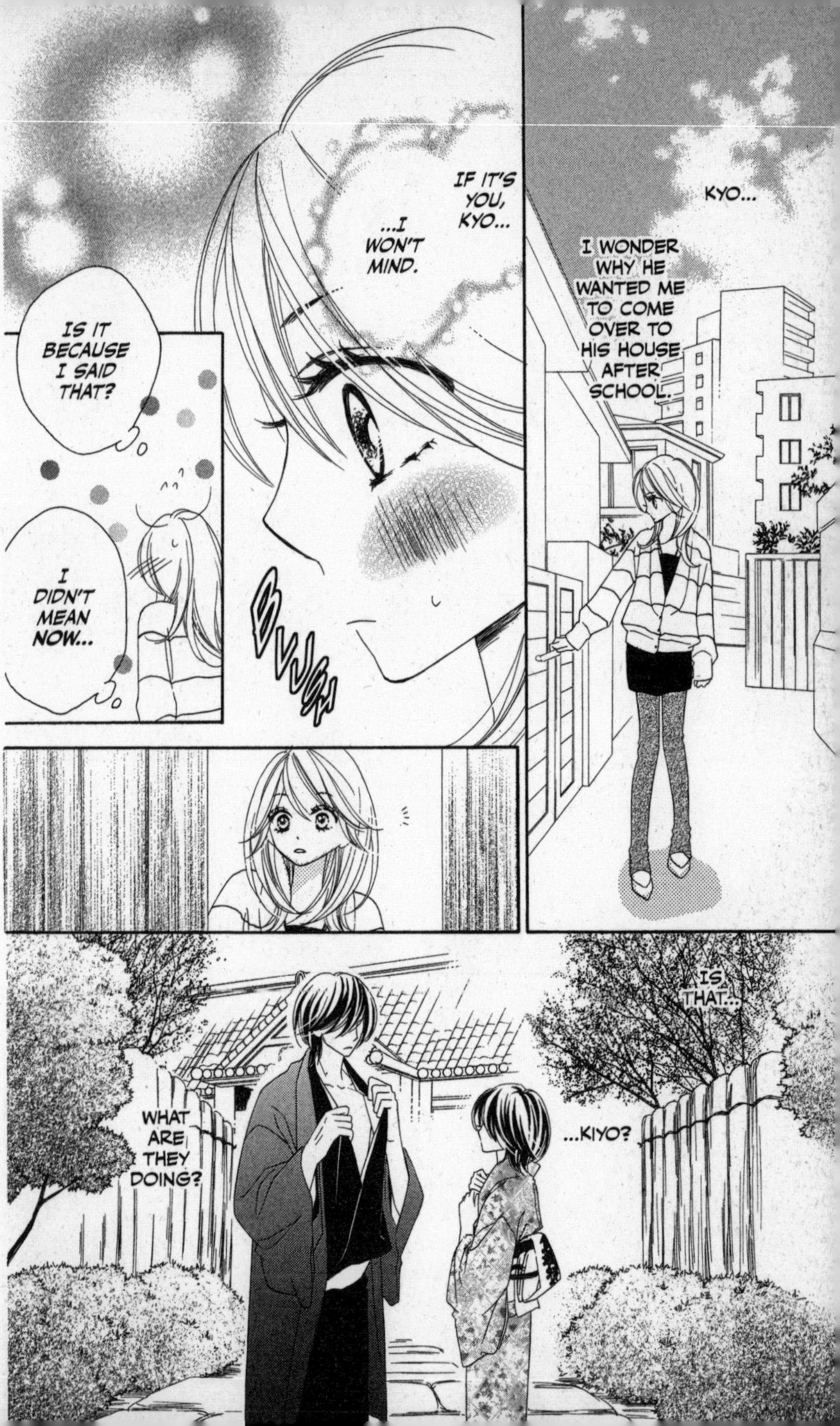
KYO...
I WONDER WHY HE WANTED ME TO COME OVER TO HIS HOUSE AFTER SCHOOL.
IF IT'S YOU, KYO...
...I WON'T MIND.
IS IT BECAUSE I SAID THAT?
I DIDN'T MEAN NOW...
IS THAT...
...KIYO?
WHAT ARE THEY DOING?

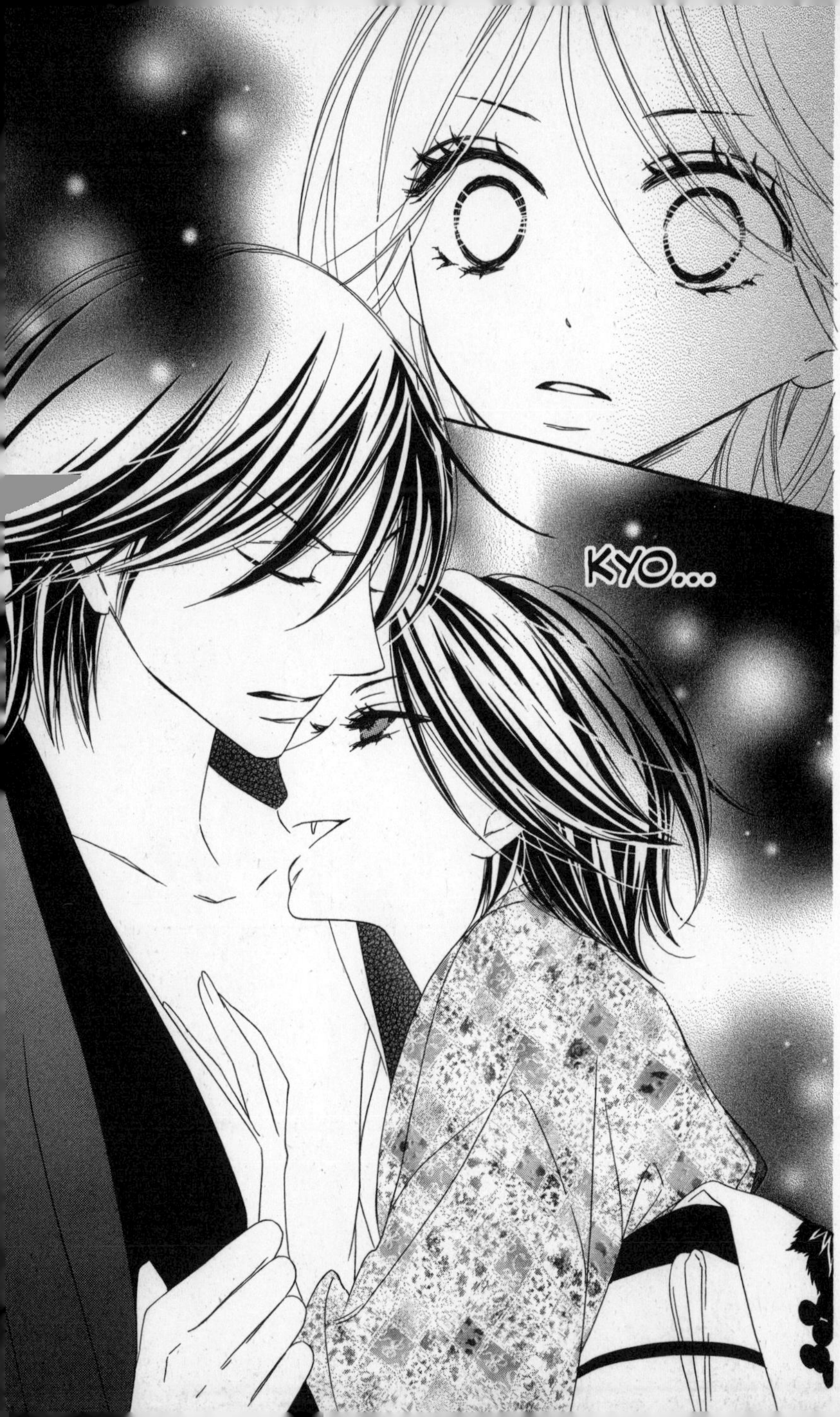
KYO...

Fan Page Number Two
"Zenki should say this."

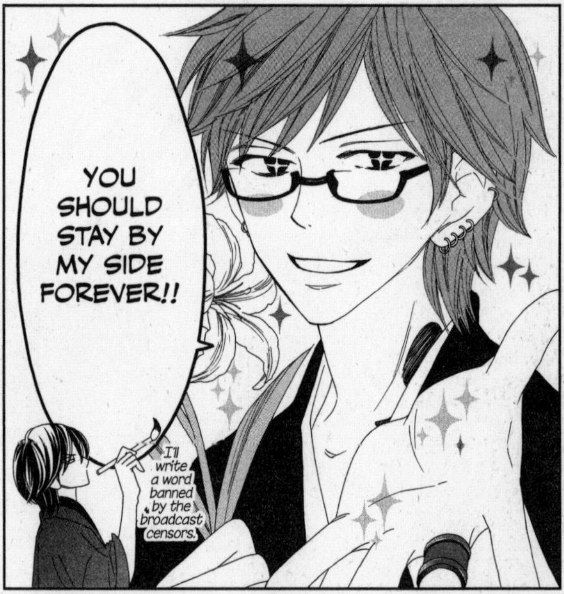
YOU SHOULD STAY BY MY SIDE FOREVER!!
I'll write a word banned by the broadcast censors.

Oops, I thought I was supposed to write what I wanted in the bubble.
That is why Kyo is saying that.
I'm happy to see that Zenki is rather popular.

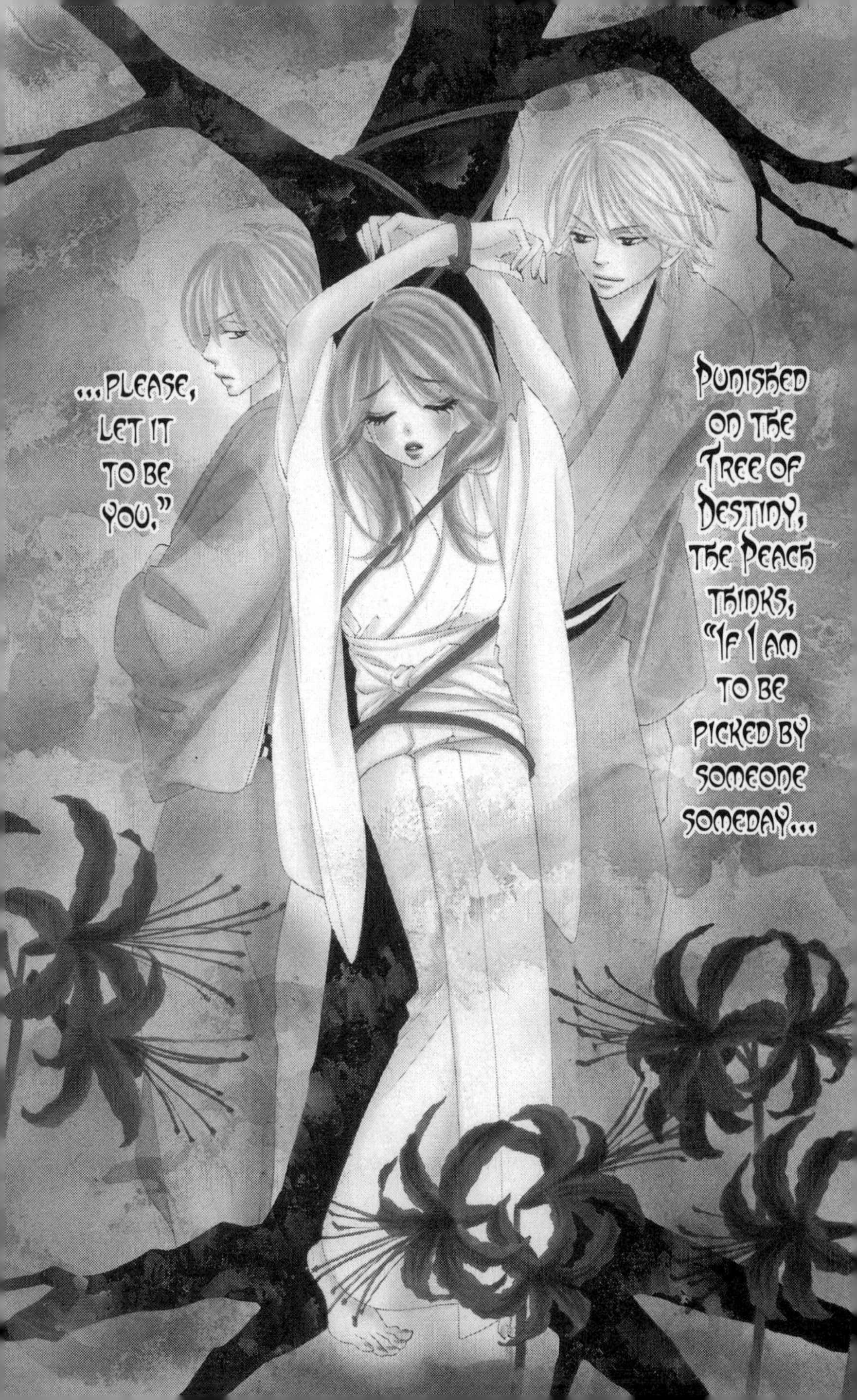
Punished on the Tree of Destiny, the Peach thinks, "If I am to be picked by someone someday...
...please, let it to be you."

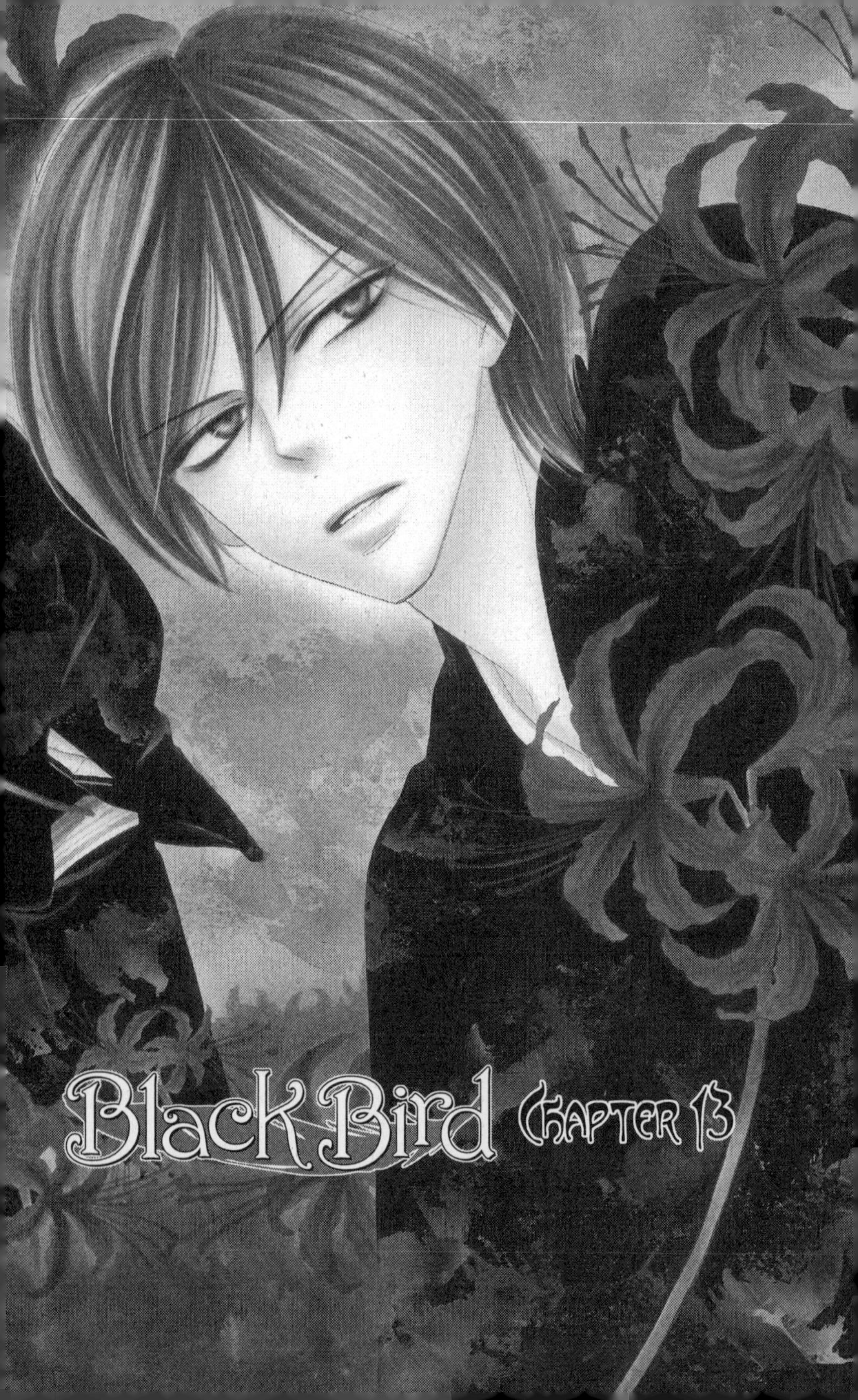
Black Bird
Chapter 13

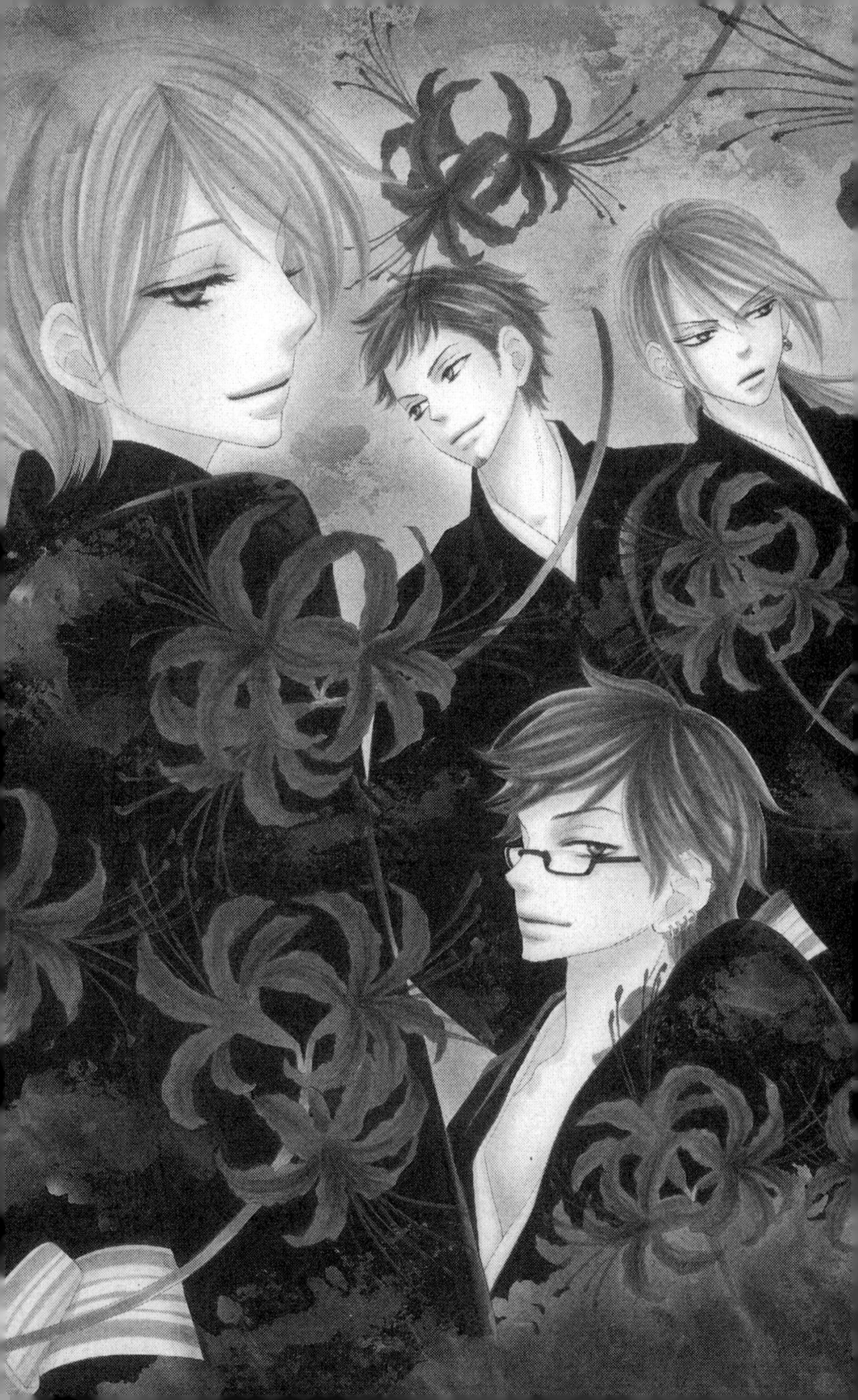

Fan Page Number Three.
I knew this was coming.
"The Butlers"

Welcome
home,
my lady. ♡

It's not that I'm crazy about butlers...
I think Buzen looks best dressed like this,
but I guess Sagami fits the role best.
Hoki is probably the gardener and Zenki
the stable master.

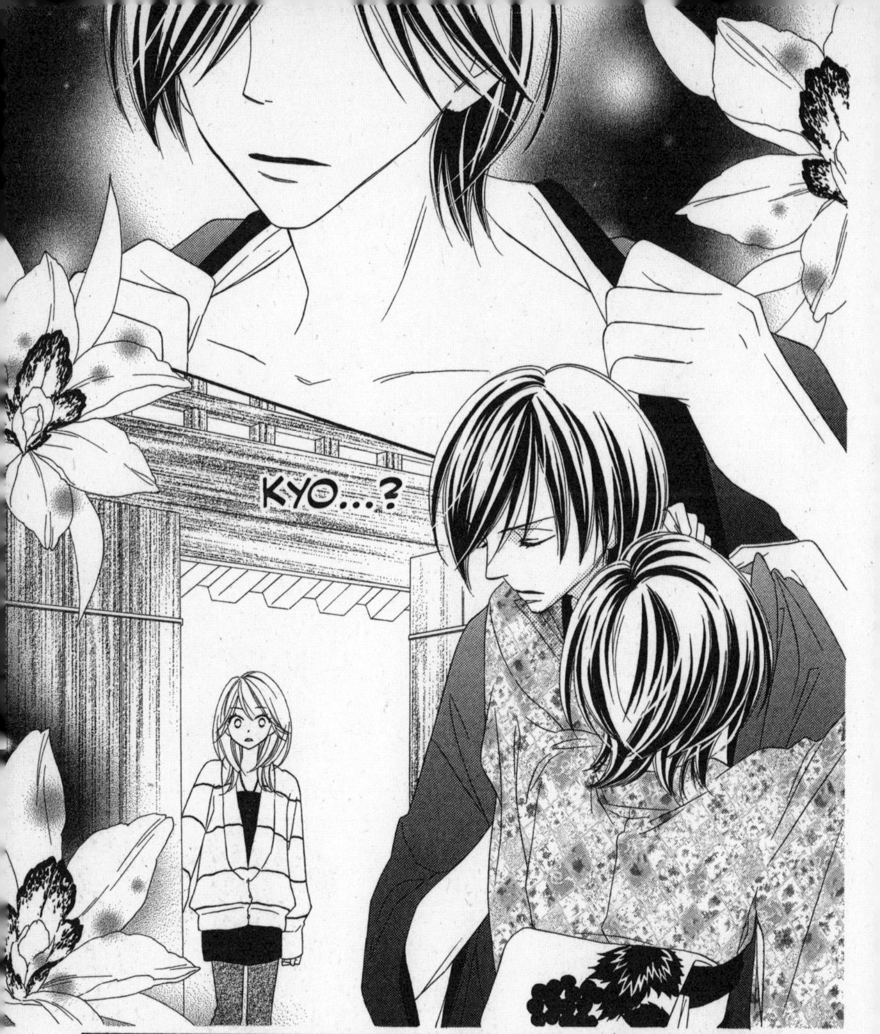
KYO...?

I have a website.

Visit me at

http://sakurakoujien.lolipop.jp

I haven't done much aside from updating the blog...

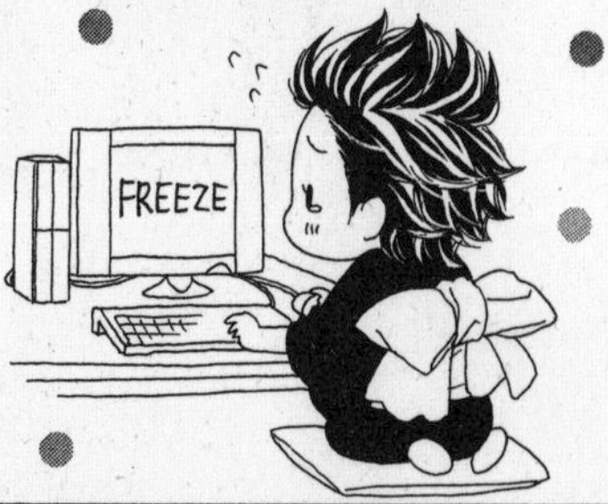
FREEZE

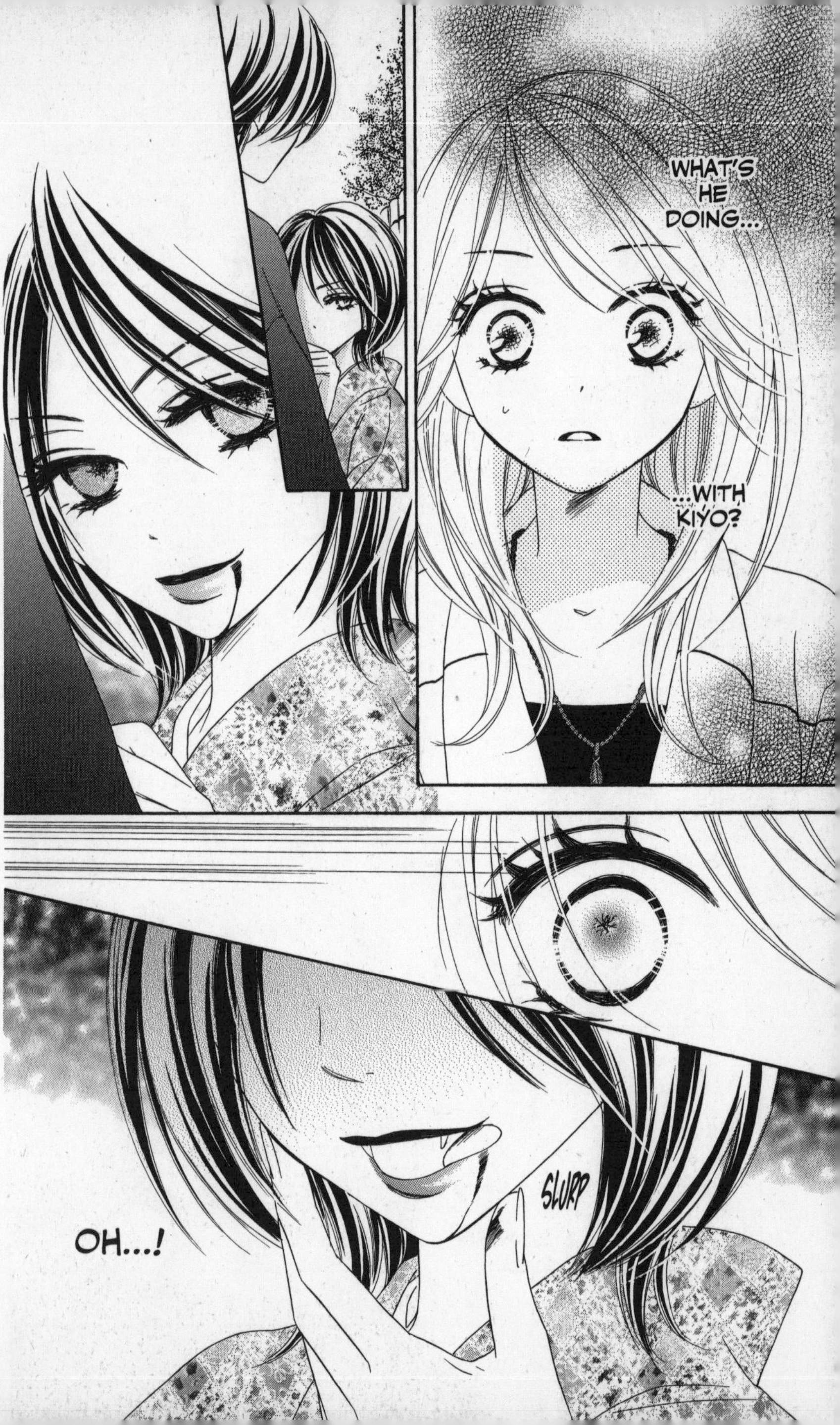
WHAT'S HE DOING...
...WITH KIYO?
SLURP
OH...!

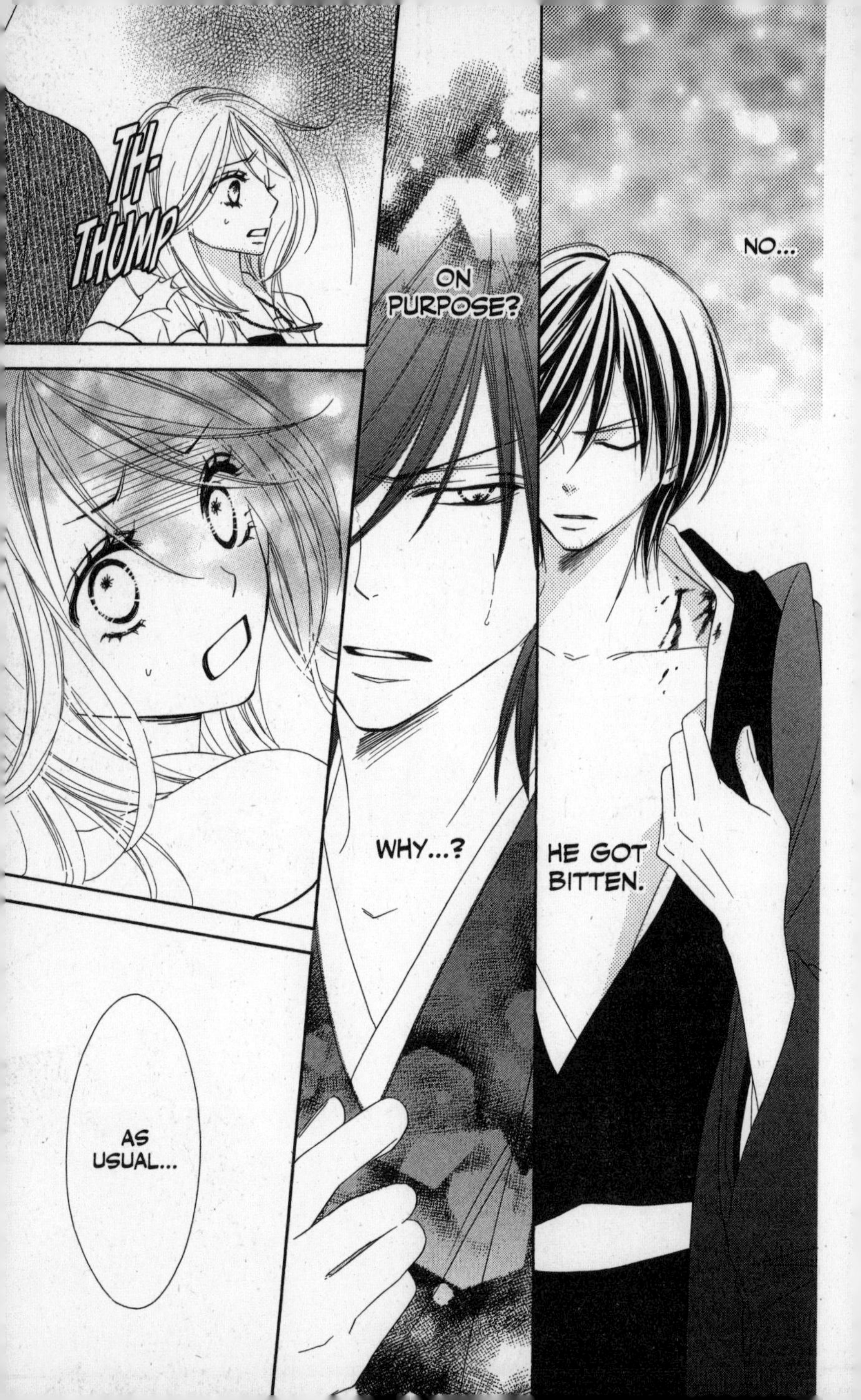
NO...
HE GOT BITTEN.
ON PURPOSE?
WHY...?
TH-THUMP
AS USUAL...

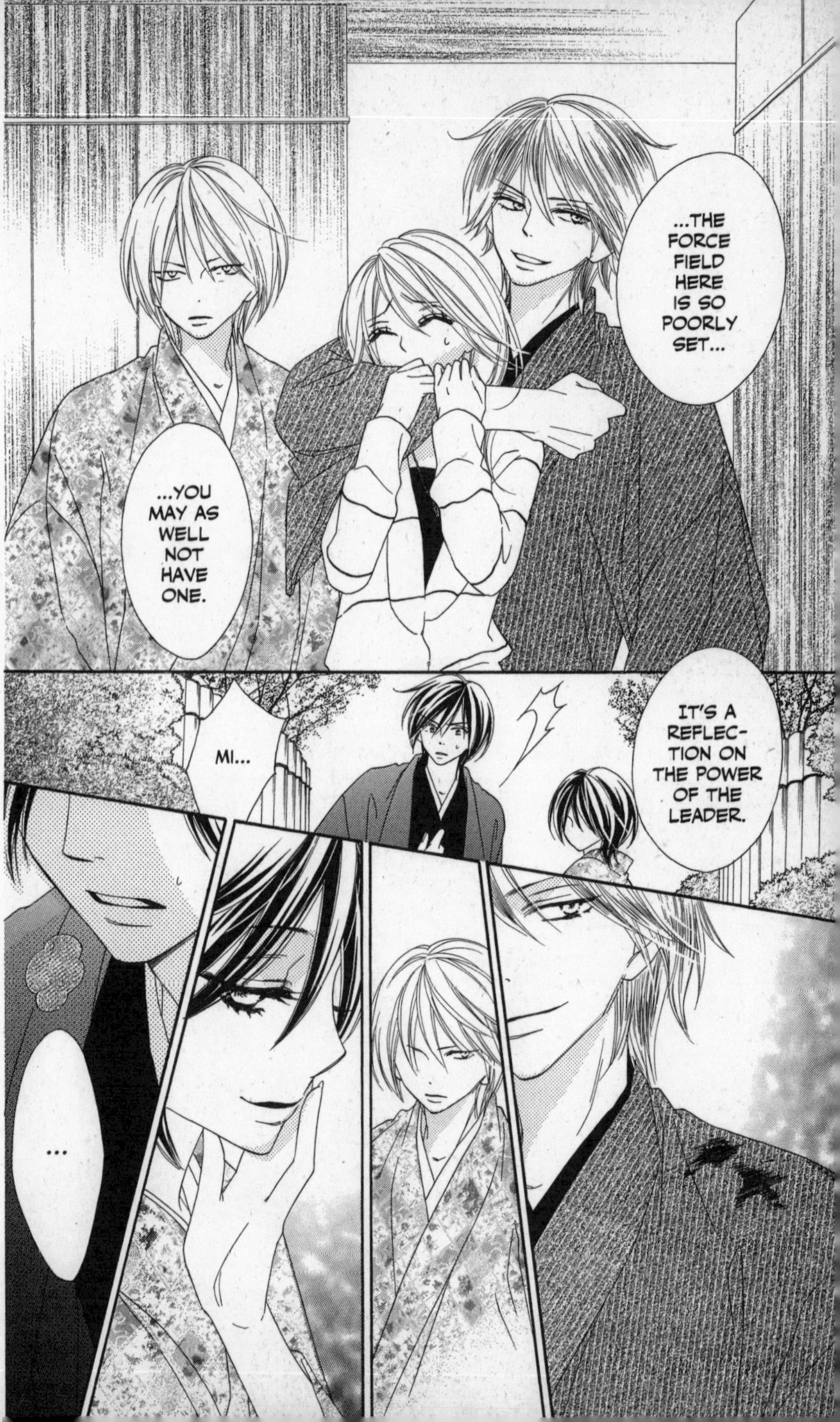
...THE FORCE FIELD HERE IS SO POORLY SET...
...YOU MAY AS WELL NOT HAVE ONE.
IT'S A REFLECTION ON THE POWER OF THE LEADER.
MI...
...

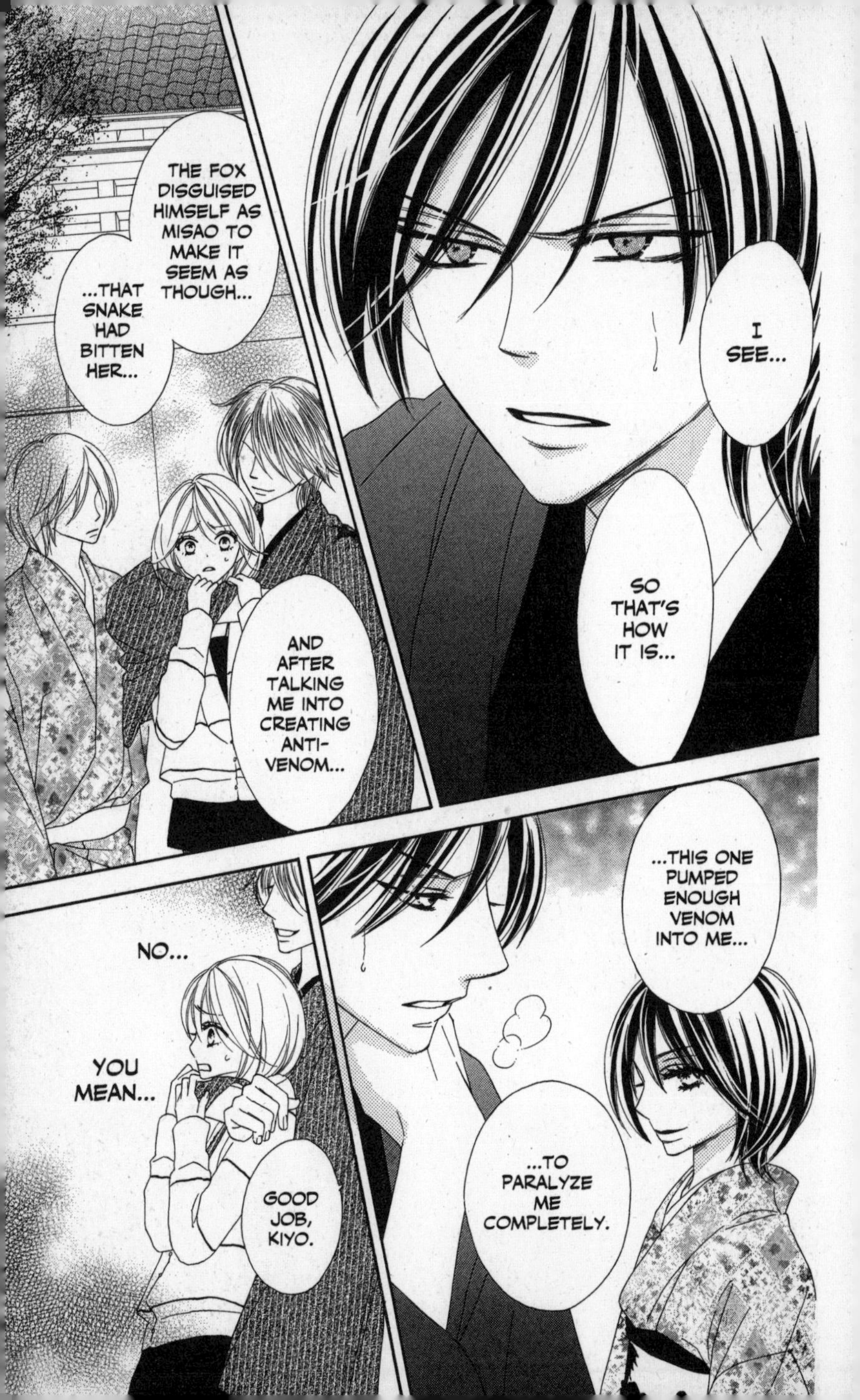
I SEE...
SO THAT'S HOW IT IS...
THE FOX DISGUISED HIMSELF AS MISAO TO MAKE IT SEEM AS THOUGH...
...THAT SNAKE HAD BITTEN HER...
AND AFTER TALKING ME INTO CREATING ANTI-VENOM...
...THIS ONE PUMPED ENOUGH VENOM INTO ME...
...TO PARALYZE ME COMPLETELY.
NO...
YOU MEAN...
GOOD JOB, KIYO.

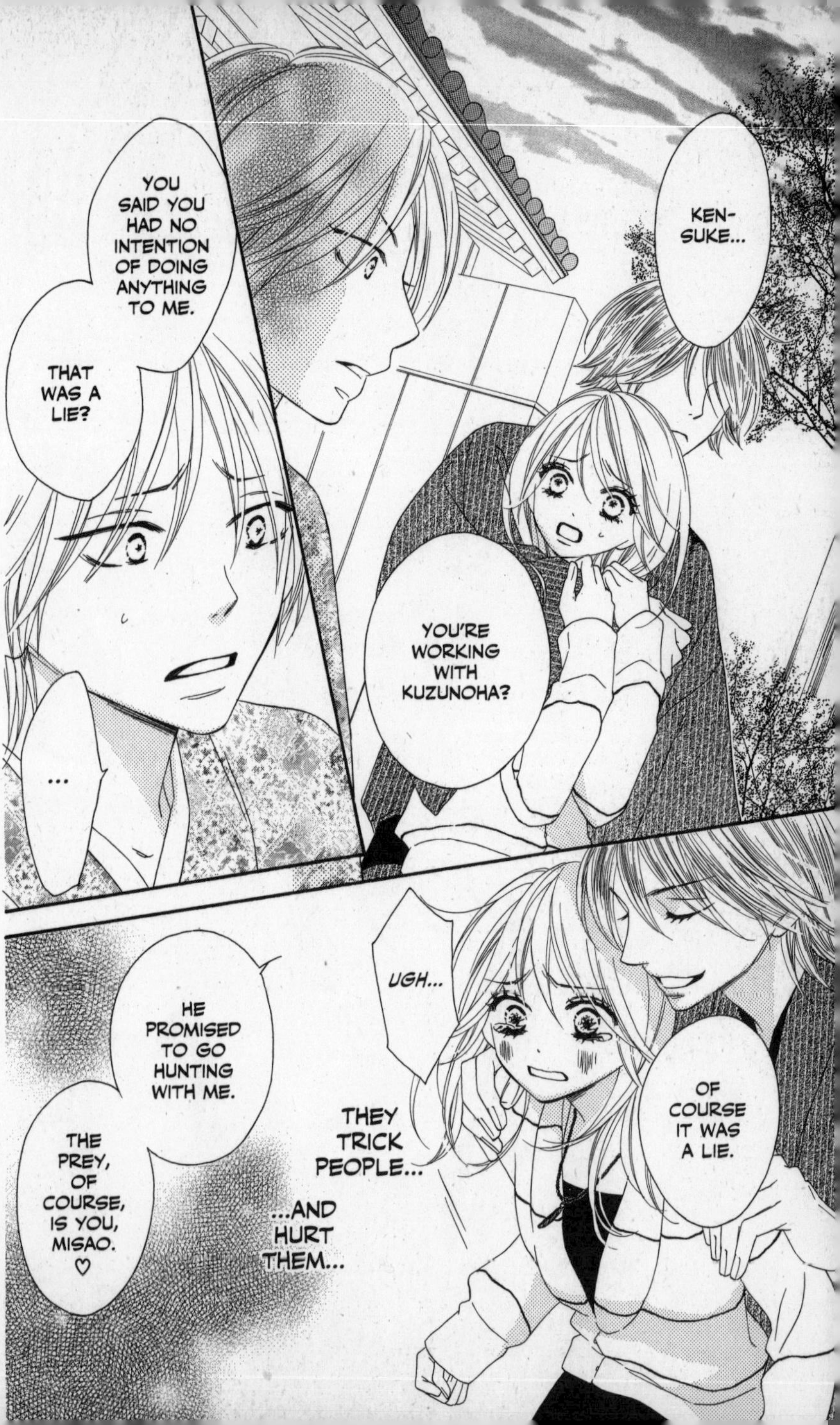
KEN-SUKE...
YOU'RE WORKING WITH KUZUNOHA?
YOU SAID YOU HAD NO INTENTION OF DOING ANYTHING TO ME.
THAT WAS A LIE?
...
OF COURSE IT WAS A LIE.
UGH...
THEY TRICK PEOPLE...
...AND HURT THEM...
HE PROMISED TO GO HUNTING WITH ME.
THE PREY, OF COURSE, IS YOU, MISAO. ♡

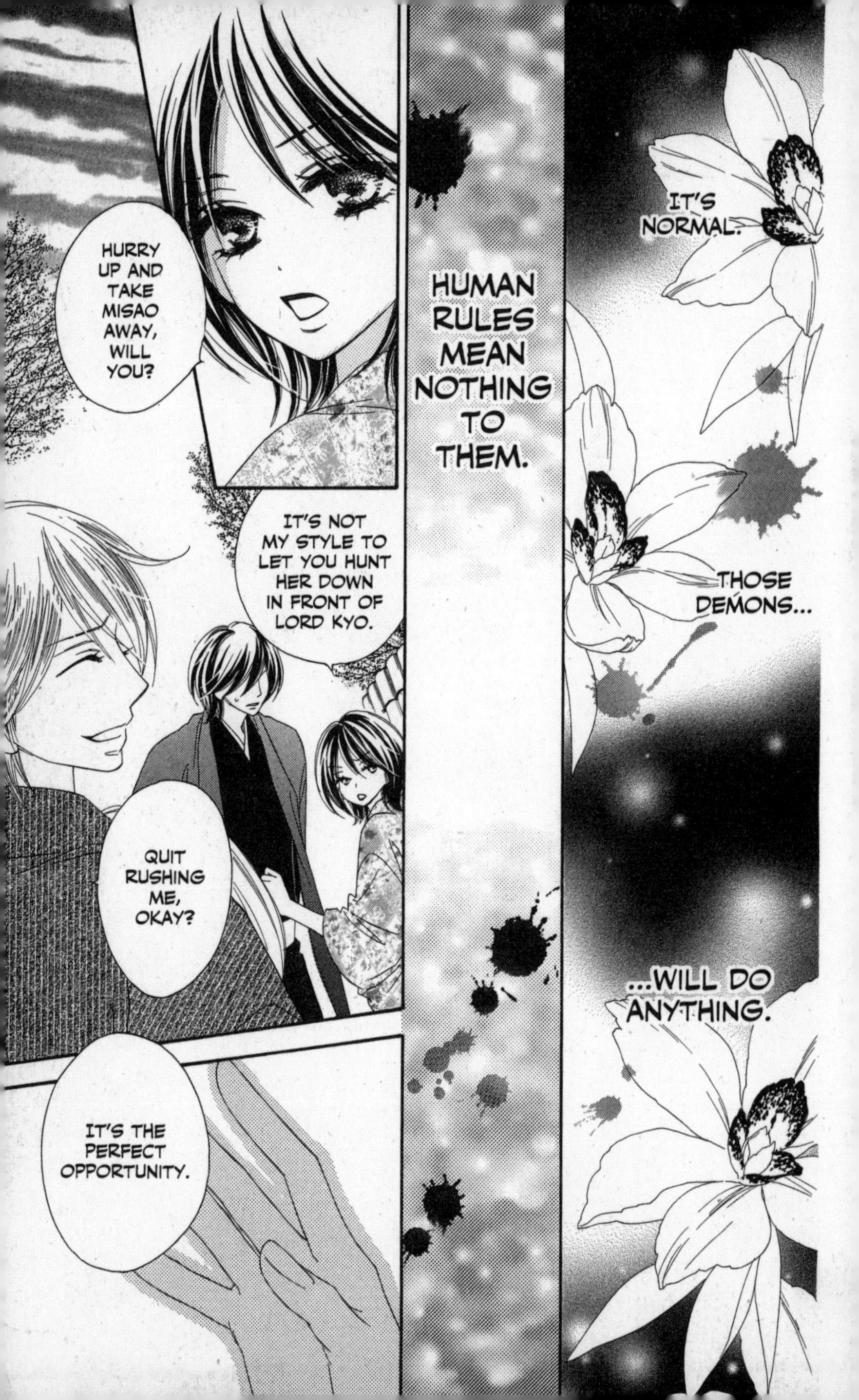
IT'S NORMAL.
THOSE DEMONS...
...WILL DO ANYTHING.
HUMAN RULES MEAN NOTHING TO THEM.
HURRY UP AND TAKE MISAO AWAY, WILL YOU?
IT'S NOT MY STYLE TO LET YOU HUNT HER DOWN IN FRONT OF LORD KYO.
QUIT RUSHING ME, OKAY?
IT'S THE PERFECT OPPORTUNITY.

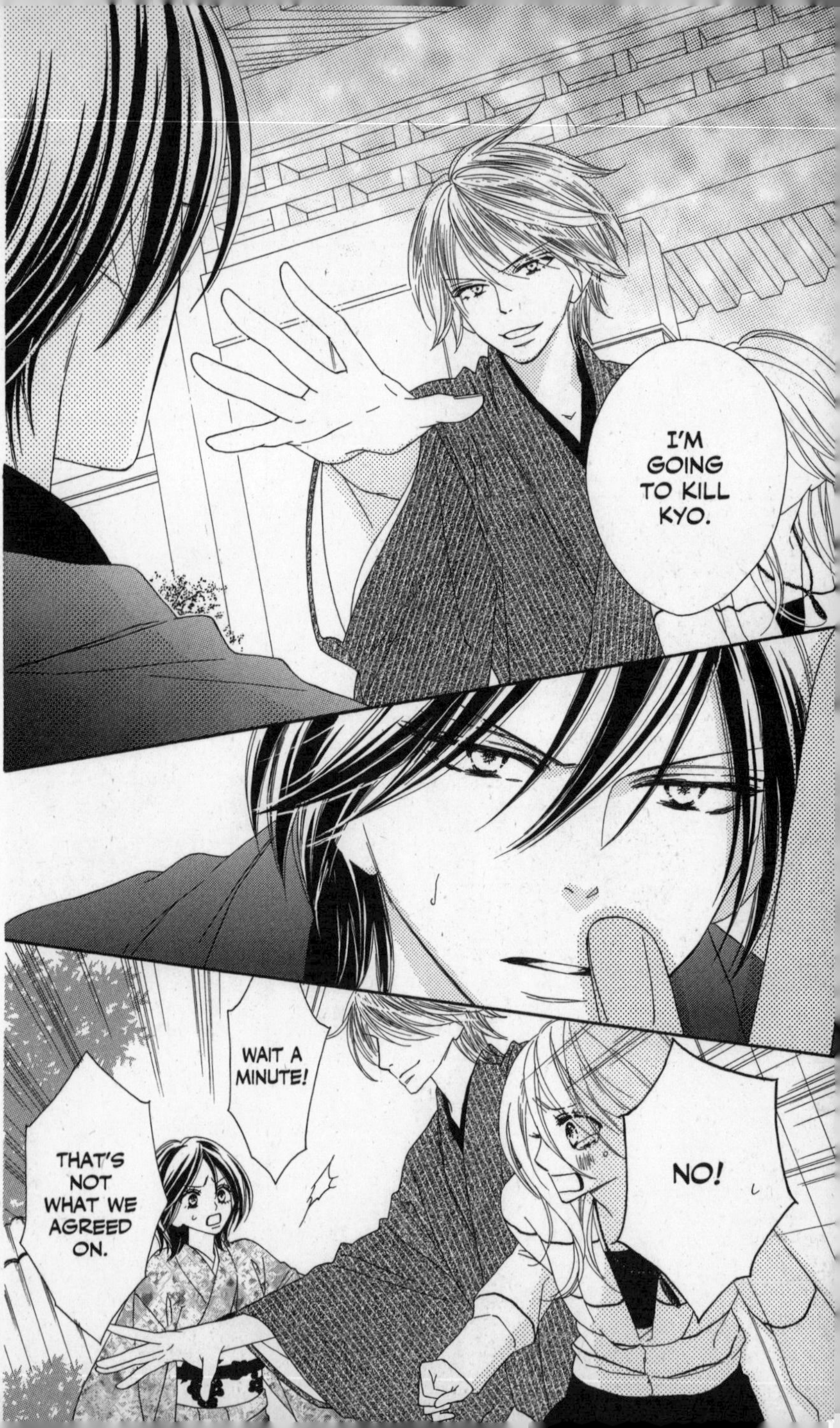
I'M GOING TO KILL KYO.
NO!
WAIT A MINUTE!
THAT'S NOT WHAT WE AGREED ON.

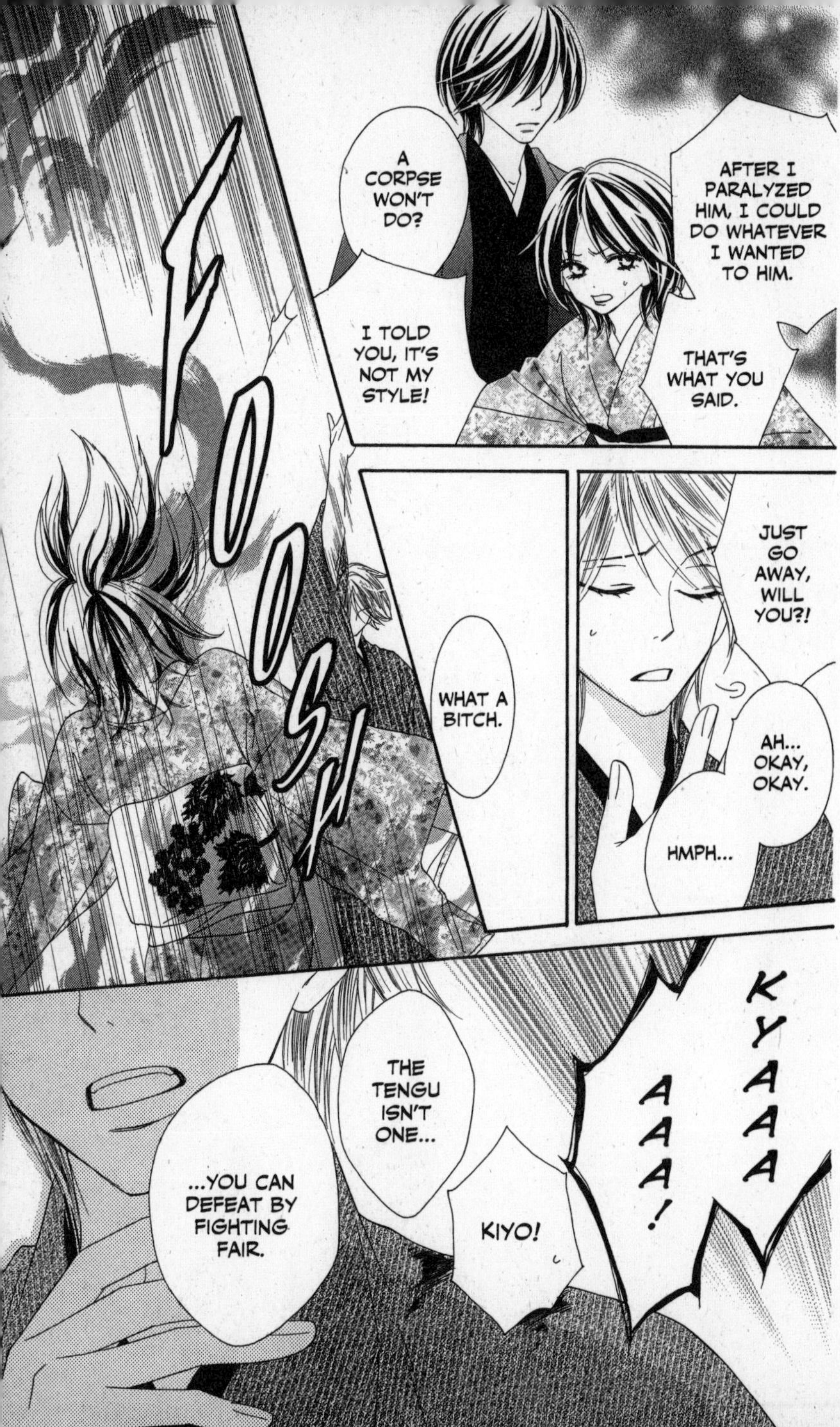
AFTER I PARALYZED HIM, I COULD DO WHATEVER I WANTED TO HIM.
THAT'S WHAT YOU SAID.
A CORPSE WON'T DO?
I TOLD YOU, IT'S NOT MY STYLE!
JUST GO AWAY, WILL YOU?!
AH... OKAY, OKAY.
HMPH...
WHAT A BITCH.
FOOSH
KYAAAAAAA!
KIYO!
THE TENGU ISN'T ONE...
...YOU CAN DEFEAT BY FIGHTING FAIR.

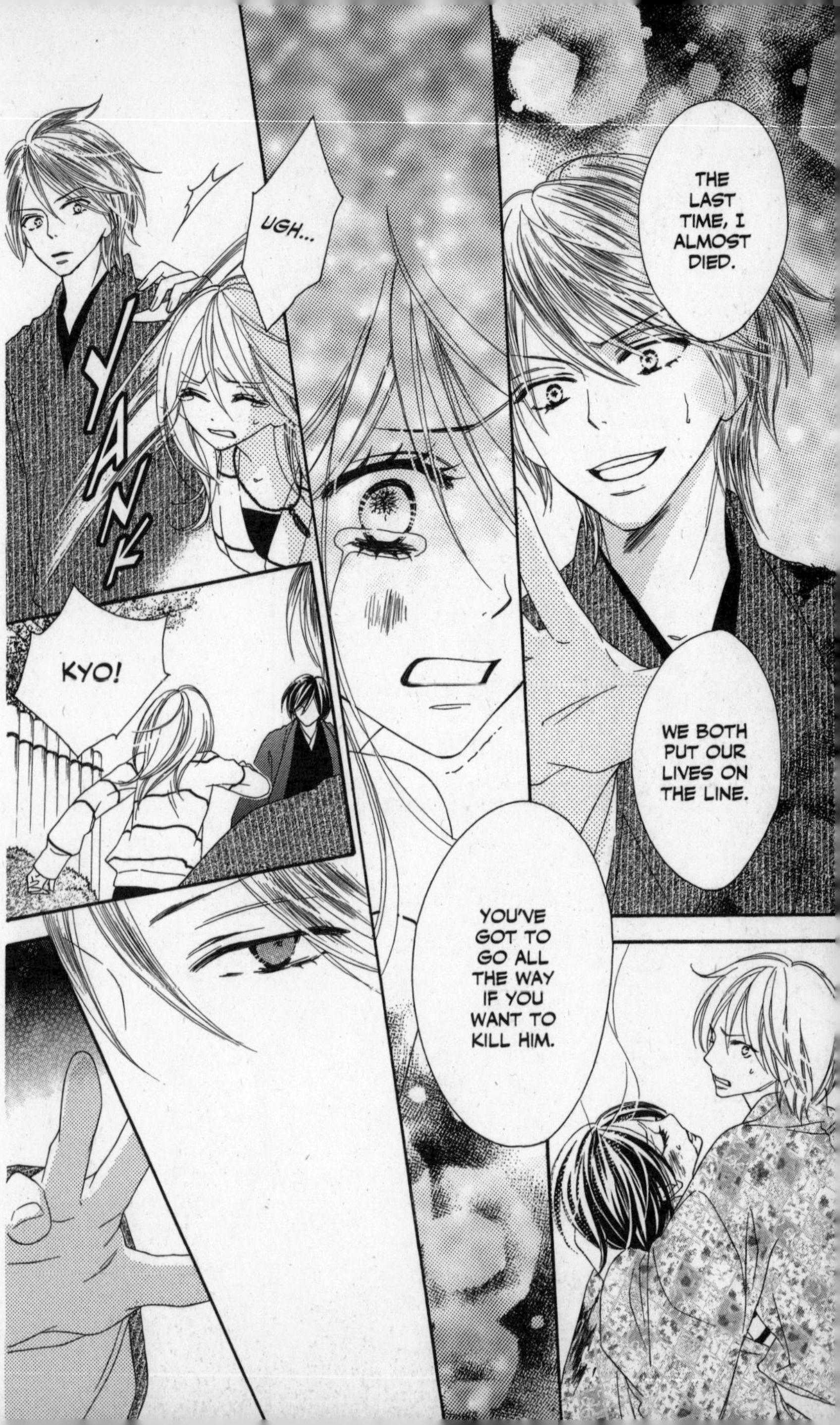
THE LAST TIME, I ALMOST DIED.
WE BOTH PUT OUR LIVES ON THE LINE.
YOU'VE GOT TO GO ALL THE WAY IF YOU WANT TO KILL HIM.
UGH...
YANK
KYO!

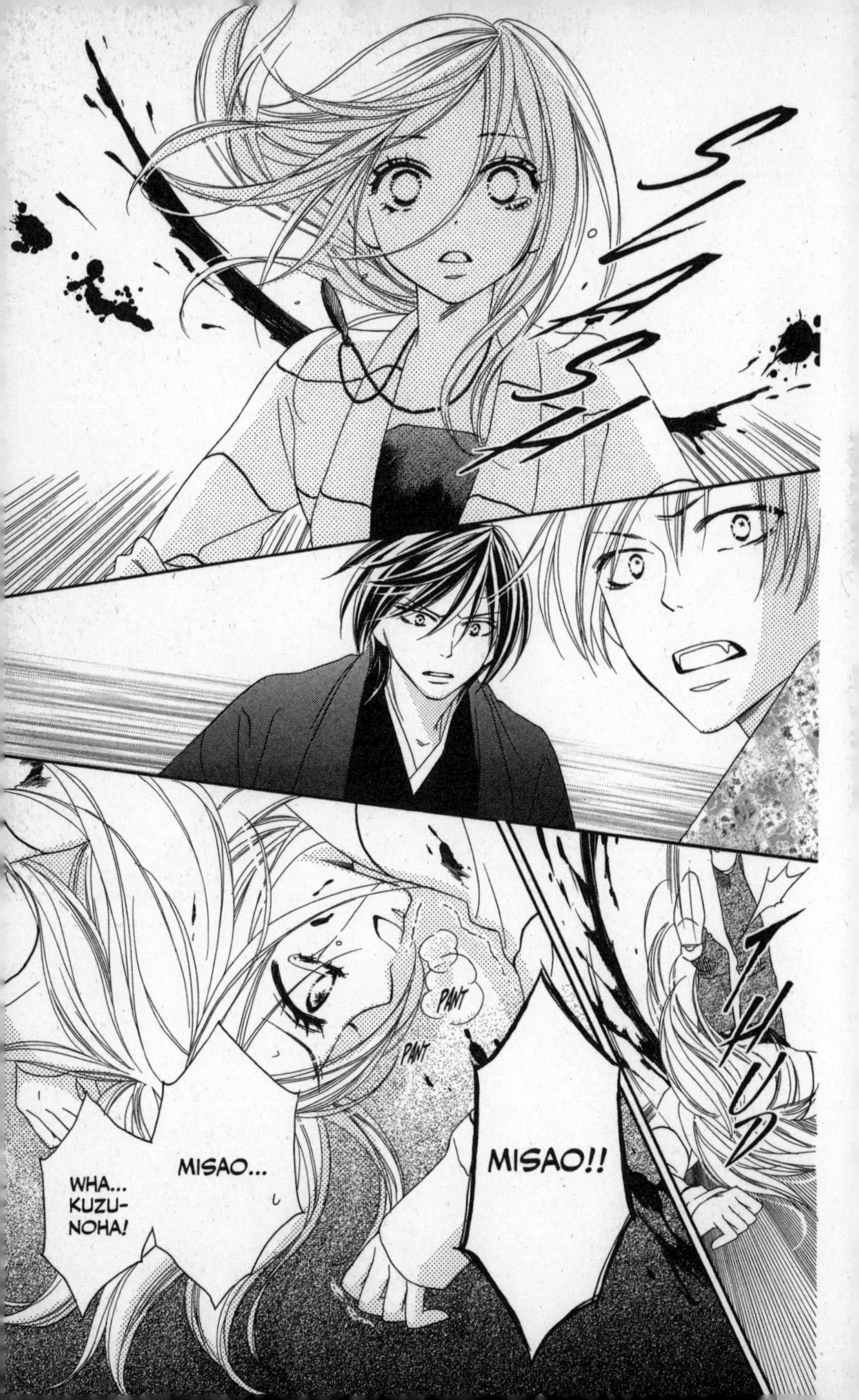
SLASH
MISAO!!
PANT
PANT
MISAO...
WHA... KUZU-NOHA!

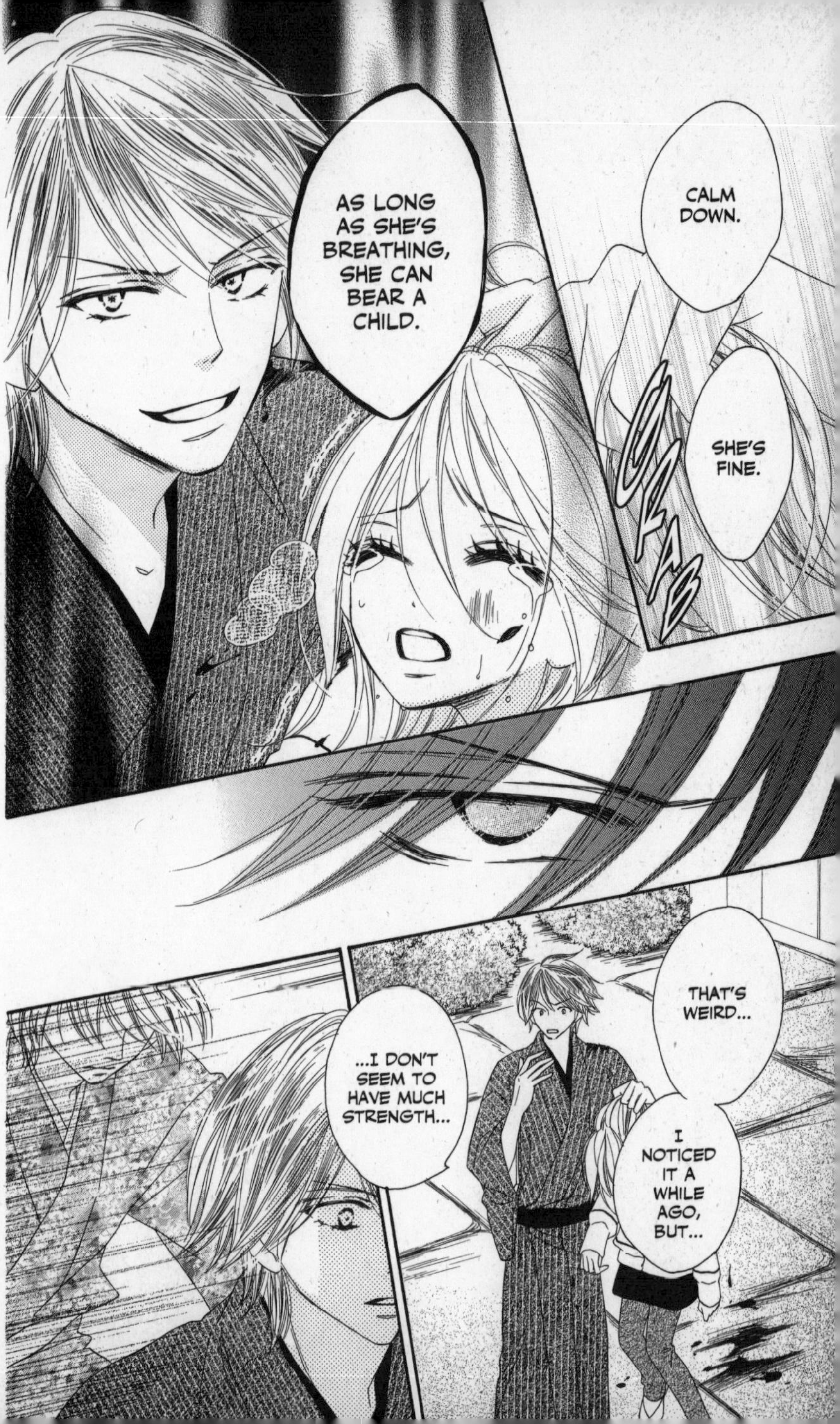
CALM DOWN.
SHE'S FINE.
AS LONG AS SHE'S BREATHING, SHE CAN BEAR A CHILD.
THAT'S WEIRD...
I NOTICED IT A WHILE AGO, BUT...
...I DON'T SEEM TO HAVE MUCH STRENGTH...

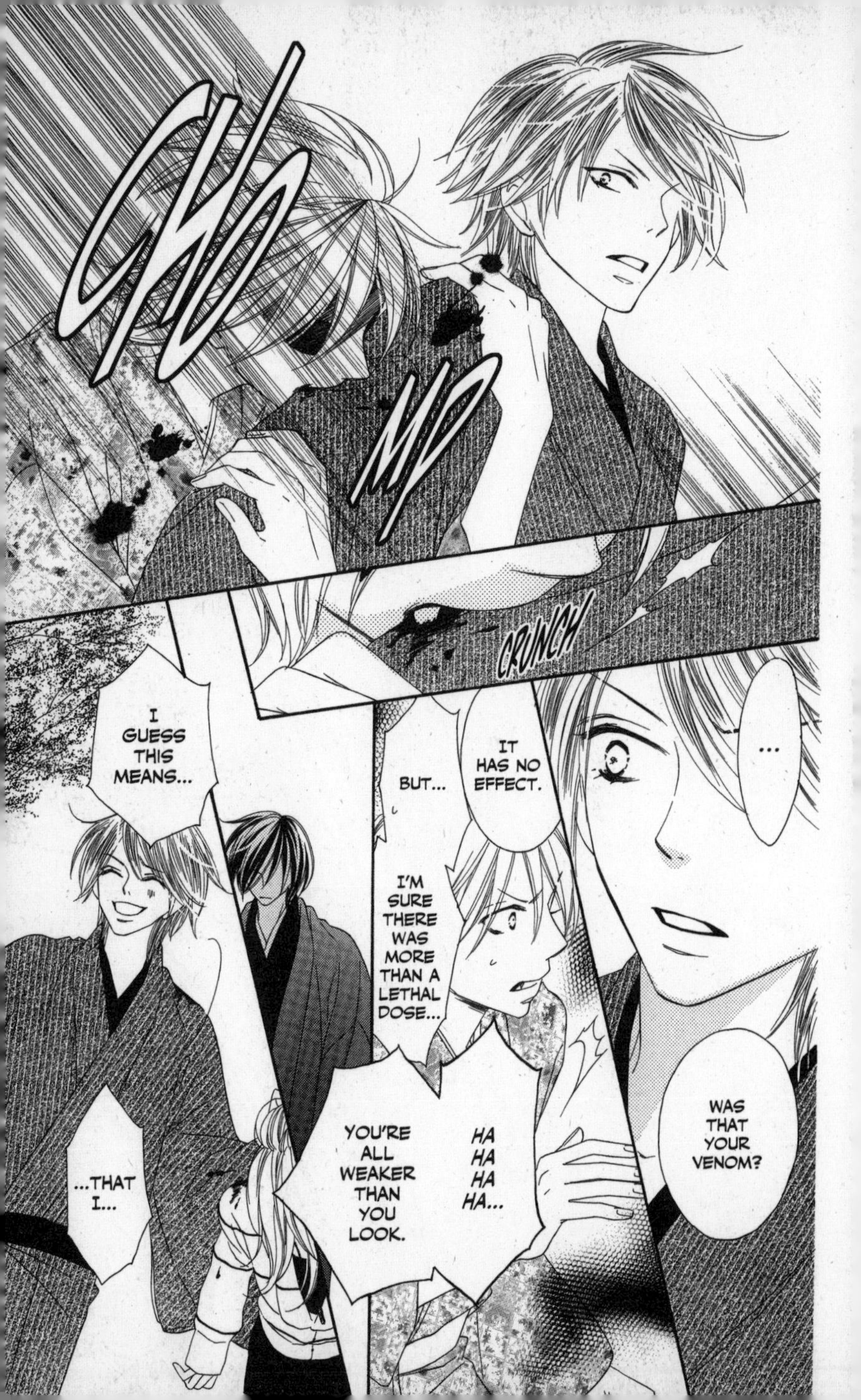
CHOMP
CRUNCH
...
WAS THAT YOUR VENOM?
IT HAS NO EFFECT.
BUT...
I'M SURE THERE WAS MORE THAN A LETHAL DOSE...
HA HA HA HA...
YOU'RE ALL WEAKER THAN YOU LOOK.
I GUESS THIS MEANS...
...THAT I...

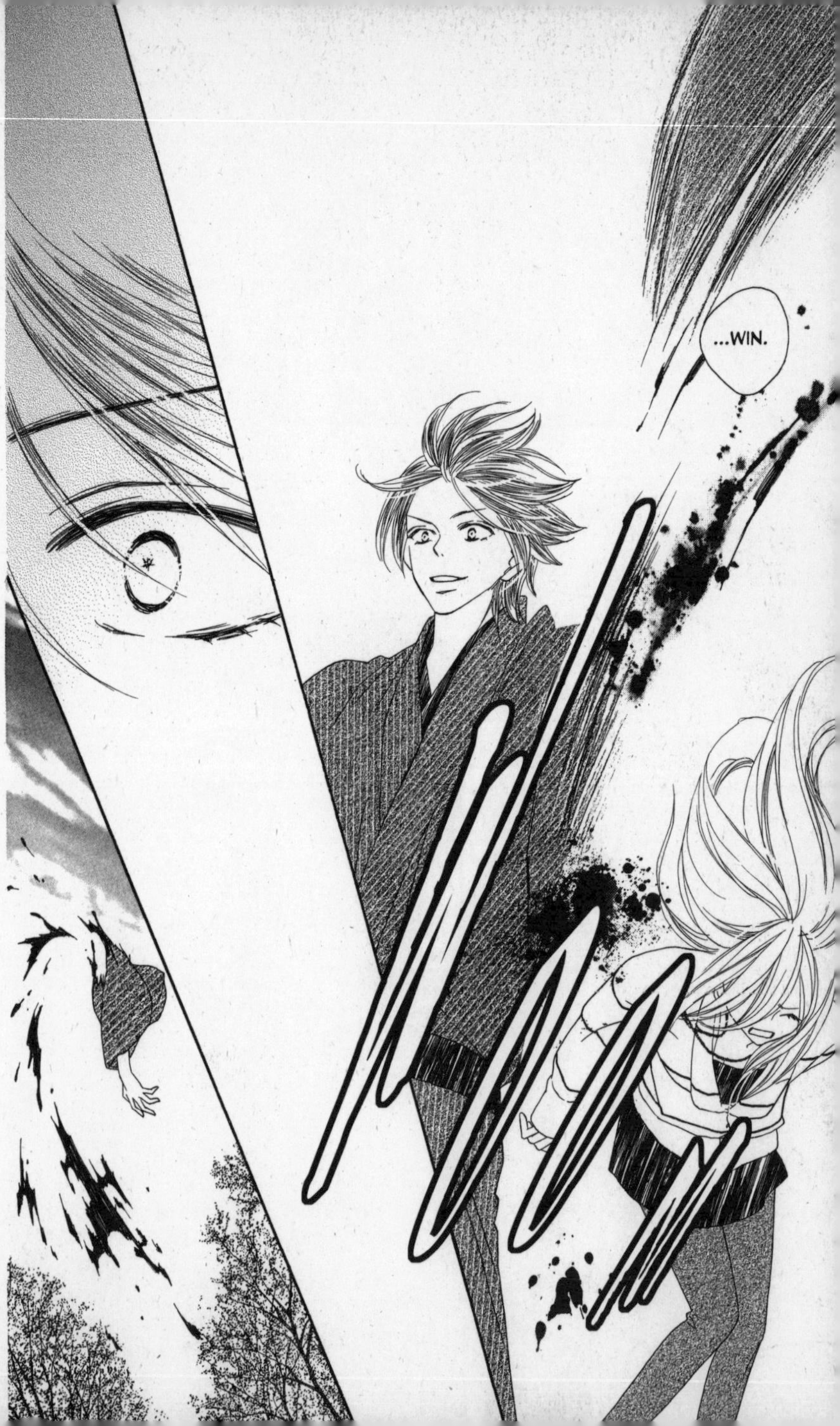
...WIN.

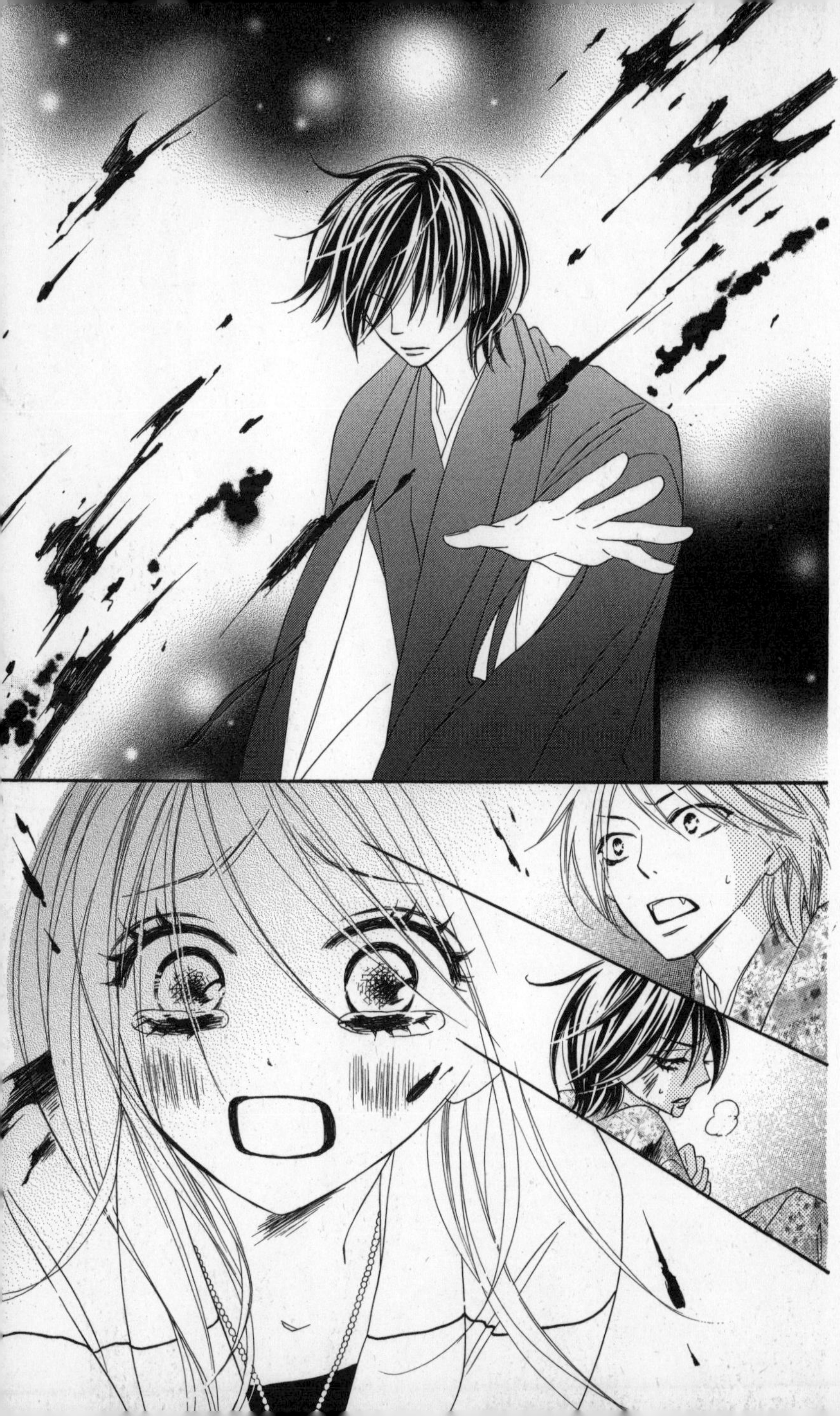

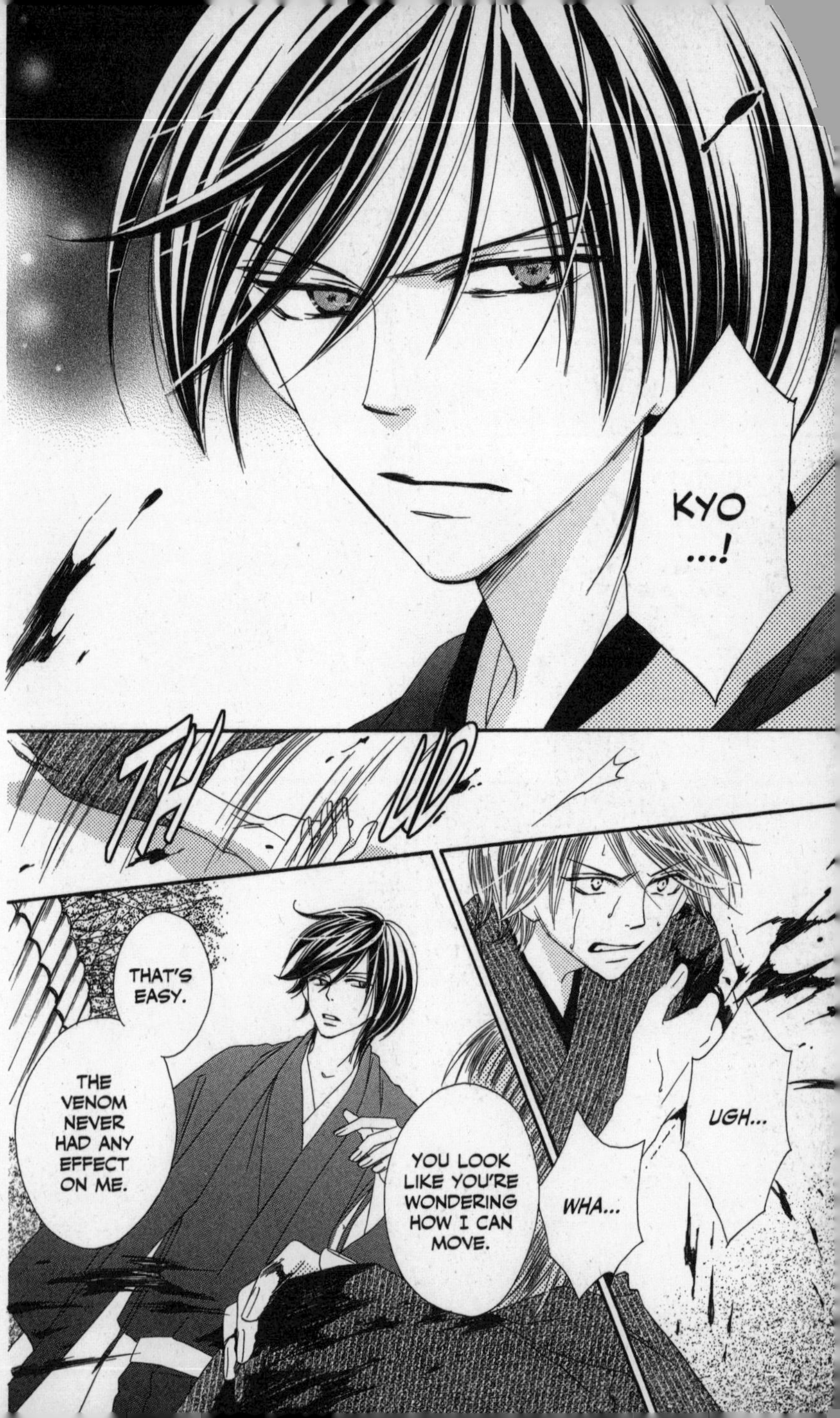
KYO ...!
THUD
UGH...
WHA...
YOU LOOK LIKE YOU'RE WONDERING HOW I CAN MOVE.
THAT'S EASY.
THE VENOM NEVER HAD ANY EFFECT ON ME.

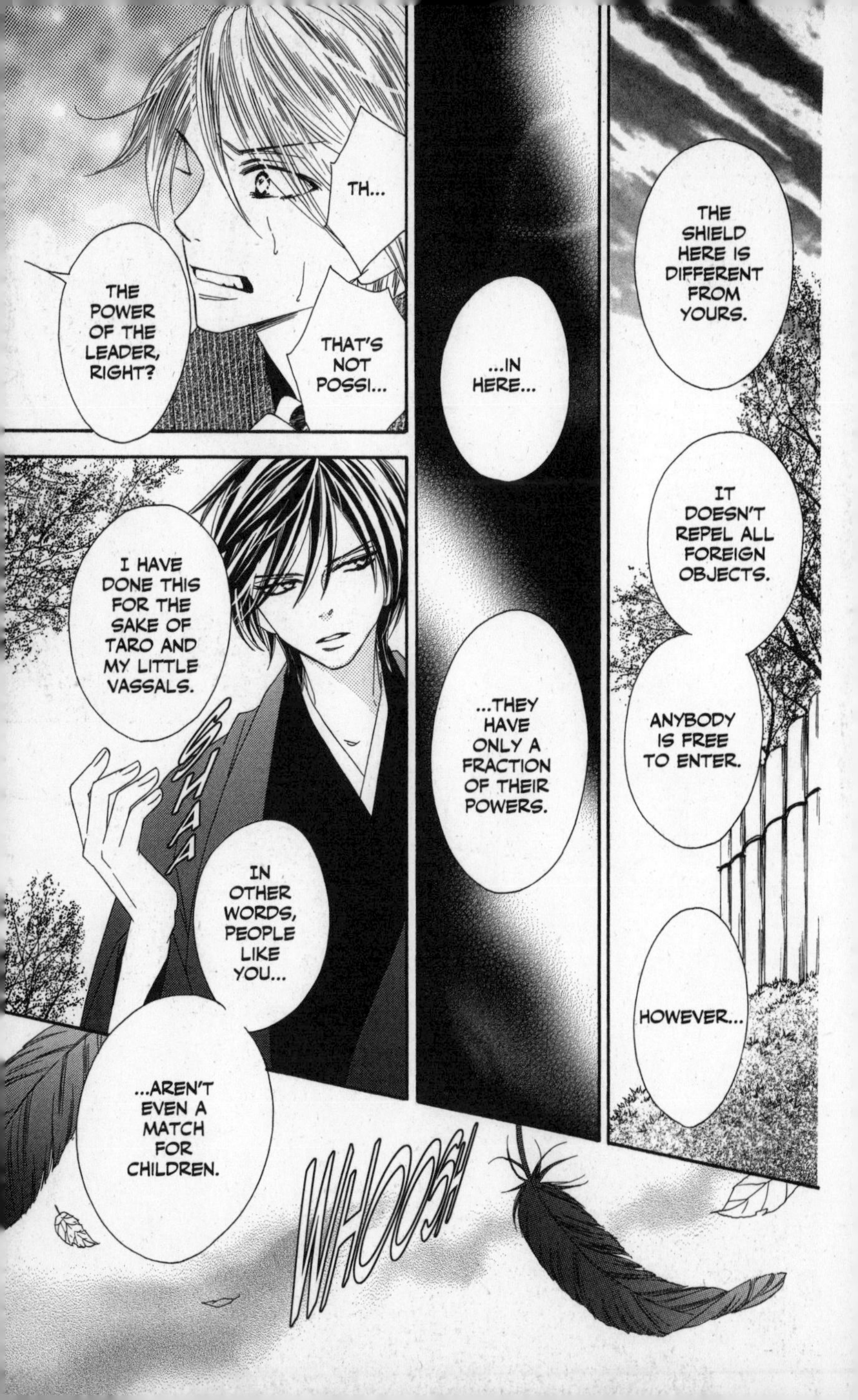
THE SHIELD HERE IS DIFFERENT FROM YOURS.
IT DOESN'T REPEL ALL FOREIGN OBJECTS.
ANYBODY IS FREE TO ENTER.
HOWEVER...
...IN HERE...
...THEY HAVE ONLY A FRACTION OF THEIR POWERS.
TH...
THAT'S NOT POSSI...
THE POWER OF THE LEADER, RIGHT?
I HAVE DONE THIS FOR THE SAKE OF TARO AND MY LITTLE VASSALS.
IN OTHER WORDS, PEOPLE LIKE YOU...
...AREN'T EVEN A MATCH FOR CHILDREN.
WHOOSH

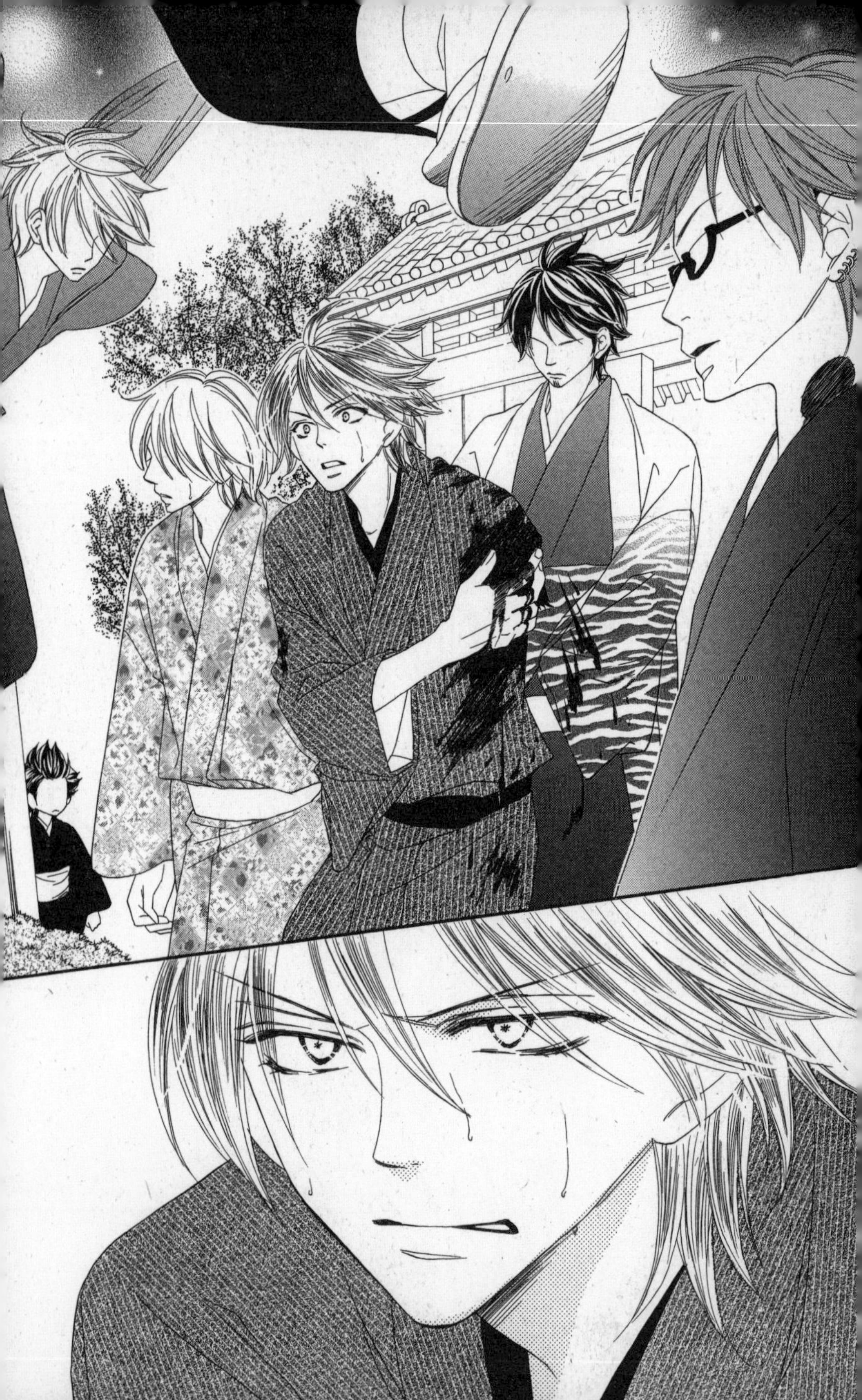

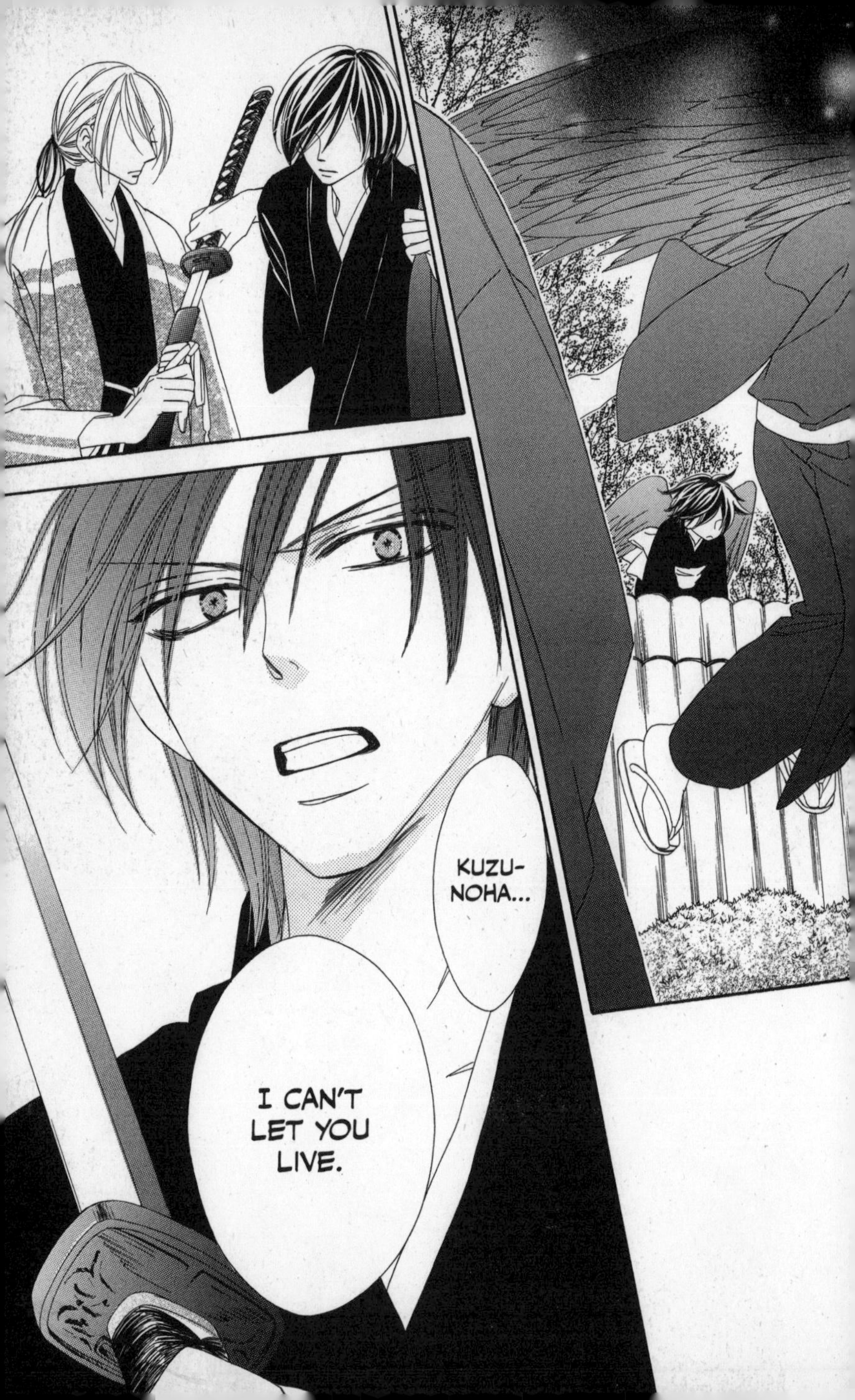
KUZU-
NOHA...
I CAN'T
LET YOU
LIVE.

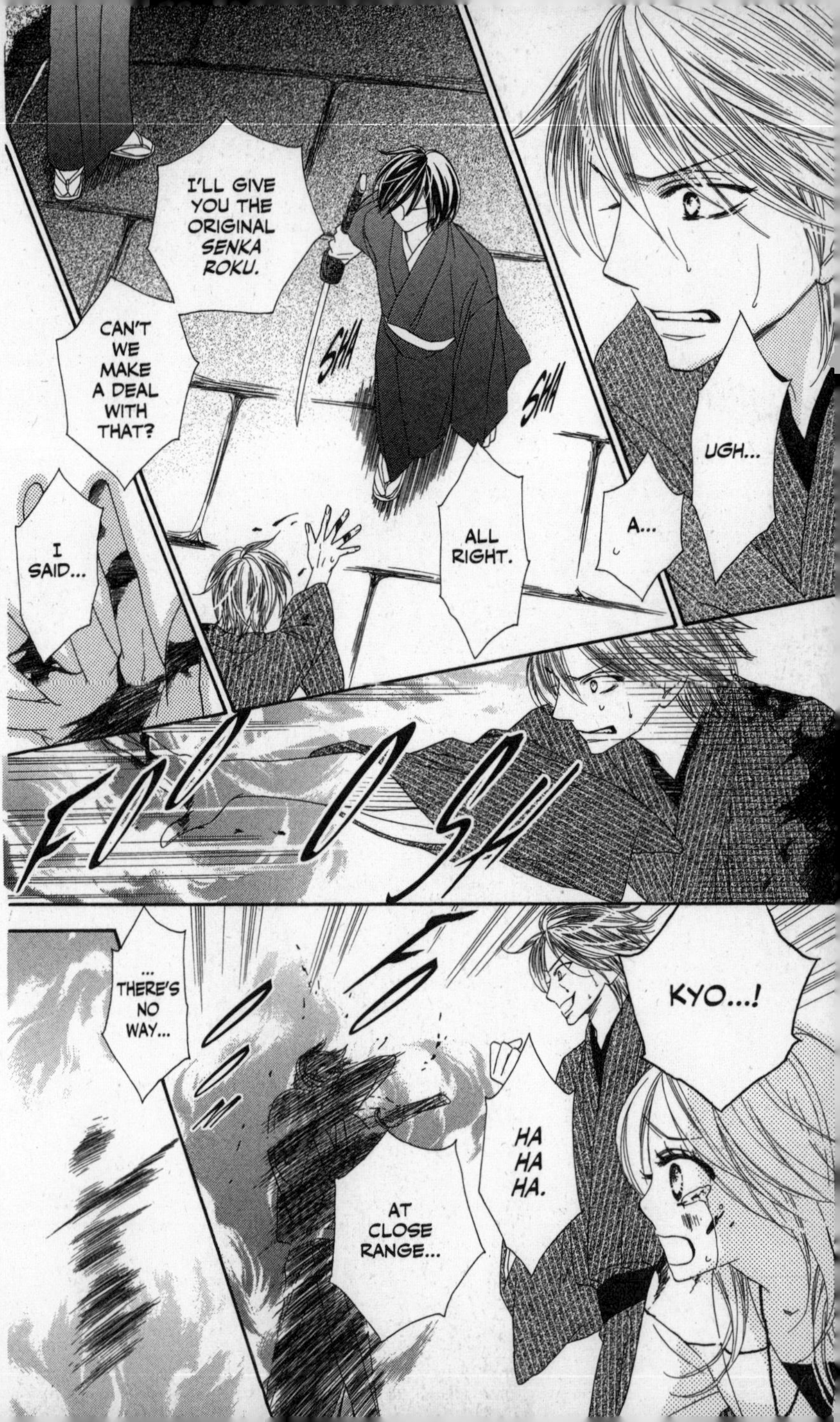
UGH...
A...
I'LL GIVE YOU THE ORIGINAL SENKA ROKU.
CAN'T WE MAKE A DEAL WITH THAT?
SHH
SHH
ALL RIGHT.
I SAID...
FWOOSH
KYO...!
HA HA HA.
...THERE'S NO WAY...
AT CLOSE RANGE...

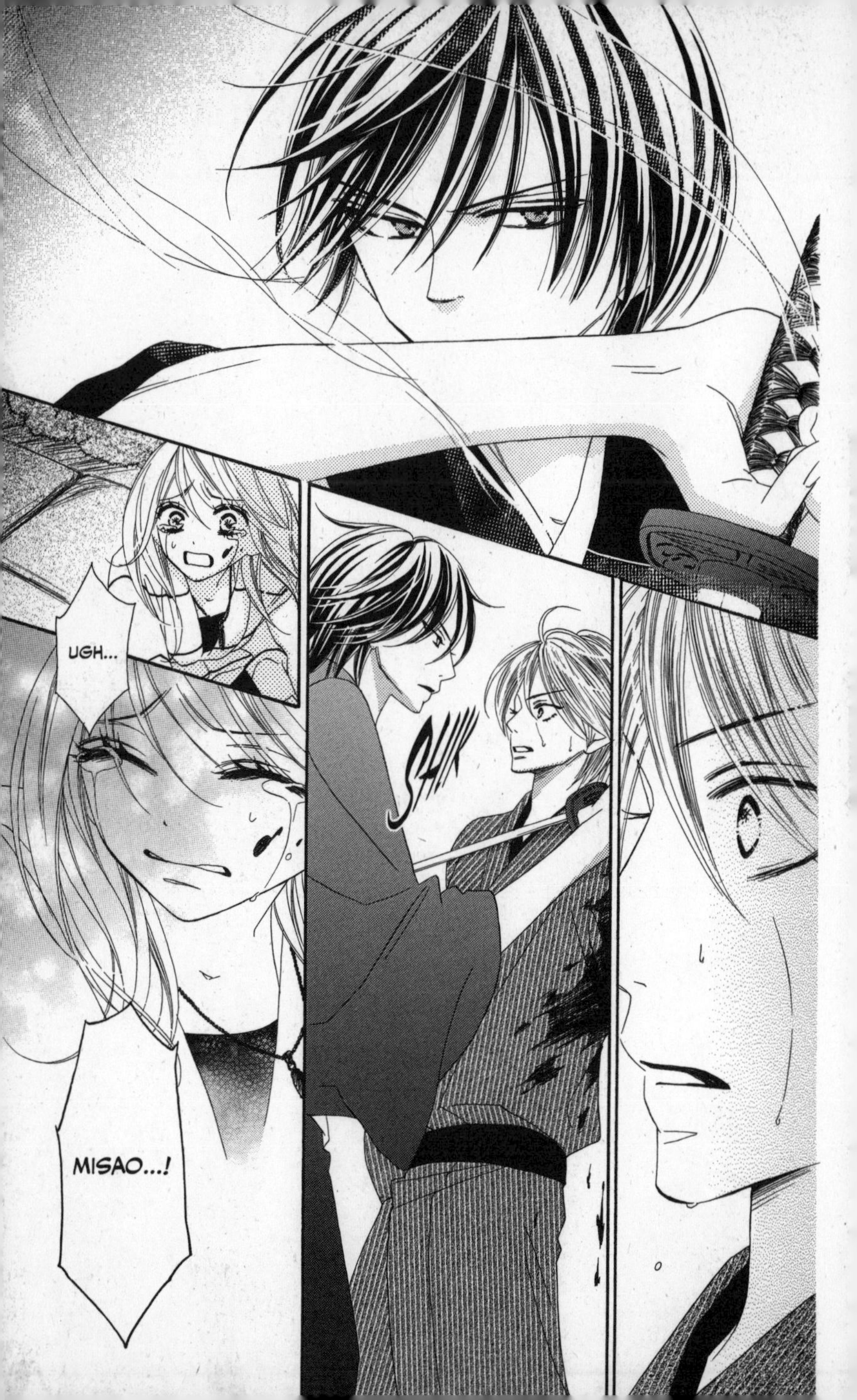
UGH...
MISAO...!

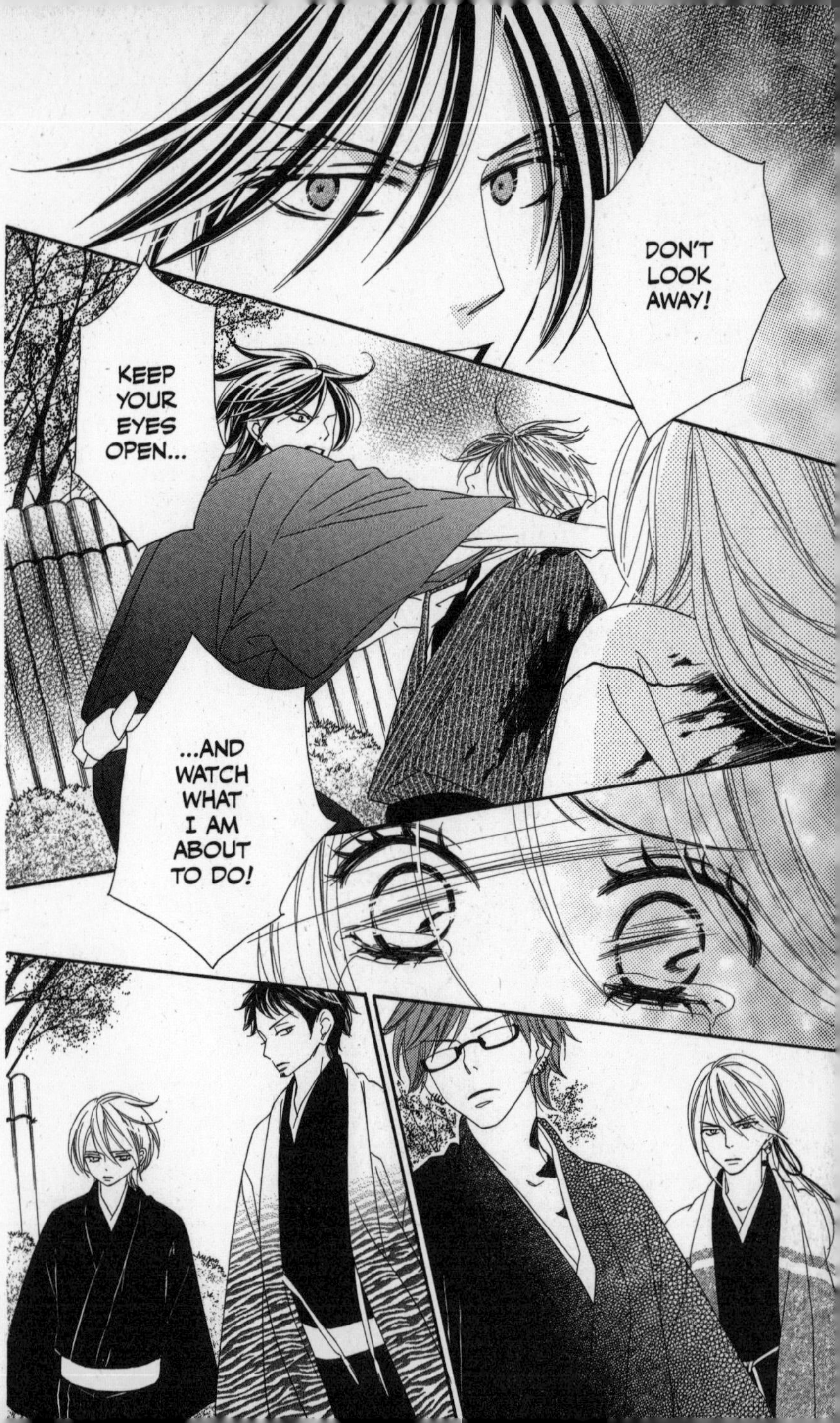
DON'T LOOK AWAY!
KEEP YOUR EYES OPEN...
...AND WATCH WHAT I AM ABOUT TO DO!

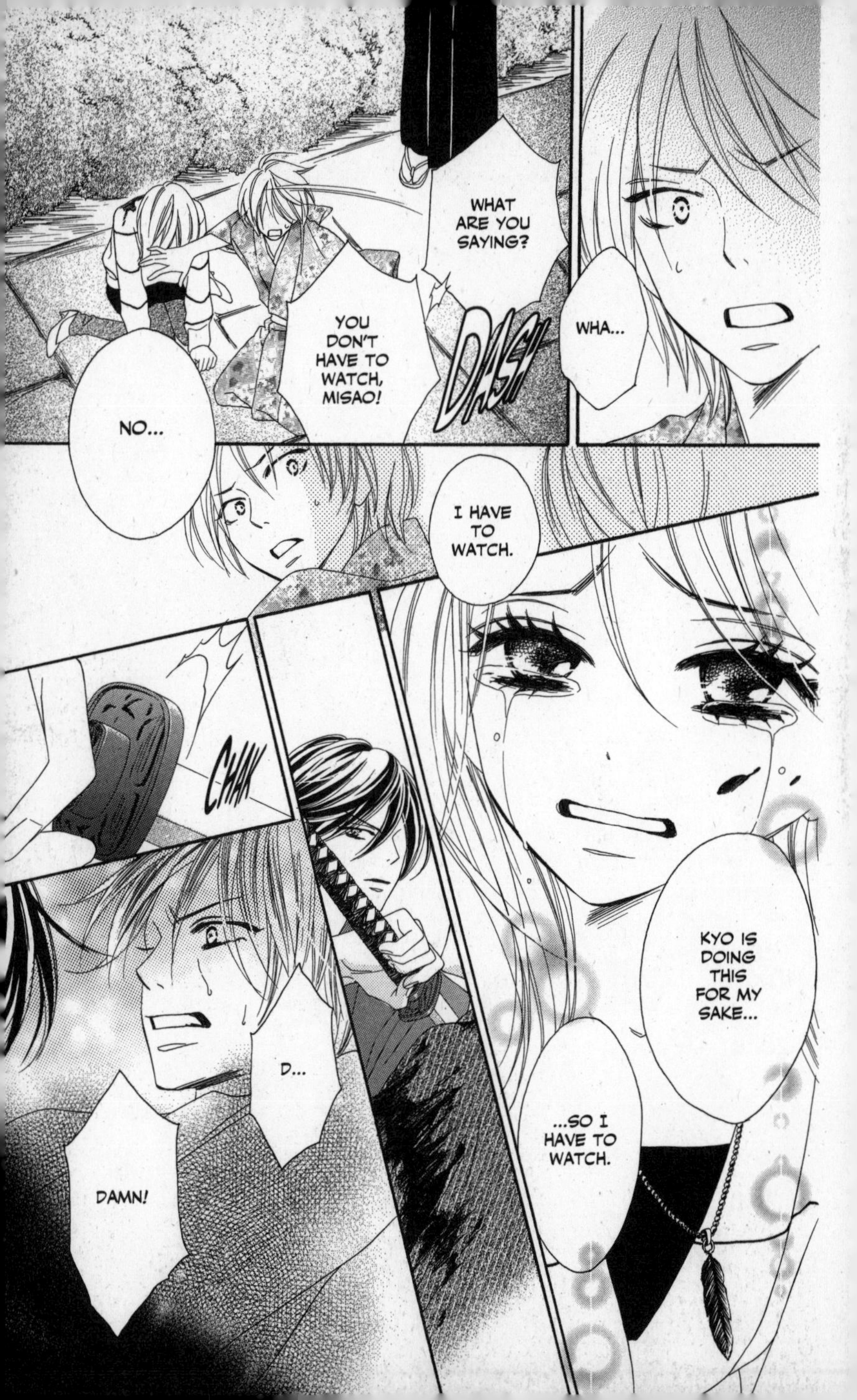
WHA...
WHAT ARE YOU SAYING?
DASH!
YOU DON'T HAVE TO WATCH, MISAO!
NO...
I HAVE TO WATCH.
KYO IS DOING THIS FOR MY SAKE...
...SO I HAVE TO WATCH.
CHAK
D...
DAMN!

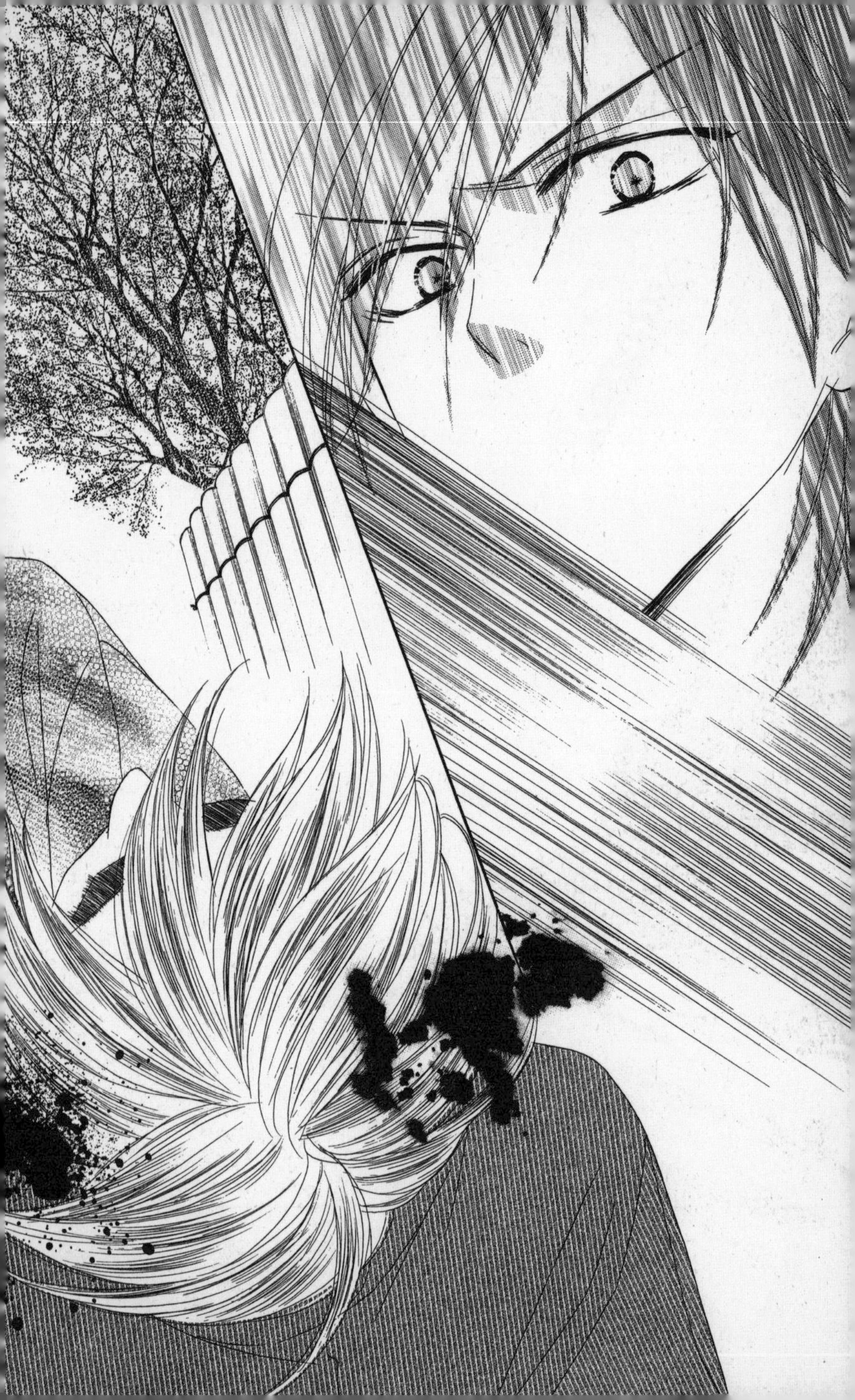

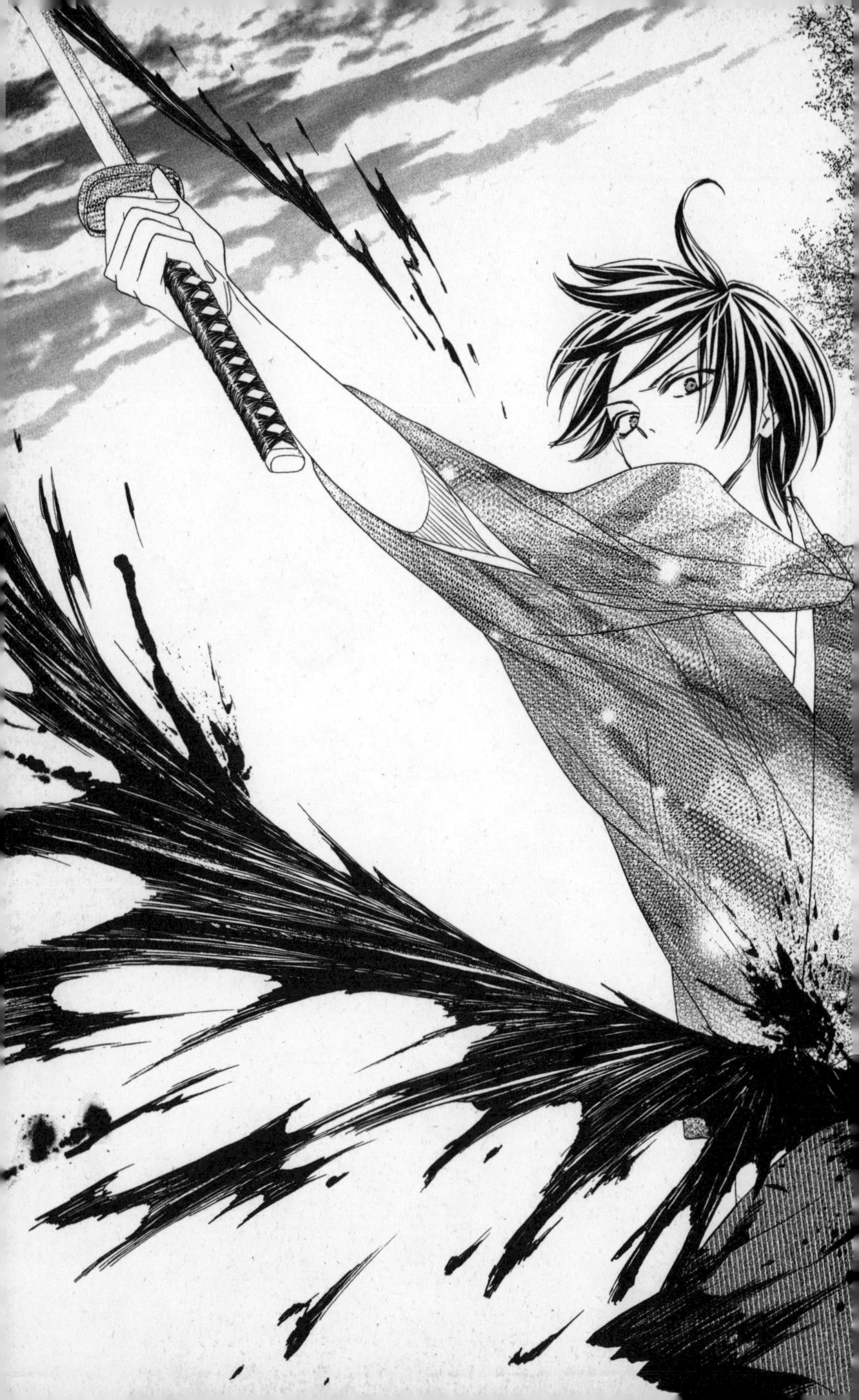

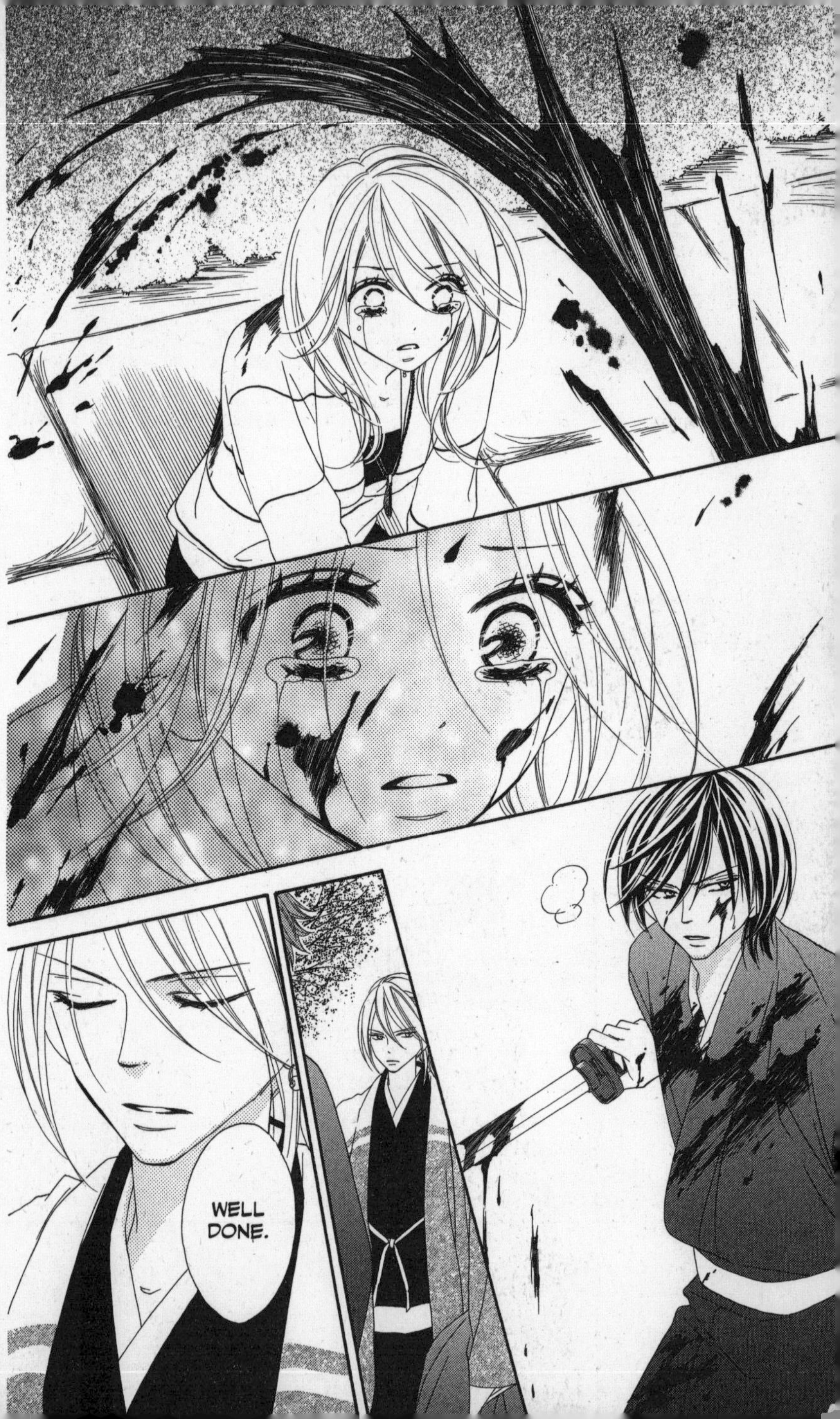
WELL DONE.

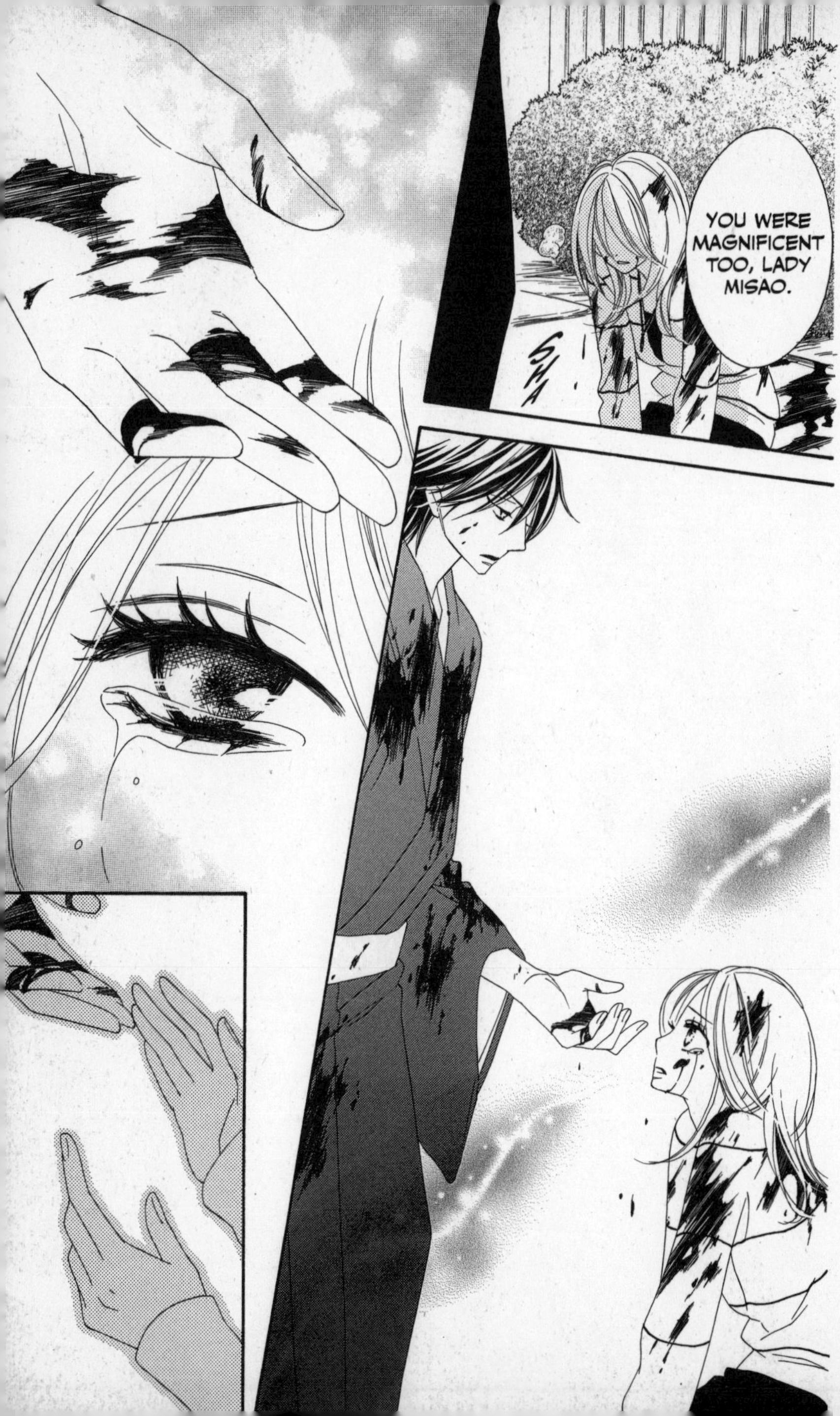
YOU WERE MAGNIFICENT TOO, LADY MISAO.
SHA

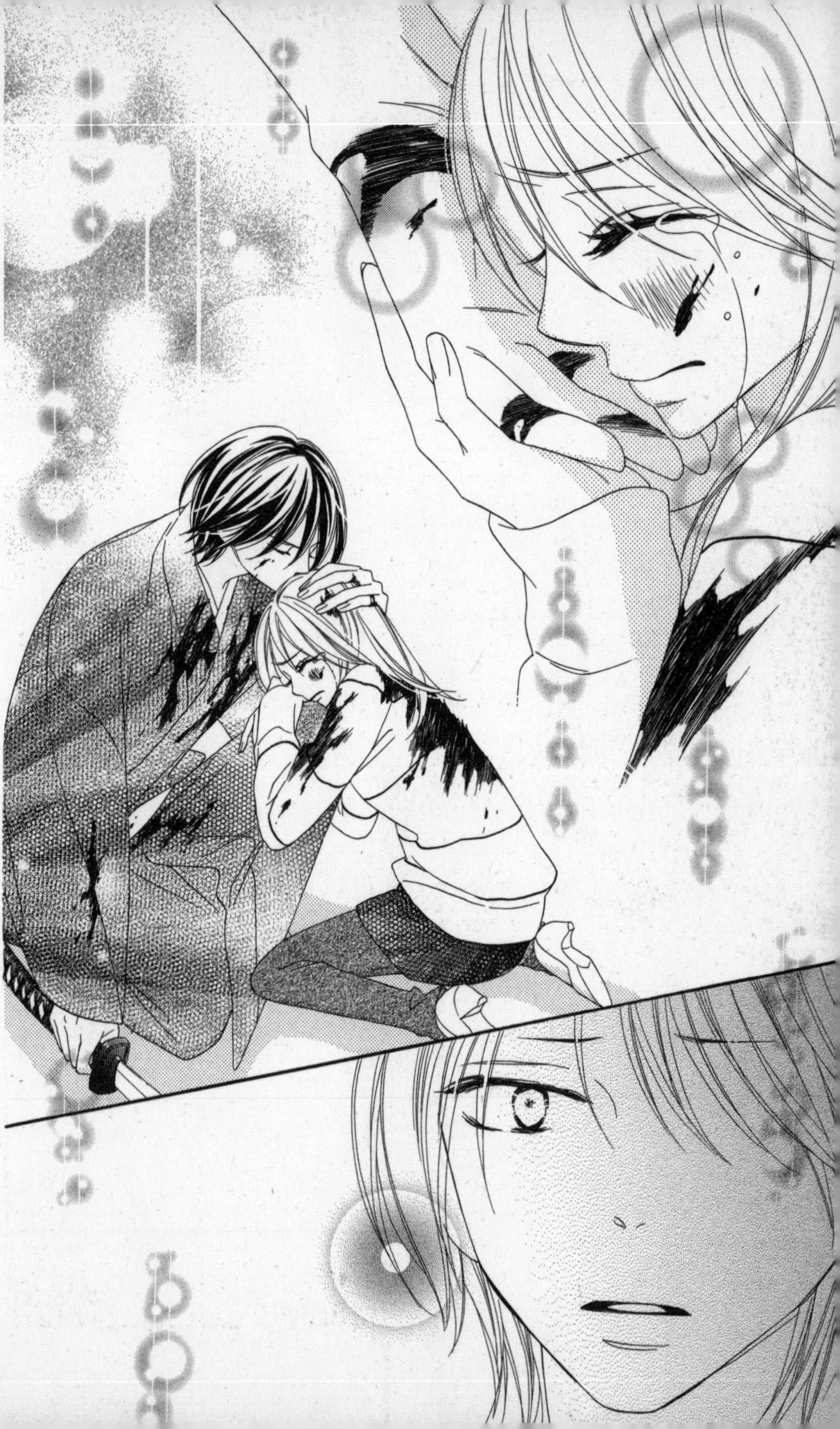

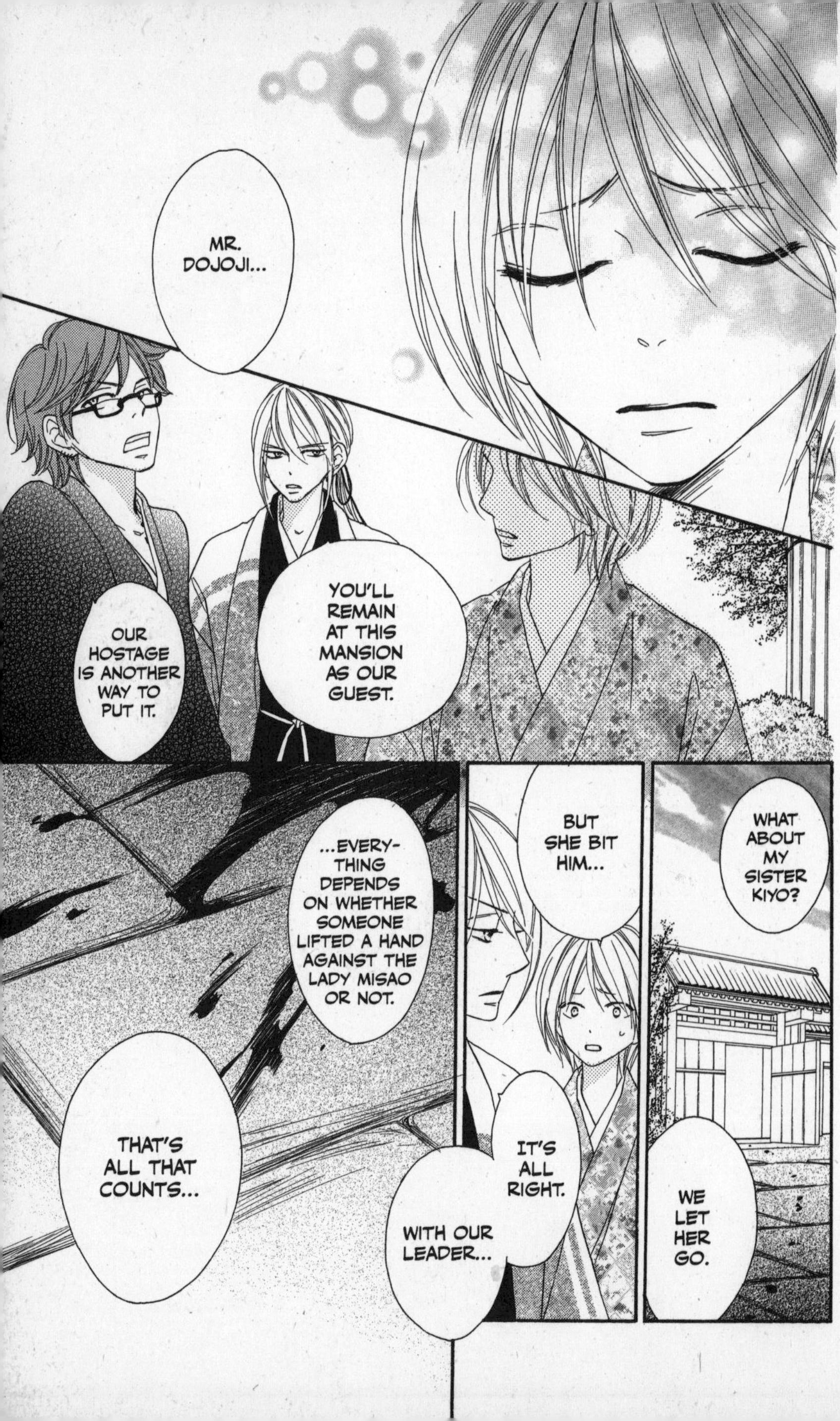
MR. DOJOJI...
YOU'LL REMAIN AT THIS MANSION AS OUR GUEST.
OUR HOSTAGE IS ANOTHER WAY TO PUT IT.
WHAT ABOUT MY SISTER KIYO?
WE LET HER GO.
BUT SHE BIT HIM...
IT'S ALL RIGHT.
WITH OUR LEADER...
...EVERY-THING DEPENDS ON WHETHER SOMEONE LIFTED A HAND AGAINST THE LADY MISAO OR NOT.
THAT'S ALL THAT COUNTS...

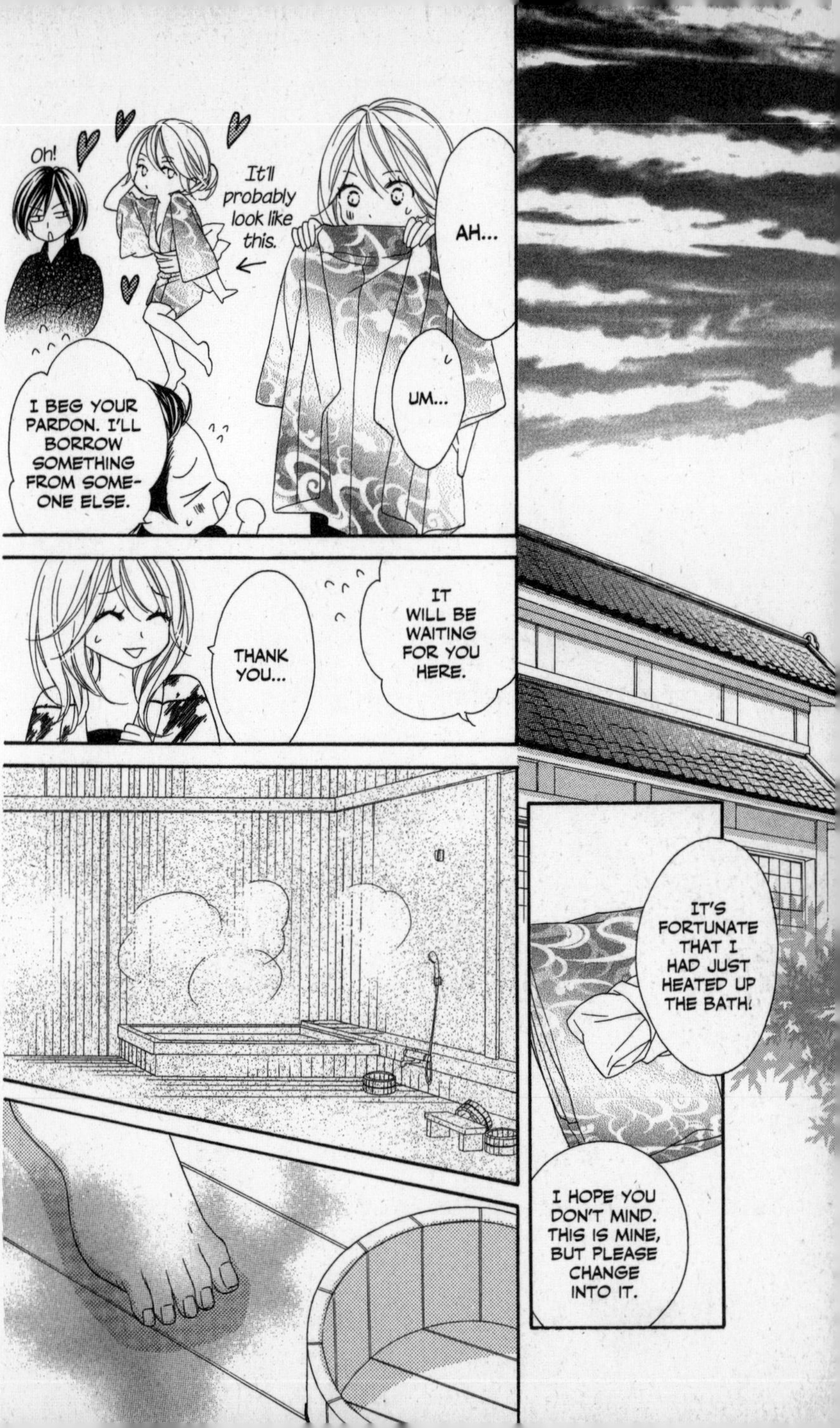
IT'S FORTUNATE THAT I HAD JUST HEATED UP THE BATH!
I HOPE YOU DON'T MIND. THIS IS MINE, BUT PLEASE CHANGE INTO IT.
AH...
UM...
It'll probably look like this.
Oh!
I BEG YOUR PARDON. I'LL BORROW SOMETHING FROM SOME-ONE ELSE.
IT WILL BE WAITING FOR YOU HERE.
THANK YOU...

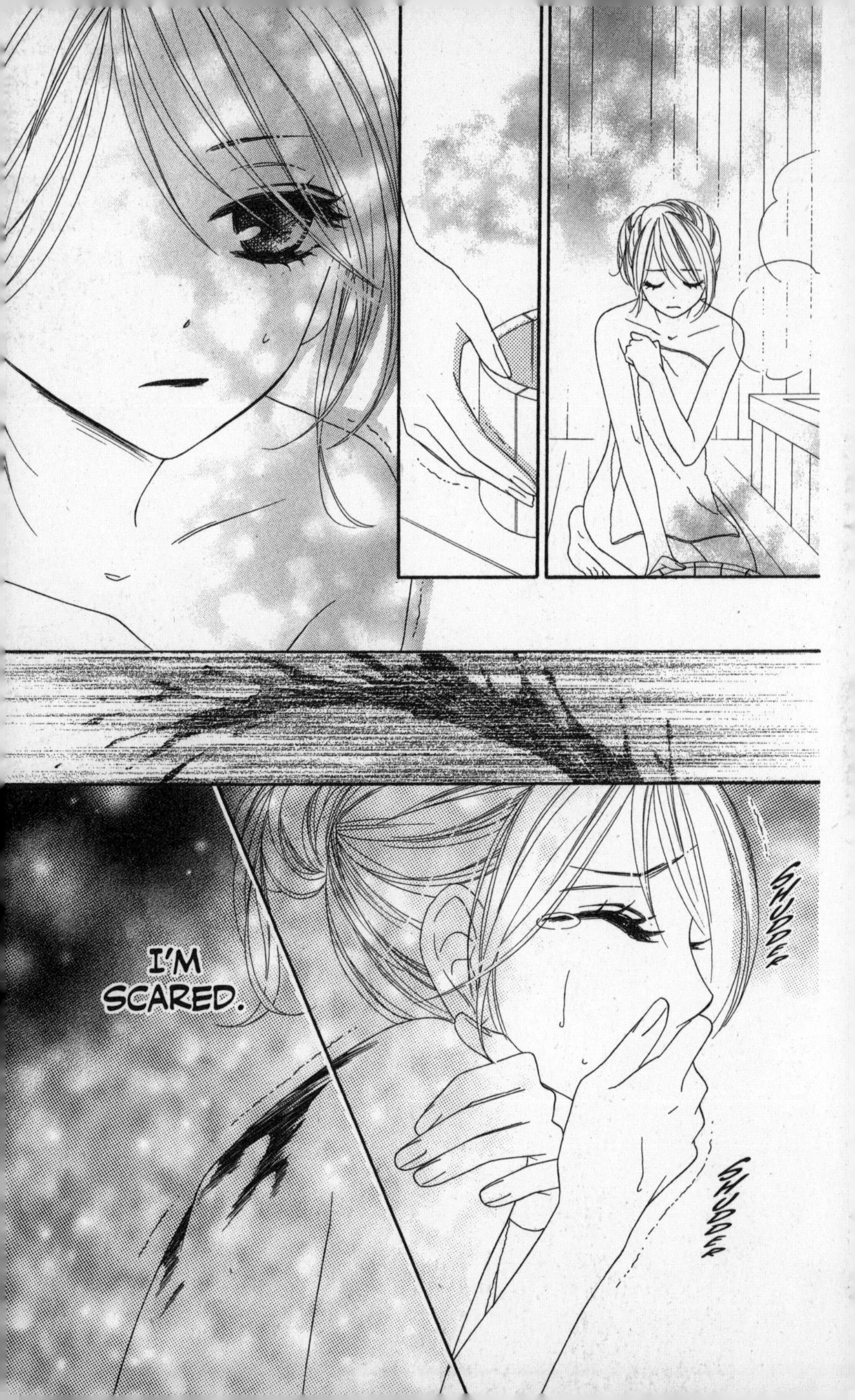
SHUDDER
SHUDDER
I'M SCARED.

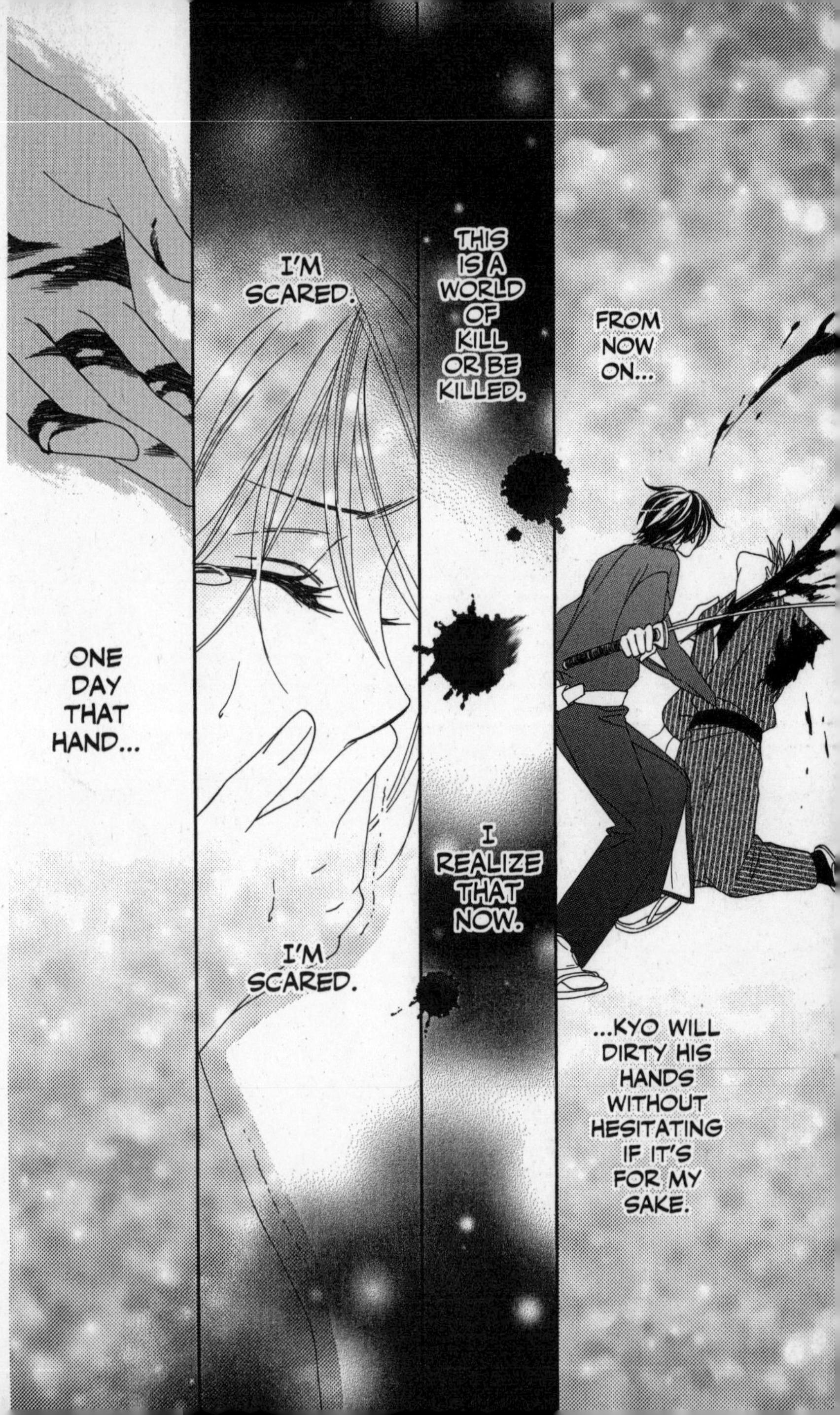
FROM NOW ON...
...KYO WILL DIRTY HIS HANDS WITHOUT HESITATING IF IT'S FOR MY SAKE.
THIS IS A WORLD OF KILL OR BE KILLED.
I REALIZE THAT NOW.
I'M SCARED.
I'M SCARED.
ONE DAY THAT HAND...

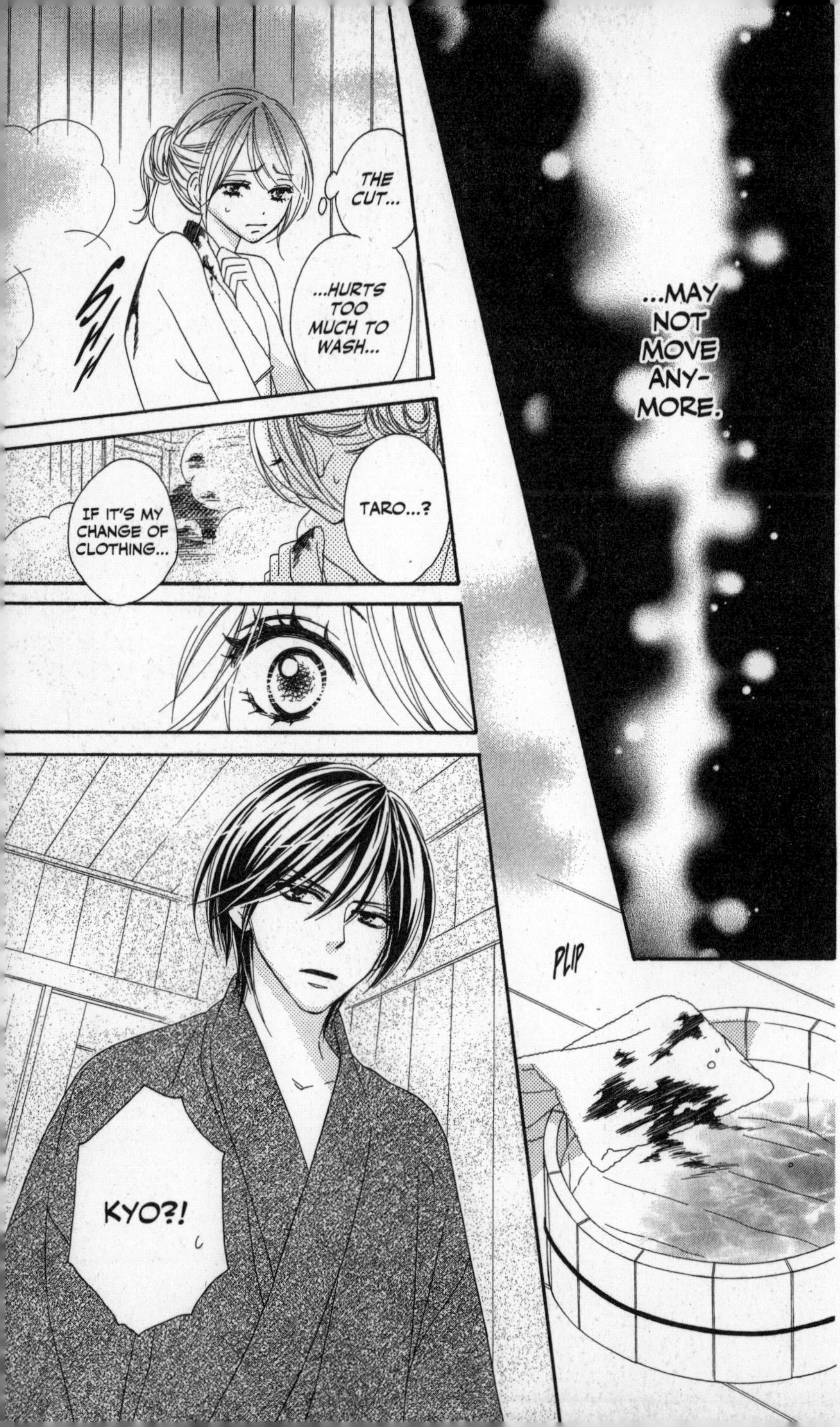
...MAY NOT MOVE ANYMORE.
PLIP
THE CUT...
...HURTS TOO MUCH TO WASH...
SHH
TARO...?
IF IT'S MY CHANGE OF CLOTHING...
KYO?!

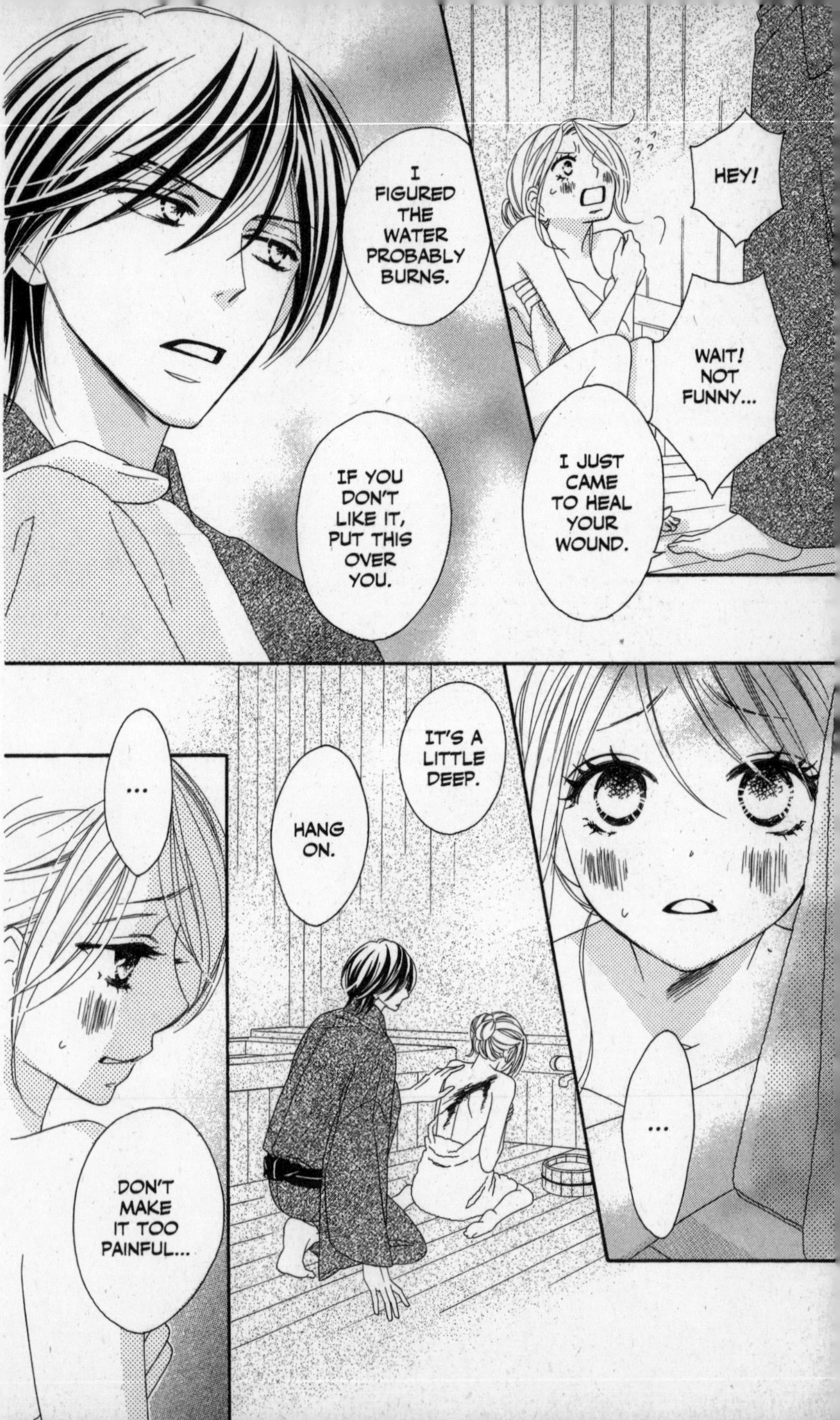
HEY!
WAIT! NOT FUNNY...
I JUST CAME TO HEAL YOUR WOUND.
I FIGURED THE WATER PROBABLY BURNS.
IF YOU DON'T LIKE IT, PUT THIS OVER YOU.
...
IT'S A LITTLE DEEP.
HANG ON.
...
DON'T MAKE IT TOO PAINFUL...

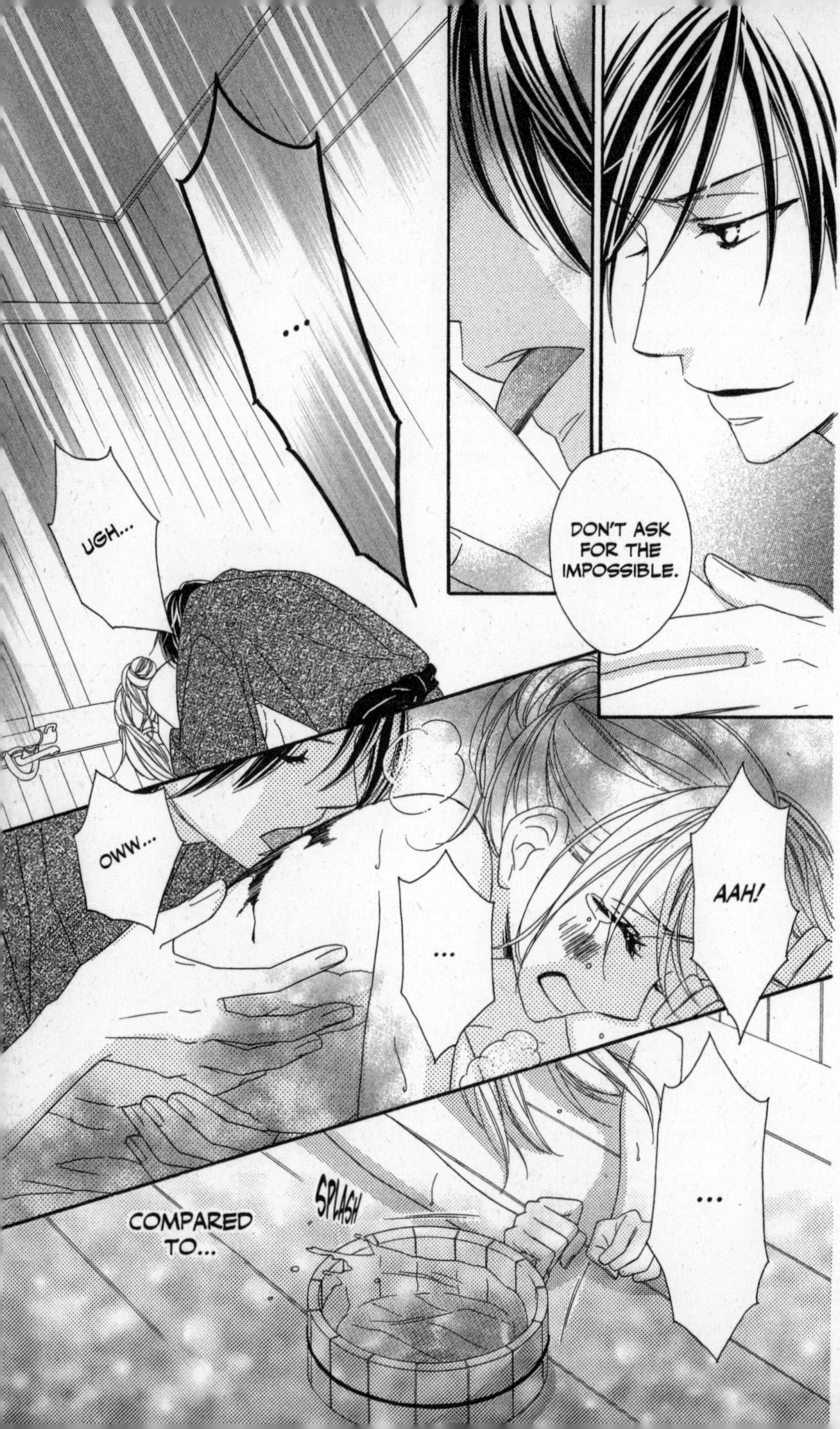
DON'T ASK FOR THE IMPOSSIBLE.
...
UGH...
AAH!
...
OWW...
...
SPLASH
COMPARED TO...

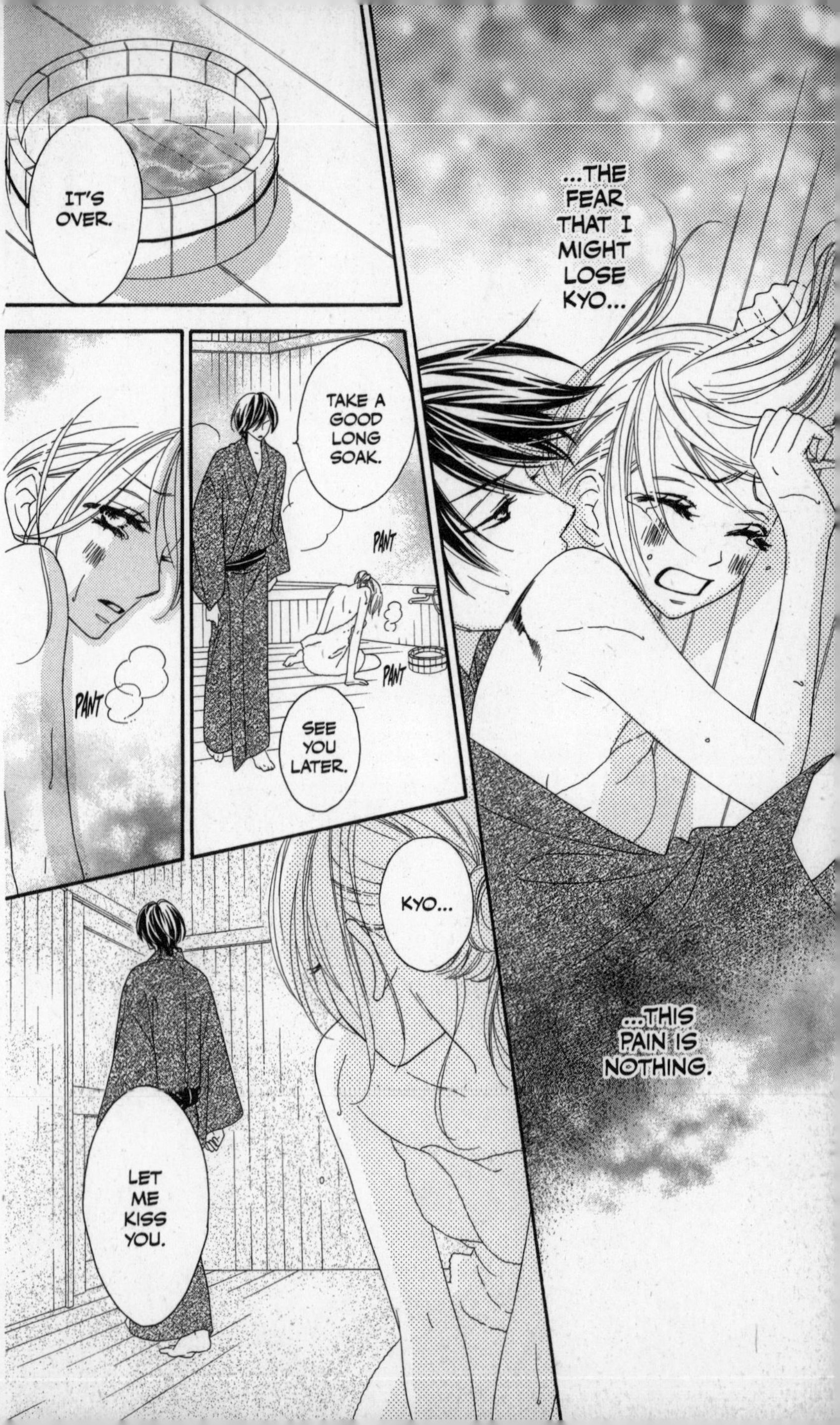
...THE FEAR THAT I MIGHT LOSE KYO...
...THIS PAIN IS NOTHING.
IT'S OVER.
TAKE A GOOD LONG SOAK.
PANT
PANT
SEE YOU LATER.
PANT
KYO...
LET ME KISS YOU.

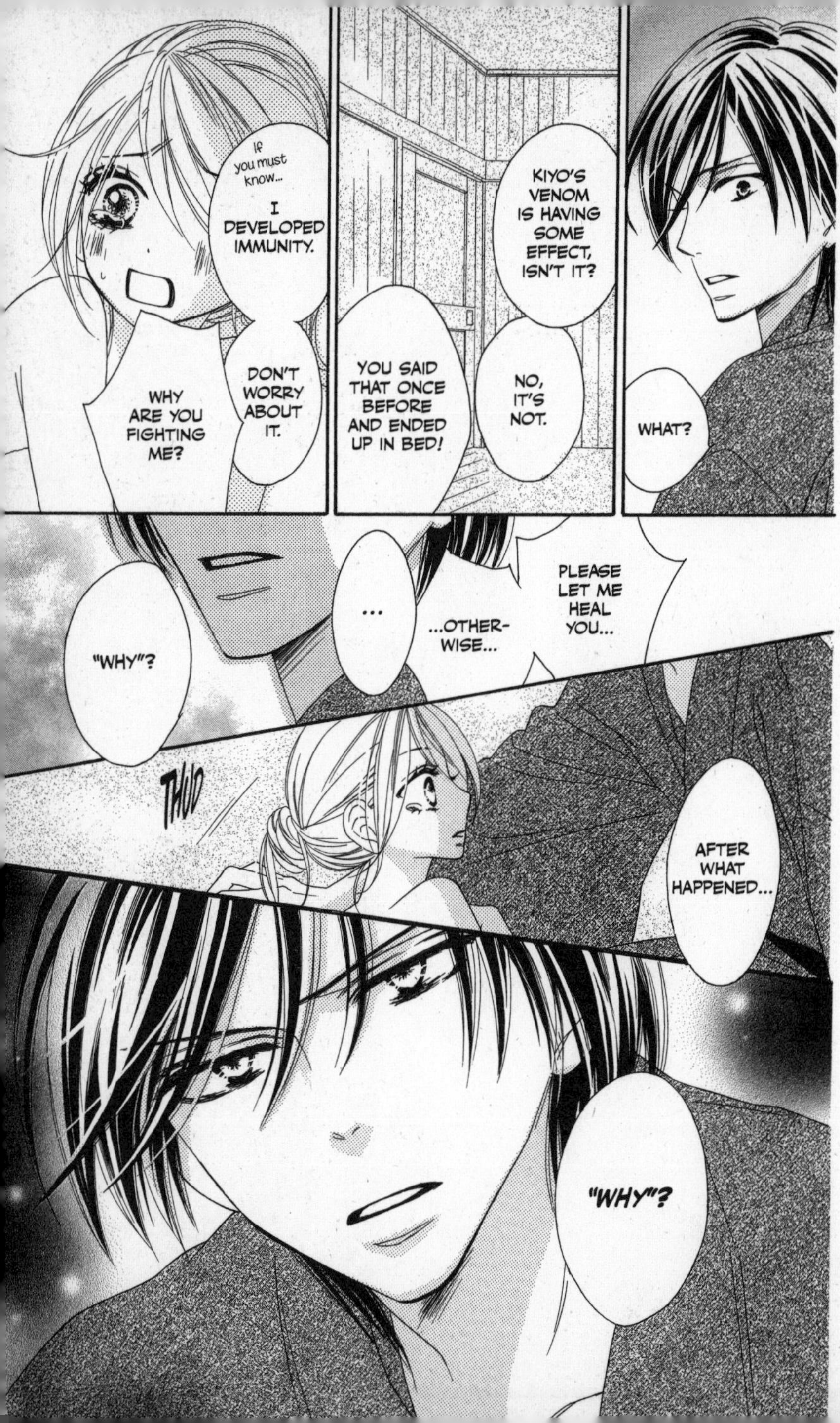
WHAT?
KIYO'S VENOM IS HAVING SOME EFFECT, ISN'T IT?
NO, IT'S NOT.
YOU SAID THAT ONCE BEFORE AND ENDED UP IN BED!
If you must know...
I DEVELOPED IMMUNITY.
DON'T WORRY ABOUT IT.
WHY ARE YOU FIGHTING ME?
PLEASE LET ME HEAL YOU...
...OTHER-WISE...
...
"WHY"?
AFTER WHAT HAPPENED...
THUD
"WHY"?

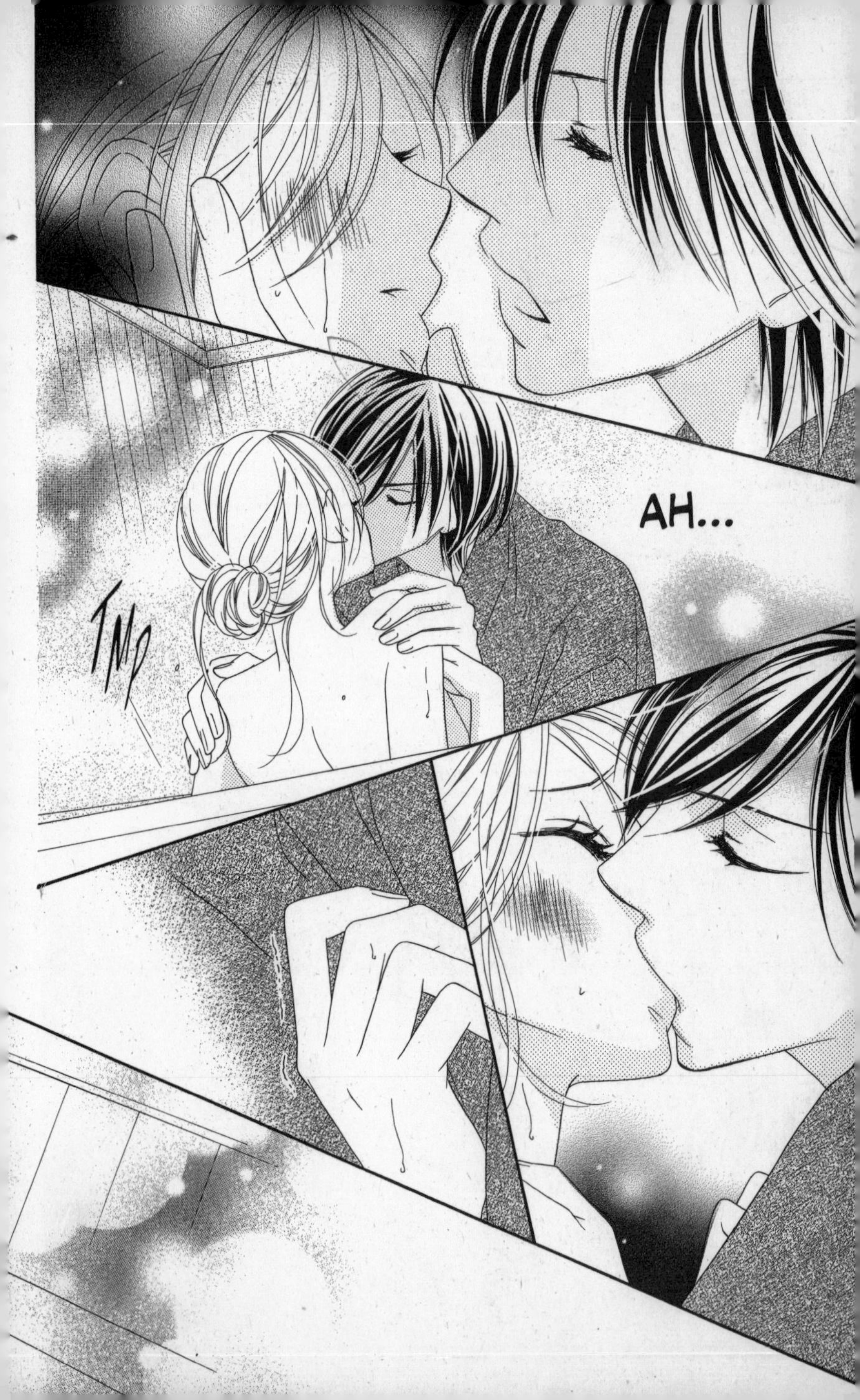
AH...
TMP

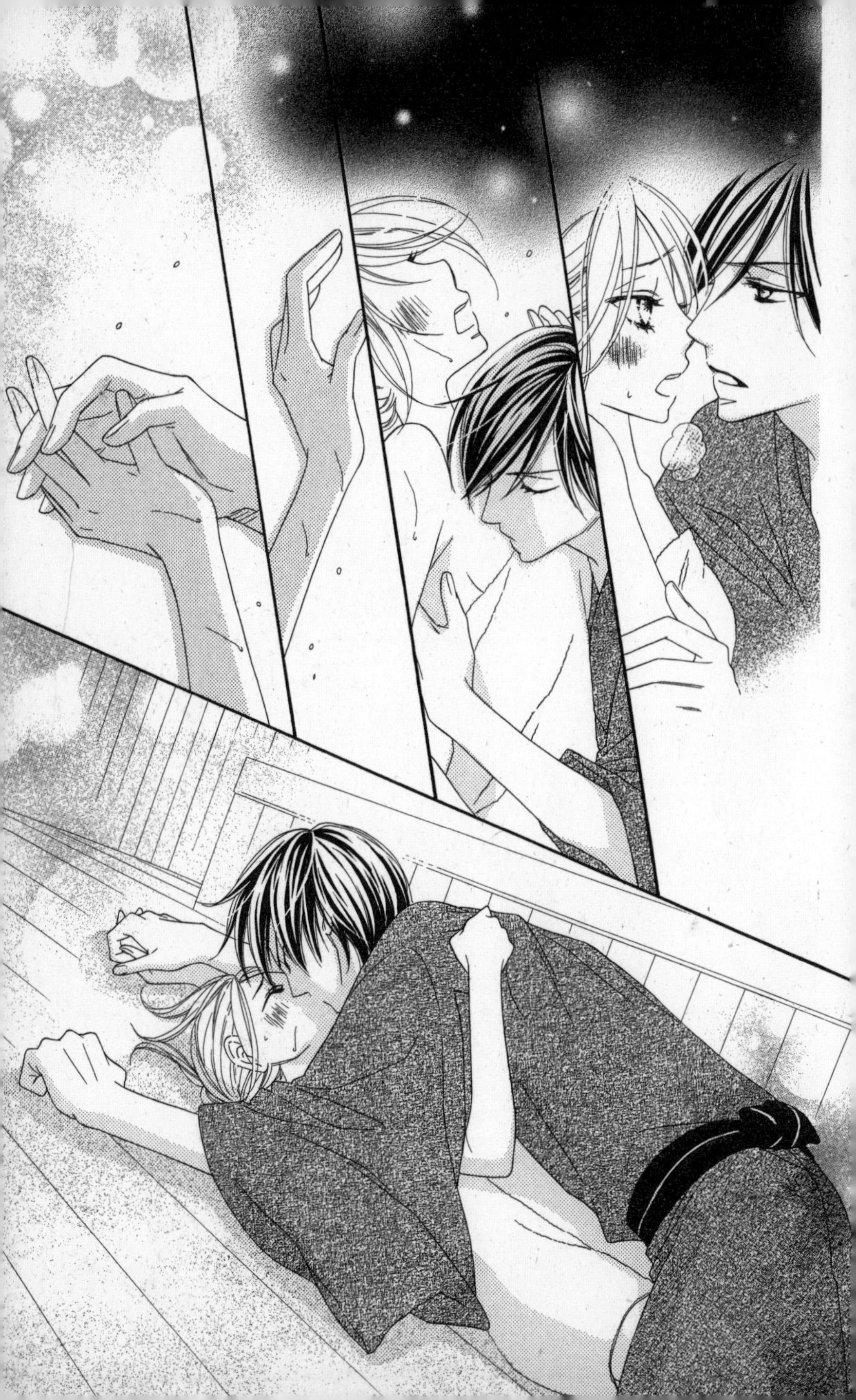

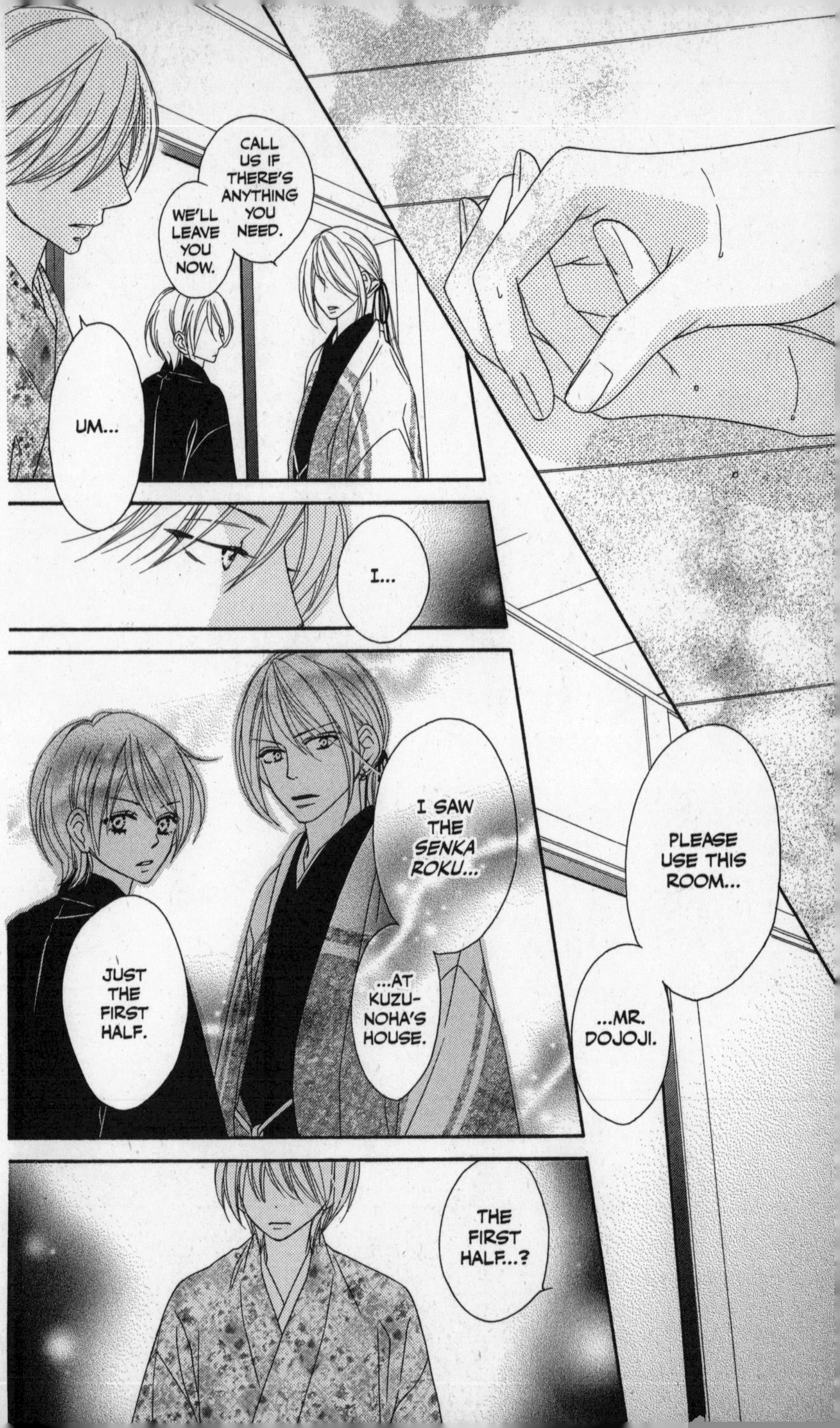
PLEASE USE THIS ROOM...
...MR. DOJOJI.
CALL US IF THERE'S ANYTHING YOU NEED.
WE'LL LEAVE YOU NOW.
UM...
I...
I SAW THE SENKA ROKU...
...AT KUZUNOHA'S HOUSE.
JUST THE FIRST HALF.
THE FIRST HALF...?

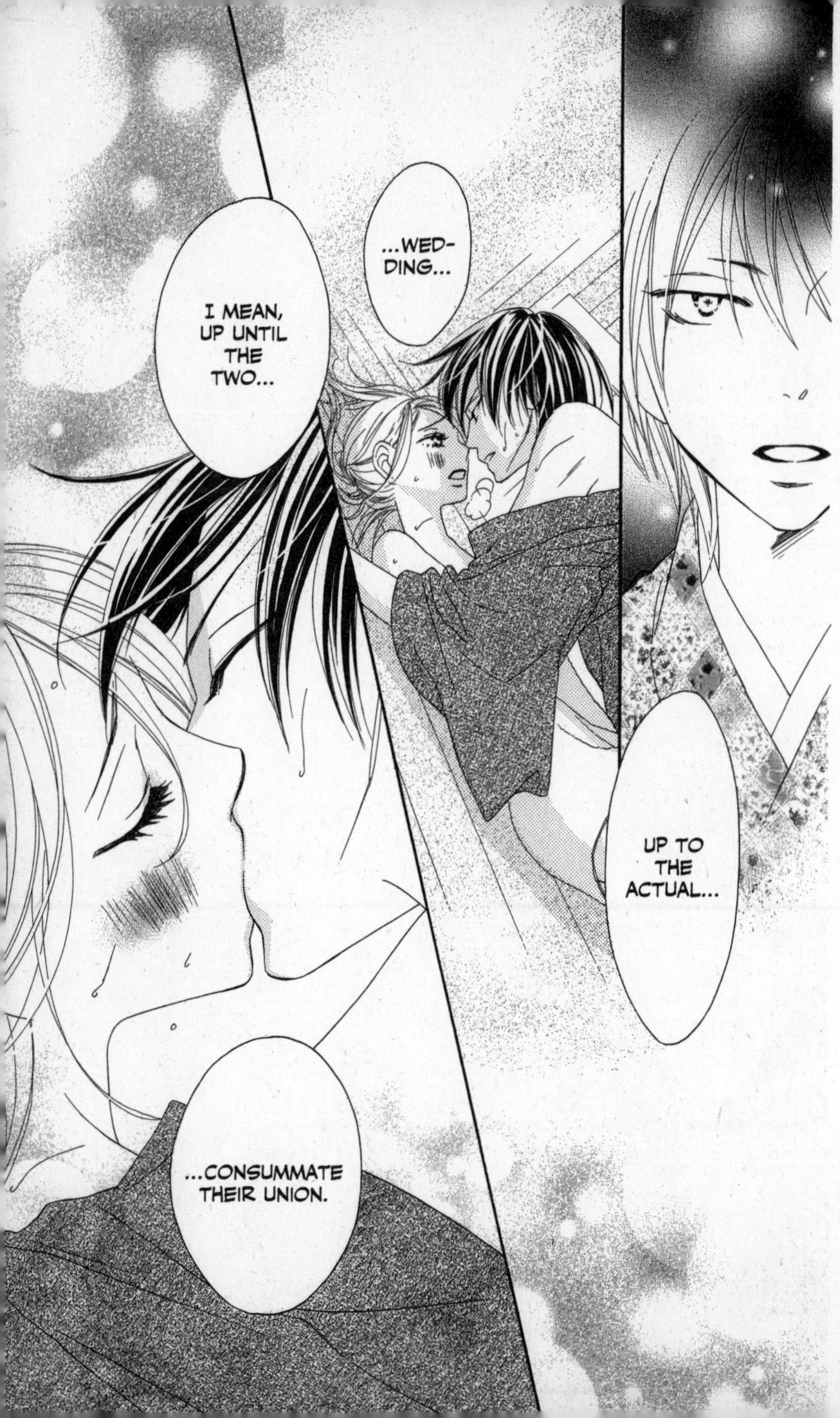
UP TO THE ACTUAL...
...WED-DING...
I MEAN, UP UNTIL THE TWO...
...CONSUMMATE THEIR UNION.

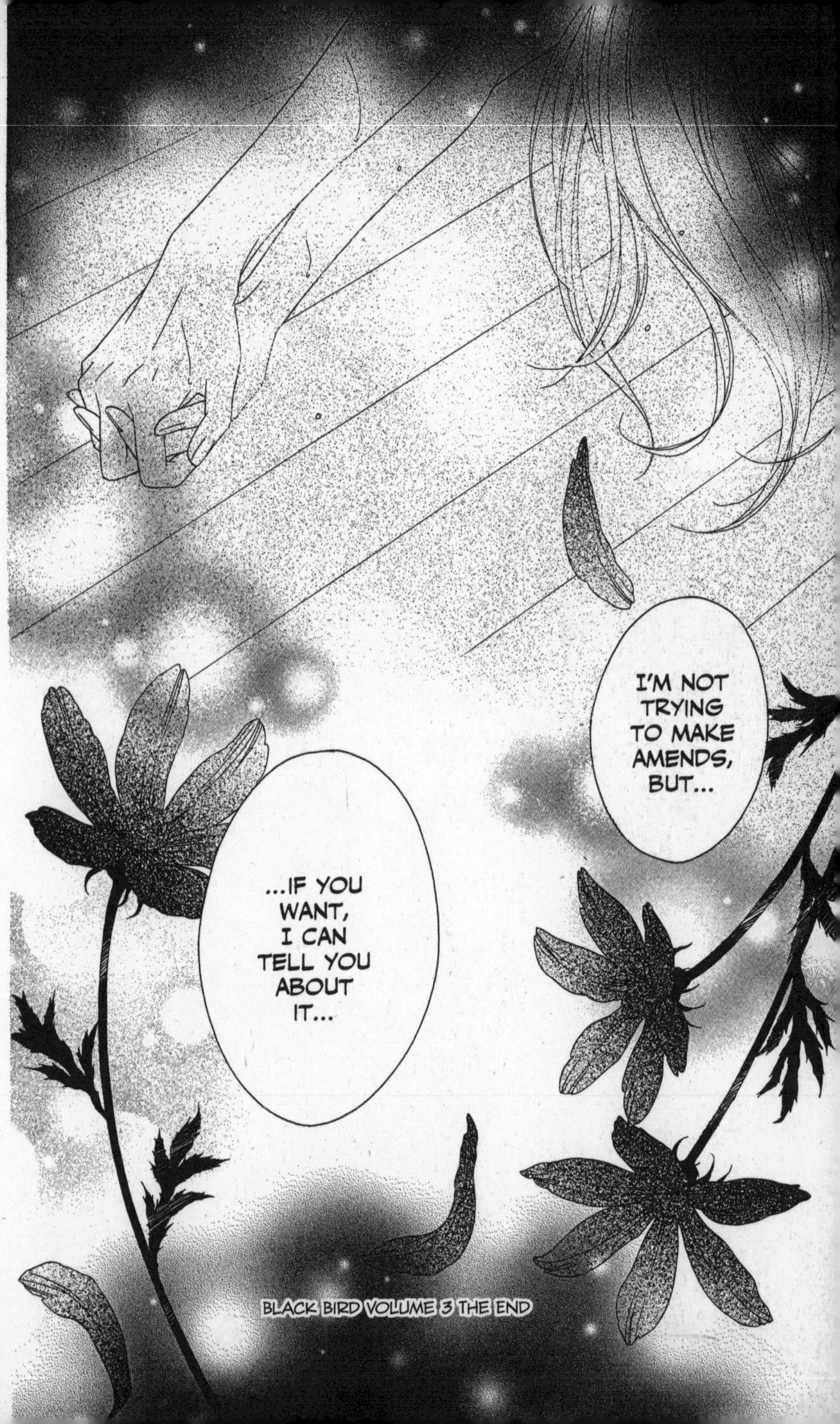
I'M NOT TRYING TO MAKE AMENDS, BUT...
...IF YOU WANT, I CAN TELL YOU ABOUT IT...
BLACK BIRD VOLUME 3 THE END

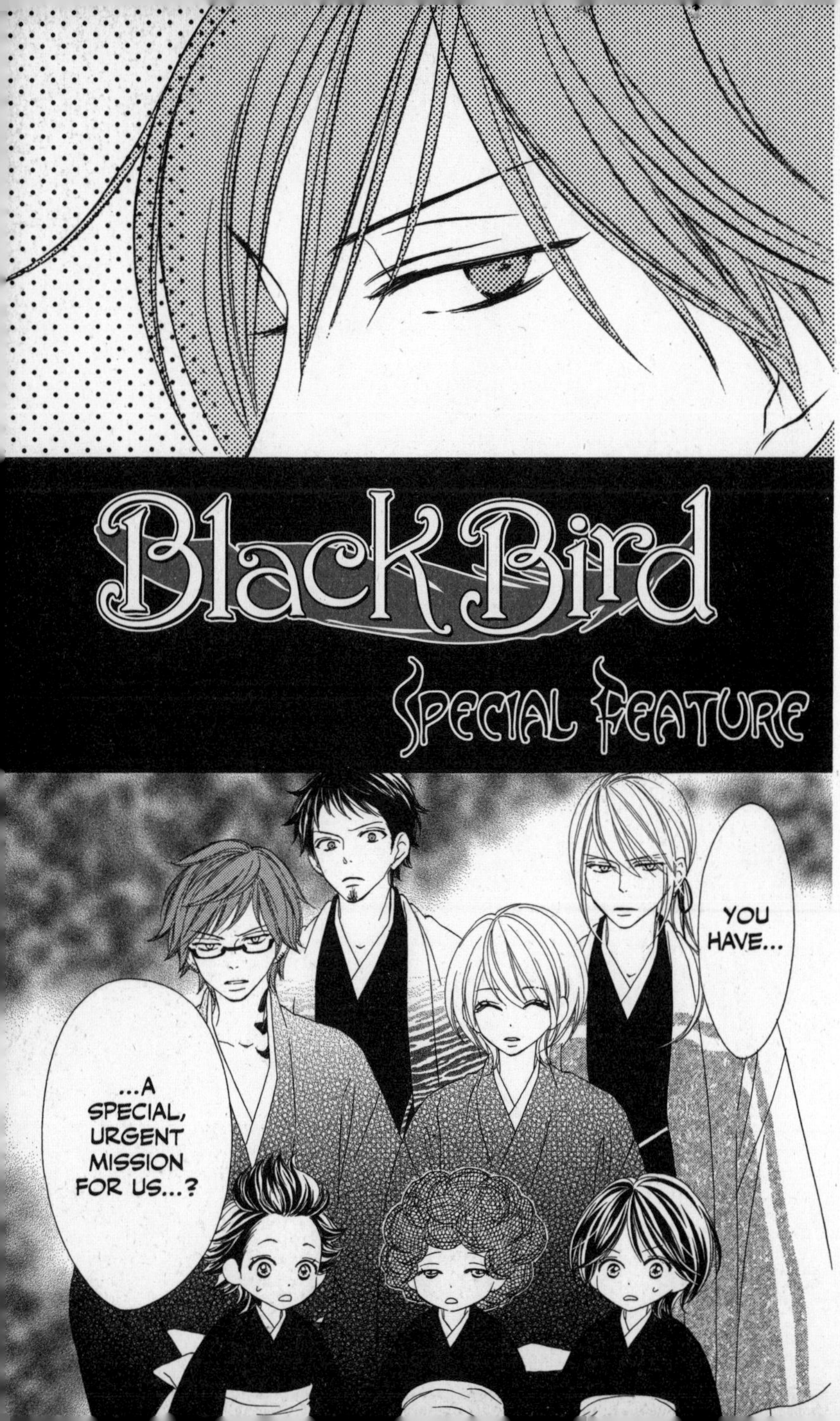
Black Bird
Special Feature
YOU HAVE...
...A SPECIAL, URGENT MISSION FOR US...?

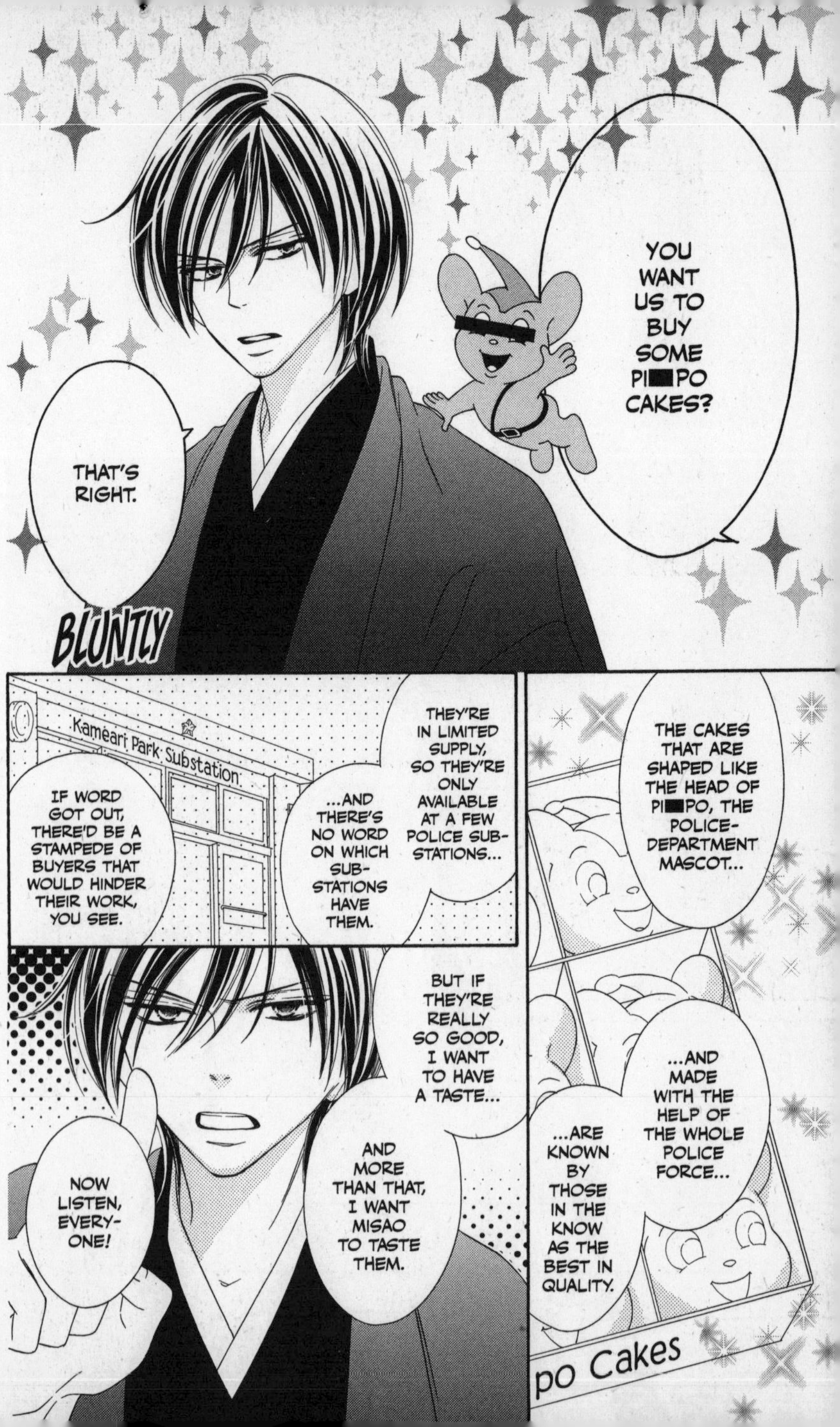
YOU WANT US TO BUY SOME PI[redacted]PO CAKES?
THAT'S RIGHT.
BLUNTLY
THE CAKES THAT ARE SHAPED LIKE THE HEAD OF PI[redacted]PO, THE POLICE-DEPARTMENT MASCOT...
...AND MADE WITH THE HELP OF THE WHOLE POLICE FORCE...
...ARE KNOWN BY THOSE IN THE KNOW AS THE BEST IN QUALITY.
po Cakes
Kameari Park Substation
THEY'RE IN LIMITED SUPPLY, SO THEY'RE ONLY AVAILABLE AT A FEW POLICE SUB-STATIONS...
...AND THERE'S NO WORD ON WHICH SUB-STATIONS HAVE THEM.
IF WORD GOT OUT, THERE'D BE A STAMPEDE OF BUYERS THAT WOULD HINDER THEIR WORK, YOU SEE.
BUT IF THEY'RE REALLY SO GOOD, I WANT TO HAVE A TASTE...
AND MORE THAN THAT, I WANT MISAO TO TASTE THEM.
NOW LISTEN, EVERY-ONE!

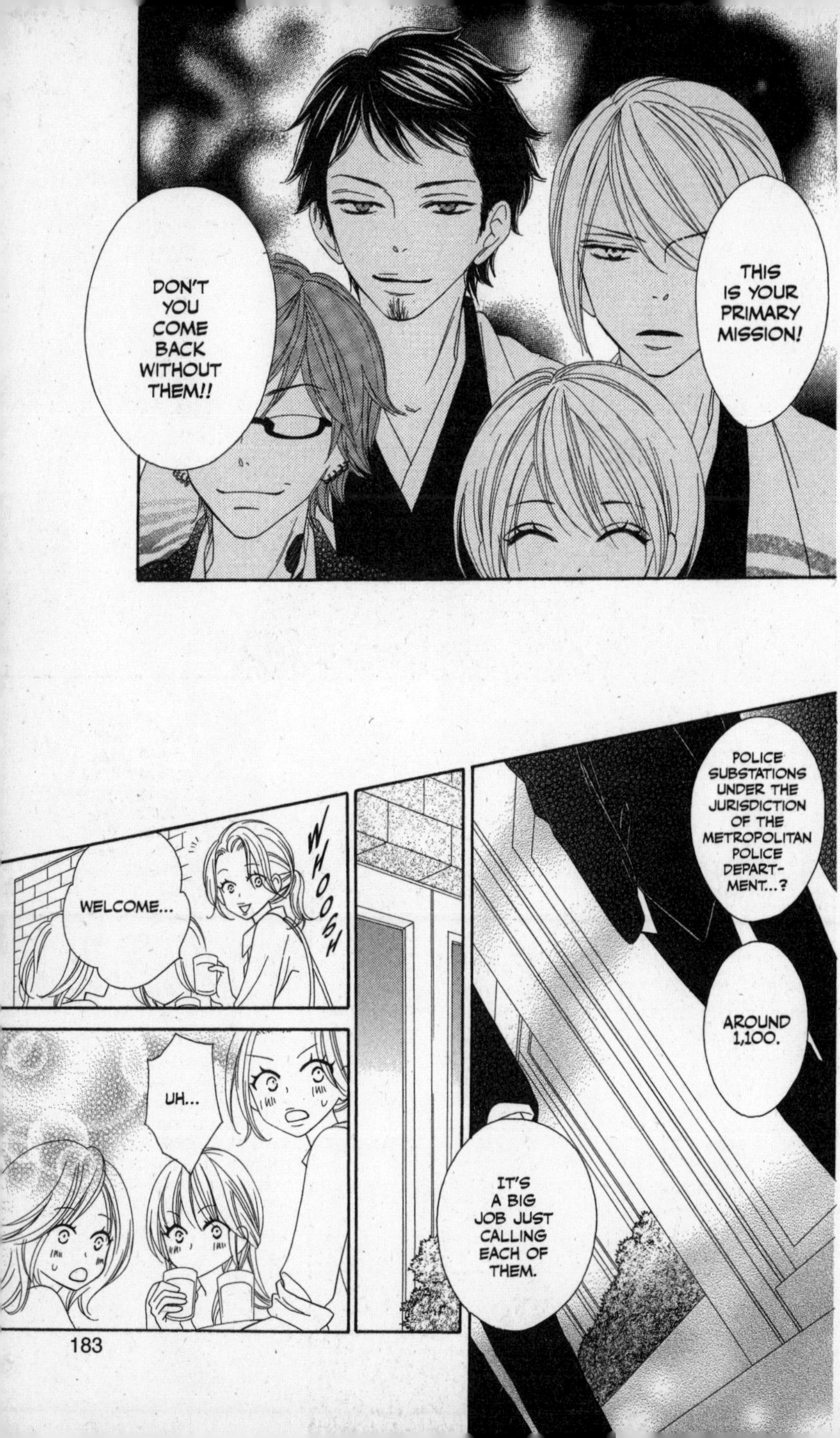
THIS IS YOUR PRIMARY MISSION!
DON'T YOU COME BACK WITHOUT THEM!!
POLICE SUBSTATIONS UNDER THE JURISDICTION OF THE METROPOLITAN POLICE DEPART-MENT...?
AROUND 1,100.
IT'S A BIG JOB JUST CALLING EACH OF THEM.
WELCOME...
WHOOSH
UH...

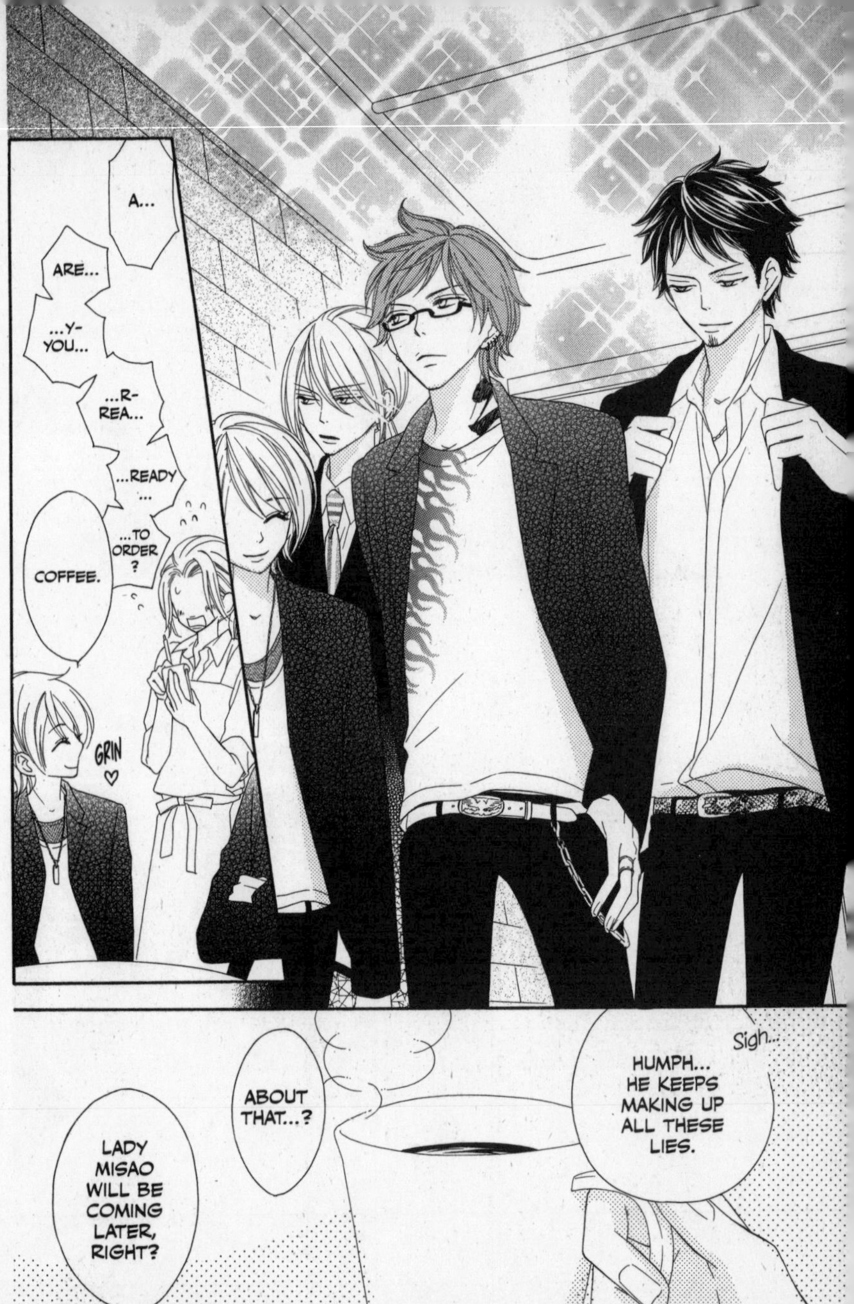
A...
ARE...
...Y-YOU...
...R-REA...
...READY...
...TO ORDER?
COFFEE.
GRIN ♡
Sigh...
HUMPH... HE KEEPS MAKING UP ALL THESE LIES.
ABOUT THAT...?
LADY MISAO WILL BE COMING LATER, RIGHT?

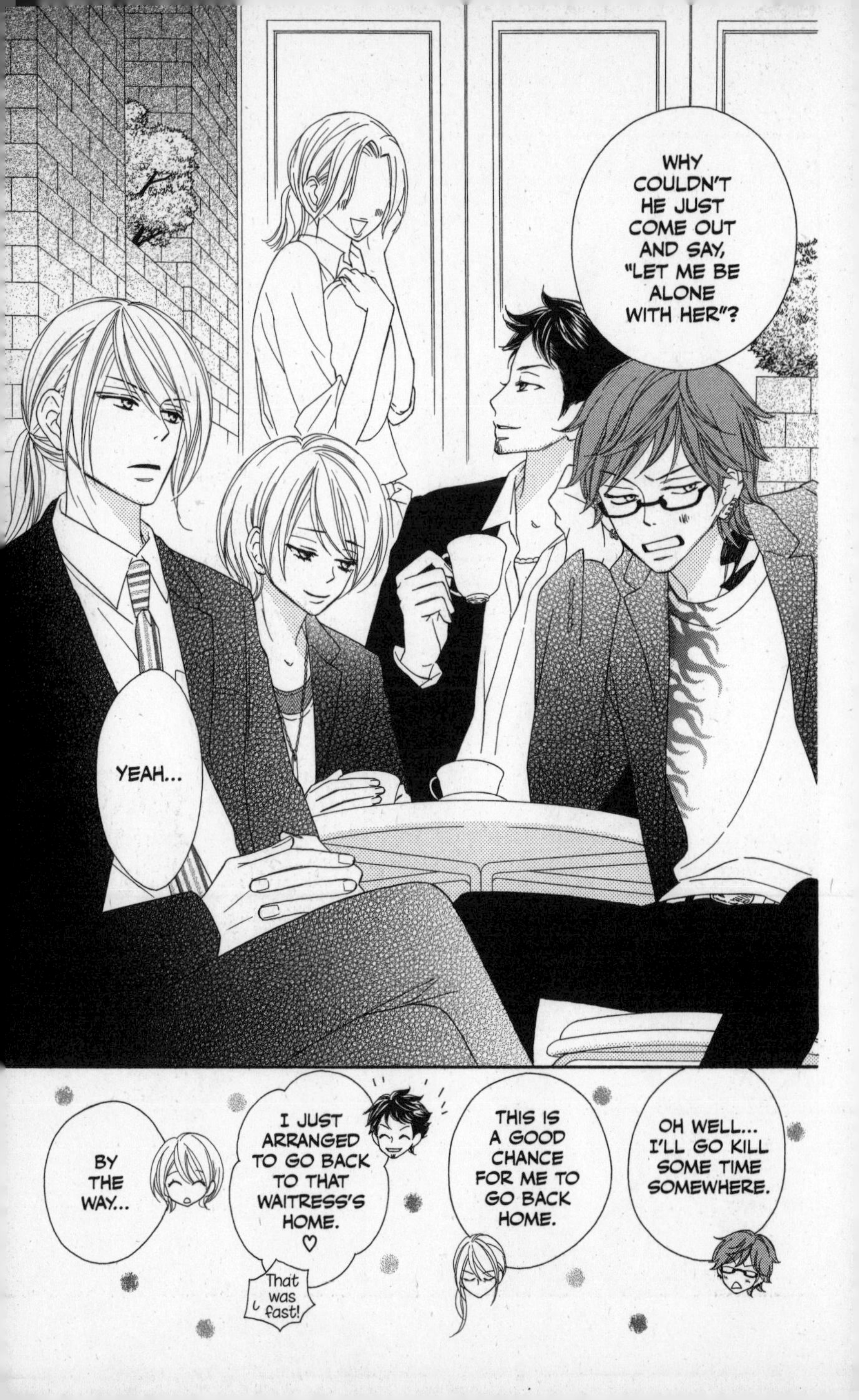
WHY COULDN'T HE JUST COME OUT AND SAY, "LET ME BE ALONE WITH HER"?
YEAH...
OH WELL... I'LL GO KILL SOME TIME SOMEWHERE.
THIS IS A GOOD CHANCE FOR ME TO GO BACK HOME.
I JUST ARRANGED TO GO BACK TO THAT WAITRESS'S HOME. ♡
That was fast!
BY THE WAY...

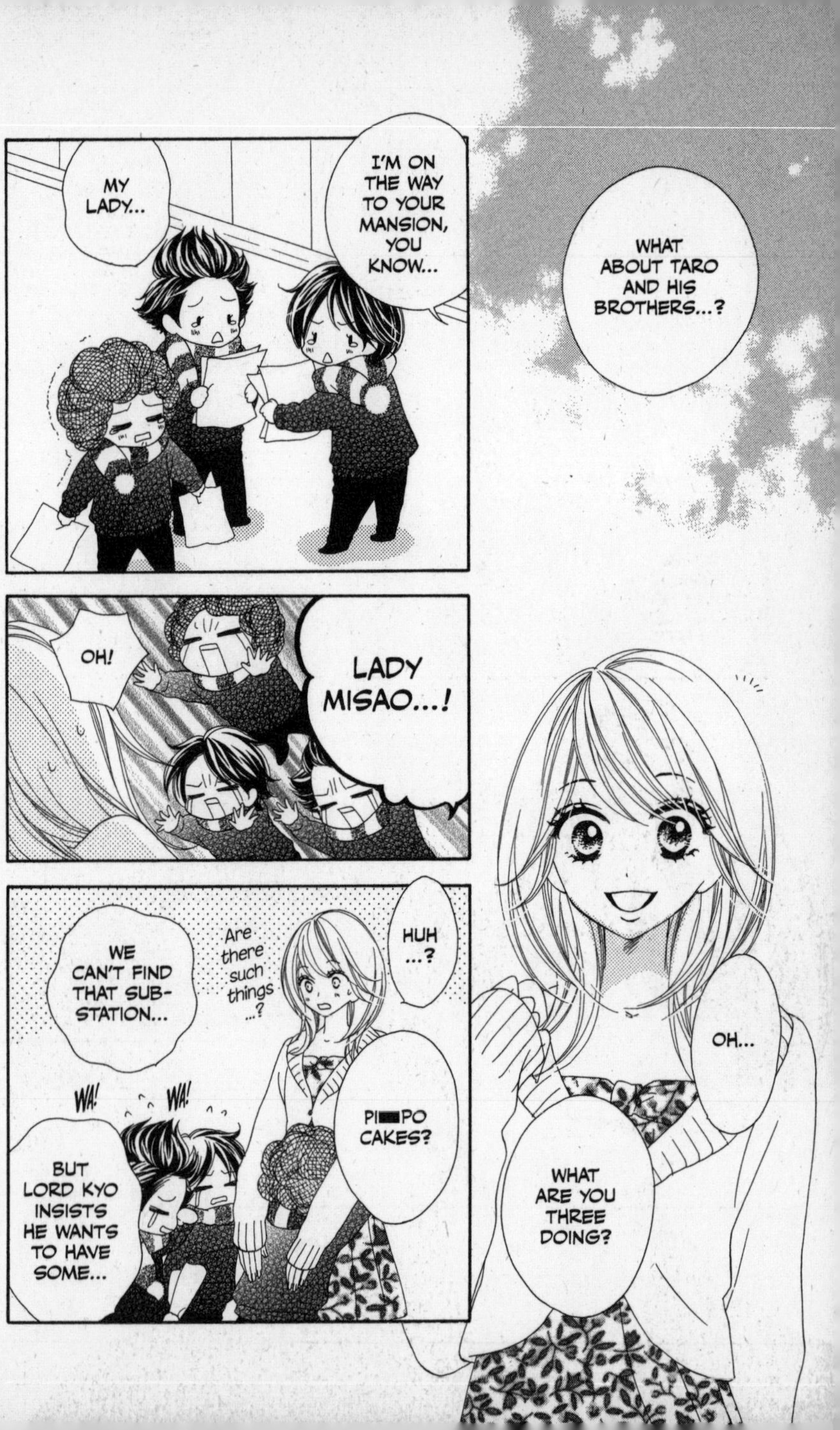
WHAT ABOUT TARO AND HIS BROTHERS...?
OH...
WHAT ARE YOU THREE DOING?
I'M ON THE WAY TO YOUR MANSION, YOU KNOW...
MY LADY...
LADY MISAO...!
OH!
HUH ...?
Are there such things ...?
WE CAN'T FIND THAT SUB-STATION...
PI[redacted]PO CAKES?
WA! WA!
BUT LORD KYO INSISTS HE WANTS TO HAVE SOME...

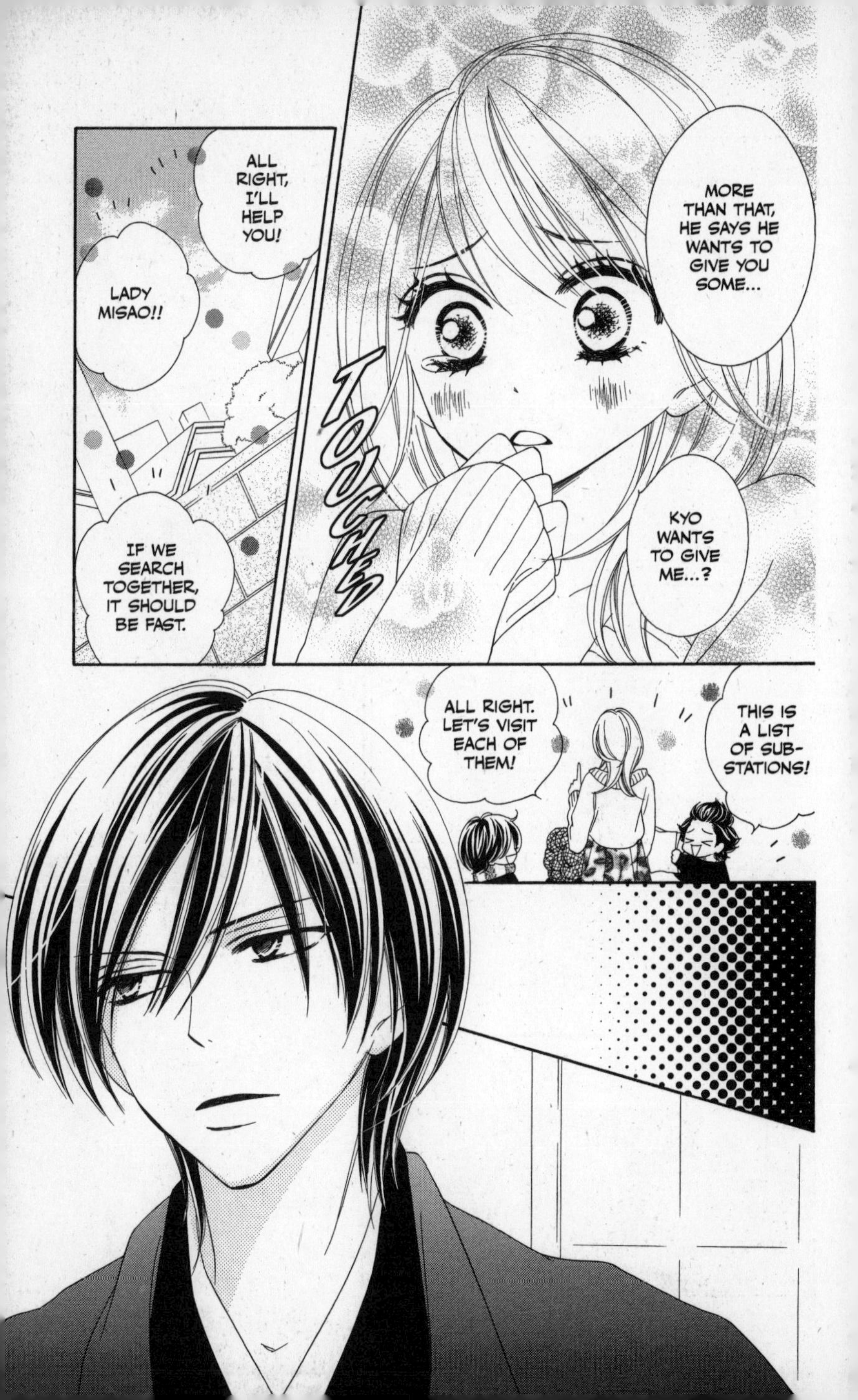

MORE THAN THAT, HE SAYS HE WANTS TO GIVE YOU SOME...
KYO WANTS TO GIVE ME...?
ALL RIGHT, I'LL HELP YOU!
LADY MISAO!!
IF WE SEARCH TOGETHER, IT SHOULD BE FAST.
THIS IS A LIST OF SUB-STATIONS!
ALL RIGHT. LET'S VISIT EACH OF THEM!

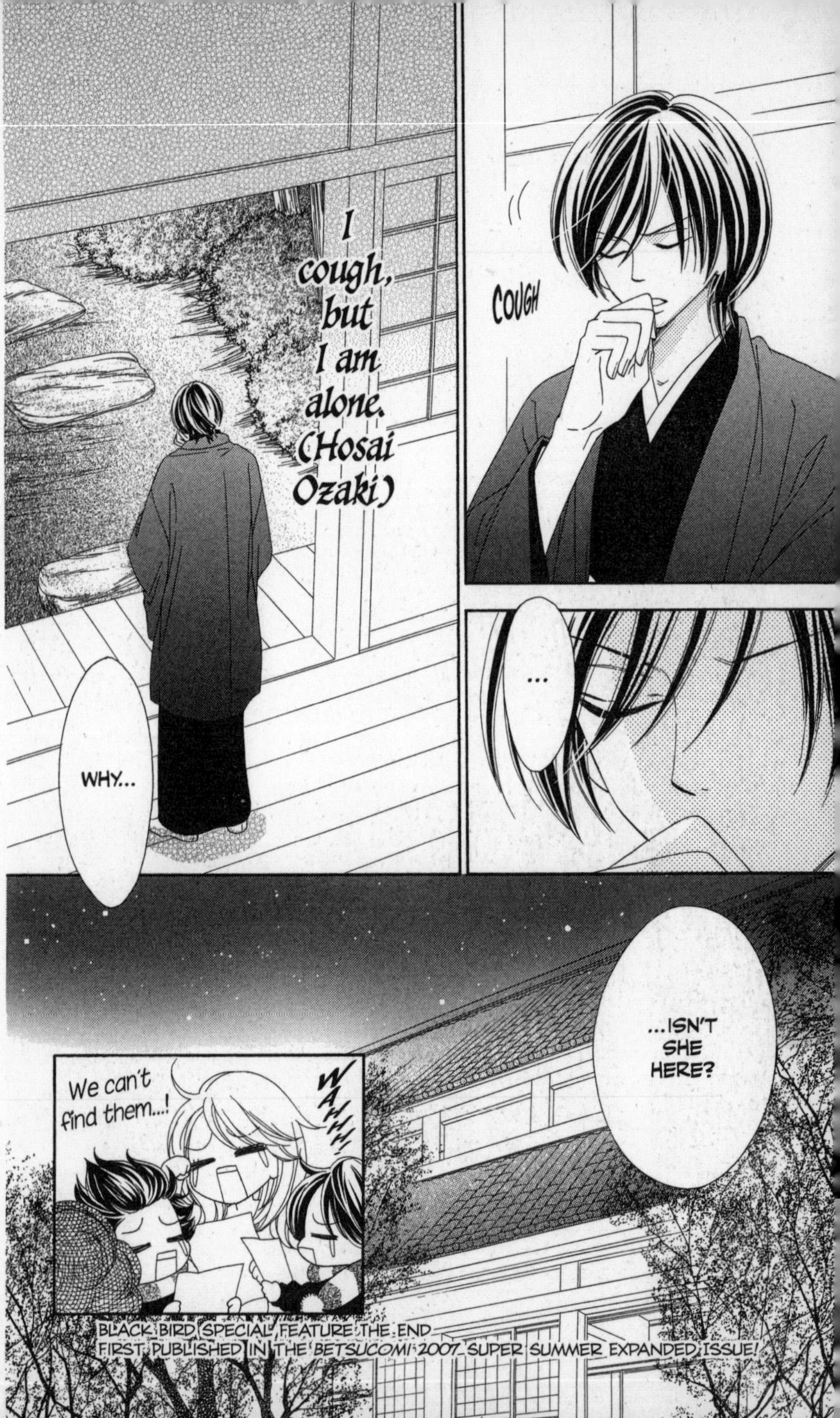
COUGH
...
I cough, but I am alone. (Hosai Ozaki)
WHY...
...ISN'T SHE HERE?
WAHHH!
We can't find them...!
BLACK BIRD SPECIAL FEATURE THE END
FIRST PUBLISHED IN THE BETSUCOMI 2007 SUPER SUMMER EXPANDED ISSUE!

The ages of the Eight Daitengu appeared in volume 2,
so here are their heights. This is what they look like lined up.

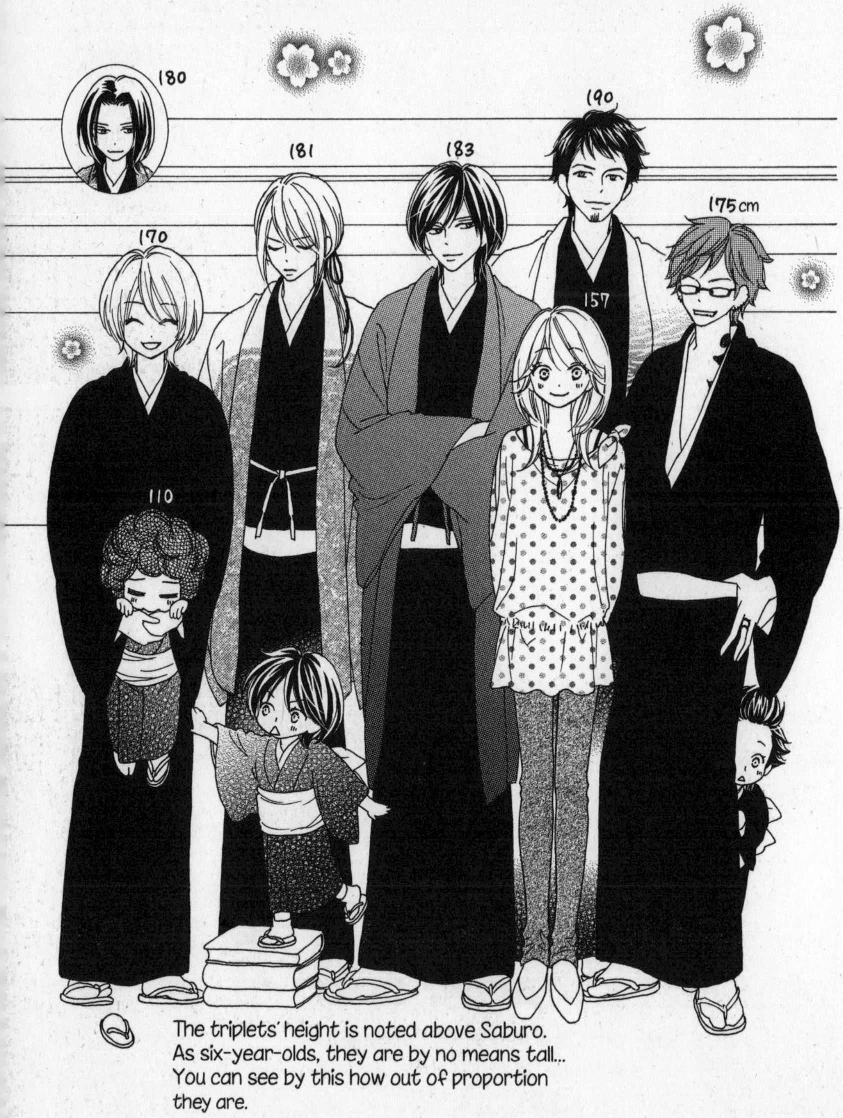
180
190
181
183
175cm
170
157
110

The triplets' height is noted above Saburo.
As six-year-olds, they are by no means tall...
You can see by this how out of proportion
they are.

● A Bonus Manga ●

Misao and Kogin

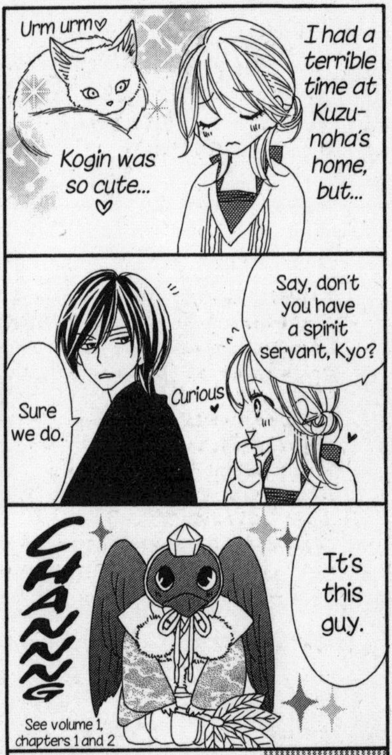
I had a terrible time at Kuzunoha's home, but...
Urm urm♡
Kogin was so cute... ♡
Say, don't you have a spirit servant, Kyo?
Curious♥
Sure we do.
It's this guy.
CHANNNG
See volume 1, chapters 1 and 2
SIGH...
Kogin...
SHOCK
...

Kyo and Kogin

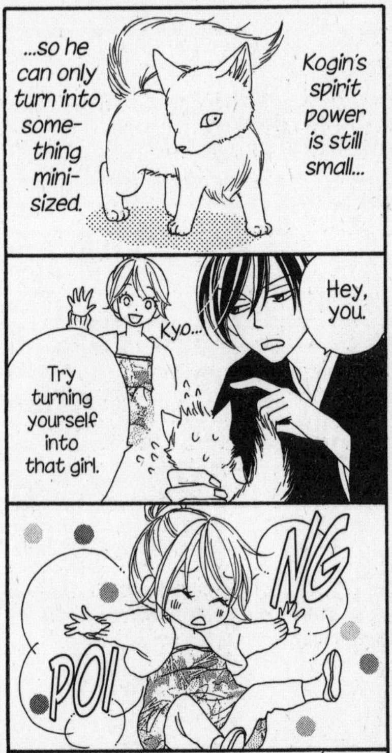
Kogin's spirit power is still small...
...so he can only turn into something mini-sized.
Hey, you.
Kyo...
Try turning yourself into that girl.
NG
POI
Misao ...!
HUG
She's exactly how she was back then... ♡
That's pathetic.
Hey ...!

I look forward to seeing you in volume 4!

September 2007 Kanoko Sakurakoji

GLOSSARY

PAGE 22, PANEL 4: *Witching hours*
The Japanese is ôma ga toki (逢魔が刻).
Ôma literally means "to meet something that is not human." *Toki* means "time."

PAGE 30, PANEL 2: *Daiginjo*
A type of premium sake that is made from highly polished rice using labor-intensive traditional steps. It is generally light with a complex, fragrant taste. Junmai Daiginjo has no added alcohol, while Daiginjo contains additional distilled alcohol.

PAGE 46: *Pink*
Momoiro (桃色) is usually translated as "pink" or "rosy," but it literally means "peach colored." It is often used to connote something lewd or amorous.

PAGE 46, PANEL 1: *The Black Tower*
A play on *Shiroi Kyotou*, which means "white tower," and is a Japanese TV drama about two doctors.

PAGE 188, PANEL 3: *Hosai Ozaki*
The pen name of Hideo Ozaki, an early 20th century haiku poet known for the loneliness of his poems.

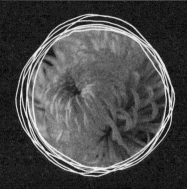

Kanoko Sakurakoji was born in downtown Tokyo, and her hobbies include reading, watching plays, traveling and shopping. Her debut title, *Raibu ga Hanetara*, ran in *Bessatsu Shojo Comic* (currently called *Bestucomi*) in 2000, and her 2004 *Bestucomi* title *Backstage Prince* was serialized in VIZ Media's *Shojo Beat* magazine. She won the 54th Shogakukan Manga Award for *Black Bird*.

BLACK BIRD

VOL. 3
Shojo Beat Edition

Story and Art by KANOKO SAKURAKOJI

Original Japanese edition "BLACK BIRD" published by SHOGAKUKAN Inc.

TRANSLATION JN Productions
TOUCH-UP ART & LETTERING Gia Cam Luc
DESIGN Courtney Utt
EDITOR Pancha Diaz

VP, PRODUCTION Alvin Lu
VP, SALES & PRODUCT MARKETING Gonzalo Ferreyra
VP, CREATIVE Linda Espinosa
PUBLISHER Hyoe Narita

Printed in the U.S.A.

Published by VIZ Media, LLC
P.O. Box 77010
San Francisco, CA 94107

10 9 8 7 6 5 4 3 2 1
First printing, February 2010

www.shojobeat.com
www.viz.com

RATED T+ FOR OLDER TEEN

PARENTAL ADVISORY
BLACK BIRD is rated T+ for Older Teen and is recommended for ages 16 and up. This volume contains violence and adult situations.

ratings.viz.com

LAND OF *Fantasy*

MIAKA YÛKI IS AN ORDINARY JUNIOR-HIGH STUDENT WHO IS SUDDENLY WHISKED AWAY INTO THE WORLD OF A BOOK, *THE UNIVERSE OF THE FOUR GODS*. WILL THE BEAUTIFUL CELESTIAL BEINGS SHE ENCOUNTERS AND THE CHANCE TO BECOME A PRIESTESS DIVERT MIAKA FROM EVER RETURNING HOME?

THREE VOLUMES OF THE ORIGINAL *FUSHIGI YÛGI* SERIES COMBINED INTO A LARGER FORMAT WITH AN EXCLUSIVE COVER DESIGN AND BONUS CONTENT

EXPERIENCE THE BEAUTY OF *FUSHIGI YÛGI* WITH THE HARDCOVER ART BOOK

ALSO AVAILABLE: THE *FUSHIGI YÛGI: GENBU KAIDEN* MANGA, THE EIGHT VOLUME PREQUEL TO THIS BEST-SELLING FANTASY SERIES

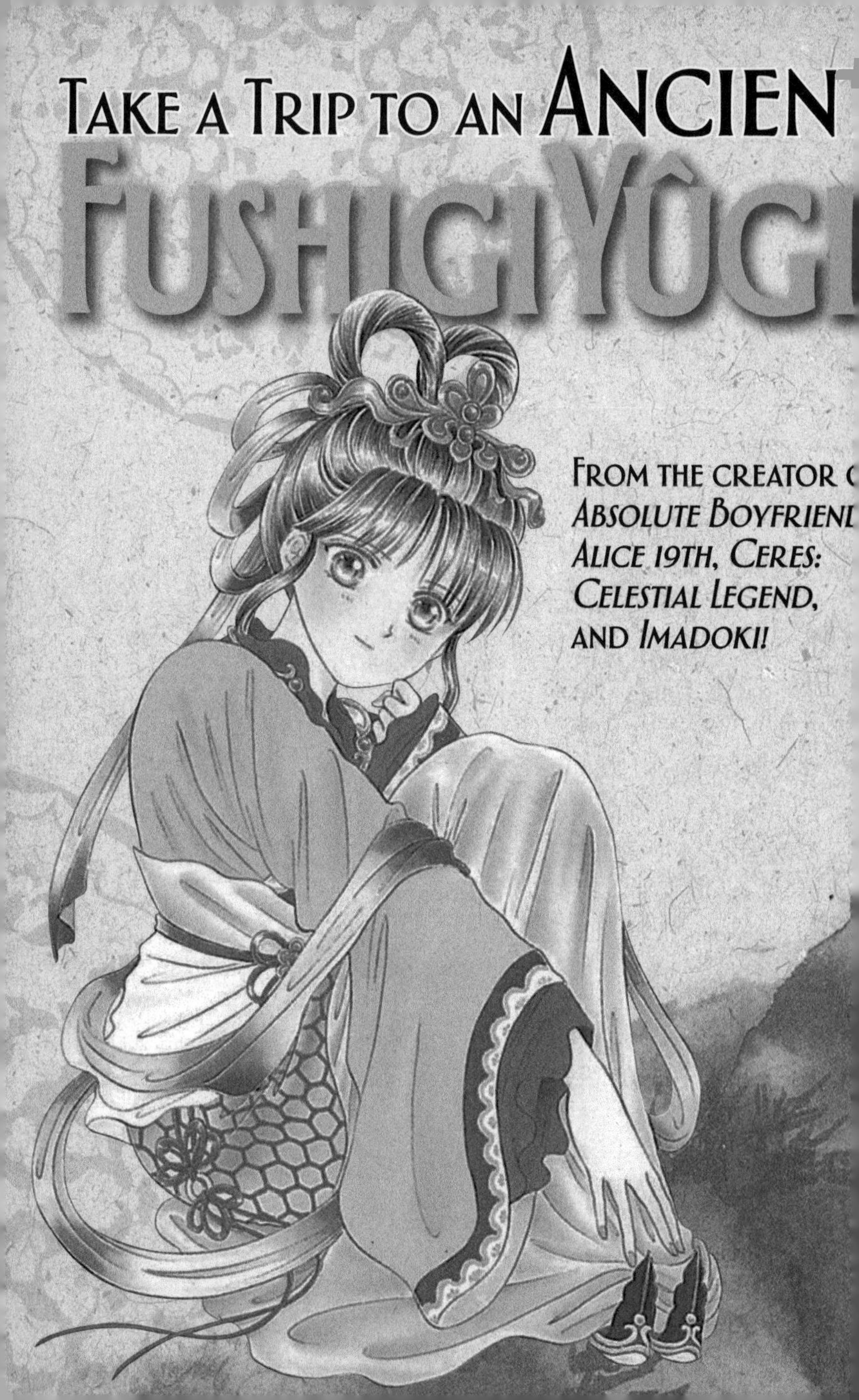
TAKE A TRIP TO AN ANCIEN
FUSHIGI YÛGI
FROM THE CREATOR
ABSOLUTE BOYFRIEN
ALICE 19TH, CERES:
CELESTIAL LEGEND,
AND IMADOKI!

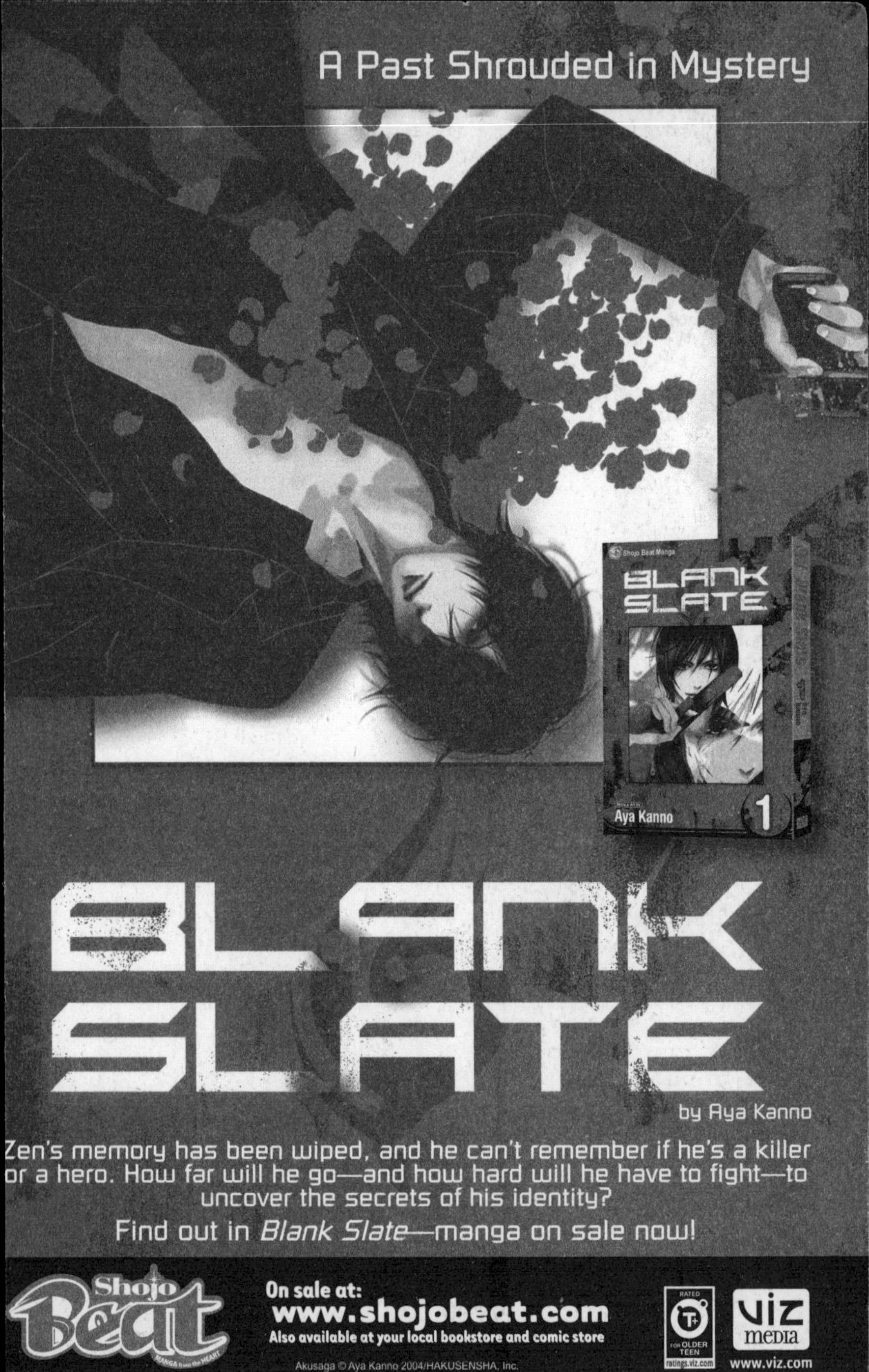
A Past Shrouded in Mystery
Shojo Beat Manga
BLANK SLATE
Aya Kanno
1
BLANK SLATE
by Aya Kanno
Zen's memory has been wiped, and he can't remember if he's a killer or a hero. How far will he go—and how hard will he have to fight—to uncover the secrets of his identity?
Find out in *Blank Slate*—manga on sale now!
Shojo Beat
MANGA from the HEART
On sale at:
www.shojobeat.com
Also available at your local bookstore and comic store
RATED
T+
FOR OLDER TEEN
ratings.viz.com
viz media
www.viz.com
Akusaga © Aya Kanno 2004/HAKUSENSHA, Inc.

Story and Art by Miki Aihara | *Creator of* Honey Hunt *and* Tokyo Boys & Girls

Three volumes of the original manga combined into a larger format with an exclusive cover design and bonus content

Full-length novel with an alternate ending and a bonus manga episode

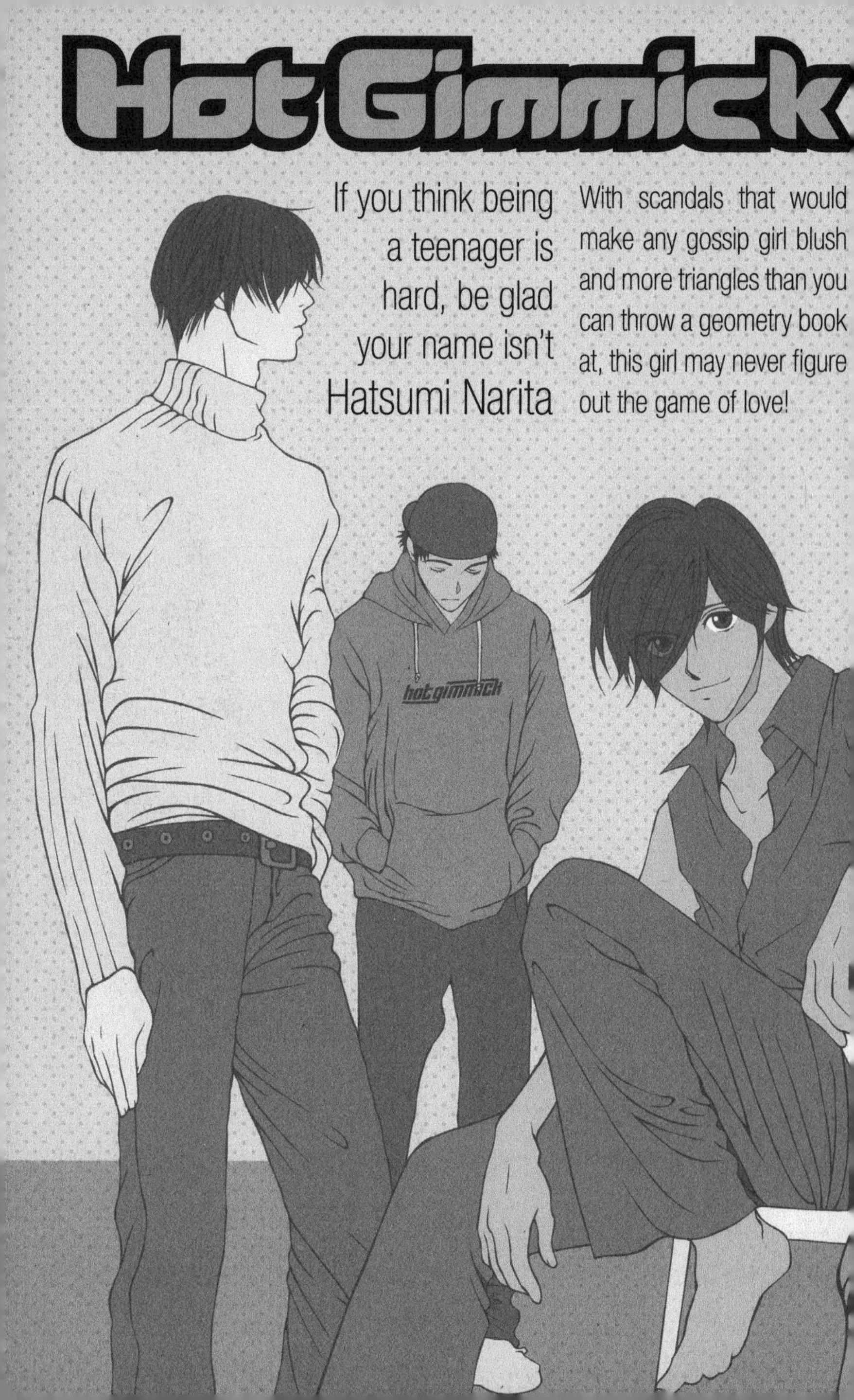
Hot Gimmick
If you think being a teenager is hard, be glad your name isn't Hatsumi Narita
With scandals that would make any gossip girl blush and more triangles than you can throw a geometry book at, this girl may never figure out the game of love!
hot gimmick

Tell us what you think about Shojo Beat Manga!

Our survey is now available online. Go to:

shojobeat.com/mangasurvey

Help us make our product offerings better!

THE REAL DRAMA BEGINS IN...